Congress and the Emergence
of Sectionalism

Perspectives on the History of Congress, 1801–1877

Donald R. Kennon, Series Editor

Congress and the Emergence of Sectionalism:
From the Missouri Compromise to the Age of Jackson,
edited by Paul Finkelman and Donald R. Kennon

Congress and the Emergence of Sectionalism

From the Missouri Compromise to the Age of Jackson

Edited by Paul Finkelman and Donald R. Kennon

PUBLISHED FOR THE
UNITED STATES CAPITOL HISTORICAL SOCIETY

BY OHIO UNIVERSITY PRESS • ATHENS

Ohio University Press, Athens, Ohio 45701
www.ohioswallow.com
© 2008 by Ohio University Press

To obtain permission to quote, reprint, or otherwise reproduce or distribute material
from Ohio University Press/Swallow Press publications, please contact our rights and
permissions department at (740) 593-1154 or (740) 593-4536 (fax).

Ohio University Press books are printed on acid-free paper ⊗ ™

15 14 13 12 11 10 09 08   5 4 3 2 1

Library of Congress Cataloging-in-Publication Data

Congress and the emergence of sectionalism : from the Missouri compromise to the age of
Jackson / edited by Paul Finkelman and Donald R. Kennon.
     p. cm. — (Perspectives on the history of Congress, 1801–1877)
  Includes bibliographical references and index.
  ISBN-13: 978-0-8214-1783-6 (cloth : alk. paper)
  ISBN-10: 0-8214-1783-5 (cloth : alk. paper)
   1. Sectionalism (United States)—History—19th century. 2. United States. Congress—
History—19th century. 3. United States—Politics and government—1815–1861. I. Finkelman,
Paul, 1949– II. Kennon, Donald R., 1948–
  JK316.C66 2008
  973.5—dc22

                                                                                    2007048418

Contents

Preface

The essays in this volume explore national political issues from the end of the War of 1812 to the Age of Jackson. These chapters were first given as papers at two conferences sponsored by the United States Capitol Historical Society (USCHS). Donald Kennon of the USCHS and I directed these conferences. For more than three decades the USCHS has sponsored conferences on U.S. history, with a special focus on national politics and, where appropriate, the nation's capital. The USCHS started with the bicentennial of the Revolution and worked through the bicentennial of the Constitution, the Bill of Rights, and the first federal Congress. This collection inaugurates a new set of volumes that Don Kennon and I will edit. We began with a conference on Congress and the capital from the end of the War of 1812 to the Age of Jackson. Our second conference was on Congress, politics, and Jacksonian America. We will end this series with the sesquicentennial of the Civil War, discussions of the Lincoln administration, Congress and the war, emancipation and black freedom, and Reconstruction.

Putting together a book like this requires the efforts of many people. First, I thank my coeditor, Don Kennon, who is a delight to work with. Working with Don reminds me of the old athletic shoe advertisement about the athletes who knew their sports. Don knows Congress. Don knows history. And Don knows how to put on a conference. We both owe a debt to Don's staff, especially Felicia Bell and Lauren Borchard. We are also terribly indebted to our editor at Ohio University Press, Gillian Berchowitz. Gill is able to push authors and editors with great humor and fabulous advice. She makes the whole process of putting together a collection of essays fun, even when we are pretty sure it is not supposed to be fun. The staff at Ohio University Press, especially our project editor, Rick Huard, added immeasurably to the quality of this book.

Most of all, we owe a debt to our colleagues and authors. The chapters in this book speak for themselves. They are insightful, meticulously researched, smartly argued, and carefully crafted. These chapters reflect cutting-edge scholarship and, in some cases, a lifetime of devotion to the field. Working with these authors was in fact a great deal of fun, as well as deeply educational. Don and I learned much from editing these chapters, as we expect all readers of this book will.

Paul Finkelman

Congress and the Emergence
of Sectionalism

Paul Finkelman

Introduction

Congress, the Rise of Sectionalism,
and the Challenge of Jacksonian Democracy

IN 1815 THE United States was a proud and confident nation. Its second war with England had come to a successful conclusion. As they had four decades earlier, the plucky Americans had somehow managed to fight the most powerful nation in the world to a standstill. It is true that the nation's new capital, Washington, D.C., had been captured and partially burned, but that temporary defeat did not force an unfavorable peace treaty. Moreover, that humiliation was avenged by Andrew Jackson's spectacular victory at New Orleans in January 1815. It did not matter to Americans that the Battle of New Orleans took place after the war was technically over. No one in America knew about the peace treaty yet, and so the great victory boosted national morale, even though it did not influence the outcome of the conflict.

After the war, Americans seemed united as never before. The Federalist party had virtually destroyed itself by opposing the war. With the exception of the chief justiceship, Republicans held all important offices in the government. The virtual end of party politics led to a reexamination of public policy issues that had previously been tainted by party competition.

Illustrative of the changing nature of politics was the creation of the Second Bank of the United States. In 1791 James Madison had strenuously opposed Alexander Hamilton's proposed Bank of the United States. Madison considered the Bank to be bad policy then. He also believed it was unconstitutional for Congress to charter a bank. By 1814, however, his views had changed. The Bank was no longer a party issue because the Federalist party was virtually defunct. Thus, in 1814 Congress passed legislation chartering a new bank. In January 1815 James Madison, now President Madison, vetoed this bill because he felt it did not "answer the purposes of reviving the public credit, of providing a national medium of circulation, and of aiding the Treasury" in collecting taxes. In his veto message Madison made it clear that he was not rejecting the bill on policy grounds. He clearly wanted a national bank—the government had been embarrassed by not having such an institution during the War of 1812. He simply felt the 1815 bill did not create what the government needed. Nor did he veto the bill on constitutional grounds. Indeed, Madison declared he was "waiving the question of the Constitutional authority of the Legislature to establish an incorporated bank as being precluded in my judgment by repeated recognitions under varied circumstances of the validity of such an institution in acts of the legislative, executive, and judicial branches of the Government, accompanied by indications, in different modes, of a concurrence of the general will of the nation."[1]

Congress quickly complied with Madison's request for a different and better bank bill that would answer America's need for a stable financial institution that could operate in all the states. The chairman of the House Committee on Currency, John C. Calhoun of South Carolina, introduced this bill. Calhoun would ultimately become the symbol of Southern sectionalism and nullification, as well as a relentless opponent of the Bank. But in 1816 this future states' rights champion found no constitutional or political objections to the Bank. With relative ease the Congress, in 1816, chartered the Second Bank of the United States.[2]

Calhoun's support for the new bank symbolizes the sectional harmony within the nation as the War of 1812 came to an end. For a brief moment—no more than five years—sectional competition seemed to have disappeared. Slavery was not a pressing moral issue for most white Americans, and the controversy over the status of slavery in the territories was not yet on the horizon. Politicians from all sections supported the Bank and federal funding of internal improvements. Madison vetoed a bill funding internal improvements only because he felt it was unconstitutional. In principle he liked the idea of

[1]James D. Richardson, ed., *A Compilation of the Messages and Papers of the Presidents, 1789–1897,* 10 vols. (Washington, D.C., 1897), 1:540.
[2]An Act to Incorporate the Subscribers of the Bank of the United States, ch. 44, 3 Stat. 266 (1816).

the national government playing an active role in economic development, but he did not think Congress had the power to do this. Thus, he urged Congress to send a constitutional amendment to the states that would allow the national government to use its surplus funds to build roads, bridges, canals, and other public works. In the House and Senate were young men who would soon come to dominate Congress—and symbolize sectional and political strife. But, in the aftermath of the War of 1812, these men—Henry Clay, Daniel Webster, and John C. Calhoun—were all nationalist members of the same party.

This harmony—what historians once called the "Era of Good Feeling"—was not illusory. But it was also not stable. One-party government could not persist for long in a vibrant democracy full of ambitious politicians. Sectional harmony was possible only as long as no one asked any hard questions about slavery, race, western expansion, or economic development. The chapters in this book illustrate how things would fall apart when the glow of postwar harmony and nationalism wore off. Within a decade slavery would emerge as a central issue of politics; western expansion would lead to internal political fights over slavery and the future of American Indians; and political parties would reemerge, coalescing around economic development, the Bank of the United States, and Indian policy. Politics would center on Congress in the 1820s. In the 1830s a new kind of politics would emerge when, for the first time, Congress challenged presidential authority and simultaneously the president challenged Congress. As much as anything else, the disharmony between Congress and the president symbolize the Age of Jackson.

The chapters in this book explore these themes. These chapters are not a summary of the period. They do not take us over the familiar highlights of this period, even though many deal with themes—such as the Missouri Compromise, the Bank War, slavery and politics, the Tariff of Abominations, nullification, and Indian removal—that are the standard signposts for American history from 1815 to the late 1830s. Each author, while dealing with a well-known and well-studied topic, offers us new insights, new understandings, and new information about the subject. Some of the material will surprise readers and surely all readers will learn much from what is here. Part 1 deals with Congress and the emergence of sectionalism in the aftermath of the War of 1812 through the end of the 1820s. Part 2 follows this story into the Age of Jackson.

Sectionalism

Looming underneath the Era of Good Feeling were deep conflicts that had been smoothed over by prosperity and patriotism, but they had not been buried. Sectionalists were more than politicians who supported policies that favored their state or region; that sort of political behavior is expected in a republic, especially in one as large as the United States. Sectionalism implies a willingness to undermine national policy, or even the nation itself, in order to protect a narrow interest that is not only tied to one part of the nation but also seen as detrimental to the rest of the nation. Slavery, and Southern demands for its special protection, is the most important example of antebellum sectionalism. In the end, Southerners were willing to leave the Union and destroy the nation in order to gain unlimited security for slavery.

Southern threats of disunion over slavery began almost as soon as the Union was established. In debating the Articles of Confederation, Benjamin Franklin and South Carolina's Thomas Lynch sparred over slavery. When James Wilson of Pennsylvania suggested that slaves be taxed as free people were, the South Carolinians at the Congress were adamant that slaves should not be counted for taxation because they were property and taxes were only based on people. Thomas Lynch of South Carolina flatly declared: "If it is debated, whether their slaves are their property, there is an end of the confederation. Our slaves being our property, why should they be taxed more than the land, sheep, cattle, horses, &c.?" Benjamin Franklin both wisely and sarcastically answered that "slaves rather weaken than strengthen the State, and there is therefore some difference between them and sheep; sheep will never make any insurrections."[3] This brief little discussion symbolized the way slavery would affect the Union, at least until the mid-1830s. The debate here was not about the morality of slavery. Rather, the essence of this debate was about money and the distribution of power and responsibility in the new nation. However, the undertones of both Lynch and Franklin suggest the huge moral problems that slavery imposed on the nation. Lynch understood that some people were uncomfortable with the idea that people could be held as property—even though all the states at this time allowed

---

[3]Worthington C. Ford et al., eds., *Journals of the Continental Congress, 1774–1789*, 34 vols. (Washington, D.C., 1904–37), 6:1080.

slavery. Franklin noted the political dangers of slavery—that it made the nation unstable. Already, slaves were flocking to the British army to fight against their masters. Moreover, Franklin acknowledged the threat that slavery posed to the body politic because of the inherent contradiction of holding people in bondage in a nation that had just asserted its right to independence on the grounds, as proclaimed in the Declaration of Independence, that "all Men are created equal" and that they were all entitled to the rights of "Life, Liberty, and the Pursuit of Happiness." If the Americans could revolt against their British rulers, then slaves might also revolt against their American rulers. The moral condemnation of slavery was implicit in the American founding, as Franklin and others well knew.

As an economic, political, and ultimately moral issue, slavery was at the root of sectionalism. Although slavery was legal in all of the thirteen colonies that fought against the British, by 1812 every state north of Delaware had either ended slavery outright or was doing so through gradual abolition. As Jan Lewis's chapter in this book shows, well before 1812 slavery had been an issue at the Constitutional Convention.[4] The three-fifths clause bedeviled Northerners, who saw it as giving the South an unfair and powerful political advantage. New Englanders fully understood that their candidate in 1800, John Adams, would have been reelected president if the three-fifths clause had not given Thomas Jefferson extra electoral votes based on the number of slaves in the South.[5] The Hartford Convention listed the three-fifths clause as one of the reasons why New England should consider leaving the Union. The War of 1812 ended any talk of disunion in that region—at least until the 1830s, when William Lloyd Garrison's radical abolitionist society adopted the slogan "No Union with Slaveholders"—but dissatisfaction with the three-fifths clause remained strong.

Although the three-fifths clause would never again determine the outcome of a presidential election, it certainly had a dramatic affect on congressional politics. As the North's population growth outstripped the South's, the three-fifths clause became more significant. Had congressional apportionment been based entirely on the free population, the South would have

---

[4]See also Paul Finkelman, *Slavery and the Founders: Race and Liberty in the Age of Jefferson*, 2d ed. (Armonk, N.Y., 2001).

[5]Paul Finkelman, "The Proslavery Origins of the Electoral College," *Cardozo Law Review* 23 (2002):1145–57.

been overwhelmed in the House of Representatives. But, the South's rapidly growing slave population gave the region a significant number of congressmen to help fend off total dominance by the North. The Missouri Compromise, discussed by Robert P. Forbes in this volume, illustrates the importance of the three-fifths clause. Without that clause it is hard to imagine how the South could have successfully negotiated the Compromise, which brought Missouri into the Union as a slave state over the objection of most Northern members of the House. The 1820 Compromise set the stage for other compromises and other congressional acts strengthening slavery. In each one of these—Texas annexation, the Compromise of 1850, the Kansas-Nebraska Act—the congressional seats created by the three-fifths clause were essential for the South in gaining new slave states and new territories where slavery was allowed.

Slavery was not the only major sectional interest. Tariff policy and Indian policy were also essentially sectional, although they were tied at least indirectly to slavery. Because of slavery the South understood itself to be at an economic disadvantage in trade, commerce, and manufacturing. Hence, most Southerners reflexively opposed high tariffs, or even tariffs at all. This Southern understanding of commerce was articulated in the Constitutional Convention when Gen. Charles Cotesworth Pinckney of South Carolina declared that "it was the true interest of the S. States to have no regulation of commerce."[6] In that speech Pinckney then declared that he would support allowing Congress to regulate commerce because the New England states had supported his demand for protection of the African slave trade. But, despite this support, the reality was that the South was wary of economic regulations that raised the price of imported goods. By the 1820s Northerners, as Peter Onuf explains, equated protectionist tariffs with patriotism, because they saw a direct connection between domestic production and what we would today call national security. As one proponent of high tariffs, Alexander Everett, noted, "The home market," which had to be protected by tariffs, was "the palladium of home itself in all its most endearing and ennobling political and social relations; without which we have no common country, but should be reduced to the condition of dismembered and defenceless provinces."[7] There may have been a great deal of truth to this argument,

---

[6]Max Farrand, *The Records of the Federal Convention of 1787*, 2 vols. (New Haven, 1966), 2:449.
[7][Alexander Everett], *Address of the Friends of Domestic Industry, Assembled in Convention, at New York, October 26, 1831, To the People of the United States* (Baltimore, 1831), p. 39.

but as a matter of economics such policies favored one section—the North —and disfavored the South. Thus, tariff policy continued to exacerbate internal stresses of the nation even as it may have made the nation economically, militarily, and diplomatically stronger.

Another great sectional tension concerned the status—and fate—of American Indians. By 1820 most Indians in the Northeast had died out, become assimilated, been forced west, or been isolated on reservations. The Indian was no longer a threat to most Americans in the Northeast or Mid-Atlantic. Illustrative of the Indian in the Northeast was James Fenimore Cooper's best-selling novel *The Last of the Mohicans*, published in 1826. The Indian was no longer a living threat; he was a quaint heroic figure of a novel, entertaining Americans as his people—the Mohicans—disappeared. In the Ohio valley, Indians had more recently been a threat, but the War of 1812 eliminated the Indians in Ohio and Indiana as a force. The rapid settlement of the lower Midwest in this period underscored the impotency of the native population.

In the South—Georgia, Tennessee, the new state of Alabama, and Mississippi—the situation was very different. In the aftermath of the War of 1812 and the Creek War, Gen. Andrew Jackson managed to persuade, coerce, and bribe most of the bands of the Creeks, Choctaws, and Chickasaws to move west into present-day Oklahoma.[8] The First Seminole War did not defeat that tribe, but it did force most of the Seminoles to retreat into the swamps of Florida or to accept removal. But the Cherokees, based mostly in northern Georgia, were disinclined to give up their lands and their way of life. The most acculturated of the five civilized tribes, they avoided conflict with the United States.

The Georgia Cherokees were certainly no military threat to anyone, but they were a cultural threat to the people of Georgia, who coveted their land and desperately wanted to remove this large, free, and increasingly prosperous nonwhite population from their midst. The reality of nonwhites controlling their own destiny, profitably farming their own lands, and maintaining their own government posed an unacceptable challenge to the white supremacy that was the basis of Southern society. Removal was about land, but it was also about racial hierarchy and racial control. Georgia simply would not tolerate large numbers of free nonwhites living in the state. Many Northerners,

---

[8]See generally Robert V. Remini, *Andrew Jackson and His Indian Wars* (New York, 2001).

however, vigorously opposed Indian removal. They were shocked at this apparently brutal land grab against a peaceful minority in an isolated part of the state. Thus, as Tim Garrison shows in his essay, the Indian removal, while taking place only in the South, was a variant of the growing sectional crisis.

Garrison begins his chapter with a long quotation from Congressman Wilson Lumpkin of Georgia, who denounced Northern opponents of removal as "intermeddlers and disturbers of the peace and harmony of society" who unfairly "depicted his constituents, the people of Georgia, as 'Atheists, Deists, Infidels, and Sabbath-breakers, laboring under the curse of slavery.'" Lumpkin denounced this sectionalism but blamed it squarely on the "*cant and fanaticism,* emanating from the land of steady habits; from the boasted progeny of the Pilgrims and Puritans."[9]

The papers in the first part of this volume illustrate the nature of sectionalism as it emerged in the 1820s. While we normally think of antebellum sectionalism as a fight over slavery, these essays show that slavery was not the only issue driving sectional rift. The only great debate over slavery in that decade was over the admission of Missouri into the Union. The other conflicts—over the tariff and Indian removal—were not essentially about slavery.

Other sectional debates in the period support this notion. Members of Virginia's states' rights elite, known as the "Richmond Junto," were deeply hostile to the Supreme Court's nationalist jurisprudence. The Virginians particularly despised their neighbor, Chief Justice John Marshall. Just after the War of 1812 Virginia's highest court adamantly refused to accept that the U.S. Supreme Court could review its opinions. In *Fairfax's Devisee v. Hunter's Lessee,*[10] the U.S. Supreme Court had ordered that certain lands once owned by Thomas, Lord Fairfax, be returned to his heirs. In 1815 the Virginia Court of Appeals refused to follow this decision, declaring instead that the U.S. Supreme Court lacked the power to review its cases. A year later Justice Joseph Story wrote one of the strongest nationalist opinions in Court history in *Martin v. Hunter's Lessee,*[11] once again overruling Virginia's highest court. Eventually Virginia partially accepted some of this outcome, and the parties themselves negotiated a settlement.

---

[9] Quoted in Garrison, chapter 4, note 1.
[10] *Fairfax's Devisee v. Hunter's Lessee,* 11 U.S. (7 Cranch) 603 (1813).
[11] *Martin v. Hunter's Lessee,* 14 U.S. (1 Wheat.) 304 (1816).

Virginia's states' rights advocates were equally appalled by Chief Justice Marshall's opinion in *McCulloch v. Maryland*,[12] which upheld the constitutionality of the Second Bank of the United States. Marshall found expansive powers for Congress in the "necessary and proper clause" of Article I of the Constitution. Judge Spencer Roane and John Taylor of Caroline,[13] a former U.S. senator from Virginia, denounced Marshall, and Marshall defended himself in essays that he signed "A Friend of the Constitution." An aging Thomas Jefferson privately said that Chief Justice Marshall was like a miner, "constantly working underground to undermine the foundations of our confederated fabric." Similarly, James Madison complained that the decision would "convert a limited into an unlimited Government."[14] Two years later Marshall further antagonized the Virginia sectionalists by reviewing the prosecution of two men for selling lottery tickets, in *Cohens v. Virginia*.[15] Here the court affirmed the Virginia decision. But the very act of reviewing a Virginia state case infuriated Virginians. Once again Roane and Taylor attacked Marshall in print, while privately Jefferson called the court an "irresponsible body."

The responses to these cases, like the responses to the tariff and to those who opposed Indian removal, indicate the growing problem of sectionalism in the 1820s. These areas—tariff policy, Indians, court jurisdiction, or the Bank—do not on their face have anything to do with the great sectional issue—slavery. But, slavery was at the root of all of these. Southerners understood that a strong national government could, and ultimately would, threaten slavery, in part because they understood that the population of the North was growing far more rapidly than that of the South and that the North soon would be able to outvote the South in Congress and in presidential elections. Thus, a strong national government that could build banks, tax imports to protect domestic industries, review state court decisions, or extensively regulate commerce, could also threaten slavery. Thus in his book-length attack on the Marshall Court, *Construction Construed and Constitutions*

---

[12]*McCulloch v. Maryland*, 17 U.S. (4 Wheat.) 316 (1819).

[13]Taylor's name was so common that he always added a reference to his home county—"of Caroline"—so everyone could know which John Taylor was writing.

[14]Jefferson and Madison quoted in Melvin I. Urofsky and Paul Finkelman, *A March of Liberty: A Constitutional History of the United States*, 2d ed., 2 vols. (New York, 2002).

[15]*Cohens v. Virginia*, 19 U.S. (6 Wheat.) 264 (1821).

Vindicated (1820), Virginia's John Taylor of Caroline argued that if Congress had the power to incorporate a bank, as Marshall claimed, then it would also have the power to free the slaves in the South. Sectionalism was about many things, but ultimately it would be about slavery.

Congress in the Age of Jackson

The controversial issues of the 1820s did not disappear in the next decade. Indeed, they reemerged and were fought over once again. The outcomes, however, were different as the politics changed. Thomas Jefferson called his election the "Revolution of 1800," but it was surely a minor revolution compared to the election of 1828. Jefferson and Adams may have had different political agendas, but both were from the elite of society and traveled in the same circles. They were equally cultured, well educated, and refined. By contrast, John Quincy Adams, the loser in 1828, and Andrew Jackson, the winner, had almost nothing in common. John Quincy, like his father, was a Harvard graduate and a worldly man. He was a sophisticated intellectual who had been to Europe, spoke foreign languages, and understood the intricacies of banking, taxation, and international law. John Quincy was the last of the patrician founders.

Andrew Jackson was a new kind of president—barely educated, uncouth, rough, poor from birth, and self-made. As William W. Freehling points out in this volume, Jackson was "the first president with a nickname," and he stood for "egalitarianism." He was our first commoner to be president. Although born in South Carolina, he was raised on the frontier, and when elected president he lived in Tennessee, making him the first president from west of the Appalachians. He had been a soldier, lawyer, and Indian fighter. Like Adams he had been a diplomat, but even here the differences were striking. Adams negotiated treaties and agreements with other diplomats and heads of state in European capitals, at state dinners, and in fancy drawing rooms and palaces. Jackson met with Indian chiefs at campgrounds or rough-hewn cabins to hammer out treaties using gifts, threats, his mercurial temper, and, when necessary, outright bribes, to force the Creek, Choctaw, Seminole, and Chickasaw to give up their lands. During the Monroe administration Jackson had pursued British agents into Spanish Florida, where he captured and summarily hanged them. He left it to the secretary of state—ironically, his future rival, John Quincy Adams—to find a rule of international law that convinced the British not to use this as a pretext to once again go to war with the United States.

John Quincy Adams, refined and dignified, had been a lawyer, senator, and secretary of state before running for president. Although Jackson was also an attorney and had held public office, his real profession was as a soldier. He also made money as a land speculator and planter. Jackson had a long and distinguished career as a soldier and was the hero of the Battle of New Orleans. He was quick-tempered and capable of verbal and physical violence. Other presidents—Washington and Monroe—had seen violent death close-up during the Revolution. But only Jackson had killed a man with his own hands while fighting a duel, had personally presided over executions, or had led troops in battle and supervised the killing of the enemy at close range. Like all other presidents, except the Adamses, he was a Southern slave owner. But, unlike the other early slaveholding presidents, he had acquired his many slaves and his plantation through hard work and cunning, not through inheritance. Unlike all other slaveholding presidents, Jackson had no doubts about the propriety or good policy of bondage.[16]

Jackson was not only a common man from a common background but also the voice, the spirit, and the hero of ordinary Americans. Jackson's support came from small farmers all over the country, particularly from western settlers. His policies would in part reflect their needs and goals. As Jenny Wahl's chapter reminds us, Jackson's war on the Bank of the United States may indeed have led to disastrous economic consequence, but it was politically very popular.

In many ways Jackson was our first modern president. The essays in this section suggest the development of an independent presidency led by a charismatic leader disdainful of Congress and impatient with the cumbersome process of legislation. Jackson used the veto in a new way. Other presidents had vetoed legislation rarely and with care. Madison, for example, had

---

[16]Washington, a lifelong slave owner, refused to buy and sell slaves and freed his own slaves at his death; Madison refused to sell slaves throughout most of his life and did so only as an old man when he could no longer afford to maintain his many slaves on his small landholding. Jefferson sold slaves frequently, defended the necessity of slavery, and articulated the first "scientific" arguments that justified the enslavement of blacks on the grounds of racial inferiority. However, he also expressed his doubts about the safety and fundamental morality of slavery. See generally, Finkelman, *Slavery and the Founders*.

vetoed the first bill to create a Second Bank of the United States because he thought the bill did not accomplish what was needed. But in his Bank War Jackson's aggressive use of the veto was a frontal attack on Congress and the commercial interests in the nation that supported the Bank. As Daniel Feller shows, his Bank veto and his other vetoes, his subsequent removal of federal deposits, and his use of interim appointments to his cabinet, including Secretary of the Treasury Roger B. Taney, led to an ongoing war with the Senate. Jackson's actions illustrate a new kind of politics that prefigured, in some ways, the modern presidency. But, for his opponents, he was, perhaps with good reason, seen as "King Andrew." His use of interim appointments to avoid Senate confirmations he could not win rightly infuriated members of Congress, who saw Jackson as flouting the Constitution to further his narrow partisan agenda. He was haughty, imperious, and disdainful of the traditional relationship of the president to Congress. As a general he had never deferred to anyone (except perhaps the president), and he surely did not think he needed to defer to a Congress full of politicians who could never match his life experiences. But, however imperious, Jackson, unlike a king, had been overwhelmingly elected by the people. And he was one of them. He was truly a commoner, even if his opponents accused him of being King Andrew.

The causes of Jackson's turbulent relationship with Congress were complicated by personalities, egos, and politics. Jackson always blamed his loss in the 1824 presidential election on Henry Clay. Jackson had led in the popular and electoral votes but lacked a majority of the electoral votes. Thus the election was decided by the House of Representatives. Clay, who ran fourth and was thus not eligible to be considered by the House, used his influence in the House of Representatives to secure the presidency for Adams. As long as Clay remained a leader in the Senate, it was probably impossible for the quick-tempered and often angry Jackson to get along with that body. Similarly, at least in his first term, most of the leaders in the Congress probably underestimated Jackson's political skills and his fearless brinksmanship. A different president and a different Congress might have worked out a compromise over the Bank of the United States. Such a compromise might have led to an end to the Bank and even a withdrawal of federal deposits, but in a more orderly manner. Jackson, the general and Indian fighter, however, was not accustomed to compromise, and the leaders of Congress believed they could force the politically inexperienced Jackson to sign the bank bill because on the eve of a presidential election he could not afford an economic catastrophe that would follow a veto. The leaders of Congress were of course wrong. Whether the Bank issue caused the Panic of 1837 or only exacerbated it, the Bank's demise, in the manner in which it took place, was surely a major fiasco for Americans, even if it enhanced Jackson's popularity with his constituents.

Despite historians' interest in the Bank, most modern Americans probably do not remember the Bank veto. Even fewer Americans recall Roger B. Taney's role in Jackson's administration and in the Bank crisis. Taney served as attorney general and drafted Jackson's veto message for the bank bill, earning him the enmity of many in the Congress. After the veto, Jackson ordered Secretary of the Treasury Louis McLane to remove all federal deposits from the Bank. McLane refused to do this, and Jackson replaced him with William Duane, who was fired when he too refused to remove the deposits. Jackson then turned to Taney, giving him a recess appointment to the Treasury. Taney dutifully began to remove federal money from the Bank, an act that led to economic chaos.

In 1834 the Senate, furious at the withdrawal of the deposits from the Bank, refused to confirm Taney as secretary of the Treasury, and Taney returned to his private law practice. In early 1835 Jackson nominated Taney for the Supreme Court, but the Senate once again refused to confirm him to office. Jackson, never one to run from a fight, nominated Taney as chief justice in December of that year, and a few months later the Senate finally confirmed him. If Jackson had had better relations with Congress, the Senate might have confirmed Taney to the Treasury, and that is where he would perhaps have remained when the Supreme Court positions opened up. Had the Senate confirmed Taney to the Court in the first round, he would probably not have been elevated to chief justice the next year. Thus, Jackson's ongoing war with Congress helped lead to Taney's becoming chief justice. This book goes to press at the 150th anniversary of Taney's decision in *Dred Scott v. Sandford* (1857). As we remember that almost universally condemned decision, it is worth recalling that one of the costs of Jacksonian Democracy, and perhaps a by-product of Jackson's stormy relationship with Congress, was Chief Justice Taney.[17]

---

[17]For a discussion of the general condemnation of that case, see Paul Finkelman, *Dred Scott v. Sandford: A Brief History with Documents* (Boston, 1995).

Debates over slavery, sectionalism, and states' rights did not end with the Missouri Compromise. In the 1820s a number of small events set the stage for the great debates over slavery in the next three decades. In the early part of the decade South Carolina began to arrest free black sailors whose ships entered the state. In *Elkison v. Deliesseline*,[18] U.S. Supreme Court Justice William Johnson condemned this practice but was unable to stop it. South Carolina put the nation on notice that it would not respect the Constitution, the Supreme Court, or Congress if the state's leaders felt that slavery or the state's racial order might be undermined by any policy, law, or constitutional provision. In 1829 Southerners were deeply shaken by the appearance of David Walker's *Appeal to the Colored Citizens of the World*, in which this almost unknown black activist urged slaves to revolt against their masters. Two years later the modern abolitionist movement began, with the publication of William Lloyd Garrison's *Liberator*. Southerners were further shaken by Nat Turner's Rebellion that summer, which led to the death of more than a hundred blacks and whites in rural Virginia. On the heels of these events came the nullification crisis.

Nullification was ostensibly about tariffs. In reality, as William W. Freehling taught us some forty years ago,[19] and as he and Michael Les Benedict remind us in this volume, nullification was rooted in slavery, fears of abolition, and a declining slave-based economy in South Carolina. Jackson's response to nullification was his shining moment. As Freehling notes, "Jackson's anti-nullification performance featured all the elements that define presidential greatness (and were missing in his banking performance): a major crisis, fully solved; superb tactics, perfectly designed to achieve pristine goals; a disinterested initiative, risking trouble for his class and party; and a long-term impact, bolstering the best of his civilization." Here Jackson suppressed a direct assault on the nation and the Constitution, and as Michael Les Benedict shows, he helped redefine the meaning of federalism. Jackson's success was of course not complete. Nullification and secessionist tendencies would not disappear. Ironically, Jackson's own chief justice would have a hand in unleashing nullification forces with his opinion in *Dred Scott v. Sandford*, which in effect "nullified" the Missouri Compromise. The crisis of the 1850s was about more than just *Dred Scott*, and it would be wrong to blame it all on Taney. However, Taney's decision certainly set the stage for Lincoln's victory in 1860,

---

[18]*Elkison v. Deliesseline*, 8 F. Cas. 493 (C.C.D.S.C. 1823) (No. 4,366).
[19]William W. Freehling, *Prelude to Civil War: The Nullification Controversy in South Carolina, 1816–1836* (New York, 1966).

which in turn led to secession. The further irony is that in his early career Lincoln was a Whig and a fervent supporter of Henry Clay. When he faced the secessionists, however, Lincoln found his model in Jackson, whose face he immediately put on a postage stamp, elevating Jackson to the iconic level of Washington, Jefferson, and Benjamin Franklin.[20]

If Jackson is most praised for his actions in the nullification crisis, he is surely most condemned for his Indian policy. Yet, as Tim Garrison points out, Jackson's Indian policy is profoundly complex. Had he been the geno-cidal Indian hater his fiercest critics claim he was, it is doubtful there would be large number of Indians in Oklahoma today living on tribal lands with a good deal of autonomy, operating businesses, and serving in public office, in-cluding the U.S. Congress. Jackson was, if nothing else, an efficient and ruth-less military commander capable of obliterating all of the Indians he fought. But, as it turns out, Jackson was not the prototype of the late-nineteenth-century cavalry that massacred women and children at Sand Creek and Wounded Knee. He was something else. He was surely a white supremacist who owned slaves and removed Indians from the Southeast. But he was also a paternalist, operating under a code of honor that led him to ally with Indians, to adopt an Indian orphan whom he raised as his only son, and to work hard to make sure the Indians had a place to live away from white so-ciety. While modern critics might accuse him of ethnic cleansing, his was not the cleansing of the Bosnian killing fields. He removed Indians to Ok-lahoma, not Auschwitz.

Jackson surely wanted the Indians out of the Southeast. He believed they were a military threat to the nation. During the War of 1812 a number of Indians had sided with the British. Moreover, in the Southeast, Jackson had to fight two wars, one against the British and the other against the Creek. His experience in the Creek War convinced him that the Indians might ally with Britain if another war with the mother country took place.[21] And he believed their fertile land would be best farmed by whites. He also believed that if Indians stayed in the East they would be either decimated physically

---

[20]Before the Civil War all postage stamps had borne the images of Franklin, Washington, and Jefferson. When the Civil War began, the U.S. Post Office demonetized all existing stamps because so many were in Confederate hands. The Lincoln administration issued a new set of stamps that included one with Jackson for sending mail within the same city, a common use of the post office at the time. The message was clear: Jackson had stood up to the nullifiers, and Lincoln was standing up to the secessionists.

[21]Similarly, while the Lincoln administration was occupied with fighting the Confederacy, the president also had to send troops to suppress Indians in Minnesota.

or culturally absorbed so that they would cease to be Indians. His paternalistic admiration for Indian culture led him to want a third alternative: Indians safely removed from the East, where they could neither help an invading British army nor be harmed by white Southerners who wanted their land.

The more interesting question, perhaps, is what would have happened if Jackson had supported the Cherokee treaties and met Georgia's challenge. Could he have mustered the political and military power to protect the Cherokee in Georgia? It seems unlikely he could have done so. Jackson was able to defeat South Carolina's nullification because the nullifiers had no support outside the Palmetto State, and because Jackson had support from Georgia and Tennessee. That support was tied to the promise of removal. But, a reverse strategy would probably not have worked. Had Jackson stood up to Georgia, it is likely that South Carolina and other Southern states would have come to Georgia's defense, in part on states' rights grounds, but also because they wanted Indian removal as well.

It is unlikely that Jackson anticipated the rough and brutal Trail of Tears that implemented the final removal. As Tim Garrison reminds us (and as so many historians forget), he was not president when the removal actually took place. His successor, Martin Van Buren, was president during the removal, and Van Buren understood little about Indians or the way the army operated. This is just one more irony of Jackson and his era. If we take him at his word, as Garrison points out, Jackson thought removal would protect and save Indians from cultural annihilation or physical destruction at the hand of Southern whites who were hungry for land and unconcerned about the rights of nonwhites. In the end, however, Jackson failed to put in place any conditions that might have prevented the horrible suffering and death of the Trail of Tears. That, too, is part of his legacy.

The essays in this book explore the emerging sectionalism of the 1820s and the political issues of the Jacksonian era. The authors revisit, in important new ways, the role of the three-fifths clause in the Constitution, the politics of the Missouri Compromise, the nature of the tariff debates, Jackson's legacy on the Bank, nullification, and Indian removal. Together, these essays help us better understand the relationship between Congress, the executive branch, and the states from the end of the War of 1812 through the Age of Jackson. It was an era of complexity, confusion, and great national growth. It set the stage for territorial expansion in the next decade and a final crisis of the Union in the 1850s and 1860s.

1: Sectionalism

Jan Lewis

The Three-Fifths Clause
and the Origins of Sectionalism

H OW EARLY CAN we find the origins of American sectionalism? Some historians have traced them to the founding of the colonies, created for different purposes by different sorts of people in different regions with different climates.[1] Yet, by definition, there could not be sections until there was a nation, and so, if we want to trace the origins of American sectionalism back to their starting place, we should begin with the Continental Congress. Certainly, by the time the Constitution was written, a little more than a decade later, American leaders had developed a language of sectionalism. Madison's comments at the Federal Convention of 1787 are well known: "He contended that the States were divided into different interests not by their difference of size, but by other circumstances; the most material of which resulted partly from climate, but principally from [the effect of] their having or not having slaves. These two causes concurred in forming the great division of interests in the U. States. It did not lie between the large & small States: it lay between the Northern & Southern."[2]

Madison's account of sectional difference is so clear and put forth so self-confidently that it is tempting to conclude that he was describing what everyone could see—a simple statement of fact. Hence, sectional difference came

---

[1]See in particular David Hackett Fischer, *Albion's Seed: Four British Folkways in America* (New York, 1989).

[2]Max Farrand, ed., *The Records of the Federal Convention of 1787*, 4 vols. (1911; reprint ed., New Haven, 1966), 1:486.

into being with the nation, and there never existed a time in the nation's history before there was a profound and obvious difference between the North and South.

Yet, if we place Madison's observation about sectionalism in its context—a high-stakes argument in the Constitutional Convention about the basis for representation in the new nation, which had been preceded by another argument in Congress about the basis for apportioning the costs of the Revolution—we can see that this early formulation of sectionalism was, as much as anything, a political tactic, more a means to an end than a simple statement of fact. To put it another way, the discussions of sectional difference in the Continental Congress and the Federal Convention were not so much descriptions of reality as carefully calculated attempts to achieve particular political ends. This is not to suggest that Madison *created* sectional difference, or even the idea of sectionalism—that would be preposterous—but rather that he used the idea of fundamental sectional difference as a political tool, in the process giving those sectional differences a legitimacy that they would not have otherwise had.

We can see how this process worked if we focus on those moments in the founding—at the Continental Congress, its successor Confederation Congress, and in the Constitutional Convention—when the delegates discussed sections in the kind of terms that Madison used: a "great division of interests" based upon whether they had slaves or not. These are the moments when slavery made its way into the discussion. It should be noted that no one—or almost no one—in Congress or at the convention really wanted to discuss slavery. In each case, the delegates had what seemed to them more pressing questions—declaring independence, fighting and winning the Revolution, and creating a new national government. If any message emerges from the discussions in Congress from 1774 on, it is that the delegates hoped that slavery would go away. In 1774, Congress agreed, without leaving any record of a discussion, to discontinue the slave trade. (This was part of a set of resolutions that cut off imports from Britain.)[3]

---

[3]Worthington C. Ford et al., eds., *Journals of the Continental Congress, 1774–1789*, 34 vols. (Washington, D.C., 1904–37), 1:77 (hereafter *JCC*); Donald Robinson, *Slavery in the Structure of American Politics, 1765–1820* (New York, 1971), p. 79. Why the separate paragraph on slaves? The first of the resolutions declared that the signatories would "not import" from Britain "any goods, wares, or merchandise whatsoever." The second resolution specified that neither would they "import nor purchase, any slave imported. . . . We will wholly discontinue the slave trade" (*JCC*, 1:76–77). Donald Robinson suggests that since all trade was to be suspended

Two years later, when Thomas Jefferson tried to insert into the Declaration of Independence a paragraph condemning King George III for carrying on the slave trade, Congress removed it. Jefferson later explained that the clause was deleted to placate South Carolina and Georgia, "who had never attempted to restrain the importation of slaves, and who in the contrary still wished to continue it." He speculated too that "our Northern brethren . . . felt a little tender" on the topic, given their prominent role as slave traders.[4]

Congress, then, was willing to curtail the slave trade but not to condemn it. These are the signs of discomfort, suggestions that the collective hope was simply to keep the problem out of sight. Given this context, it is hard to imagine that Congress—or the Constitutional Convention—would have discussed slavery qua slavery unless it was absolutely necessary.

That, in fact, became the case once the issue of apportioning expenses among the states came up—in shorthand, taxation. Congress wrangled with this issue for several years. Each of these discussions was complicated. Not only was this the first time that representatives from all of the states had met together, but most of the delegates were trying out their ideas as they went along. Think of a multiplayer card game, in which each player makes his bids and tries to play his hand without yet knowing the rules of the game. Rather than take you through all the moves—which would be dizzying— we will focus on a few moments, snapshots rather than streaming video.

---

anyway, why not gain a moral advantage by singling out slaves?: "It would be a mistake to assume that these agreements to suspend the slave trade represent the triumph of moral principle over interest and desire" (p. 79). Yet, simply to ask whether slaves were comprehended in the phrase "any goods, wares, or merchandise," as the delegates must have done, was to confront troubling questions about the nature of slavery. By giving slaves their own clause, the delegates recognized, if subtly, the anomalous nature of property in slaves. See also William W. Freehling, "The Founding Fathers and Slavery," *American Historical Review* 77 (1972):81–93. Although Freehling does not mention this particular action, he argues that the Founding Fathers engaged in a strategy of "attack[ing] slavery where it was the weakest, thereby driving the institution south and vitiating its capacity to survive" (p. 86). The slave trade represented one of the institution's weakest points.

[4]Julian P. Boyd et al., eds., *The Papers of Thomas Jefferson*, 31 vols. (Princeton, N.J., 1950–2004), 1:314–15. Some years later, John Adams partially verified Jefferson's account, telling Timothy Pickering, "I was delighted with [the Declaration's] high tone and the flights of oratory with which it abounded, especially that concerning Negro slavery, which, though I knew his Southern brethren would never suffer to pass in Congress, I would never oppose." He described the deleted paragraph as "a vehement philippic against slavery" (John Adams to Timothy Pickering, Aug. 22, 1822, in *Letters of Members of the Continental Congress*, ed. Edmund C. Burnett, 31 vols. [Washington, D.C., 1921–36], 1:515–16).

Our first moment: In Congress, 1775, Benjamin Franklin offers a preliminary draft of articles of confederation to the Continental Congress. He suggests basing both representation and apportionment of expenses upon the
"Number of Male Polls between 16 and 60 Years of Age."[5] What might appear an innocuous formula was in fact Franklin's awkward—and ultimately
unsuccessful—attempt to forge a compromise between North and South.
Representatives from the big states repeatedly argued for proportional representation on democratic and self-serving grounds—and each time went
down to defeat, but not before they had had an opportunity to air their
democratic theories. As Franklin knew, the small states would never countenance proportional representation. Hence, the only part of his proposal that
stood a chance was the suggestion to apportion assessments on the basis of
adult male taxables, not female ones. This formulation actually represented
something of a concession to the South. In the colonies, poll taxes were typically levied on adult men, but in the South they also were assessed on black
women as members of the labor force.[6] In a pattern that would become familiar, an antislavery Northerner from a big state, Franklin, offered a concession to the South. This proposal and, indeed, the attempt to forge articles
of confederation went nowhere, however; the delegates had more pressing
matters at hand.

Our next moment: In 1776, a week after the Declaration of Independence
has been signed, John Dickinson presented his draft of articles of confederation, with an array of concessions to the various interests. For the slave states,
each state's quota of troops were to be based on the white population only.
Congress readily agreed. Dickinson's formulas for representation and allocation of expenses, however, differed from Franklin's. In Dickinson's proposal,
each state received one vote, while expenses were allocated on the basis of
the total population, including slaves.[7] Samuel Chase, from the slave state of
Maryland, objected immediately to the counting of slaves in the basis for
taxing the states. His logic was far too convoluted to recapitulate here.[8]

---

[5] *JCC*, 2:195–97.

[6] Robinson, *Slavery in the Structure of American Politics*, p. 488 n. 39.

[7] *JCC*, 5:546–56. The draft articles were presented on July 12, 1776, and Congress began
debating them on July 30.

[8] Jonathan Elliot, ed., *The Debates in the Several State Conventions on the Adoption of the Federal
Constitution in 1787*, 5 vols. (1888; reprint ed., New York, 1968), 1:70–71. See also Boyd, *Papers of
Thomas Jefferson*, 1:330–31.

John Adams quickly steered the discussion back on track, in the process laying out what would become the default Northern position, which was that "numbers of people"—population—was just an "index of wealth" and that slaves should be counted because, like free laborers, they contribute to the state's wealth. Adams also moved the discussion onto the terrain of political economy, suggesting that slaves were just as productive as free laborers.[9] Hence, when Virginia's Benjamin Harrison offered a compromise—"two slaves should be counted as one freeman"—he justified it by explaining "that slaves did not do as much work as freemen, and doubted if two effected more than one."[10]

Once Adams shifted the discussion, each section took a position that one may think counterintuitive: Northerners insisted that slave and free labor were equally productive, while Southerners claimed that slave labor was less productive than free. Self-serving though it was, the Southern argument rested on good authority: the world's best political economists also thought that slave labor was comparatively unproductive—and hence on the road to extinction. (James Oakes has recently labeled this the "bourgeois critique of slavery.")[11] Thus, by arguing that slave labor was less productive than free, Southern delegates not only justified lower assessments for their states, but they also made themselves appear almost as abolitionists. Slavery, they implied, would be its own undoing. South Carolina's Edward Rutledge, for example, said that he would "be happy to get rid of the idea of slavery. The slaves do not signify property; the old and young cannot work." Similarly, North Carolina's William Hooper insisted, "I wish to see the day that slaves are not necessary." He thought free labor at least four times as valuable as slave.[12]

Let us skip ahead to another moment, 1783, when this question was revisited. In 1777, the delegates had decided that assessments should be based

---

[9]Elliot, *Debates*, 1:71–72. Adams wrote in his diary that "Chace [*sic*] is violent and boisterous. . . . He is tedious upon frivolous points" (L. H. Butterfield et al., eds., *Diary and Autobiography of John Adams*, 4 vols. [Cambridge, Mass., 1962], 2:172).

[10]Elliot, *Debates*, 1:72.

[11]James Oakes, "The Peculiar Fate of the Bourgeois Critique of Slavery," in *Slavery and the American South*, ed. Winthrop D. Jordan (Oxford, Miss., 2003), pp. 29–48. Oakes notes that until about 1820, the best minds in the South believed that slave labor was inferior to free and hence slave labor was on its way to extinction.

[12]*JCC*, 6:1080.

upon the value of land.[13] When it became clear that a new method of levying assessments was needed, nationalists in Congress returned immediately to the idea of taxing population. The question now was how to count slaves. In a letter to Congress, Robert Morris, the superintendent of finance, suggested a one-dollar tax on "all freemen, and all male slaves between 16 and 60," excepting those who were in the army or unfit for service. Like Benjamin Franklin's proposal in 1775, which it resembled, Morris's plan would have exempted female slaves, normally subject to poll taxes in the South.[14] Connecticut's Oliver Wolcott proposed something similar on the floor of Congress. He thought that the number of inhabitants should be the "rule," but, in a bow to the political economy argument, he "admit[ted] the difference between freemen & blacks; and suggest[ed] a compromise by including in the numeration such blacks only as were within 16 & 60 years."[15] Like Morris,

---

[13]There were simply too many disagreements among the delegates to make possible a compromise on how to count slaves. Some thought land a better index of wealth. See, for example, Cornelius Harnett to the governor of North Carolina, Oct. 10, 1777, and Nov. 30, 1777, in Burnett, *Letters of Members of the Continental Congress,* 2:514, 578; and Richard Henry Lee to Roger Sherman, Nov. 24, 1777, in *Letters of Delegates to Congress, 1774–1789,* ed. Paul H. Smith, 26 vols. (Washington, D.C., 1976–2000), 8:320. As a rule, Southerners preferred to assess land, and Northerners population, but some Northern delegates were unwilling at this point to give the South a discount for their slaves. Likewise, some Northerners had difficulty comprehending the argument that the South was making about the nature of slavery itself. As Nathaniel Folsom of New Hampshire wrote to the president of that state, "In the first place it appears to me that one third part of the welth [*sic*] of the Southern States which consists in negroes, is entirely left out and no Notice taken of them, in determining their ability to pay taxes, notwithstanding it is by them that they procure their wealth." He was objecting to Article VIII, which assessed land, the proxy the delegates had decided upon for wealth, but the same objection could be applied to population: The South had a most peculiar system in which *labor* was also *property,* and the instruments of Southern wealth were in themselves wealth. Northerners and Southerners both struggled for analogies. Were slaves like horses or cattle? Like white dependent laborers? They were neither; slavery was like nothing else. Nathaniel Folsom to Meshech Ware, Nov. 21, 1777, in Smith, *Letters of Delegates to Congress,* 8:299.

[14]William T. Hutchinson et al., eds., *The Papers of James Madison,* 17 vols. (Chicago, 1962–91), 6:153 n. 35.

[15]Ibid., 6:215. In their earliest discussions, the delegates seemed to be looking for a formula that would use age as the basis for providing a discount for slaves. North Carolina's delegates reported home about a recommendation of a "Poll Tax of half a Dollar on all male Slaves from 16 to 60 & all free men from 16 to 21 & a Dollar on all free men from 21 to 60 except those in the federal army &c." (North Carolina delegates to Alexander Martin, Oct. 22, 1782, in Smith, *Letters of Delegates to Congress,* 19:290). Half a year later, North Carolina's delegates reported a new proposal "to exclude all Slaves under 16 Years, which would be rating two slaves for one free men [*sic*]" (North Carolina delegates to Alexander Martin, Mar. 24, 1783, ibid., 20:91). Hence, although there seemed to be a general willingness to give the South some consideration for its supposedly less productive slave population, the basis for the judgment of

he was offering the South a discount for slaves, implicitly because he agreed that they were less productive than free people or less able to contribute to the general welfare.

The only question was how great the South's discount should be. As James Madison explained to Thomas Jefferson in early March 1783, "A recommendation is to be included for substituting numbers in place of the value of land as the rule of apportionment. In this all the States are interested if proper deductions be made from the number of Slaves."[16] Congress's *Report on Public Credit* incorporated a variant on Wolcott's proposal, excluding all those "who are bound to servitude for life according to the laws of the State to which they belong, other than such as may be between the ages of [ ]"— and the space was left blank, for Congress to fill in later. Congress had begun to wrestle with the proper formula in 1775, when Harrison suggested counting two slaves for every free person. Now it was struggling with the way to say "slave" without using the word.[17] Within a few weeks, Congress had found, for the moment, a formula and a more concise way to avoid saying "slave": assessments should be levied "in proportion to the whole number of free inhabitants & one half of the number of all other inhabitants of every age sex and condition except Indians not paying Taxes in each State."[18]

Now that a formula and terminology—and the need to arrive at some compromise—were on the floor, the debate could begin in earnest.[19] Let us follow the debate, as James Madison rendered it in a kind of shorthand. The committee had suggested "that two blacks be rated as one freeman. Mr. Wolcot [Oliver Wolcott, Connecticut] was for rating them as 4 to 3. Mr. Carroll [Charles Carroll, Maryland] was for rating them as 4 to 1." North and

---

lower productivity was not entirely clear. Was it that younger and older slaves were less productive than whites of the same age? Or was it that black workers of the same age were less productive than their white counterparts? The discussion implicitly moved from the first proposition to the second.

[16]Hutchinson, *Papers of James Madison*, 6:310–11.

[17]Ibid., 6:313–14. The text comes from Madison's notes. He had originally written and then crossed out the two words "deemed slaves" and penned in the much more awkward locution, the obvious forerunner of the three-fifths clause's "all other persons" (6:316 n. 16).

[18]Ibid., 6:406. Note also that Madison had originally written "free white" and then crossed out "white," reflecting a change made in the debates in Congress (6:407 n. 3). It is worth noting that the terms *white* and *free* were generally used interchangeably, as were the terms "slave" and "black," but that once the discussion moved from debates to formal resolutions, the words "slave," "white," and "black" generally disappeared.

[19]For the political context, see Jack N. Rakove, *The Beginnings of National Politics: An Interpretive History of the Continental Congress* (New York, 1979), esp. pp. 297–329.

South were bickering over the size of the slavery discount. "Mr. Williamson [Hugh Williamson, North Carolina] sd. he was principled agst. slavery; & that he thought slaves an incumbrance to Society instead of increasing its ability to pay taxes." Here, once again, was the South's strategic use of political economy: slavery is less productive than free labor; we hate slavery; we shouldn't have to pay as much because we have slaves. Stephen Higginson, from Massachusetts, responded not with an argument but with a return to Wolcott's initial bid—"4 to 3." South Carolina's John Rutledge offered a compromise—"2 to 1, but he sincerely thought 3 to 1 would be a juster proportion." Then Samuel Holten and Samuel Osgood, both from Massachusetts, implicitly rejected it, instead reiterating Wolcott's 4 to 3.

It appeared that the North, having offered the South a small discount, was unwilling to yield any more. Madison then "said that in order to give a proof of the sincerity of his professions of liberality he wd. propose that the Slaves should be rated as 5 to 3." Rutledge, another Southerner, immediately seconded this motion, and then Pennsylvania's James Wilson said that he would "sacrifice his opinion to this compromise."[20] The haggling was over; the compromise had been struck—as a measure of wealth, five enslaved black workers were the equivalent of three free white ones.

In 1783, everyone seemed to agree that slavery was less productive than free labor. As Madison explained in his summary of the debate, even Northerners agreed that slaves' "[i]ndustry & ingenuity were below those of freemen." But Northerners also insisted that it cost less to feed and clothe slaves. Moreover, the South had the additional advantage of a better climate. Southerners replied that—and here their debt to the bourgeois critique of slavery is particularly clear—"having no interest in their labor," slaves "did as little as possible, & omitted every exertion of thought requisite to facilitate & expedite it."[21] Northerners and Southerners now had agreed that slave labor was less productive than free; the only argument was about how much less. There was no pretense that Congress had accurately assessed the relative value of free and slave labor. As Congress explained to the states when asking them to ratify this amendment to the original articles: "The only material difficulty which attended [the new rule] in the deliberations in Congress, was to fix the proper difference between the labor and industry

---

[20]Hutchinson, *Papers of James Madison,* 6:408.
[21]Ibid. Again, see Oakes, "Bourgeois Critique of Slavery."

of free inhabitants, and of all other inhabitants. The ratio ultimately agreed on was the effect of mutual concessions, and if it should be supposed not to correspond precisely with the fact, no doubt ought to be entertained that an equal spirit of accommodation among the several Legislatures, will prevail against little inequalities which may be calculated on one side or on the other."[22]

Although the states never ratified this amendment, Congress had demonstrated that it was able to compromise on the issue of slavery. The delegates agreed that slave labor was less productive than free and hence that the South deserved a discount. The North, it might appear, had won the moral point, and the South the practical one, but the compromise was more complicated than that. By persuading Northerners to accept the proposition that slave labor was less productive, Southerners conceded that slavery was tainted. In a nation as bourgeois as the new United States, to state that slave labor was inferior, an "incumbrance," was quite a concession.[23]

Even though the South had gained important concessions on troop and tax quotas, the North thought it had struck a fair deal. Not only had the fledgling union been preserved—always the first priority—but slavery itself also seemed on the road to extinction. Northerners believed that their concessions to the South, accommodating the peculiar institution of slavery, would thus turn out to be temporary expedients, necessary for holding the new nation together. This is why those early concessions that the South made on the slave trade were so important. Not only had the South agreed to discontinue importing slaves, at least for the time being, but also a Southern slaveholder had tried to insert into the Declaration of Independence a condemnation of the slave trade so fiery that even Northern delegates winced. Now that Southerners were telling them that slave labor was so inefficient that two slaves could barely do the labor of one free man, who could fault Northerners for believing that slavery would die a quiet death?

Some Northerners still thought, in spite of what Southern delegates told them, that slavery was an enormously profitable institution. And of course

---

[22]Hutchinson, *Papers of James Madison*, 6:492. Madison, Nathaniel Gorham (Massachusetts), and Alexander Hamilton (New York) wrote the report. See also James Madison to Edmund Randolph, Apr. 8, 1783: "The deduction of 2/3 was a compromise between the wide opinions & demands of the Southern & other States" (6:440).

[23]It should be noted that slavery was, in fact, enormously profitable and that the South at the time was the wealthiest section of the new nation. On this point, see Oakes, "Bourgeois Critique of Slavery."

they were right. But the Southerners sold them a dream, a fantasy that freed them from the contradictions of slavery and freedom and people as property. In the fall of 1783, Rhode Island delegates William Ellery and David Howell reported back to Gov. William Greene about the proposed change in Article VIII. They had doubts about its fairness. "If numbers are to be the rule ought not all the blacks in the Southern States to be taken into the census? The nett [sic] produce of the labour of a black man in those States is, at least, double to that of a common white labourer in the eastern States."[24] They were still not convinced that slave labor was inferior to free, but by 1785 David Howell had changed his mind. He still thought that all of the slaves should have been counted, but he recognized that some compromise had been necessary. More important, history itself would eventually make the point moot. "An attention to the actual Situation & population of the Southern States where the blacks are most numerous will suggest a probability that in time the proposed rule of apportionment will become less objectionable." He then gave his governor a lesson in geography and political economy as he now understood them. "Once you leave the Sea co[a]st" of the Southern states "and pass on westward . . . the lands are cultivated by white people, whose method of life & manners are similar to the middle & northern States. . . . So that the number of blacks compared with the whites even in those States will probably diminish in the future. . . . And even the ratio of the States, in which the blacks are numerous . . . will gradually diminish as the tide of population rolls westward & new States arise peopled from Europe where the Slavery of the blacks is unknown, or from the northern States where it is reprobated." Thus, Howell could confidently conclude, "On all these accounts the proposed rule . . . will probably in future approximate to justice."[25] Greatly to their advantage, Southerners had persuaded their Northern brethren that slavery was a slowly dying institution, for that is what Northerners wanted to believe. North and South shared a common fantasy, one that offered them an escape from the dilemma that slavery presented.

ONLY FOUR YEARS later, many of the same men—Madison, Wilson, and Franklin, as well as Alexander Hamilton and Nathaniel Gorham—were in Philadelphia as delegates to the Constitutional Convention. Once again,

---

[24]Rhode Island delegates to William Greene, Sept. 8, 1783, in Smith, *Letters of Delegates to Congress,* 20:642.

[25]David Howell to William Greene, Aug. 23, 1785, ibid., 22:587.

slavery was an issue, and it came up just as it had in the Continental Congress. The delegates were discussing something else and then, all of a sudden, there it was—slavery. That something else was representation.

On Monday June 11, the delegates were debating the provision of the Virginia Plan, introduced two weeks earlier, which established the basis for suffrage in the proposed Congress. In fact, the Virginia Plan had dodged this issue, saying that representation in both houses should be proportional—but giving the delegates a choice about how the representatives and senators were to be proportioned: whether by "quotas of contribution, or [by] the number of free inhabitants."[26] Clearly, this formulation was an allusion to the earlier discussions in the Continental Congress, and it would have signaled something specific to the delegates who were familiar with what had transpired there. "Quotas of contribution" was a synonym for wealth that came with its own ready-made formula for measurement: all of the free people (except Indians) and three-fifths of the slaves.

When the delegates turned to this question, they immediately addressed the two issues that had been combined in this clause of the Virginia Plan: whether representation in *both* houses should be proportional, and, if the representation in either or both houses *was* to be proportional, how were those proportions to be determined? These two issues were almost inextricably connected in the minds of the Framers, and they raised questions about both state and regional interests as well as underlying political philosophy.

Connecticut's Roger Sherman began the day's discussion by proposing that representatives to the lower house should be apportioned "according to the respective numbers of free inhabitants," while in the second branch, each state should have one vote. Sherman would have had one house highly undemocratic, just as Congress had been, and the other house seemingly quite democratic but clearly favoring the North by counting only free persons. Sherman offered a representation of states and of persons, with no allowances made for slavery at all. In 1777, when Congress was discussing the apportionment of state quotas, Sherman had told Virginia's Richard Henry Lee that "as to the Negros, [*sic*] I Should be willing to do what appears equitable," and he suggested a formula for excluding some slaves from the count.[27] A decade later we see the realpolitik of the convention at work. We should regard Sherman's proposal as an opening bid in what he

---

[26]Farrand, *Records of the Federal Convention*, 1:20.
[27]Ibid., 1:196; Richard Henry Lee to Roger Sherman, Nov. 24, 1777, in Smith, *Letters of Delegates to Congress*, pp. 320–21 n. 2.

knew would be a lengthy negotiation. He had established the principle—which he would ultimately gain—of equal representation for the states in the upper house,[28] and he signaled that the South could expect no automatic consideration from the North for its peculiar institution. This was a proposal designed to serve—and balance—the interests of the small states and the large free ones.

South Carolina's John Rutledge and Pierce Butler immediately countered that representatives in the lower house should be apportioned not on the basis of number of free inhabitants, but on the basis of quotas of contribution. Sherman had taken up one of the options offered by the Virginia Plan, and the South Carolinians were taking up the other. They knew, even if they did not state so explicitly, that "quota of contribution" came, courtesy of the Congress, with a ready-made formula: all the free people plus three-fifths of the slaves. Still, there is something odd about this provision in the Virginia Plan that the South Carolinians took up. The convention had not yet discussed how or whether the states should be assessed, let alone made any decisions on this subject. And although everyone in the room knew the congressional formula for calculating "quota of contribution," the South Carolinians did not mention that it was based upon population, including a proportion of slaves. Instead, Butler explained that "quota of contribution" was a proxy for wealth. "Money was power," he asserted, and hence, "the States ought to have weight in the Govt.—in proportion to their power."[29] In terms of political theory, this proposal was really quite reactionary. No one in Congress had ever suggested that wealth per se should be represented, and no one had ever suggested previously that slaves be included in the basis for calculating representatives.

To be sure, in both Britain and America suffrage had long been associated with the ownership of property, and it was an axiom of classical political thought that officeholders should be men of property and standing who would give government stability. But those Americans who sought representation for wealth usually focused upon the Senate. Only four days earlier, John Dickinson had said that he hoped it would "consist of the most distin-

---

[28]On this point see Jack N. Rakove, *Original Meanings: Politics and Ideas in the Making of the Constitution* (New York, 1996), pp. 61, 68. The equal representation of the states in the Senate is usually regarded as a triumph of the small states. As Rakove notes, however, it also proved a boon to the slave states, which retained control of the Senate long after the North's more rapidly expanding population gave the free states control of the House (see p. 93).

[29]Farrand, *Records of the Federal Convention*, 1:196.

guished characters, distinguished for their rank in life and their weight of property, and bearing as strong a likeness to the British House of Lords as possible." Similarly, Madison believed that "the Senate ought to come from, & represent, the Wealth of the nation."[30] But now the South Carolinians were arguing that not only the Senate but the House, too, should represent wealth and that it should do so not by filtering out distinguished characters to hold office or even by restricting suffrage to property holders but by giving the wealthier states more representatives.

In Congress, the question had been whether states were to be represented or people. Franklin, Wilson, and John Adams, representing the populous states of Pennsylvania and Massachusetts, had advocated proportional representation on democratic and nationalist grounds, while representatives from small states, such as New Jersey's John Witherspoon and Rhode Island's Stephen Hopkins, warned that the confederation would fall apart unless the small states were guaranteed equal representation. The closest anyone came to arguing that representation should be based upon wealth was when Franklin observed sardonically that "if we vote equally we ought to pay equally: but the smaller states will hardly purchase the privilege at this price." Indeed, Wilson had made clear a distinction that the South Carolinians were now, in 1787, fast eroding: "Taxation should be in proportion to wealth, but that representation should accord with the number of freemen."[31] The point bears repeating: no one in Congress had ever suggested that wealth per se should be represented, and, certainly, no one had ever suggested that slaves be included in the basis for calculating representatives.

With the South Carolinians' proposal, the Constitutional Convention now had before it more theories—and more houses of Congress—than it could deal with at one time. Several members suggested that the discussion focus for the moment only on the House of Representatives, where representation should be "according to some equitable ratio of representation."[32] At this point, some of the Northern delegates seemed willing to consider the South Carolinians' suggestion that representation should be based upon wealth. It

[30]Ibid., 1:150, 158. See also Gordon S. Wood, *The Creation of the American Republic, 1776–1787* (Chapel Hill, 1969), pp. 554–55. For theories of representation at the time, see also J. R. Pole, *Political Representation in England and the Origins of the American Republic* (Berkeley, Calif., 1966); John Phillip Reid, *The Concept of Representation in the Age of the American Revolution* (Chicago, 1989); and Rakove, *Original Meanings.*

[31]*JCC*, 6:1102–6.

[32]Farrand, *Records of the Federal Convention*, 1:196.

is worth noting that they seemed to think that they were talking about how much each state would contribute to the national coffers rather than a measure of population that might include slaves.[33] This was too much for Franklin, who began in a conciliatory but disingenuous way by noting that he had originally thought that each state should have the same number of representatives but that he now believed in proportional representation: "The number of Representatives should bear some proportion to the number of the Represented: and that the decisions shd. be by the majority of members, not the majority of States." After all, "[t]he Interest of a State is made up by the interests of its individual members."[34] In fact, Franklin had given much the same speech in 1776, and then, as now, it served two purposes: a statement of democratic principles and a brief for the large states.

It was at just this moment that Pennsylvania's James Wilson suggested that representation in the lower house should be based upon an "equitable ratio of representation . . . in proportion to the whole number of white & other free Citizens and inhabitants of every age sex & condition including those bound to servitude for a term of years and three fifths of all other persons not comprehended in the foregoing description, except Indians not paying taxes."[35]

Wilson had just proposed what has come to be called the Three-Fifths Compromise; yet a very odd and even incongruous compromise it was. True, it was an attempt to reconcile Sherman's suggestion that representation in the lower house be based upon free population and the South Carolinians' that it be based upon wealth. Wilson was merely inserting the formula for calculating wealth that had been adopted four years earlier by the Continental Congress; conveniently, it happened to be a formula also for counting persons. On the face of it, this was a nice compromise—but compromise usually comes late in the game, when the players are exhausted and everyone knows that something must be surrendered. Why did Wilson's proffer come so early? The delegates had been meeting in earnest for only two weeks, and this part of the discussion—about how to apportion representation in the House—had been going on for less than a day. Thus far, only six other men had spoken.

---

[33]John Dickinson of Delaware and Rufus King of Massachusetts.
[34]Farrand, *Records of the Federal Convention,* 1:197–99, 204–5, 207–8. See also *JCC,* 6:1102–3.
[35]Farrand, *Records of the Federal Convention,* 1:201.

Why did Wilson give so much away? The seeming compromise was barely a compromise at all. The South Carolinians had asked for "quota of contribution," and Wilson helpfully offered them the formula by which "quota of contribution" should be calculated. They could not reasonably have dreamed of more.[36]

And why did Wilson toss slavery, already the new nation's apple of discord, into the gathering? It has sometimes been argued that compromise on the issue of slavery was necessary in order to create the Union—that South Carolina and Georgia would not have joined had they not gained certain concessions.[37] Indeed, later in the summer the delegates from the Deep South would make their threats. But they had not made them yet, nor had any delegates, at least in public, said the first thing about slavery. The word had not yet even been mentioned. Not only was Wilson giving the South Carolinians just what they had asked for, but he was also signaling to them that they could now, as they had in Congress, make demands on the basis of slavery.

Wilson, an ardent nationalist and a shrewd politician, was playing a dangerous—but ultimately successful—game. The compromise he laid down was one of those upon which, when all was said and done three months later, the Constitution itself hinged. By throwing slavery into the discussion and by signaling to South Carolina and Georgia that here was a Northerner who was willing to make concessions even before they asked for them, he altered the calculus of those discussions. What had, until that moment, been a conflict between the small and the large states now became one also between states that were slave and those that were substantially free. It is in this context that we can come to understand Madison's claim that the principal division was not between the large states and the small, but between the slave states and the free. In fact, on June 11, when Wilson introduced what would become the three-fifths clause, the fault line ran between the

---

[36]Indeed, Charles Cotesworth Pinckney later told the South Carolina House of Representatives, "We thus obtained a representation for our property; and I confess I did not expect that we had conceded too much to the Eastern States, when they allowed us a representation for a species of property which they have not among them" (ibid., 4:253).

[37]See, for example, William W. Freehling, *The Road to Disunion: Secessionists at Bay, 1776–1854* (New York, 1990), p. 584 n. 28, and idem, "Founding Fathers and Slavery," pp. 81–93; Lance Banning, *The Sacred Fire of Liberty: James Madison and the Founding of the Federal Republic* (Ithaca, 1995), pp. 459–60 n. 48; Don E. Fehrenbacher, *The Dred Scott Case: Its Significance in American Law and Politics* (New York, 1978), pp. 20–27; Howard A. Ohline, "Republicanism and Slavery: Origins of the Three-Fifths Clause in the United States Constitution," *William and Mary Quarterly*, 3d ser., 28 (1971):563–84.

big and small states, not along the Mason-Dixon line; by throwing slavery into the equation, however, he created a new divide, one that Madison was happy almost three weeks later to invoke. Creating a second fault line complicated the politics of the Constitutional Convention and made it easier for big-state nationalists to secure their objectives.

As an opponent of slavery, Wilson did not want to give any encouragement to the institution; but as a nationalist and a veteran of the Continental and Confederation Congresses, he considered the small states—which had threatened to dissolve the confederation unless they had an equal vote— as a greater menace to the new nation than the slave states. In fact, when Sherman had proposed that each state should have one vote in the Senate, he had justified his proposal in terms that must have made Wilson fear that the small states would be just as obstructionist in the new national government as they had been under Congress.[38] Wilson calculated that he could use his proposal to build a coalition between the large states and the smaller ones of the Deep South. Counting three-fifths of the slave population would give the slave states a bonus, one that would make proportional representation more attractive to them by increasing their weight in Congress.[39] If this strategy were successful, the small states of the North would be isolated. In fact, shortly after making his proposal, Wilson and Alexander Hamilton— another big-state nationalist—suggested that representation in the Senate as

---

[38]Farrand, *Records of the Federal Convention*, 1:196. Sherman offered a more elaborate and constitutionally grounded defense of the one-state, one-vote proposition than anyone had offered in Congress, where the threat to dissolve the confederation had been sufficient to win the point. His theory was a modification of British constitutional thought, which held that Parliament embodied the three orders of British society. To justify his proposal that each state should have one vote in the upper house, Sherman compared the states to the English nobility. Like the aristocracy, the "States would remain possessed of certain individual rights," which they ought to be able to protect, without being trampled by the larger states. "The House of Lords in England he observed had certain particular rights under the Constitution, and hence they have an equal vote with the House of Commons that they may be able to defend their rights." This was clearly a limited, indeed, an antiliberal notion of "individual rights" that defined them not as the minority rights of individual citizens, but as the corporate interests of individual states. What Sherman gave with one hand—a broad representation of persons, rather than property, in the lower house—he took away with the other—an upper-house check upon majority rule. Jack N. Rakove has argued that Madison's objective was to create an extended republic that would solve the problem that had been presented to national government by self-interested and obstructionist small states. Sherman was proposing the structure that could perpetuate just such obstructionism in the name of "individual rights." See Rakove, "Great Compromise."

[39]For evidence that this was Wilson's conscious calculation, see Farrand, *Records of the Federal Convention*, 2:10–11, in which Wilson voiced his fear that "the small States . . . may controul the Govt. as they have done in Congs."

well as the House should be proportional to population.[40] This was a clear signal to the small states of the North, just in case they had missed the earlier one, that the large states were on the offensive.

Wilson justified his proposal not in pragmatic terms, however, but in the democratic ones that he and others had laid out at the Continental Congress more than a decade before and had reiterated in the Federal Convention. In fact, when he offered his proposal—I still hesitate to call it a compromise, as there was nothing yet to be compromised between North and South—he was repeating a point he himself had made two days earlier when he argued that representation should be based upon population: "As all authority was derived from the people, equal numbers of people ought to have an equal no. of representatives, and different numbers of people ought to have different numbers of representatives."[41] The South Carolinians had asked for representation of wealth. Wilson was giving them what they asked for, but explaining it as the democratic representation of people.

---

[40]Farrand, *Records of the Federal Convention*, 1:202. As J. R. Pole has shown, Madison was thinking along similar lines. In April, before the convention had even begun, he explained to Edmund Randolph why he thought that proportional representation would win out: "The Northern States will be reconciled to it by the *actual* superiority of their populousness: the Southern by their *expected* superiority in this point" (Pole, "The Emergence of the Majority Principle in the American Revolution," in *Paths to the American Past* [New York, 1979], p. 50). Of course, giving the Southern states a bonus for their slave populations would make proportional representation all the more appealing to them. Drew R. McCoy has noted that "the southern delegates to the Philadelphia Convention . . . overwhelmingly [took] the large state position on the matter of proportional representation. That the delegates from Georgia, which actually had a quite small population, and North Carolina, which was middling in demographic size, would join Virginia (a bona fide large state) vividly confirms the power of southern expectations" ("James Madison and Visions of American Nationality in the Confederation Period: A Regional Perspective," in *Beyond Confederation: Origins of the Constitution and American National Identity*, ed. Richard Beeman, Stephen Botein, and Edward C. Carter [Chapel Hill, 1987], p. 246). Garry Wills has recently suggested that the South's attendant bonus in the Electoral College was responsible for Thomas Jefferson's election in 1800 (Wills, *The Negro President: Jefferson and the Slave Power* [New York, 2003]). As Paul Finkelman has demonstrated, when the convention decided that the executive should be chosen by an Electoral College whose composition would be based on each state's representation in Congress, it was consciously choosing to give the South extra representation for its slaves (Finkelman, "The Proslavery Origins of the Electoral College," *Cardozo Law Review* 23 [2003]: 1145–57). Yet, by June 11—rather early in the proceedings—Wilson, an important Northern antislavery nationalist, had offered the South a significant inducement to agree to proportional representation: a bonus, allowing them to count 60 percent of their slaves. Moreover, by making the offer so early, he signaled a willingness to make other concessions on slavery.

[41]Farrand, *Records of the Federal Convention*, 1:179. Rakove notes another dimension to this fundamentally democratic principle: that new states should be brought into the Union on the same terms as the original states (Rakove, *Original Meanings*, p. 74).

Wilson had just conflated two discussions that had taken place a few years earlier in the Continental Congress: how representatives should be apportioned and how taxes should be levied. Or, to be more precise, he had taken the ideas developed in one context—a discussion about taxation—and applied them in another—a discussion about representation. The three-fifths ratio was a compromise on taxation, not representation, and there the discussion turned on questions of political economy. The states had always accepted that their quotas of contribution should bear some relation to their wealth. When in 1783 they decided to use population as a proxy for wealth, the only argument had been over the productivity of slave labor. When Wilson proposed using the same formula for representation, he was at once altering the terms of the discussion and muddying them. He himself had trouble making sense out of what he had proposed. And hence, the big debates about slavery came *after* the three-fifths clause was proposed, not before.

For all its calculation and cunning, Wilson's proposal was also stunningly radical. With good reason, the three-fifths clause has long been considered an embarrassment, a blot on the Constitution, a source of national shame.[42] Yet, odious as the clause was, it was also, for the time, a radical statement about the nature of representation. As Jack N. Rakove has recently suggested, "It was . . . the closest approximation in the Constitution to the principle of one person, one vote."[43] Although, as several historians have shown, Revolutionary-era democrats were beginning to insist that persons, not property were the proper basis for representation, not until the federal Constitution did any government in America base representation upon inhabitants rather than taxpayers or adult men.[44] The closest any government

---

[42]See William M. Wiecek, "The Witch at the Christening: Slavery and the Constitution's Origins," in *The Framing and Ratification of the Constitution*, ed. Leonard W. Levy and Dennis J. Mahoney (New York, 1987), pp. 167–84; Paul Finkelman, "Slavery and the Constitutional Convention: Making a Covenant with Death," in Beeman, Botein, and Carter, *Beyond Confederation*, pp. 188–225; and Edward Countryman, *Americans: A Collision of Histories* (New York, 1996), pp. 83–84. See also, for example, John Chester Miller, *The Wolf by the Ears: Thomas Jefferson and Slavery* (New York, 1977), pp. 222–3l; James Oakes, "The Rhetoric of Reaction: Justifying a Proslavery Constitution" (paper presented to symposium on Bondage, Freedom, and the Constitution, Cardozo School of Law and Yeshiva University, New York, Feb. 19–20, 1995).

[43]Rakove, *Original Meanings*, p. 74.

[44]J. R. Pole, *Political Representation in England and the Origins of the American Republic* (1966; reprint ed., Berkeley, Calif., 1971), pp. 204, 274–75; Rosemarie Zagarri, *The Politics of Size: Representation in the United States, 1776–1850* (Ithaca, 1987), pp. 39–42, 57–60; and Peter S. Onuf, "The Origins and Early Development of State Legislatures," in *Encyclopedia of the American Legislative System*, ed. Joel Silbey, 3 vols. (New York, 1994), 1:175–94.

had come was with the Northwest Ordinance, which linked representation to the number of "free male inhabitants, of full age."[45] Basing representation on population, then, was a significant democratic innovation.

Wilson had grafted a formula for calculating wealth, one that enumerated human beings as property, onto an expansive theory of government—and in the process implied that slaves were at least partial members of the political community. As political theorists Benedict Anderson and Michael Walzer remind us, the political community is both imagined and bounded.[46] Here we see the Framers, led by James Wilson, imagining the political community to include all white people, all free blacks, and all indentured servants, regardless of age or sex—*and* setting its boundaries by excluding 40 percent of the slaves and untaxed Indians.

The delegates to the Constitutional Convention understood immediately that this was the implication, indeed the intellectual underpinning, of Wilson's proposal. It was not Wilson's intent to insist that slaves were members of society or to make an issue out of slavery. Those historians who have argued that slavery was not the primary issue dividing the delegates are substantially right. Slavery was—and this point bears repeating—so divisive an issue that no one who seriously wanted to create a federal union would have brought it up had he been able to avoid it. But Wilson was a democrat who believed that representation should be based upon population, and if he wanted to win that point, he was going to have to bring up slavery. First, there was the matter of realpolitik. As we have seen, Wilson—and like-minded big-state democrats—needed some way to outflank the small-state delegates who were already clamoring for one state, one vote, and insisting that "individual rights" pertained to states, not to persons. Second, to say that representation should be based upon population was necessarily to raise the issue of whether slaves should be counted as persons. In the context of the Federal Convention, democracy and slavery were thus inevitably and inextricably joined.

But democracy and slavery were also a contradiction, or so it seemed to the Northern state delegates especially. No sooner had Wilson made his proposal than Elbridge Gerry of Massachusetts immediately asked, "Why

---

[45]"Northwest Ordinance," in *The Founders' Constitution,* ed. Philip B. Kurland and Ralph Lerner, 5 vols. (Chicago, 1987), 1:27.

[46]Benedict Anderson, *Imagined Communities: Reflections on the Origin and Spread of Nationalism* (1983; reprint ed., New York, 1991); and Michael Walzer, *Spheres of Justice: A Defense of Pluralism and Equality* (New York, 1983), esp. pp. 28–30.

then shd. the blacks, who were property in the South, be in the rule of representation more than the cattle & horses of the North?"[47] New Jersey's William Paterson later made a similar point, in the process offering a succinct definition of freedom: "He could regard negroes slaves in no light but as property. They are no free agents, have no personal liberty, no faculty of acquiring property, but on the contrary are themselves property, & like other property entirely at the will of the Master."[48] The authors of the Constitution understood the theoretical implications of including slaves partially in the basis of representation; it meant that slaves were—in theory at least—to be represented in part by the new federal government. The first impulse of a number of Northern delegates was to recoil from the incongruity of grafting a formula for calculating wealth onto an expansive definition of the polity. Ironically—or perhaps it is not so ironic, if one considers the interests that were being advanced—Northerners insisted that slaves should not be represented because they were property.

The South Carolinians responded by insisting that it was wealth that was being represented, not persons; hence there was no inconsistency. "Property," Rutledge said, "was certainly the principal object of Society," and Butler echoed that "property was the only just measure of representation. This was the great object of Governt."[49] Pennsylvania's Gouverneur Morris objected, however, to the "incoherence" of the clause. If representation was to be based upon wealth, then the clause should say just that; and if representation was to be based upon the number of inhabitants, then all the slaves should be counted. He asked the question in mid-July, and he asked it again in early August: "Upon what principle is it that the slaves shall be computed

[47]Farrand, *Records of the Federal Convention*, 1:201. For well-informed narratives of the proceedings in the Federal Convention, see Don E. Fehrenbacher, *The Slaveholding Republic: An Account of the United States Government's Relations to Slavery* (New York, 2001), pp. 28–38; and Rakove, *Original Meanings*, pp. 57–93.

[48]Farrand, *Records of the Federal Convention*, 1:561. This point was repeatedly made by Antifederalists in the debates over ratification in the press and in the ratifying conventions. See, for example, Luther Martin, "The Genuine Information," in *The Complete Antifederalist*, ed. Herbert J. Storing, 7 vols. (Chicago, 1981), 2.4.45; "Essays of Brutus," 2.9.39; "A Letter from a Gentleman in a Neighbouring State to a Gentleman in This City," 4.2.3; "Letters of a Republican Federalist," 4.13.22; "Speeches by Melancton Smith," 6.12.8; as well as "Debate in Massachusetts Ratifying Convention," Jan. 17–19, 1788, reprinted in *Founders' Constitution*, 2:122. The debate on the three-fifths clause had resumed on July 9, about a month after Wilson's original proposal. For an informed narrative of deliberations in the interim, see Rakove, *Original Meanings*, pp. 60–72.

[49]Farrand, *Records of the Federal Convention*, 1:534, 542.

in the representation? Are they men? Then make them Citizens & let them vote. Are they property? Why then is no other property included?"[50]

Here was the intellectual problem presented by the three-fifths clause, and try as they might, its supporters could not wrest coherence out of the inconsistency of counting slaves as both inhabitants to be represented and a measure of wealth.[51] James Wilson admitted as much. He told the convention that he "did not well see on what principle the admission of blacks in the proportion of three fifths could be explained. Are they admitted as Citizens? Then why are they not admitted on an equality with White Citizens? Are they admitted as property? then why is not other property admitted into the computation?"[52] James Madison, reluctant to give up on his dream of proportional representation in both houses, thought he saw a way out of the dilemma: base representation in the lower house on the number of free inhabitants, and in the upper—"which had for one of its primary objects the guardianship of property"—the whole number of persons, including slaves.[53] Under this plan, slaves would have been counted entirely as property and not at all as the represented. The small states, however, as many historians have demonstrated, were not willing to agree to any sort of proportional representation in the upper house; instead, the three-fifths formula, which based representation on both wealth and persons, became part of the Constitution.

The compromise was struck, then, just as Wilson had suggested on June 11. After all the threats had been made, the delegates agreed on the need to agree. But the logic of this particular compromise still eluded some of the Northern delegates. They could not understand how or why slaves—whom the Southerners continued to define as "wealth" or "property" could be represented. Curiously, it was Gouverneur Morris, perhaps the clause's most vehement critic, who suggested a way for the troubled Northerners to reconcile themselves to the incoherence. On July 12, he offered a "proviso that taxation shall be in proportion to Representation."[54] In one sense, he was merely reiterating the South Carolinians' suggestion of a month before that

---

[50]Ibid., 1:603–4; 2:222.

[51]The convention eventually settled on a compromise by which slaves would be counted at the ratio of 5 to 3 for purposes both of representation and taxation. See Finkelman, "Slavery and the Constitutional Convention."

[52]Farrand, *Records of the Federal Convention,* 1:587.

[53]Ibid., 1:562.

[54]Ibid., 1:591–92.

representation should be in proportion to "quotas of contribution." Morris was now proposing language that, after editing, became part of Article I, Section 8, of the Constitution: "Representatives and direct taxes shall be apportioned among the several states" by the formula that we have been discussing at such length. Morris's amendment served two purposes. First, it made it appear as if the slave states were going to have to pay, literally, for their bonus: if they got more representatives, they would also have to pay more in taxes. As Morris himself later noted, his proposal was something of a sham. It was almost inconceivable that the federal government would "stretch its hand directly into the pockets of the people scattered over so vast a Country."[55] The sham, however, served as a crutch for hobbled Northerners. Wilson caught on immediately, noting that "less umbrage would perhaps be taken agst. an admission of the slaves into the Rule of representation, if it should be so expressed as to make them indirectly only an ingredient in the rule, by saying that they should enter into the rule of taxation: and as representation was to be according to taxation, the end would be equally attained." A few weeks later, Morris suggested removing the clause about direct taxation, as "he had only meant it as a bridge to assist us over a certain gulph" that had now been crossed, but he later reconsidered. He thought the clause still necessary "in consequence of what had passed on this point; in order to exclude the appearance of counting the Negroes in *the Representation*."[56]

In that rhetorical wave of the hand—"in consequence of what had passed on this point"—Morris alluded to the convention's bitter debates over slavery, one of the most fierce of which he himself had provoked with his original proposal to link representation with taxation. No sooner had Morris proposed the clause than South Carolina's Butler, no doubt already recognizing that the taxation part of it was a sham, proposed that representation should be based upon the full number of inhabitants, "including all the blacks." Morris, snapping out of his conciliatory mood, replied that "the people of Pena. will never agree to a representation of Negroes." Charles Pinckney, another South Carolinian, turned Butler's suggestion into a formal motion.[57] Butler and Pinckney had made the same proposal the day before, without causing as much of a stir as it now did. One cannot help sur-

---

[55]Ibid., 2:223.
[56]Ibid., 1:595, 2:106, 607. No one could ever have accused Morris of making a fetish of consistency.
[57]Ibid., 1:591–97.

mising that when the South Carolinians brought up the proposal again on the twelfth, their purpose was not to gain the point but to appear as obstinate as possible.

The first time Butler proposed counting all the slaves, he claimed that "the labour of a slave in S. Carola was as productive & valuable as that of a freeman in Massts." In fact, that was the best argument the South Carolinians could come up with. Unfortunately for them, it was directly contrary to what they had argued just a few years before in the Confederation Congress when they were demanding a discount for their supposedly less productive slave labor. The irony of the situation was not lost on North Carolina's Hugh Williamson, who observed that when they were arguing about taxation, Southerners had said that slave labor was inferior to free and Northerners that it was equal.[58] Having earlier insisted—to their advantage—that slave labor was relatively unproductive, the Southerners could not effectively mount the opposite argument.[59] They were reduced to simple bullying and a naked assertion of self-interest. As Rutledge later put it, in another argument about slavery, "Interest alone is the governing principle with Nations —The true question at present is whether the Southn. States shall or shall not be parties to the Union."[60]

On July 12, the argument was so heated that delegates from both the North and South, including Morris himself, threatened to walk out. Now the delegates were having just the sort of argument that normally leads to a difference-splitting compromise such as the one that Wilson had proposed a month earlier. But having offered his compromise a month earlier, Wilson could do nothing more now than to try to make sense out of his own proposal and to reassert the importance of compromise. "If numbers be not a

---

[58]Ibid., 1:580–81.

[59]In this light, Madison's famous speech of July 11, in which he predicted that population in the United States would naturally flow away from the crowded states of the Northeast to the less populated territory takes on an interesting meaning. Asserting the labor theory of value upon which the Confederation's 1783 compromise on taxation rested—and which he had written—Madison stated that "the value of labour, might be considered as the principal criterion of wealth and ability to support taxes; and this would find its level in different places where the intercourse should be easy & free. . . . Wherever labour would yield most, people would resort" (ibid., 1:585). Implicitly, this was a free-soil vision, similar to the one that David Howell had shared with his governor: which free white men would voluntarily migrate to a region where they would have to compete with slaves? In spite of Butler's bluster, and the South Carolinians' and Georgians' insistence that the slave trade remain open until 1808, the convention generally accepted the premises of the bourgeois critique of slavery.

[60]Ibid., 2:364.

proper rule, why is not some better rule pointed out. . . . In 1783, after elaborate discussion of a measure of wealth all were satisfied then as they are now that the rule of numbers, does not differ much from the combined rule of numbers & wealth." Wilson simply defined the problem away by insisting that this particular formula for including wealth did not materially alter the outcome. Then he reasserted, as if they had not been altered by the compromise, his general principles: that "again he could not agree that property was the sole or the primary object of Governt. & Society. . . . [that] numbers were surely the natural & precise measure of Representation," but that numbers were a close enough approximation of wealth.[61] And then the delegates voted, accepting the three-fifths clause. Not even its own author had been able to render it coherent.

Having settled this point, the delegates would argue seriously about slavery only one more time. The issue then, in late August, was the slave trade. The Committee of Detail, chaired by South Carolina's John Rutledge, reported out a draft of the Constitution that not only explicitly permitted the slave trade but also prohibited taxing either the trade or slaves themselves, which would have made slaves the only import exempt from taxation. This time the opposition was led by delegates from the Upper South; Maryland's Luther Martin thought the proposals "inconsistent with the principles of the revolution and dishonorable to the American character." Once again, the South Carolinians resorted to bullying; John Rutledge said that "the true question at present is whether the Southn. States shall or shall not be parties to the Union."[62]

This time South Carolina and Georgia found allies in the delegation from Connecticut, which urged the rest of the convention to heed the Southerners' warnings. Besides, as Roger Sherman put it, "the abolition of slavery seemed to be going on in the U.S. & . . . the good sense of the several States would probably by degrees compleat it."[63] Oliver Ellsworth came up with his own twist on the bourgeois critique of slavery: the climate in South Carolina and Georgia was so deadly to slaves that those two states had to keep importing

---

[61]Ibid., 1:605–6.

[62]Ibid., 2:183, 364.

[63]Ibid., 2:364–75. See also Fehrenbacher, *Slaveholding Republic,* pp. 33–37, and Rakove, *Original Meanings,* pp. 85–89. This discussion was part of a larger debate about regulation of trade. In committee, Southern delegates were willing to agree to let Congress regulate imports so long as their trade in slaves could be exempted.

them. Time, however, would solve even this problem. "As population increases[,] poor laborers will be so plenty as to render slaves useless." Here
it was, a sort of Gresham's law of labor in reverse: free labor would drive
out slave. "Slavery in time," Ellsworth continued, "will not be a speck in
our Country."[64]

Of course, this argument made no sense. There was only one conceivable
way in which the continued importation of slavery could not strengthen the
institution, and that was if the punishments of the institution killed off more
slaves than the Deep South could import. If that is what Ellsworth believed,
he was implicitly delivering a more damning indictment of the institution
than any of its most outspoken foes. But Ellsworth and his Connecticut colleagues were not trying for consistency. They seemed to think it was enough
to point to the eventual demise of the institution. And they urged their colleagues to give in to the Deep South's threats. Roger Sherman "said it was
better to let the S. States import slaves than to part with them [i.e., South
Carolina and Georgia] if they made that a sine qua non."[65] The matter was
referred back to another committee, which offered a compromise seemingly
much less favorable to the Deep South: the slave trade could not be banned
until 1800, and slave imports could be taxed. With very little discussion—
and none of South Carolina's blustering or threats—the delegates approved
two amendments, moving the date forward to 1808 and setting the tax at no
more than ten dollars per slave.[66]

---

[64]Ibid., 2:369–71. See also Fehrenbacher, *Slaveholding Republic*, pp. 33–37, and Rakove, *Original Meanings*, pp. 85–89.

[65]Farrand, *Records of the Federal Convention*, 2:374.

[66]Ibid., 2:400, 415–17. It is, of course, an interesting question why the South Carolinians (and the Georgians, their silent junior partners) cut this particular deal with the commercial states of the North, one that brought them into conflict with the Virginians Mason and Randolph. True, the South had won a ban on export duties, but the two Virginians had also wanted to require a two-thirds majority in Congress for import duties as well. In the end, the South Carolinians agreed to a simple majority for import duties in return for the reopening of the slave trade and the ten-dollar cap on each slave brought into the country. A little more than forty years later, South Carolina would object strenuously to national import duties—the so-called Tariff of Abominations—and develop the novel doctrine of nullification to oppose them. One won-
ders if, had they been able to see so far ahead, the South Carolinians would have made the bargain they did, trading away an impediment to import duties for keeping the slave trade open another twenty years. The point, however, is that none of the participants in the convention knew how events would turn out—but who ever does? They made a series of calculations based upon their perceptions of their best interests, their expectations about the future, and their understandings of political theory. Sometimes their calculations turned out right, and sometimes they didn't.

It has been observed that this was a compromise between two extremes—a complete ban on the importation of slavery and no restriction whatsoever, but South Carolina and Georgia got, by far, the better end of the deal.[67] It is hard not to believe that this was the purpose of all of their truculence earlier in the summer. At the moment the compromise was struck, every state except Georgia had either banned or suspended the slave trade or effectively curtailed it with prohibitive duties.[68] The convention had now reversed the tide against the slave trade, guaranteeing any state that wanted to import slaves that right and preventing states—now denied the power to regulate commerce—from blocking the trade with high duties.[69] Just before the delegates approved the clause, Madison commented sardonically that "twenty years will produce all the mischief that can be apprehended from the liberty to import slaves. So long a term will be more dishonorable than to say nothing about it in the Constitution."[70] His prediction was correct. In the twenty-one years before a ban on slavery finally was enacted, thousands of African slaves were imported into the United States.[71]

Neither Madison nor Wilson was happy with this compromise. But it was late August, the delegates were tired, the South Carolinians were still raging, and the Constitution was almost finished. They restrained themselves, making only a few brief but bitter comments. Wilson, ever alert to Deep South hypocrisy, "observed that if S.C. & Georgia were themselves disposed to get rid of the importation of slaves in a short time as had been suggested, they would never refuse to Unite because the Importation might be prohibited." Madison struggled to keep any explicit recognition of slavery out of the Constitution. He "thought it wrong to admit in the Constitution the idea that there could be property in men."[72] Both men sincerely disliked slavery and hoped that it would disappear. They, like many other democrats of the period, thought that it might be on the road to extinction. As many historians have noted, they were probably indulging in fantasy. Even without the thousands and thousands of Africans imported into the South in the next two decades, slavery was far too entrenched and the opposition to it far too weak to make its peaceful elimination a realistic prospect.

---

[67]Fehrenbacher, *Slaveholding Republic*, p. 35.

[68]Robinson, *Slavery in the Structure of Politics*, pp. 297–99.

[69]Oakes, "Rhetoric of Reaction."

[70]Farrand, *Records of the Federal Convention*, 2:415.

[71]Helen Hornbeck Tanner, ed., *The Settling of North America: The Atlas of the Great Migrations into North America from the Ice Age to the Present* (New York, 1995), p. 51.

[72]Farrand, *Records of the Federal Convention*, 2:372, 417.

Still, there is a certain logic to the words and actions of these nationalist democrats. It is in this context that Jefferson's florid passage condemning the slave trade in the draft of the Declaration makes a certain kind of sense: if the slave trade had been halted, or if it could be curtailed right now, perhaps slavery would die a natural death. The bourgeois critique of slavery suggested that free labor would prevail because it was both morally and economically superior. Cut off the slave trade, encourage white immigration, open the West to settlers, and the rapidly increasing free white population would eventually overshadow the black. This is one reason why Madison and other nationalists were so committed to the opening of the West, so insistent that the new states be brought in on equal terms with the older ones: the West was where slavery would disappear. Later, both Madison and Jefferson consoled themselves with a dream of "diffusion"—the idea that if only the institution of slavery were left alone, it would die out, somewhere in the West. For Jefferson especially, the dream of diffusion became a shibboleth to use against the abolitionists.[73]

It is sometimes observed that creating a national government was so formidable a task that compromise was a fundamental necessity. It is unreasonable of us, with our modern notions of freedom and racial equality, to have expected the Founders to have done more than they possibly could do. They gave us a federal government, a Bill of Rights, and a body of ideas that set slavery on the road to extinction.[74] The Founders kept the Constitution as neutral on slavery as they could; it is as much, therefore, an antislavery document as a proslavery one.[75] Such arguments have some truth in them—if we stop the clock in mid-July, just after the Three-Fifths Compromise has finally been agreed to. If one thought, as Wilson did and Madison did, and as David Howell did in the Confederation Congress, that slavery was

---

[73]On this point, see Drew R. McCoy, *The Elusive Republic: Political Economy in Jeffersonian America* (Chapel Hill, 1980), pp. 251–52; idem, *The Last of the Fathers: James Madison and the Republican Legacy* (New York, 1989), pp. 267–76; and Onuf, *Jefferson's Empire*, pp. 185–87.

[74]Most explicitly, see Thomas G. West, *Vindicating the Founders: Race, Sex, Class, and Justice in the Origins of America* (Lanham, Md., 1997), p. 16. More nuanced versions of this argument can be found in Gordon S. Wood, *The Radicalism of the American Revolution* (New York, 1992), p. 187, and Fehrenbacher, *Slaveholding Republic*, p. 47. It is implicit, I think, in Banning, *Sacred Fire of Liberty*, a very fine book that, however, pays too little attention to the issue of slavery.

[75]This seems to have been Madison's reasoning, although in the Virginia convention he walked a very fine line, arguing both that Virginians' property in slaves was secure and that allowing the importation of slaves for another twenty years, while distasteful, would do no harm. He believed that the Constitution offered the best hope for securing liberty, and in that context he argued that certain concessions to South Carolina and Georgia were necessary to keep those two states in the Union (Elliot, *Debates*, pp. 453–61).

on the road to extinction, then the bonus given to the South for slavery—whether as a discount on the national tax bill or as a little extra representation in the House—would soon be moot: once slavery faded away, the South would lose its temporary advantage.

But if we move the clock forward, to late August, after the concession on the slave trade (and after an additional one on a fugitive slave clause), then the compromises take on a different cast. The institution of slavery itself has been given encouragement. More slaves can enter the country. The institution will grow. The dream of extinction or diffusion becomes more fantastic by the day. In June and even in July, Wilson's calculation may have appeared shrewd. By September, when an emboldened Deep South had secured even more, we may wonder about its wisdom.

Moreover, not only did the democratic nationalists such as Wilson and Madison enhance the power of the slave-owning states, they authorized—in both senses of the term—sectionalism itself. By anticipating the claims of the Deep South, they encouraged that region to make excessive demands in the Constitutional Convention, which they, in turn, had no choice but to satisfy. And they gave those claims legitimacy, denominating them a legitimate interest and helping a section come into being.

The great abolitionist William Lloyd Garrison once called the Constitution a "covenant with death" and an "agreement with hell."[76] Surely, this is not what antislavery nationalists such as Wilson and Madison intended. But the road to hell, as my father used to say, is paved with good intentions.

[76]Quoted in Finkelman, "Slavery and the Constitutional Convention," p. 188.

Peter S. Onuf

The Political Economy of Sectionalism

Tariff Controversies and Conflicting Conceptions of World Order

THE DEBATES OVER American commercial policy following the War of 1812 revolved around the prospects for future wars. Optimistic revolutionaries conceived of their federal union of free republics as a peace plan for the New World that would insulate them from the perpetual conflicts that characterized the history of the European balance of power. But they also recognized that Europe remained a powerful, destabilizing presence in America and that transatlantic trade relations remained vital to the new nation's prosperity and power. The visionary ideal of a complete separation between New World and Old stood in stark counterpoint to the reality of continuing entanglement.

The final spasm of the Napoleonic wars, the Americans' War of 1812, showed how easily the United States could be drawn into European conflicts. When the devastation finally came to a halt with the Treaty of Ghent in 1815, a broad coalition of Jeffersonian Republicans rallied behind policy initiatives—a new national bank, internal improvements, and a protective tariff—that would prepare the new nation to better meet future threats to its vital interests and very survival. When the next war failed to materialize, however, the coalition began to fall apart: "National" Republicans remained convinced that the new nation's independence was still at risk, if not from conventional attack then from the more insidious and ultimately more devastating threat of British commercial domination. Meanwhile, "Old" Republicans, reflexively suspicious of all concentrated power, gained new recruits among skeptical merchants and staple producers who advocated free trade and discounted the threat of war.[1]

American revolutionaries understood that peace in the New World depended on peace in—and with—the Old. After all, the 1783 Peace of Paris terminating the wider European war that the American colonial rebellion had initiated constituted the true beginning of American national history.[2] In subsequent decades, American statesmen avoided European entanglements as much as possible, hoping to persuade the belligerent powers to adhere to the canons of neutrality, a controversial principle not yet fully incorporated in the modern law of nations, at the very time when the European balance and the legal regime it had supported was collapsing.[3] From the Quasi-War with France in the 1790s to commercial warfare during the Jefferson and Madison administrations and finally to a second war for independence in 1812, the new nation's destiny remained subject to the vagaries of European diplomacy and war. Recent history thus gave little reason to hope that the Treaty of Ghent in 1815 would inaugurate a lasting peace, particularly in view of the failure of negotiators to resolve the full range of maritime and commercial issues that had led to war in the first place.[4]

Yet if the history of chronic warfare underscored the need for military preparedness and economic self-sufficiency, the logic of foreign trade relations pulled in the other direction, toward greater involvement in the world trading system in order to promote American prosperity and greater reliance on international commercial interdependence to mitigate the threat of war. The two tendencies—toward withdrawal from and further integration into the Atlantic trading system—could be reconciled only as long as protection was seen as temporary: tariff barriers would promote national security by

---

[1]For a superb analysis of the Founders' intentions, see David C. Hendrickson, *Peace Pact: The Lost World of the American Founding* (Lawrence, Kans., 2003). See also Peter Onuf and Nicholas Onuf, *Federal Union, Modern World: The Law of Nations in an Age of Revolutions, 1776–1814* (Madison, Wis., 1993). For harsh assessments of the failure of Jeffersonian commercial diplomacy, see Bradford Perkins, *The Creation of a Republican Empire, 1776–1865*, Cambridge History of American Foreign Relations, vol. 1 (New York, 1993), p. 111; and Doron S. Ben-Atar, *The Origins of Jeffersonian Commercial Diplomacy* (New York, 1993). My analysis of Republican divisions in the postwar period is indebted to James E. Lewis, Jr., *The American Union and the Problem of Neighborhood: The United States and the Collapse of the Spanish Empire, 1783–1829* (Chapel Hill, 1998). See also idem, *John Quincy Adams: Policymaker for the Union* (Wilmington, Del., 2001).

[2]David Armitage, "The Declaration of Independence and International Law," *William and Mary Quarterly*, 3d ser., 59 (2002):39–64.

[3]Onuf and Onuf, *Federal Union, Modern World*.

[4]For a review of the new nation's international history, see Peter S. Onuf and Leonard J. Sadosky, *Jeffersonian America* (Oxford, 2002), chap. 4.

developing national resources while forcing recalcitrant trading partners to offer commercial concessions. The memory of recent war and the expectation of future war sustained the balance between diverse interests and conflicting policy prescriptions in the Republican alliance. Improving prospects for peace and stability in the postwar years fractured the party, however, as protectionist-minded nationalists sought to promote home manufactures while free traders insisted that permanent peacetime trade barriers were counterproductive provocations to war rather than preparations for war.[5]

National Republicanism grew out of the Madison administration's embarrassments in conducting the War of 1812 and the expectation that other wars would inevitably follow. Without an efficient or energetic central government, without even a bank to manage the national revenue (the charter of the First Bank of the United States had expired on the eve of the war), the United States had barely survived its second war for independence. The rapid emergence of domestic manufactures during the interruption of foreign trade from the onset of the embargo in 1807 to the end of the war in 1815—the one bright spot in the American record—was the inadvertent consequence of the *failure* of Jeffersonian commercial diplomacy. At war's end, National Republicans hoped to protect this emerging manufacturing sector from the anticipated flood of cheap British imports, recognizing the strategic importance of a balanced, interdependent, and independent national economy in future international conflicts. War cut off revenue from import duties when it was most desperately needed; so, too, a nation that depended on foreign trade for vital war materiel, even for textiles to clothe its soldiers, could not claim to be truly independent.

Tariff protection was the centerpiece of a broader, neo-Hamiltonian program of nation building that included chartering the Second Bank of the United States in 1816 and federal funding for internal improvements, thwarted by President Madison's stunning veto of the bonus bill in 1817 on constitutional grounds.[6] Madison believed that the proposed expansion of

---

[5]The best study of commercial policy, partisan political competition, and sectionalism is Brian Schoen, "The Fragile Fabric of Union: The Cotton South, the Federal Union, and the Atlantic World, 1787–1860," Ph.D. diss., University of Virginia, 2003. On the nexus between commercial agriculture and foreign policy, see Drew R. McCoy, *The Elusive Republic: Political Economy in Jeffersonian America* (Chapel Hill, 1980).

[6]John Lauritz Larson, "Jefferson's Union and the Problem of Internal Improvements," in *Jeffersonian Legacies*, ed. Peter S. Onuf (Charlottesville, 1993), pp. 340–69; idem, *Internal Improvement: National Public Works and the Promise of Popular Government in the United States, 1783–1862* (Chapel Hill, 2001); Bray Hammond, *Banks and Politics in America: From the Revolution to the Civil War* (Princeton, N.J., 1957).

federal powers was critical for national security but could be authorized only by a constitutional amendment. Seizing on Madison's scruples, Old Republican opponents of nationalist initiatives were increasingly successful in downplaying the national security concerns that had originally framed the debate. The real issue, they insisted, was not the new nation's place in a hazardous, war-prone world, but rather the perpetuation of a federal union that "presumes a perfect equality and community of interests among all the parties concerned."[7] Would policies ostensibly designed to secure collective interests against external threats instead subjugate one part of the country to the tyranny of another, provoking Thomas Cooper and his fellow Southerners "to calculate the value of our union; and to enquire of what use to us is this most unequal alliance?"[8]

The success of tariff proponents in sustaining a moderately protective tariff in 1820 and progressively higher rates in 1824 and 1828 (the infamous Tariff of Abominations) generated a powerful backlash among staple export producers and transatlantic traders. As the threat of renewed war apparently receded, free traders became convinced that the tariff constituted a tax on the most productive sectors of the economy, diverting capital from agriculture to manufactures that would not survive, much less compete effectively, without protection. Through the 1820s, free traders were able to sustain an intersectional coalition, mirroring the alliance of protected interests —including Louisiana sugar producers—that gave Henry Clay and his fellow tariff proponents congressional majorities. But the tendency of tariff politics was increasingly sectional, as John Taylor of Caroline and other precocious Old Republican critics had recognized from the outset.[9]

Daniel Webster's famous Senate debate with Robert Hayne over the character of the Union reflected a critical sectional realignment. Webster's great speech against protection in 1824 had made him the darling of free traders

---

[7]"Cotton Manufacture," in *The Examiner, and Journal of Political Economy; Devoted to the Advancement of the Cause of State Rights and Free Trade,* ed. Condy Raguet, 2 vols. (Philadelphia, 1834–35), 1:135 (Nov. 27, 1833).

[8]Speech of Thomas Cooper, July 27, 1827, in *Niles' Weekly Register,* Sept. 8, 1827, reprinted in *The Nullification Era: A Documentary Record,* ed. William W. Freehling (New York, 1967), p. 25.

[9]For a succinct account of the history of the tariff, see Jonathan J. Pincus, "Tariff Policies," in *Encyclopedia of American Political History,* ed. Jack P. Greene, 3 vols. (New York, 1984), 3:1259–70. For a fuller history of antebellum tariff battles, see Maurice Baxter, *Henry Clay and the American System* (Lexington, Ky., 1996), pp. 16–33; Merrill D. Peterson, *The Great Triumvirate: Webster, Clay, and Calhoun* (New York, 1987), pp. 68–84, 146–64; J. J. Pincus, *Pressure Groups and Politics in Antebellum Tariffs* (New York, 1977).

across the country, but he now followed the lead of influential constituents who abandoned free trade and embraced protection as their capital shifted from commerce to manufacturing. Meanwhile, the rapid expansion of cotton production, the new nation's most lucrative export, sectionalized support for free trade and exacerbated a developing sense of sectional grievance that culminated in the great political-constitutional crisis of nullification (1828–33).[10] South Carolinians threatened to bolt from the Union, asserting their right to nullify an "unconstitutional" protective tariff that encroached on their state's sovereignty and thus threatened to destroy the Union. The nullifiers may have lost the battle—at least, that is the conventional interpretation of President Andrew Jackson's vigorous vindication of federal authority—but they won the war.

The Compromise Tariff of 1833 was a victory for free traders. Clay, its author, insisted that the progressive reduction of tariff rates over the next nine years to a revenue level that would offer only incidental protection did not jettison the protective principle. Though it was certainly true that manufacturers were given plenty of time to prepare for the new regime, Clay's protestations strained credibility. Mathew Carey and Hezekiah Niles, the most ardent and influential spokesmen for tariff protection, were devastated: the "price of the Union" would not be paid by cotton planters, the self-styled victims of high tariffs, but rather by the free labor of the Northeast and free farmers of the West.[11] Protection enjoyed a brief revival in 1842, as the briefly ascendant Whigs enacted the last protective tariff in the antebellum years. But the Democrats' Walker Tariff of 1846 marked the definitive triumph of free trade and final demise of the protective principle.

---

[10]Webster's speeches are reprinted in Charles M. Wiltse, ed., *The Papers of Daniel Webster: Speeches and Formal Writings*, 14 vols. (Hanover, N.H., 1974): on the tariff, Apr. 1–2, 1824, 1:113–60; second reply to Hayne, Jan. 26–27, 1830, 1:285–348. See also Peterson, *Great Triumvirate*, pp. 171–79, and, for the best study of the nullification controversy, William W. Freehling, *Prelude to Civil War: The Nullification Controversy in South Carolina, 1816–1836* (New York, 1965).

[11]On the Compromise of 1833, see also Peter B. Knupfer, *The Union As It Is: Constitutional Unionism and Sectional Compromise, 1787–1861* (Chapel Hill, 1991), pp. 102–18. On protectionists' responses to the compromise, see Kenneth Wyer Rowe, *Mathew Carey: A Study in American Economic Development* (Baltimore, 1933); Philip R. Schmidt, *Hezekiah Niles and American Economic Nationalism: A Political Biography* (New York, 1982). Carey conceded defeat in a letter to Duff Green, editor of the *Daily Telegraph*, on March 29, 1833: "I have withdrawn from the arena in consequence of the utter destitution of co-operation throughout the whole of last year, on the part of those vitally interested, and the hopelessness of any in future" (reprinted in *Niles' Weekly Register*, Apr. 13, 1833, p. 104).

The history of tariff politics is usually cast in terms of conflicting interests, while the deepening polarization over slavery—the paramount interest of the Southern states—roils just beneath the surface. Yet the very definition of these interests was predicated on assumptions about the future of American foreign trade relations—and the likelihood that they would be interrupted by war. If cotton producers were convinced that dismantling tariff barriers would promote world peace and prosperity, they also feared that protection would lead to commercial warfare—countervailing tariffs, embargoes, and other sanctions, perhaps war itself—as other trading states sought to secure their own vital interests. Alternatively, Britain and France, the leading customers of Southern cotton, might develop new sources of supply, with devastating results for both regional and national economies.[12]

For their part, protectionists would prepare for war in order to secure true national independence and a more durable peace. And as the threat of an early resumption of war receded, protectionists persuaded themselves that this peace was merely nominal, a disguise for a British commercial empire that had already blighted Ireland and India and ultimately threatened the United States as well.[13] Free traders and protectionists sought to promote their own interests, recognizing that control of the federal government, and therefore of national commercial policy, was the great desideratum. But they also developed dialectically opposed, ultimately irreconcilable understandings of the way the world had worked in the past and would work in the future. Fundamental principles were implicated in these opposing worldviews.

Republican divisions pivoted on differing assessments of the likelihood that the nations of the world would turn away from the "barbarous" policies of the past, promote an expanding regime of free trade, and eschew recourse to war. In their increasingly bitter controversies, Jeffersonians divided among realists and idealists, exponents and opponents of vigorous state action, nationalists and cosmopolitans. These divisions were further and more profoundly complicated by the politics of federalism: as Americans argued about the new nation's proper relation to the world at large, they were forced to reconsider the character of their own federal union.

---

[12]The best treatment of this theme is in Schoen, "Fragile Fabric of Union."

[13]Bernard Semmel, *The Rise of Free Trade Imperialism: Classical Political Economy, The Empire of Free Trade and Imperialism, 1750–1850* (Cambridge, 1970).

History and Theory

Free trade principles were broadly appealing in an export-driven colonial economy long before the publication of Adam Smith's *Wealth of Nations;* revolutionary patriots who mobilized against British imperial trade regulations were naturally predisposed to endorse his arguments against mercantilism.[14] Americans were flattered to read in Smith that "the most sacred rights of mankind" were at stake in their struggle against mercantilism.[15] Dismantling the colonial monopoly would vindicate American rights, but it would also benefit the entire trading world, including Britain. Smith thus provided a rationale for American independence and affirmed the Revolution's world historical significance. Not surprisingly, Smith's stock rose steadily in the United States throughout the antebellum years. "No person yet has carefully perused" *The Wealth of Nations,* Smith's American disciple Thomas Cooper wrote a half century after its publication, "without becoming a convert to his leading doctrines."[16]

In theory, every extension of the market fostered a more elaborate and productive division of labor. The free traders' Smith thus celebrated the benefits of foreign trade: "A more extensive market" provided a vent for domestic surpluses and promoted the development of a nation's "productive powers."[17] Furthermore, the mercantilists' policy of "beggaring all their neighbours" was obviously misguided: "A nation that would enrich itself by foreign trade is certainly most likely to do so when its neighbours are all rich, industrious, and commercial nations."[18] The division of labor "is highly beneficial to mankind throughout the civilized world," according to John Taylor of Caroline, an early American advocate of Smith's political economy:

---

[14]On early American free traders, see Cathy D. Matson and Peter S. Onuf, *A Union of Interests: Political and Economic Thought in Revolutionary America* (Lawrence, Kans., 1990). On the reception of Smith, see Joseph Dorfman, *The Economic Mind in American Civilization,* 5 vols. (New York, 1961), vol. 2. See also Paul Conkin, *Prophets of Prosperity: America's First Political Economists* (Bloomington, Ind., 1980), and Allen Kaufman, *Capitalism, Slavery, and Republican Values: Antebellum Political Economists, 1819–1848* (Austin, Tex., 1982). See more generally Douglas Irwin, *Against the Tide: An Intellectual History of Free Trade* (Princeton, N.J., 1996).

[15]Adam Smith, *An Inquiry into the Nature and Causes of the Wealth of Nations,* ed. R. H. Campbell and A. S. Skinner (Indianapolis, 1981), IV.7.66, p. 582.

[16]Thomas Cooper, *Lectures on the Elements of Political Economy,* 2d ed. (1830; reprint ed., New York, 1971).

[17]Smith, *Wealth of Nations,* IV.1.31, p. 447.

[18]Ibid., IV.3.38, 40, pp. 493, 495.

it was nature's design to "diffuse and equalize her blessings labours" across the globe.[19] Political economist Thomas Roderick Dew agreed. "An active and free commerce will enable each section and each latitude to produce the commodity which naturally befits it," Dew wrote, but "when the system of restriction and encouragement begins, these fair prospects are clouded; labour and capital are no longer left to take that profitable course which interest and a more humane and liberal national policy would point to would be best adapted to different climates."[20] Governments were ill-advised to interfere with market exchanges that increased the wealth of all nations by forcing the premature development of infant manufactures.

Yet if free trade ideas remained attractive for most Americans—at least in theory—the bitter experience of chronic warfare and perennial concern about the threat of British commercial domination fostered countervailing protective tendencies in American economic thought and practice. At first, protectionists found themselves at a rhetorical and ideological disadvantage in countering the free traders' reading of Smith. They could emphasize Smith's qualifications on free trade—to protect industry crucial to national security, to equalize tax burdens on imports, to retaliate against foreign trade regulations, or to prevent dumping of "cheaper foreign goods"—agreeing with him that "defence is of much more importance than opulence."[21] But these were all limited exceptions, contingent on what Smith insisted were unusual conditions: an actual state of war or an international commercial dispute that pointed toward war.

The protectionists' campaign for an activist federal state gained more leverage from Smith when they focused instead on the primacy of the American home market and compared its situation to that of Britain. *The Wealth of Nations* provided a broad historical narrative that illuminated inequalities among nations at different stages of development and emphasized the role of the state in securing vital national rights and interests. Read in the light of the *differences* among nations, *The Wealth of Nations* provided powerful arguments for tariff protection and the balanced development of interdependent interests in the domestic economy. Protectionists discovered that

---

[19]John Taylor, *Tyranny Unmasked* (1822), ed. F. Thornton Miller (Indianapolis, 1992), p. 24.

[20]Thomas Roderick Dew, *Lectures on the Restrictive System Delivered to the Senior Political Class of William and Mary College* (Richmond, 1829), p. 22.

[21]Smith, *Wealth of Nations*, IV.2.23–24, 2.31, 2.38, 2.40, 2.31, pp. 463, 465, 467, 469, 464.

Smith had anticipated their own interest in the development of the home market.[22] In the 1850s the great Whig economist Henry C. Carey offered the fullest reading of Smith in this new key, distinguishing the master from David Ricardo, Thomas Malthus, and the other "English politico-economical writers, who, while claiming to belong to [his] . . . school . . . , repudiate all his doctrines, praising what he denounced, and everywhere denouncing what he advised—to wit, the careful cultivation of the home market."[23]

American protectionists recovered the historical dimension of Smith's *Wealth of Nations,* distinguishing the circumstances of a specific nation at a particular stage of development from the long-term tendency of national markets to merge into an inclusive international market. From a British perspective, Smith's ambiguity about markets was easily overlooked: if the particular circumstances of Britain's "home market" were not yet universal, they would become so as other nations reached the same stage of development and free trade drew them increasingly into a single global market. But the distinction between nation and world was much more conspicuous from the underdeveloped periphery, in a young, developing country far removed from the European markets on which it relied. Distance in space underscored the temporal gap: the United States would have to move rapidly through the stages of its own historical development before it could secure an equal position in the trading world. Was it more likely to do so simply by throwing

---

[22]See "American System," *North American Review* 32 (1831):145: "The home trade is admitted by all, including Adam Smith, the great authority of the opponents of the protecting policy, to be a steadier, safer, and, on the whole, more eligible branch of business than the foreign; and the increase of it evidently indicates a favorable change in the general state of industry."

[23]Henry C. Carey, *The Prospect: Agricultural, Manufacturing, Commercial, and Financial. At the Opening of the Year 1851* (Philadelphia, 1851), p. 6. Carey claimed that his conversion from free trade to protectionism resulted from his analysis of the beneficent effects of the 1842 tariff and was confirmed by a "reperusal of *The Wealth of Nations,*" where he found that Smith's "essential object . . . had been to teach the people of Great Britain, that the system, against which it has been the object of protection among ourselves to guard, was not less manifestly destructive of themselves than it was violative 'of the most sacred rights of mankind'" (p. 5). See Conkin, *Prophets of Prosperity,* for discussions of protectionist economics (pp. 171–99) and Carey (pp. 267–301). On Carey, see George Winston Smith, *Henry C. Carey and American Sectional Conflict* (Albuquerque, N.M., 1951). There is no broad study of the intellectual history of protective economics equivalent to Irwin's study of free trade, cited above. But see Roman Szporluk, *Communism and Nationalism: Karl Marx versus Friedrich List* (New York, 1988), and Keith Tribe, *Strategies of Economic Order: German Economic Discourse* (Cambridge, 1995).

open its own markets, as free trade absolutists insisted?[24] Or would a regime of neomercantilist trade regulations force trading partners to offer equitable terms, thus compensating through political means for the new nation's unequal state of development?[25]

The Wealth of Nations is a rich text, profoundly informed by Smith's historical sensibility. Even Smith's apparently ahistorical passages could be read in terms of his conjectural approach to history: his axioms are empirical generalizations, glosses on economic behavior characteristic of advanced commercial societies. Yet because Smith himself believed that his generalizations prefigured the laws that govern relations under perfect market conditions, his self-appointed heirs felt amply justified in dispensing with his empirical approach and suppressing his moral historical vision. American free traders enthusiastically embraced this antihistorical reading of Smith, conflating his polemic against mercantilism with the revolutionary struggle against British imperial despotism: only the most rigorously limited state—and only the most self-effacing statesman—could avoid the onus of old-regime, mercantilist corruption.[26] In dialectical fashion, however, doctrinaire free traders invited protectionists to distinguish the "real free trade school" of "Dr. Smith" from "the system of the modern British school" and its American expositors, thus recovering the historical dimension of Smith's text and giving the conjectural history of developmental stages a new lease on life in nineteenth-century debates on political economy.[27] "Real" free trade would be achieved only through the mobilization of productive resources and perfection of markets *within* nations and *through* history.

---

[24]"Universal association and absolute free trade, may possibly be realized centuries hence," Friedrich List acknowledged, but Smith and the theorists regarded "them as realizable now. Overlooking the necessities of the present and the idea of nationality, they lose sight of the nation, and consequently of the education of a nation with a view to its independence" (*National System of Political Economy, Tr. from the German by G. A. Matile . . . Including the Notes of the French Translation by Henri Richelot . . . with a Preliminary Essay and Notes by Stephen Colwell* [1856; reprint ed., New York, 1974], p. 64).

[25]John E. Crowley, *The Privileges of Independence: Neomercantilism and the American Revolution* (Baltimore, 1993). For an excellent recent discussion of Smith's reception in the United States emphasizing his broad influence on the Founders and the relative insignificance of the free trade principles that would dominate interpretations of *The Wealth of Nations* in subsequent generations, see Samuel Fleischacker, "Adam Smith's Reception among the American Founders, 1776–1790," *William and Mary Quarterly*, 3d ser., 59 (2002):897–924.

[26]For testimonials to Smith as the founder of the "science of political economy," see Dew, *Lectures on the Restrictive System*, p. 195; Cooper, *Lectures on Political Economy*, p. 34; "The Prospect before Us . . . ," *North American Review* 13 (1823):191.

[27]*American Whig Review*, Oct. 1850, p. 353.

The great American debate about free trade and protection justified radically different readings of Smith's *Wealth of Nations*. The very title of Smith's masterpiece was subject to different interpretations. Did Smith mean nations *collectively* and was the commercial freedom he prescribed therefore now applicable to the world as a whole? "English politico-economical writers" and their American avatars had no doubt that this was the case. "By increasing the general mass of productions," Ricardo wrote, free trade "diffuses general benefit, and binds together, by one common tie of interest and intercourse, the universal society of nations throughout the civilized world."[28] Because this "universal society" already existed, the dismantling of trade barriers *anywhere* would benefit participants *everywhere*.

Significantly, however, the classical economists' optimism about global free trade was balanced by their increasingly dismal assessment of the implications of population growth, capital accumulation, and rent for the domestic economy. Protectionists reversed these tendencies, offering a more optimistic account of the progressive development of the home market, even while questioning the wisdom of liberalizing global trade relations. They insisted that Smith's primary concern was with "nation," not "nations," and that his prescriptions for the perfection of the *British* national market had to be adapted to the specific circumstances of other nations, including the United States. Ricardo's universal society would emerge only when all the nations of the world had achieved the same stage of market freedom and economic development, at the end of history.

Protectionists resisted the free traders' cosmopolitanism by situating the United States at a particular moment in its own historical development and emphasizing the new nation's vulnerability to British commercial domination. Patriotic protectionists warned that Britain would seek to gain through unequal trade relations in peacetime what she had failed to gain on the battlefield in the two American wars for independence.

They thus pitted "history"—the American experience over the previous four decades of chronic conflict—against "theory"— the economists' dogmatic insistence on the inherently rational, progressively peaceful character of the international division of labor. Dispute moved from an apparently straightforward empirical question—what had been the frequency of war in United States history or in the modern history of the European states

---

[28]Michael P. Fogarty, introduction to David Ricardo, *The Principles of Political Economy and Taxation* (London, 1965), p. 81.

system—to more fundamental questions about the character of international relations.

New York manufacturers assured Congress in 1832 that another war was inevitable: "Should the international relations of the great powers of the Christian world be on no worse a footing for the next two centuries than they have been for the two last—and it would surely be rash, whatever we may wish and hope, to reason and act on the hypothesis that the next following age will be better than the best in the history of our race—we must still calculate, as your memorialists have already remarked, that on an average, every alternate year will be one of war."[29] In 1828 the protectionist political economist Willard Phillips calculated that the United States had been involved in wars or victimized "by the wars of other nations" for eighteen of the first fifty years of national history. "Admit that the prospect in future is more favourable, and assume that we shall either be at war, or that our foreign trade will be exposed to interruption and embarrassment from foreign wars, one year out of five."[30]

Free traders were not impressed with such calculations. Protectionists assumed, with Thomas Hobbes, "that the natural state of man is WAR." But American history belied the Hobbesian dogma, as a free trade writer noted in 1834, "for we have been at war only four or five years out of the fifty-one that have elapsed since the treaty of peace which established our independence." Protectionists, this writer pointed out, perversely insisted that "we ought to foster manufactures, by high protecting duties in peace, to have them cheap and plentiful in war. In other words, that in order to diminish possible difficulties for five years, we should endure a most oppressive and unequal taxation for fifty!"[31] In any case, protectionists seemed to acknowledge that the frequency of wars was likely to decrease, for, as Thomas Cooper wrote in 1830, it was the common sense of the age that "war is seldom the interest of any nation, and is likely to be less so in future than formerly."[32] The premise of the protectionists' crude historicism, projecting past patterns into the future, was fundamentally "unphilosophical and inconclusive," Dew

[29]"Memorial of the New-York Convention, To the Congress of the United States. Presented March 26, 1832, and Referred to the Committee on Manufactures," bound with [Alexander Everett], *Address of the Friends of Domestic Industry, Assembled in Convention, at New York, October 26, 1831, To the People of the United States* (Baltimore, 1831), pp. 129–74; quotation p. 149.

[30]Willard Phillips, *A Manual of Political Economy* (Boston, 1828), p. 188.

[31]"M," "Suiting Facts to Theory," in Raguet, *Examiner,* Feb. 5, 1834, 1:216.

[32]Cooper, *Lectures on Political Economy,* p. 62.

concluded: peace, not war, was the "most natural state of nations," whatever "the past history of Europe, during its most barbarous and unsettled state."[33]

Free traders waxed eloquent about the beneficent effects of commerce for the "whole human family": free trade, Cooper asserted, makes "one family of all the nations on earth."[34] Economist Henry Vethake insisted that the progressive implementation of free trade principles contributed "to the peace of the world, and to the general progress of human civilisation," giving the lie to the mercantilist notion that one nation's gain was necessarily another's loss.[35] In the free traders' broad conception of progress, the stages of historical development were both simplified and universalized: "Free trade" was "the offspring of a grand movement, the first fruits of a rich harvest, the precursor of a mighty, world–embracing revolution."[36] In "the present enlightened and civilized age," statesmen rejected "barbarous and unenlightened" injunctions of mercantilist statecraft, now recognizing that the growing prosperity and power of nations depended on peaceful, reciprocally beneficial relations, not on conflict and conquest.[37]

The free trade revolution was nothing less than the "dawn of a new day," promising "peace on earth, and good will toward men."[38] The difference between old and new, barbarous and enlightened, was as clear as night and day. The new dispensation would secure the true wealth and welfare of all nations, exposing the fundamental mercantilist fallacy of "considering a nation in a corporative capacity, entirely distinct from the individuals who compose it."[39] "National prejudices would be corrected," and "the relations of distant people would be made so close and vital, that it would be next to impossible to foment a war."[40] There would be no more wars in a free-trading world because there would no longer be nations, at least according to the conventional definition of the term. "We do not believe that free trade could at once make the world what it should be," the editors of the *Democratic Review* acknowledged in 1841, "but it would give it the

---

[33]Dew, *Lectures on the Restrictive System*, pp. 128, 128n.

[34]Cooper, *Lectures on Political Economy*, p. 195.

[35]Henry Vethake, *The Principles of Political Economy* (Philadelphia, 1838), p. 284.

[36]"Free Trade," *Democratic Review* 9 (1841):329.

[37]Dew, *Lectures on the Restrictive System*, p. 190.

[38]Cooper, *Lectures on Political Economy*, p. iv.

[39]Dew, *Lectures on the Restrictive System*, p. 11; Cooper, *Lectures on Political Economy*, p. 16: "a nation or a community consists essentially of the individuals who compose it."

[40]Dew, *Lectures on the Restrictive System*, p. 146; "The Home League," *Democratic Review* 9 (1841):552.

opportunity to become so, and put it on the way. It would bind diverse interests into a solemn league of good–will."[41] Democrats envisioned "the moral amelioration of society"—a *single,* world society—as nation-states disappeared and diverse interests were reconciled and bound together in an all-embracing covenant.

Protective Nationhood

The polarization of positions on the prospects for war and peace generated by the tariff battles also led protectionists away from history and toward the very kinds of broad generalization, or theory, they claimed to disdain. "Nations are to them conflicting powers," a hostile critic charged, "set to jostle and tear each other in a rough contest for supremacy."[42] Protectionists did not hesitate to characterize the world in just such terms. "The globe is divided into different communities," Clay told Congress in his great speech on the tariff in 1824, "each seeking to appropriate to itself all the advantages it can, without reference to the prosperity of others." "Whether this is right or not," Clay would leave to the liberal moralists, but "it has always been, and ever will be, the case."[43] Protectionist economist Daniel Raymond insisted that nation and world necessarily constituted radically distinct moral domains. "Every nation," he wrote, must "consult its own interests exclusively, without any regard to the interests of other nations" and regardless of misguided "doctrines of universal philanthropy": "the old adage, 'charity begins at home,'" was the fundamental principle of good statesmanship. Wars were inevitable under the anarchic conditions of international society, and nations should always be ready to fight. "The romance of the Free-Trade doctrine," Whig economist Calvin Colton wrote in 1848, was "the assumption that all nations are one family, and that therefore a system of perfect Free trade would be best for their aggregate interests." This was far from the case. Quite to the contrary, Colton insisted, the premature dismantling of protective barriers would constitute a form of unilateral disarmament, making "the young and weak nations slaves to the old and strong" and ulti-

---

[41]"Free Trade," *Democratic Review* 9 (1841):341.

[42]"The Home League," *Democratic Review* 9 (1841):553.

[43]Clay, speech on tariff, Mar. 30–31, 1824, in *The Papers of Henry Clay,* ed. James F. Hopkins, 11 vols. (Lexington, Ky., 1959–92), 3:712.

mately giving "one nation, probably Great Britain, an ascendency over all the rest."[44] This was the peace of total capitulation and defeat, a new, more insidious, and subversive form of the universal monarchy that the despots of old sought to establish by force of arms.

At the peak of the tariff controversy in 1831, Alexander Everett elaborated the key premises of the protectionists' quarrel with free trade cosmopolitanism. The free trade position was predicated on idealized and unrealistic conceptions both of human nature and of the unity of mankind. The "imaginary condition of individual independence . . . absurdly called the state of nature" never existed, Everett charged, except "in the dreams of poets and philosophers."[45] If men were not naturally independent, then the philanthropists' corollary, that there was a universal society of all mankind, was equally fallacious. The distribution of "mankind into different communities" or nations, Everett insisted, was natural, even providential. Mankind would have descended into a Hobbesian state of nature if men had not been "separated originally by confusion of tongues, and prevented from all rushing together into the most favored latitudes, by local attachments and foreign antipathies, which are the germs of national preservation, by means of national emulation."[46]

Friedrich List, the founding father of "national economics," blasted Cooper and the free traders for failing to grasp the reality of the nation. Cooper argued that the idea of the nation as a moral entity was sheer mystification, a merely "grammatical being . . . clothed in attributes that have no real existence except in the imagination of those who metamorphose a word into a thing."[47] "But the American nation," List responded, was no abstraction: "it has all the qualities of a *rational being* and real existence. It has body and real possessions; it has intelligence, and expresses its resolutions to the members by laws, and speaks with its enemy—not the language of individuals, but at the mouth of cannon." As free traders deconstructed the nation, protectionists put it back together again, insisting first that individuals and nations were utterly dissimilar, but then imputing to nations a transcendent organic unity, or corporative capacity, analogous to that of the

---

[44]Calvin Colton, *Public Economy of the United States* (New York, 1848), p. 62.

[45]"Memorial of the New-York Convention," reprinted in [Everett], *Address of the Friends of Domestic Industry*, p. 165.

[46][Everett], *Address of the Friends of Domestic Industry*, pp. 21–22.

[47]Cooper, *Lectures on Political Economy*, p. 28.

individual. The simple difference was that real individuals depended on society for their very existence—property, the foundation of individual rights claims in modern times, was "itself . . . the creation of society"—while the independence and individuality of nations was, in a crucial sense, more natural and less imaginary (or conventional) than that of individual men.[48]

Cosmopolitan free traders imaginatively banished the nation, only to have the repressed concept return with a vengeance in protectionist rhetoric. The full-blown, romantic conception of the nation grew out of this transvaluation of values, in the imaginative embodiment of particular national societies *as if they were individuals* and in opposition to the economists' enlightened vision of the universal society of mankind. List's idea of the nation thus filled in the space "between the individual and the whole human race" that Cooper and the "cosmopolitical" economists sought to empty.[49] Proceeding from Smith's focus on the home market, national economists emphasized the interdependence of sectors of the economy, classes, and regions. Smith did not need to distinguish the *British* home market from that of other nations: clearing away the rubbish of mercantilism clearly would promote "natural liberty" at home and promote the emergence of an international free trade that inevitably would benefit Britain. Protectionist economists had to work out the implications of Smith's teachings for less happily situated nations, subject to the commercial domination of better-developed metropolitan economies, namely Britain itself.

In making the case for the nation as more than a legal entity, one *gens* among many, national economists invested the home market with layers of meaning, suggesting that the nation was an organic whole, a *natio*, uniquely

---

[48]Friedrich List, *Outlines of American Political Economy in a Series of Letters to Charles J. Ingersoll, Esq.* (1827), reprinted in Margaret Esther Hirst, *Life of Friedrich List and Selections from His Writings* (New York, 1965), pp. 216–17.

[49]List, *National System of Political Economy*, p. 263: "Between the individual and the whole human race there is the nation with its special language and literature, with its own origin and history, with its manners and habits, its laws and its institutions; with its claims to existence, its independence, its progress, its duration, and with its distinct territory; an association having not only an entirely separate existence, but having an intelligence and interest peculiarly its own, a whole existing for itself, acknowledging within itself the authority of the law, but claiming and enjoying full exemption from the control of similar associations, and consequently in the actual state of the world, able to maintain its independence only by its own strength and proper resources. As an individual acquires chiefly by the aid of the nation and in the bosom of the nation, intellectual culture, productive power, security, and well-being, human civilization can only be conceived as possible by means of the civilization and development of nations."

defined by a common historical experience and sharing common interests mediated through attachments to the land. This was not Smith's nation, but its genealogy could be traced to his conception of the home market in *The Wealth of Nations* and the efforts of history-minded readers to adapt its teachings to their own circumstances. The corporate spirit Smith sought to extirpate in Britain emerged with growing force over the course of the next century, notwithstanding the ascendancy of classical economics throughout the liberal world. As weaker nations sought to overcome inequalities in world political and commercial systems, they discovered the countervailing moral-historical dimension of Smith's teachings; as nationalists leveled distinctions and created the homogenous space *within* the nation that enabled market relations to flourish, they also revived and rehabilitated the corporate spirit in the world of nations.

Protectionists insisted that the progressive liberalization of international trade relations would reduce the United States and all the other nations of the world to a condition of servile dependence on Britain. Under these unnatural conditions, nations ultimately and inevitably would struggle to assert their independence, bursting the chains of commercial domination and inundating the world in "rivers of blood." "The experience of all mankind forbids us to hope for an exemption" from future wars, protectionist Mathew Carey warned in 1819. Free trade on necessarily unequal terms would retard the development of national resources, rendering the nation weak and vulnerable. Under the specious pretense of liberality and reciprocity, Henry Brougham and his fellow British free traders wanted to strangle America's "rising manufactures . . . in the cradle." Free trade was nothing less than war by other, more insidious means. If we mean to be "really" and not merely "nominally independent," Carey concluded, we must recognize that "the cause of the manufacturers . . . is the cause of the nation."[50]

Protectionists argued that free trade constituted an insidious form of warfare that subverted national independence: "after having expended the best blood of the nation, and millions of treasure to shake off the yoke of colonization," Carey wrote, "we have voluntarily adopted the colonial policy of England, and placed ourselves with respect to her, and in truth to most of the world, in the situation of colonies." "Who can contemplate the result

---

[50][Mathew Carey], *Addresses of the Philadelphia Society for the Promotion of National Industry,* 5th ed. (1820; reprint ed., New York, 1974), pp. iv, 74, 152.

[of free trade] without horror? . . . The wealth of the country would be swept away, to enrich foreign, and probably hostile nations, which might," he ominously predicted, "at no distant period, make use of the riches and strength thus fatuitously placed in their hands, to enslave the people who had destroyed themselves by following such baneful counsels."[51] Free trade, Clay concluded, leaves us "essentially British, in every thing but the form of our government."[52] We will not "possess a real national existence," a writer in the *North American Review* explained; we cannot claim to be "a self-subsisting substantive community" until "we shall have succeeded in relieving ourselves from the sort of colonial relation in which we have hitherto stood to the mechanical and intellectual workshops of Europe—when we shall have acquired an economical and moral, as well as a political independence."[53]

Protectionists saw opportunities for commercial exploitation in the national differences that, for free trade economists, gave rise to a providentially benign international division of labor. "As a municipal principle," Everett acknowledged, "there is no question of the great advantages of Free Trade," but "as between foreign nations, there is no free trade—there never was—there never can be—It would contravene the arrangements of Providence."[54] The possibility of "a *perfect reciprocity*" in foreign trade, Niles explained, "must remain Utopian, until it shall please the Great Creator of all things to give the same soil and climate, wants and wishes, governments and customs, to all the human race."[55] Thus, as free traders calculated the value of the Union, protectionists insisted that union was the necessary precondition of a genuinely free trade. As List pithily summarized the protectionist position: "Political union always precedes commercial union." "In the actual state of the world," he added, "free trade would bring forth, instead of a community of nations, the universal subjection of nations to the supremacy of the greater powers in manufactures, commerce, and navigation."[56]

---

[51] Ibid., pp. 189, 18.

[52] Clay, speech on tariff, Mar. 30–31, 1824, in Hopkins, *Papers of Henry Clay*, 3:722–23.

[53] "American System," *North American Review* 32 (1831):129.

[54] [Everett], *Address of the Friends of Domestic Industry*, p. 21.

[55] [Hezekiah Niles et al., Central Committee, Convention of the Friends of Domestic Industry], *Memorial to the Senate of the United States* (Baltimore, July 4, 1832), reprinted in Everett, *Journal of the Proceedings of the Friends of Domestic Industry*, p. 180.

[56] List, *National System of Political Economy*, p. 201.

Free Trade and Strict Construction

In the antebellum era, nationalists followed Smithian precepts in seeking to preserve and perfect a continent-wide free trade zone. The "freedom of interior commerce" had been the key to Britain's economic power, Smith explained, "every great country being necessarily the best and most extensive market for the greater part of the productions of its own industry."[57] But the efforts of the Marshall court to fulfill Smith's mandate, to make a nation by perfecting its market—most notably through broad constructions of the Constitution's commerce clause—raised the specter of a powerful central government that would obliterate states' rights and destroy the federal union.[58] Doctrinaire free traders thus tended to be strict constructionists, challenging the elastic clauses of the Constitution that nationalists invoked in their campaign to expand the powers of the federal state.[59]

In the view of John Marshall and like-minded nationalists, the perfection of the market in America entailed the *expansion* of the federal state's powers at the expense of other, putatively subordinate jurisdictions, not its progressive withering away. A powerful central government would, in turn, be able to promote the national interest—which, in circular fashion, could be said to exist only if there was a home market in the first place—by exercising effective power in the Atlantic states' system. An assertive, neomercantilist commercial diplomacy thus could promote the international political conditions under which a free trade regime would *ultimately* flourish, just as the development of the home market would promote market freedom domestically.

By contrast, critics feared the enlargement of the federal state, its interference with free trade, and the inevitably corrupting consequences. They

---

[57]Smith, *Wealth of Nations*, V.2.2, p. 900.

[58]R. Kent Newmyer, *John Marshall and the Heroic Age of the Supreme Court* (Baton Rouge, La., 2001), pp. 210–66; idem, *Supreme Court Justice Joseph Story: Statesman of the Old Republic* (Chapel Hill, 1985), pp. 115–54, 305–43; G. Edward White, *The Marshall Court and Cultural Change, 1815–1835*, abridged ed. (New York, 1991), pp. 595–673.

[59]The "general welfare" theme was a central pivot of Calhoun's constitutionalism: "For Congress . . . to undertake to pronounce what does, or what does not belong to the general welfare—without regard to the extent of the delegate powers—is to usurp to highest authority—one belonging exclusively to the people of the several States in their sovereign capacity" (Calhoun, *Discourse on the Constitution and Government of the United States*, in *Union and Liberty: The Political Philosophy of John C. Calhoun*, ed. Ross M. Lence [Indianapolis, 1992], pp. 246–47). For a sustained effort to link constitutional and political economic issues, see Condy Raguet, *The Principles of Free Trade, Illustrated in a Series of Short and Familiar Essays; Originally Published in the Banner of the Constitution* (Philadelphia, 1835).

borrowed liberally from Smith's strictures against mercantilism and insisted on the universal applicability of the axioms of market behavior they drew from the opening chapters of *The Wealth of Nations.* Free exchange in a global context was their great goal, and they fervently embraced the Smith who sought to open "the whole world for a market to the produce of every sort of labour."[60] From their global perspective, efforts of nationalists to promote balanced and integrated development in the home market were fundamentally misguided. The conduct of foreign commercial policy thus proved increasingly controversial to American free traders, even though this was one area where the federal government had a clear constitutional mandate. If the market that mattered was transatlantic in scope, efforts to promote the home market at the expense of a direct free trade with foreign trading partners were fundamentally misguided. The great achievement of Southern statesmen, culminating in John C. Calhoun's theory of the "concurrent majority," was to translate sectional grievances about the unequal impact of tariff policy into constitutional language, thus calling into question the value of the Union—and eventually its survival. In doing so, Southern disunionists enacted another Smithian script, looking beyond a factitious American nation toward full integration in a dynamic, expansive, and interdependent global market.[61]

For Smithian cosmopolitans, an overly energetic federal government was the problem, not the solution. The machinations of bankers, internal improvement advocates, and protection-minded manufacturers showed that the federal government, not the states, was most vulnerable to capture by corrupt alliances of partial interests. Concerns about congressional corruption raised more profound questions about majority rule and minority rights.[62] Majority rule, as the framers of the Constitution so acutely understood, was not a sufficient safeguard against abuses of government and the true interests of the people as a whole. It was axiomatic, Cooper acknowledged, that *"every political community or nation, ought to be considered as instituted for the good and*

---

[60]Smith, *Wealth of Nations,* I.3.4, pp. 33–34.

[61]Jesse T. Carpenter, *The South as a Conscious Minority, 1789–1861: A Study in Political Thought,* with a new introduction by John McCardell (1930; reprint ed., Columbia, S.C., 1990), pp. 77–126.

[62]James H. Read's forthcoming study of Calhoun's political and constitutional thought offers a fresh perspective on the crucial theoretical issues. See also Lacy K. Ford, Jr., "Inventing the Concurrent Majority: Madison, Calhoun, and the Problem of Majoritarianism in American Political Thought," *Journal of Southern History* 60 (1994):19–58.

the benefit of the MANY who compose it, and not of the FEW who govern it." The peculiar vulnerability of republics was that interests that sought to use state
power to their particular advantage could form a coalition, or what Madison
called "majority faction"—as protectionists did in 1824 and, most notoriously, in 1828—that could gain control of Congress and enable the corrupted "MANY" to exploit, impoverish, and subjugate "the FEW."[63] The
Southerners' solicitude for minority rights (meaning the right to exploit slave
labor) may not commend itself to modern democrats, but it underscored a
fundamental tension between republican majoritarianism and the liberal
determination to secure property rights and market exchanges from state
interference. The need to keep these domains inviolate inspired revolutionary patriots to break with the British Empire; a later generation of states'
rights advocates, reinforced by the teachings of Smith and the economists,
elaborated the distinction in a more rigorous, doctrinaire fashion as they
sought to sustain the liberal-republican synthesis.[64]

The identification of the Union *as a states' system* with the international
system was a logical response to the protectionists' emphasis on the in-
evitability of war and therefore on the persistence of a state of war in the
larger world. Strict constructionists of the Old Republican school were
predisposed toward such an identification in any case. As Calhoun later
explained in his *Discourse on the Constitution and Government of the United States*,
the federal Constitution was "a treaty—under the form of a constitutional
compact—of the highest and most sacred character" that governed "the
exterior relations of the States among themselves."[65] The presumption was
that, in the absence of such a treaty, the disunited states would seek to promote their conflicting interests by making war on one another, just as independent sovereignties presumably did—or so protectionists claimed—in the
Atlantic world.

At first blush, free trade advocates and jealous defenders of states' rights
might seem to offer radically divergent accounts of the natural tendency of
political communities toward war and peace. But the point of securing states'

---

[63]Cooper, *Lectures on Political Economy*, p. 33.

[64]My understanding of Southern liberalism is indebted to Jan Ellen Lewis, "The Problem
of Slavery in Southern Discourse," in *Devising Liberty: Preserving and Creating Freedom in the New
American Republic*, ed. David Thomas Konig (Stanford, Calif., 1995), pp. 265–97.

[65]Calhoun, *Discourse on the Constitution and Government of the United States*, in Lence, *Union and
Liberty*, p. 147.

rights was to prevent legislation that would bear unequally on different parts of the Union and thus interfere with free trade both within and beyond the Union. The most immediate and insidious threat to a liberal trading system thus came from within, as manufacturers and other beneficiaries of federal largesse sought to rig national commercial policy in ways that would perpetuate and promote their privileged interests. "The Cause of State Rights and Free Trade" was thus a single cause, as Philadelphia economist Condy Raguet insisted.[66] Mirroring the identification of part (manufacturers) and whole (the nation) in protectionist rhetoric, Raguet argued that the sovereign states—the Union's constituent parts—played a critical defensive role in preempting the concentration of power in the federal government that jeopardized the peace and prosperity of the whole union.

The Old Republicans' defense of a strictly construed federal Constitution had the paradoxical effect of calling into question the very union it was supposed to perfect and perpetuate. Their crucial move was to relocate the source of threat. A benign view of a progressively enlightened, stable, and peaceful world order organized around reciprocally beneficial market relations thus was juxtaposed to a federal political arena in which the "weaker party" was dominated "by the stronger."[67] Of course, strength and weakness in the Union did not reflect the real wealth—and potential power—of its separate members, but rather the domination of an adventitious and artificial majority. In effect, the Constitution made strong states weak by disarming them, and the predictable result was a kind of war through the scheme of unequal, redistributive taxation that the tariff authorized.

In the absence of a genuine foreign threat, the Union was therefore worse than useless, as Gov. George McDuffie of South Carolina explained in his 1835 inaugural address: "The rights and liberties of the minority States . . . are in much greater jeopardy from the majority States, acting through the federal government, under an assumed and practical omnipotence, than they possibly could be, if there existed no compact of Union, and each were separate and independent." McDuffie "conscientiously believe[d] that the smallest state on the continent of Europe, amidst the gigantic struggles of warring monarchies, holds its rights and liberties by much surer guaranties,

---

[66]In the title of his journal, *The Examiner, and Journal of Political Economy; Devoted to the Advancement of the Cause of State Rights and Free Trade*, cited above. On Raguet and his circle, see H. Arthur Scott Trask, "The Constitutional Republicans of Philadelphia, 1818–1848: Hard Money, Free Trade, and State Rights," Ph.D. diss., University of South Carolina, 1998.

[67]"Adjournment of Congress," in Raguet, *Examiner*, Mar. 9, 1831, 1:276.

under the laws of nations, than South Carolina now holds her rights and liberties, under the federal constitution, subject to a construction which absolutely inverts its operation, rendering it a chain to the oppressed, and a cobweb to the oppressor."[68]

McDuffie's horrific vision of constitutional warfare relocated the anarchic state of nature from the world at large, where consensual relations premised on reciprocal interest now governed, to the operations of the federal system itself. Free traders did not banish the specter of war: they simply displaced it. Under the ostensible forms of majority rule, the federal government provided an arena for an insidious form of warfare that would subvert liberty and property, the foundations of republican self-government itself. In this deeply skeptical view, the peace and prosperity Americans supposedly enjoyed within their federal union was itself only nominal, depending finally on the capacity of its members to enforce "that equality of protection to which all the citizens of the Union are justly entitled."[69] From the free traders' perspective, "oppressive and unequal taxation" that promoted the development of one sector of the economy—or section of the Union—at the expense of others was the moral equivalent of war. The protectionists' claim that the promotion of manufactures served the national interest, their identification of the part with the whole, was thus called into question: a high tariff was inherently redistributive, taking from one sector—or one section—and giving to another. This is, of course, what nations at war sought to achieve with respect to each other, though much less efficiently and without the legitimacy that the presumed consent of the victims through representation in Congress conferred on the transaction.[70]

---

[68]McDuffie's inaugural address, in Raguet, *Examiner,* Jan. 7, 1835, 2:185–86. According to Calhoun, "no two distinct *nations* ever entertained more opposite views of policy than these two *sections* do" (Fort Hill address, July 26, 1831, in Lence, *Union and Liberty,* p. 386), my emphasis. Calhoun elaborated on this theme in his *Discourse on the Constitution and Government of the United States* (1851): "Never was there an issue between independent States that involved greater calamity to the conquered, than is involved in that between the States which compose the two sections of this Union. The condition of the weaker, should it sink from a state of independence and equality to one of dependence and subjection, would be more calamitous than ever before befell a civilized people" (p. 267).

[69]"The American Tariff," *Edinburgh Review,* Dec. 1828, quoted in [Alexander Everett], *British Opinions on the Protecting System, Being a Reply to Strictures on that System Which Have Appeared in Several Recent British Publications* (Boston, 1830), reprinted in Alexander Everett, *Journal of the Proceedings,* p. 15.

[70]The classic and most influential statement of this argument may be found in Taylor, *Tyranny Unmasked.* The protective "system pretended to be leveled against foreigners, has only hit ourselves"; "this new war is to be carried on by foreign and native capitalists" at the expense of the great agricultural majority" (quotations on pp. 48, 179).

Skeptical critics depicted protectionist advocates of preparedness as war-mongers who magnified the threat of future conflict in order to justify en-croachments on states' rights and individual liberties. A strong federal state conjured up images of the kind of despotic imperial authority the Ameri-can revolutionaries thought they had destroyed.[71] Protectionists proceeded on the premise that foreign trade was inherently unequal and conflictual, that one nation's gain was always at another's expense. Free traders pointed out that this was the same fundamentally fallacious premise that had led mercantilists astray. Obsessed with bullion flows and the balance of trade, old-regime policy makers kept up a constant state of war in order to beggar their rivals and achieve economic autarky—or what protectionists now called "independence." Cooper complained that the mercantilist beast that Smith and his followers had slain was, incredibly, now resurrected in the protec-tionists' "*manufacturing system;* a system equally absurd and selfish, and equally jealous lest our neighbours should profit as well as ourselves."[72]

Protectionism, Cooper explained, was the second coming of mercantilism, "a system of monopoly, exclusive privilege, restriction, and prohibition; a system, which professes to make its gain, by depressing as far as possible the efforts of every other nation who using its natural advantages, seeks to make a profit by commerce and manufacture as well as ourselves." Such systems were unnatural: they distorted foreign trade—which, like exchanges in the home market, should be reciprocally beneficial—by subordinating it to the interests of belligerent states seeking to dominate one another. "Manufac-tures and commerce," when protected and promoted by neomercantilist governments, "are the great and perpetual sources in modern days of na-tional quarrels. They are war-breeders. Three fourths at least of the wars in Europe for these one hundred and fifty years, have originated from the jealousies of trade, from the stupidity, and the selfishness of merchants and manufacture[r]s."[73]

Preparing for war, as the protectionists urged, was thus tantamount to making, or breeding, war. And it was just such preparations that most jeop-ardized republicanism. The revolutionary generation conceptualized the

---

[71]This theme is elaborated in Peter S. Onuf, "Federalism, Republicanism, and the Origins of American Sectionalism," in *All Over the Map: Rethinking American Regions,* ed. Edward L. Ayers et al. (Baltimore, 1996), pp. 11–37.

[72]Cooper, *Lectures on Political Economy,* p. 10.

[73]Ibid., pp. 62, 131–32.

threat in terms of standing armies, the consolidation of political authority, and high levels of taxation and indebtedness. The economists of Cooper's later career offered a more sophisticated analysis: the confusion and therefore corruption of the distinct domains of politics and economics, the illegitimate interference of governments in the private business of citizens, inevitably subverted the foundations of republican government. This monopolizing, despotic impulse had provoked American patriots to rise up in revolt; during the nullification crisis it justified resistance to the tariff in South Carolina.

Two Nations

The worldviews of protectionists and free traders mirrored one another. Protectionists looked abroad—and particularly toward Britain—and saw a world of nations in perpetual conflict. They challenged the rosy projections of liberal cosmopolitans who imagined that the dismantling of trade barriers—indeed, the dismantling of nations themselves—would inaugurate a regime of world peace and prosperity. Peace, they insisted, was deceptive: it was best understood either as an interval in an unending succession of wars—the plausible premise of Mathew Carey and the first generation of protectionists—or as a cover for more insidious assaults on the independence of young, undeveloped, commercially dependent nations such as the United States. There could be no real, lasting peace among unequal states at different stages of development. By contrast, the federal union secured free trade, prosperity, and peace among the American state-republics, regardless of discrepancies of size, population, and wealth.

Free traders inverted protectionist logic at every point. Optimistic about the prospects for peace of an increasingly interdependent, peaceful, and prosperous trading world, free traders saw the federal union as a zone of danger, an arena for warlike assaults on the vital interests and fundamental rights of embattled minority interests. Safety depended on a rigorous, constitutional distinction between the realms of economics and politics, putting "freedom of commerce . . . beyond the reach of any combined or corrupted majority in a central or consolidated Congress."[74] Free traders' logic

---

[74]"The Cotton Manufacture," in Raguet, *Examiner,* Nov. 27, 1833, 1:139.

subverted their faith in the efficacy of republican government to secure liberty and property and of the Union to guarantee states' rights. Without the kinds of constitutional protections Calhoun's concurrent majority offered, Southerners would be better off seceding from the Union altogether.

Yet free traders could not escape from profound anxieties about the threat of war, however much they imagined the trading world a peaceful place. Their skeptical assessment of protectionists' motives underscored the likelihood of conflict in the event of disunion: if their fellow Americans constructively made war on them *within* the Union, what would restrain them from more overt, violent assaults in the *absence* of union? Strict constructionist free traders had no reason to question the wisdom of the Founders in constructing a union that would guarantee peace among potentially hostile states, for hostility and suspicion among Americans had never been more conspicuous. If, when they looked abroad, free traders could imagine that enlightened nation-states would coexist in peace, progressively withering away, they had no illusions about the future of American politics. The idea that states were sovereign—with a legitimate claim to the rights of fully independent states in an international society—and the displacement of the idea of the nation from the whole American people to the separate nationalities of the particular states and finally to two hostile, united sections constituted an implicit acknowledgment of the Founders' wisdom. Americans experienced the imaginative demolition of the Union in the tariff debates and in subsequent sectional crises as a kind of virtual war—and as a rehearsal for the actual bloodbath that would finally fulfill the Founders' most awful imaginings.

Controversy over commercial policy reflected—and, to a significant extent, precipitated—the deepening crisis of the American union. The Founders' primary goal had been to preempt the possibility of war, whether with foreign powers or among the American states themselves. Ironically, their successful efforts to demonstrate the endemic threats to peace and security, to depict the inexorable tendency of disunited states to slide into an anarchic state of nature, paved the way toward subsequent conflict and confusion. The need to meet *external* challenges to American independence by establishing a more energetic federal regime was broadly appealing to most Americans, even moderate Antifederalists—and future Jeffersonian Republican oppositionists—who feared the concentration of power in a potentially despotic central government. But the Federalists' emphasis on the dangers of interstate—and intersectional—conflict, however effective it may have been in countering Antifederalist concerns about consolidation, underscored and even reinforced anxieties about *internal* threats to the American peace. In other words, the very premise of the new federal peace plan was that war threatened in all quarters, whether from the counterrevolutionary great powers of Europe or from conflicts among states or sections in the Union. Under such dire circumstances, the very survival—much less the perfection—of the Union was indeed something of a miracle. But it was a miracle that depended on a spirit of compromise and concession that proved increasingly difficult to sustain under the strain of sectional conflict.

The paradoxical effect of the post–War of 1812 campaign to bolster American independence and prepare for future wars was to call into question the legitimacy of the federal Constitution and the value of the Union. Opponents of this campaign did not instantly forget the Founders' warnings about the dangers of disunion and the likelihood of war among disunited states. However they might embrace the free traders' inspiring vision of an increasingly peaceful and prosperous *world* order, their resistance to nationalist initiatives revealed fundamental conflicts of interest—and belligerent tendencies—that only union could hold in check. Disunion meant war, and, as the National Republicans had insisted, the threat of war required energetic national government. Critics of the American System thus accepted the Founders' logic. They simply disagreed on the source of threat to the American peace.

Agreement on the Founders' wisdom sustained powerful commitments to the Union, despite deepening intersectional divisions. The deepest division was over the chief source of danger to liberty and union. Did it come from foreign powers in a dangerously anarchic European states' system or from the consolidation of power by a corrupt alliance of ambitious interests *within* the Union? Unionist sentiments could not contain or suppress sectional tensions —particularly when, despite the disclaimers of its most fervent exponents, unionism took on an increasingly pronounced sectional inflection—and intersectional antipathies prepared the way for the emergence of two hostile nations in the place of one. Successive crises of the Union did not banish the idea of the nation or lead Americans to imagine that they could transcend the threat of war. To the contrary, just as free traders displaced the threat of war from the larger world to the federal arena itself, the idea of the nation was displaced—first to the separate nationalities of sovereign states, prepared like nullifying South Carolina to mobilize its military force against Yankee consolidationists, and then to an emergent Southern nation.

The route toward Northern nationhood was apparently more direct, beginning with the defense of the Union and a harmonious, interdependent balance of interests in the home market and extending to a romantic conception of the American people as one great, inclusive family. "The home market," the protectionist Everett wrote in 1831, "is the palladium of home itself in all its most endearing and ennobling political and social relations; without which we have no common country, but should be reduced to the condition of dismembered and defenceless provinces."[75] But of course this fervent nationalism was predicated on the denial of the deepening divisions among Americans, most notably over the future of slavery as a domestic institution, that had long since alienated Southerners. Northern nationalism was thus fixated on the preservation of the Union, not on the acknowledged sense of sectional difference—and grievance—that inspired sectional nationalists in the South.

[handwritten margin notes:] how tariff philosophy related to ideas of world order / Constitutional order. Free traders - believe it promotes international harmony but free oppression within the chain protectionists - peace deceptive, Great Britain uses free trade to exploit us (i.e. economically dependent U.S.) Believe fed. gov't should protect nation & Constitution authorizes it.

---

[75][Everett], *Address of the Friends of Domestic Industry,* p. 39.

Robert P. Forbes

The Missouri Controversy
and Sectionalism

IT HAS BEEN said that the Missouri crisis brought the South into being. In fact, one can be even more specific: the South came into existence on Saturday, February 13, 1819, around 4:30 in the afternoon. At that moment, Rep. James Tallmadge of New York introduced an amendment to the Missouri statehood bill providing "[t]hat the further introduction of slavery or involuntary servitude be prohibited . . . ; and that all children of slaves, born within the said state . . . shall be free at the age of twenty-five years."[1] This amendment instantaneously sparked an explosion that would consume Congress for two years and bring the Union closer to dissolution than at any time prior to the firing on Fort Sumter.

Why was the Missouri question so explosive? In reality, of course, Representative Tallmadge did not create the South; instead, by knowingly or unknowingly aiming a blow at the South's most sensitive spot, his amendment pulled the plug on an upsurge of Southern nationalism after the War of 1812. The frenzied response of Southerners, Virginians in particular, to an attempt to limit the transfer of slaves from the exhausted plantations of the Old Southeast to the fertile lands of the New Southwest, vividly displayed the degree to which slavery had gained a stranglehold over Southern policy that trumped all other national interests and values.

---

[1] *Annals of Congress*, 15th Cong., 2d sess., p. 1170 (hereafter *Annals*).

This was not news to Southerners, of course; but it was a revelation to the country as a whole. As historian George Dangerfield put it, "The paradox—the very complicated and difficult paradox—that slavery could have a legal existence in a land of free men was now . . . fully open to inspection. It would be too much to say that the country as a whole was willing to inspect it; the country as a whole was willing only to be surprised by it."[2] From this revelation a fissure opened—not between North and South, initially, but between those Americans who could make peace with this paradox and those who ultimately could not.

The Missouri controversy involved two distinct issues, extending over two years and culminating in two separate compromises. The second phase of the crisis stemmed from a provision in Missouri's constitution to bar free blacks and mulattoes from the state. Henry Clay's deliberately ambiguous compromise, holding that the controversial clause in the Missouri constitution should not be interpreted as in conflict with the U.S. Constitution, left the door open to the claim that persons of African descent were not citizens of the United States—an interpretive wedge that defenders of slavery would drive throughout the antebellum period, that would explode into the forefront of politics in the Dred Scott decision of 1857, and that would shape American social and political life long after the Civil War.

Southerners' sense of apprehension within the American polity went deeper than the check to the expansion of slavery threatened by the Missouri crisis or even the strong Northern opposition to slavery that it disclosed. A largely unreported episode during the debates over Missouri convinced many slaveholders that slavery could come under assault even in the states where it was already established and that the very land of the United States itself constituted a dangerous threat.

Given the history of sectionalism during the War of 1812, it is hardly surprising that many of the strongest nationalists were from the South. Virginians, the once and future champions of states' rights, lent many voices to this nationalist chorus. After all, the chair of the federal executive had been their exclusive property for all but four years of the republic's existence. Thomas Jefferson may have been the oracle of states' rights and strict construction, but it was his purchase of Louisiana that turned America into a continental power. War Hawks Henry Clay of Kentucky and John C. Calhoun and

---

[2]George Dangerfield, *The Era of Good Feelings* (New York, 1952), p. 200.

William Lowndes, both of South Carolina, led the nationalist chorus for the War of 1812, when New Englanders, not Southerners, spun schemes of secession. While Madison's conduct of the war did not earn him many plaudits, he could hardly be charged with sectional tendencies. As early as 1815, the Richmond *Whig* printed paeans to internal improvement, sentiments echoed in the Charleston *Courier* and other Southern papers.[3]

To some Southerners, particularly those in the slave-majority states of South Carolina and Georgia, a strongly nationalist outlook stemmed less from ardent patriotism than from a visceral pragmatism. Quite simply, many slaveholders believed that no other institution in America possessed the force to defend their dangerous human property. "Without the aid and countenance of the whole United States," insisted diehard South Carolina Unionist James Chesnut, Sr., "we could not have kept slavery. I always knew the world was against us. That is one reason I was a Union man. I wanted all the power the United States gave me—to hold my own—&c&c."[4]

Other nationalist Carolinians, such as Langdon Cheves, president of the Second Bank of the United States, diplomat Joel Poinsett, and Sen. William Lowndes, played more constructive and edifying roles on the national stage (while never shirking their responsibility to their state's paramount interest). No politician's career more vividly illustrated the dilemma of the Carolina nationalist, however, than that of John C. Calhoun.

From the outset of his career, Calhoun seemed intent on fashioning himself as a truly national figure. Hailing from the newly settled backcountry of his native state, Calhoun started life very nearly as much a western frontiersman as Andrew Jackson. To this rugged beginning, Calhoun added the polish of a Connecticut education at Yale and the new Tapping Reeve Law School. In addition to his universally acknowledged brilliance, inexhaustible energy, and almost mystical powers of fascination, the young statesman truly seemed to represent the nation itself rather than the particular interests of his home state. John Quincy Adams, his colleague in the cabinet of James Monroe, famously described Calhoun as "a man . . . of enlarged philosophical views,

---

[3]See Robert F. Durden, *The Self-Inflicted Wound: Southern Politics in the Nineteenth Century* (Lexington, Ky., 1985), p. 12; *Charleston Courier,* Mar. 8, 1819.

[4]C. Vann Woodward., ed., *Mary Chesnut's Civil War* (New Haven, 1981), p. 421. Colonel Chesnut's position (as transmitted by his daughter-in-law) is in line with the view of Paul Finkelman and other modern historians who regard the Constitution as a proslavery document, although Chesnut's peers regarded his views as outdated.

and of ardent patriotism . . . above all sectional and factious prejudices more than any other statesman of this Union with whom I have ever acted."[5] The nationalist Calhoun embodied an almost unique pairing of characteristics: he was a charismatic technocrat, a coolly rational zealot of American progress. It was to Calhoun that Monroe turned to transform the War Department into an engine of nationalist influence.[6] It was to Calhoun, as well, that New Yorkers turned as a symbol of reform in their efforts to break the electoral stranglehold of the state's Bucktail faction prior to the election of 1824. Calhoun had devoted followers as well in Connecticut, Pennsylvania, Massachusetts, Ohio, and other states. As late as 1832, Calhoun evidently viewed himself as a figure with national appeal; he was reported as angling for the nomination for president of the Northern-based, evangelical-influenced, antislavery-oriented Antimasonic party. By that time, however, the exigencies of slave-state politics had long since forced Calhoun to repudiate his expansive nationalism and adopt positions that foreclosed the possibility of a national political career. In the words of his former Yale professor Benjamin Silliman, "when sectional jealousies arose . . . the high-minded, honorable patriot became the antagonist of internal improvement, and was narrowed down to a South Carolina politician."[7]

Perhaps nothing illustrates more vividly the destructive effect on nationalism of slavery than the self-immolation of Calhoun the nationalist. Calhoun saw no conflict between American nationalism and slavery. In a sense, this was his true tragic flaw. Recognizing no contradiction himself, he displayed a striking inability to comprehend that others might see one. For Calhoun, at the heart of the conflict between Northerners and Southerners was a simple matter of misunderstanding. Better communication would inexorably produce a harmonizing of outlook, bringing the sections together. Indeed, this conception stood at the heart of Calhoun's passion for internal improvements. On the subject of "national power," Calhoun demanded, what "can be more important than a perfect unity in every part, in feelings and senti-

---

[5] C. F. Adams, ed., *Memoirs of John Quincy Adams*, 12 vols. (Philadelphia, 1874–77), 5:361.

[6] It seems likely as well that Monroe picked Calhoun as secretary of war with the intention of forwarding Calhoun's signature project of internal improvements, especially a national system of roads, under the rubric of national security and thereby circumventing constitutional objections. This was precisely the method employed by Dwight D. Eisenhower, Monroe's closest modern counterpart as a "hidden-hand" president, in the construction of the modern interstate highway system.

[7] George P. Fisher, *Life of Benjamin Silliman, M.D., LL.D.*, 2 vols. (New York, 1866), 1:309.

ment?" With "a perfect system of roads and canals," Americans could "conquer space," and "a citizen of the West" could "read the news of Boston still moist from the press." "The mail and the press," he continued, were "the nerves of the body politic," by which "the slightest impression made on the most remote parts" would be "communicated to the whole system; and the more perfect the means of transportation, the more rapid and true the vibration."[8] It did not then occur to the man who two decades later called for draconian punishment of abolitionists sending literature through the postal system that such instantaneous communication between communities with profoundly different mores would be as likely to engender anger and moral outrage as to promote harmony and understanding.

What can we learn from the collapse of Calhoun's nationalist dreams? On the one hand, it reaffirms Speaker Thomas P. O'Neill's famous dictum that "all politics is local." No politician, not even one as brilliant as Calhoun, can successfully present himself as a national figure without being firmly rooted in his local base. His influence, founded on his personal magnetism, delayed South Carolina's turn to full-fledged sectionalism for several years, helping to ensure that when it arrived there (in the wake of the aborted Denmark Vesey insurrection), it would be particularly ferocious. Indeed, the rest of antebellum history can be viewed in large part as waiting for the rest of the South to catch up with the conclusions of South Carolina.

More fundamentally, Calhoun's nationalist failure tells us that there was at base, in Southern eyes at least, a contradiction between activist American nationalism and the safety of slavery that even a figure as forceful as John C. Calhoun could not overcome. Calhoun was the ultimate test case of the proslavery nationalist; if anyone could have made the case for the compatibility of a powerful, centralized national government and the defense of slavery, he should have. Instead, he beat a retreat into the kind of "strained and forced constructions" of the Constitution that he had once deprecated, and he became the chief promoter of the "belief in the slave holding States, that it is the intention of the other States gradually to undermine their property in their slaves," which he had earlier denounced as "so dangerous a mode of believing" that "no one can calculate the consequences."[9]

---

[8]Calhoun, speech on the bonus bill, Feb. 4, 1817, *Annals*, 14th Cong., 2d sess., pp. 853–54.
[9]Calhoun to V[ergil] Maxcy, Aug. 12, 1820, in *The Papers of John C. Calhoun*, ed. Clyde N. Wilson and Shirley Bright Cook, 28 vols. (Columbia, S.C., 1959–2003), 5:327.

We are left with the question: why did the South find nationalism so threatening to slavery? Why were they so willing to believe that Northerners were intent on stripping them of their slave property with the machinery of the federal state? Why, for example, did South Carolina's governor, Whitemarsh Seabrook, denounce the ubiquity of antislavery propaganda in every form of literature, even children's books, during the era known as the "neglected period of anti-slavery in America?"[10] Why did some Southern leaders attack the American Colonization Society, understood by contemporary abolitionists and modern historians alike to have been the sanctimonious handmaiden of the planter interest? Why was Virginia's governor, John Floyd, so fearful of federal power that he rejected the assistance of the United States military to subdue Nat Turner and his followers because of the dangerous precedent it would set, even while white Virginians cowered in their homesteads? Why did Southern leaders such as Nathaniel Macon and John Randolph regard the assertion of Congress's power to build roads and canals as tantamount to claiming its power to abolish slavery? The examples of Southerners' apparently unrealistic fears of antislavery sentiment in America, and especially of the threat to slavery posed by the federal government, could be multiplied endlessly. What are we to make of them?

For the most part, such responses have been chalked up to what Richard Hofstadter called "the paranoid style in American politics." Generations of historians have indicted Southerners' paranoia in tandem with the fanaticism of the Garrisonian abolitionists; but all but the most blindly partisan of scholars have acknowledged that the abolitionists had not the tiniest influence on the federal government and hardly more with the public at large. Thus the problem, it has been thought, must be with the extreme overreaction of the Southerners. Important works have tied this phenomenon to the cultural or psychological impact of the slaveholding style; to the efforts of designing Southern leaders to impose class cohesion through fear; and even (once upon a time) to the pangs of an inflamed conscience.[11]

---

[10]See Whitemarsh B. Seabrook, *A Concise View of the Critical Situation, and Future Prospects of the Slave-Holding States, in Relation to their Coloured Population* (Charleston, S.C., 1825), and A. D. Adams, *The Neglected Period in American Anti-Slavery, 1808–1832* (1908; reprint ed., Gloucester, Mass., 1964).

[11]See, for example, Richard Hofstadter, *The Paranoid Style in American Politics, and Other Essays* (New York, 1965); James Oakes, *Ruling Race: An Interpretation of American Slaveholders* (New York, 1982); Eugene D. Genovese, *The World the Slaveholders Made* (New York, 1969); and Charles G. Sellers, "The Travail of Slavery," in *The Southern as American*, ed. Sellers (Chapel Hill, 1960).

More recently, scholars such as David Brion Davis have proposed a more rational basis for Southerners' antislavery fears. Approaching the problem from an Atlantic perspective, Davis has stressed the significance of British abolitionism, noting that the heat of British rhetoric—and more important, Parliament's concrete steps against slavery, which included registration, curtailment of the slave trade among Britain's West Indian possessions, and liberation of slaves in American ships forced into British colonies' harbors —offered a pattern of behavior that Southerners monitored intensely and interpreted as components of an elaborate plot to overthrow Southern slavery —an "elaborate fantasy," Davis opines, that rested on no more than "a thin foundation of truth."[12]

Davis is surely correct that fears of a British invasion to end slavery were far-fetched, and if Southern concerns had stemmed entirely from that source, they would be easy to dismiss. But while British antislavery measures provided a *context* to slaveholders' apprehensions, they by no means constituted the whole of their *content*. Rather, Southerners recognized specific, concrete, and homegrown threats to their peculiar institution, and it is to these that we must now turn.

In the wake of the Missouri controversy, Southerners found several aspects of the affair deeply disturbing. The first was the hostility that many Americans revealed toward slavery. Slaveholding congressmen were shocked by the passion and outrage of their nonslaveholding colleagues and were mortified in particular by their implications that the involvement with slavery of the Southern states compromised their republicanism—a suggestion, by inference, that their state governments were in violation (of the spirit, in the case of the original thirteen, and of the letter, in the case of the rest) of the U.S. Constitution. Another term for this would be "un-American," fighting words in any century. As the rhetoric reached the boiling point, Northerners—who lived, after all, in a condition of demographic safety and tranquility—could easily be interpreted as endorsing slave violence against masters or at the very least of viewing themselves as neutral in such a contest.

Equally disturbing to Southern leaders, the rank-and-file of the Southern public appeared unmoved by the shocking affront to Southern honor

---

[12]David Brion Davis, *Challenging the Boundaries of Slavery* (Cambridge, Mass., 2003), p. 88. Davis was earlier one of the chief exponents of applying the Hofstadter paranoia thesis to the Northern view of the sectional crisis; see Davis, *The Slave Power Conspiracy and the Paranoid Style* (Baton Rouge, 1970).

and to Southern property that Missouri represented. In the Northern states, the Richmond *Enquirer* noted, towns of every size organized mass meetings against the spread of slavery, adding petulantly, "but in the slave-holding states, not one meeting, not one resolution."[13] To historian Glover Moore, writing on the Missouri controversy from the vantage point of the Jim Crow South, this absence of public outcry merely attested to the Southern public's complacency and passive confidence in its leaders.[14] It is hard to see how such a hypothesis could be tested.

Perhaps it is time to apply Occam's razor to the problem of Southerners' fear of a threat to slavery from the federal government: what if the fear wasn't wrong? To answer this question, we need to look again at the Missouri conflict and what it meant for Southerners.

We must begin by placing the Missouri debates in their immediate context. The Missouri crisis began as the ultimate inside-the-Beltway story. The push for restriction of slavery began in Congress, without any noticeable public pressure from constituents, and it seems likely that local developments in the District of Columbia had a major influence on its dynamics.

Ironically, the closing of the transatlantic slave trade in 1808 created a condition that made slavery in the United States considerably uglier than it had been previously. It led to vast expansion of the *domestic* slave trade—the familiar coffles of manacled slaves crisscrossing the land. One of the major national slave markets was just across the river in Alexandria, Virginia, and coffles of slaves chained together were routinely visible through the windows of the Capitol. In 1816, John Randolph of Roanoke denounced the domestic slave trade on the floor of Congress and called for a federal investigation into it.[15] Over the next several years, the movement to end the slave trade in the District of Columbia gained momentum.

At the same time, however, slavery continued to expand. The 1820 census showed a slave population in the United States of 1,538,038, an increase of approximately 30 percent over the 1810 figure. So the belief that closing the African trade would bring a gradual end to slavery—a reasonable assumption, as death rates of slaves exceeded birth rates in most plantation societies—turned out to be completely wrong in an American context.

---

[13] *Richmond Enquirer*, Dec. 3, 1819.

[14] "It was a tribute to the self-confidence of the Southerners that they did not deem it necessary to hold meetings in Missouri's behalf. They took it for granted that their section was united" (Glover Moore, *Missouri Controversy, 1819–1821*, [Nashville, 1937], p. 219).

[15] *Annals*, 14th Cong., 1st sess., pp. 1115–16.

The demographics of slavery in the United States created a curious arrangement of intersectional interests within the South. This time, unlike earlier controversies such as the closing of the African slave trade, it was Virginia that took the most strident proslavery stand, not South Carolina. The reason is straightforward. The longest-settled of the states, Virginia had exhausted the fertility of her land and possessed a tremendous oversupply of slaves for the labor required of them—a recipe for insurrection. The new western territories had virgin land and an insatiable demand for slaves. Thus the freedom to sell their slaves west without restrictions—"diffusion," planters liked to call it—was essential both to Virginians' continued prosperity and to their safety. As Spencer Roane wrote, with revealing orthography, closing territories to slavery would leave Virginians "damned up in a land of slaves."[16]

But extending slavery to the new states to be admitted across the Mississippi River would make the institution effectively impossible to abolish and would, in effect, silently put to rest the long-held hope that the nation would ultimately shed the stigma of slavery and become true to its founding principles. Although members of Congress had expressed a concern with the callousness of the domestic slave trade—particularly in the federal district, where it reflected poorly on the national honor—few congressmen gave any thought to the crucial institutional question of the status of slavery in the new states.

New York's James Tallmadge had considered the issue seriously, speaking and voting against the admission of Illinois because of the inadequacy of the sham provisions against slavery in its state constitution. With his well-pitched amendment—mild enough to appeal to a solid block of Northerners as no more than common sense—Tallmadge brought the question of the expansion of slavery in the territories to a head. Without his intervention, the polite evasion of the issue might have continued indefinitely, as slavery gained ground gradually enough to fail to provoke alarm.

Two things were especially remarkable about the reaction of the Upper South representatives to the Tallmadge amendment. The first was its violence. From the sketchy account of the session provided by the House reporter, William Seaton, supplemented by the accounts of members, it is evident that the Southern representatives—led by the moderate, consummate nationalist Henry Clay—exploded into fireworks of emotion almost

---

[16]Harry Ammon, *James Monroe: The Quest for National Identity* (New York, 1971), p. 455.

immediately upon the introduction of Tallmadge's proposal.[17] The second remarkable circumstance concerning the Upper South legislators was their almost perfect unity. With no opportunity to organize a coordinated response to an unanticipated threat, these men nonetheless presented the kind of unified front that would have been difficult to achieve on most issues even with hard-driving party whips, smoke-filled caucuses, cajolery, bribery, and threats. This is testimony at once to the deep importance of the issue to the Southern legislators and to the striking homogeneity of outlook of the men Southern voters chose to represent them in the nation's Capitol.

A similar scene played out in the Senate when the Tallmadge amendment came before that body. When one Massachusetts Federalist saw the "terror" in the faces of his slaveholding colleagues at the prospect of restriction, he "awoke as from a trance" from the dream of an antislavery South.[18] Before the end of the congressional session, all of the seats in the Capitol were filled with spectators, including many blacks, who understood that the history that was taking place had an immediate relevance to the future of their people.

It took a while for Americans outside Washington, however, to understand the implications of the storm over Missouri. Carolinians, whose interests were less directly affected than those of their Virginian compatriots, paid little attention for several months.[19] Yet even the most eagle-eyed scouts for threats to slavery, such as Virginia's Old Republican stalwart Spencer Roane, initially overlooked the significance of the Tallmadge amendment, viewing it as less dangerous than John Marshall's sweeping endorsement of a broad construction of the Constitution in *McCulloch v. Maryland*.[20] Gradually, however, Roane and like-minded Southerners recognized that the Missouri controversy and the *McCulloch* decision, each threatening to slaveholders' interests singly, constituted a far greater threat when considered in tandem.

Between February and December 1819, while Congress was out of session, the movement to restrict the spread of slavery gained momentum throughout the North. The almost completely unified Northern front against the expansion of slavery is truly stunning, especially when contrasted with

---

[17]*Annals,* 15th Cong., 2d sess., pp. 1166, 1177; *New-York Daily Advertiser,* Feb. 26, 1819.

[18]Samuel Eliot Morison, *The Life and Letters of Harrison Gray Otis, Federalist, 1765–1848,* 2 vols. (Boston, 1913), 2:226.

[19]Michael P. Johnson, "Reading between the Lines of the Missouri Debates in Charleston, South Carolina," paper delivered at the U.S. Capitol Historical Society symposium "Debates over Sectionalism," Washington, D.C., Apr. 16, 2004.

[20]Ammon, *James Monroe,* pp. 449–50.

the widespread demonstrations against abolitionists a mere decade later. Most communities of any size convened large public meetings—some of the largest held since the Revolution—and nearly every Northern legislature voted to instruct its representatives to vote against admission of new slave states. "Upon this topic there is but one opinion in Pennsylvania," asserted that state's legislature. Indeed, the chair of the anti-Missouri public meeting in Lancaster was the future president and future archetypal "doughface"— the term coined by John Randolph for a "Northern man with Southern principles"—James Buchanan.[21]

This was a momentous development, particularly for Pennsylvania. Although founded by Quakers and the first state to pass a gradual emancipation law, the Keystone State had generally sided with the South in controversies regarding slavery. "Up to this hour, she has been the faithful and steady and almost unpaid ally of the slave States," noted New York's Rufus King, the leader of the restriction movement in the Senate.[22] Now Pennsylvanians took leading roles in the restriction movement in both houses of Congress: in particular, the genteel Federalist representative from Philadelphia, John Sergeant, and the Quaker former War Hawk, Jonathan Roberts, in the Senate.[23] Because party discipline in Pennsylvania had collapsed, it now became clear that without that restraint, the expansion of slavery had no natural supporters in the state.

In the meantime, there was no such mobilization in the South. Many factors made the generation of mass public opinion difficult in that region: the lack of urban centers, paucity of newspapers (and low level of literacy), and the very real possibility, as discussed above, that nonslaveholding whites would not share the same level of concern as large slaveholders about the proposed restriction. Many small farmers in the Upper South may simply have felt that they did not have a dog in this fight. Despite all the Southern advantages on the federal level, then—of the bonus of three-fifths slave representation in House, equal representation in the Senate, and control of the White House—slaveholders faced a serious shortfall in domestic public opinion.

---

[21]*Annals*, 16th Cong., 1st sess., p. 72; *Poulson's Daily Advertiser* (Philadelphia), Nov. 29, 1819.

[22]Charles R. King, ed., *Life and Correspondence of Rufus King*, 6 vols. (New York, 1894–1900), 6:278.

[23]Roberts and Sergeant had collaborated in the previous Congress in submitting petitions against the slave trade from their Pennsylvania constituents. See *Annals*, 14th Cong., 2d sess., p. 96; *House Journal*, 15th Cong., 2d sess., Jan. 15, 1819, p. 154.

Another major problem for the slaveholding South was that it did not control the Supreme Court. Under Chief Justice John Marshall (a Virginian, but an American first), the high court continued to be as strong a nationalizing force as it had been during the Federalist period. The Court's decision in *McCulloch v. Maryland*, which cleared the way for a broadened interpretation of the Constitution on matters of federal action, was handed down within three weeks of the introduction of Tallmadge's amendment and struck fear into the hearts of slaveholding strict constructionists.

An additional problem for the South was that it did not really control the White House, either. James Monroe is usually viewed by historians as a rigid strict constructionist and in his early years, at least, as Thomas Jefferson's enforcer. In fact, by the time he acceded to the presidency, he was an ardent, if discreet, nationalist and an untroubled activist. (It is perhaps an axiom that those who do not hold power are the most concerned with the abuse of it.) Out of the public eye, he took executive decisions with as little hesitation as Andrew Jackson. During his visit to the Brainerd Cherokee School in Tennessee, for example, Monroe, impressed with its spirit but not with its facilities, ordered solid wood-frame houses to be constructed for the students out of federal funds.[24] Privately, Monroe had no qualms about other forms of federal power, such as internal improvements. After vetoing the Cumberland Road bill (appending to the veto message a ten-thousand-word essay on the importance of national roads and canals), Monroe sought a private ruling from the Supreme Court on the constitutionality of federally funded internal improvements. Justice William Johnson, a South Carolinian and Jefferson appointee who had evolved into a deep-seated nationalist himself, relayed to the president the information that the court believed unanimously that *McCulloch* meant that Congress indeed had the power to build roads and canals as well as to take other action to carry out the mandates of the Constitution. Thereafter, Monroe never vetoed another bill for internal improvements, and his successor in the White House, John Quincy Adams, evidently considered the constitutionality of the question permanently settled.

Both the patronage and the precedent offered by internal improvements constituted real potential threats to slavery. As the hypersensitive Southern

---

[24]Daniel Preston, ed., *The Papers of James Monroe*, 2 vols. to date (Westport, Conn., 2003–), 1:662–63.

leader Nathaniel Macon argued, "If Congress can build roads and canals, it may with more propriety emancipate every slave in this Union." John Randolph of Roanoke said virtually the same thing on the floor of the House.[25] Many other Southern leaders were more discreet but no less disturbed.

This was not an idle or laughable threat, as historians have believed. In the midst of the Missouri debates, the House of Representatives received a resolution to explore a proposal for the abolition of slavery that would likely have constituted the largest public undertaking in American history. On February 5, 1820, as the crisis over Missouri approached a climax, Henry Meigs, a representative from New York City, introduced the following resolution:

> Whereas slavery in the United States is an evil of great and increasing magnitude; one which merits the greatest efforts of this nation to remedy: Therefore,
>
> *Resolved,* That a committee be appointed to inquire into the expediency of devoting the public lands as a fund for the purpose of—
>
> 1st. Employing a naval force competent to the annihilation of the slave trade.
>
> 2dly. The emancipation of the slaves in the United States; and
>
> 3dly. Colonizing them in such way as shall be conducive to their comfort and happiness in Africa, their mother country.[26]

It is worth pausing to examine how sweeping and comprehensive Meigs's proposal was. First, it addressed the basic problem in any scheme of African resettlement: the ongoing slave trade, which threatened any potential colonist with reenslavement. This proposal would put an end to the slave trade itself with American force: expanding the sixty or so vessels in the service of the U.S. Navy into the kind of vast armada necessary to interdict the potent commerce. Such a force had ramifications far beyond the slave trade itself; it would give the United States a maritime strength at least equal to that of Great Britain and make it capable of imposing its military will virtually anywhere in the world.

Step two of Meigs's plan, the emancipation of the nation's slaves, would have constituted one of the largest philanthropic acts of history, as well as one of the costliest. More than a dozen years before the unprecedented British

---

[25]Noble E. Cunningham, Jr., "Nathaniel Macon and the Southern Protest against National Consolidation," *North Carolina Historical Review* 32 (1955):379–80; *Annals*, 18th Cong., 1st sess., p. 138.

[26]*Annals*, 16th Cong., 1st sess., pp. 1113–14.

emancipation of eight hundred thousand slaves at a cost of £20 million (about US$90.5 million), Meigs envisioned the compensated emancipation of nearly twice that number of American slaves. On top of this stupendous outlay, however, in step three, Meigs proposed the transportation and resettlement of the freed people in Africa—a monumental undertaking, a massive Middle Passage in reverse, made feasible only by the stupendous flotilla of naval ships constructed to put down the slave trade in step one. All of this Faustian-scale social engineering was to be financed by the sale of the public lands.

How seriously should we take this proposal? Clearly, it dwarfs any federal undertaking ever contemplated at the time; even the Louisiana Purchase cost only $15 million. Indeed, just step two alone, the emancipation of the nation's 1.5 million slaves, at the conservative rate of $400 per slave, would cost $600 million—almost three *trillion* dollars at the 2005 rate, making it by far the most costly federal expenditure ever. Meigs proposed this gargantuan outlay at a time when budget cutting—"retrenchment"—was one of the watchwords of politics; only four years earlier, nearly the entire House of Representatives had been summarily fired by their constituents for voting themselves a relatively modest increase in their compensation. Neither the Congress nor the electorate was friendly to major federal spending.

At first glance, then, this proposal seems not to merit serious consideration. Meigs's proposal was immediately tabled, and although he tried to introduce it again a few days later, the Southern representatives would have none of it.

Several circumstances make it difficult for us to reject Meigs's proposal outright, however. For one thing, it comes with the imprimatur of the most eminent surviving Founding Father. Eight months earlier, in June of 1819, almost exactly four months after Tallmadge introduced his Missouri amendment, former president James Madison responded to Pennsylvania antislavery author Robert J. Evans with a sweeping proposal for slave emancipation and removal almost identical to Meigs's. "The object to be obtained, as an object of humanity, appeals alike to all," Madison effused; "as a National object, it claims the interposition of the nation. It is the nation which is to reap the benefit. The nation therefore ought to bear the burden." Madison estimated the cost of this project at $600 million but observed serenely that "the amount of the expence is not a paramount consideration." This is because it was "the peculiar fortune, or, rather a providential blessing of the

U.S. to possess a resource commensurate to this great object" without recourse to taxation or bonding: the public lands. Responsibly managed, they were worth three times this stupendous amount.

Madison urged Evans's discretion and requested that he not be "publickly referred to" when citing the proposal.[27] This was a pro forma appeal, however, since Madison well knew that much of the value of the plan derived from his authority; what Madison did expect was that Evans would not use his name in print, and he did not. It is likely that Meigs knew of Madison's plan, whether from Evans or from Madison himself.

It is also likely that Monroe knew of Meigs's resolution ahead of time. Monroe had close ties to the Meigs family. Henry's father, Josiah, was commissioner of the U.S. Land Office, whose job was to supervise and report on the progress of the surveys of the public lands. He had also been surveyor general and was a former president of the University of Georgia. No one knew more about the nature and value of the millions of acres in the national patrimony.

Monroe's postmaster general, Return J. Meigs II, was Henry's cousin and Josiah's brother; he was also the son of the Cherokee agent who had hosted Monroe at the tribal school in Tennessee. During his tenure as postmaster, Meigs presided over a spectacular expansion of the postal system, adding in six years more than eighteen hundred new post offices to the twenty-six hundred or so that had been created over the previous fifteen and nearly doubling the mileage of designated post roads. This stupendous enterprise vastly increased the value of the public domain, and the anticipated expansion of roads and canals after *McCulloch* would increase it even more. This precious natural resource would soon be even more valuable, making possible public projects on a scale never envisioned in history.

Do we know that Monroe intended to use the power of the federal government to emancipate and transport American slaves to Africa? No. Given the man's political caution and prudence, it is hard to envision him taking such a radical step. Yet, in the aftermath of the Missouri debates, Monroe told the visiting British reformer Fanny Wright that within a few years "not a slave would be found within the limits of the United States." Likely following the opinion of Monroe, Wright cited the Meigs resolution as

---

[27]Gaillard Hunt, ed., *The Writings of James Madison*, 9 vols. (New York, 1900–1910), 8:439–47.

evidence that the project of colonization was "neither visionary nor impracticable."[28] It is also perhaps significant that the name chosen for the capital of the new colony of Liberia was Monrovia—not simply a tribute to the patronage of the president but also the name of his birthplace and his family's ancestral seat.[29]

What we can say with certainty is that opponents of emancipation had reason to fear the power of the federal government to intervene in slavery, since associates of the administration were sending clear signals that it wanted to do so. Whether Meigs's proposal was intended as a trial balloon to gauge Southern sentiment, a threat to slaveholding lawmakers to accept a compromise or face dire consequences, a personal expression of frustration with the unproductive stalemate of the Missouri deliberations, or the initial gambit of a genuine plan with the backing of the executive, it is likely to have sent a profound shock through conservative Southern circles.

Cumulatively, the Missouri struggle set the tone for Southern participation in national affairs. Obstruction became standard operating procedure for Southern congressmen on major legislative initiatives of importance to their Northern brethren. The attempt to exclude Maine from statehood during the Missouri crisis proved to be the model for this new approach; thereafter, a comprehensive national bankruptcy law, internal improvement projects, protection of manufactures, and even the federal auctions system were held hostage to Southern objectives. In some cases, the price of Southern cooperation with these projects of deep concern to Northerners was their silence or acquiescence on questions of slavery; in other cases, compromise was simply not forthcoming.

The problem of apathetic public opinion in the South was of a different nature, but in the aftermath of the Missouri controversy, it too proved to have a solution. While the broader citizenry of the slave states may have cared little about the rights of planter aristocrats to sell their slaves west, all Southern whites were concerned about the danger of slave revolt. After a relatively passive response to the early phase of the conflict, South Carolina authorities became convinced that "the Missouri question" had vented "opinions and doctrines which tend[ed] not only to diminish" the value of

---

[28]Frances Wright Darusmont, *Views of Society and Manners in America* (New York, 1821), pp. 50–51, 385.

[29]On Monroe's ancestral seat of Monrovia, see Ammon, *James Monroe*, pp. 1–2, 576.

slave property but also to threaten whites' safety. The legislature passed laws outlawing emancipation, barring free blacks from the state, and increasing the penalties for importing incendiary publications. This last was an essentially futile provision at the time, since the reporting of congressional debates —given in full on the front page of the state's major papers—reprinted all of the recorded debates over the Missouri question, including the text of speeches by New York's Sen. Rufus King that contained the most "radical declaration of slavery's illegality" made publicly by any "statesman or political leader in the world" to that date.[30]

A year after the resolution of the Missouri conflict, two Charleston slaves approached authorities with a report of a planned insurrection against the city. As the investigation into the plot unfolded, authorities revealed that a free black carpenter, Denmark Vesey, had been inspired to launch his assault on Charleston by reading Rufus King's speeches.

It is unclear whether Vesey's revolt was a genuine plot, a figment of slaveholders' fevered imaginations, or a pretext manufactured by city leaders to tighten controls over blacks and unify white opinion through terror against mounting local and national antislavery sentiment. In any case, it had the effect (like more recent terrorist incidents) of strengthening the hand of the ruling establishment by providing new tools of repression and much stronger sanctions—social as well as legal—against internal dissent. Certainly, the tie to King provided a welcome opportunity to charge a vocal Northern opponent with inciting a race war. "It is a well ascertained fact, which the late trials have developed," a South Carolina editor asserted, "that the currency given to the sentiments of those who, during the agitation of the Missouri Question, labored together in the humane vocation of rendering the slave discontented with his situation; has assisted to produce the late diabolical plot against our lives."[31] The chill caused by the accusation muffled Northern antislavery voices for a decade.

Some South Carolina defenders of slavery sought to accomplish much more than simply silencing the institution's most vocal critics. The Missouri controversy and related events, such as the rise of the American Colonization Society and Henry Meigs's proposal to emancipate and resettle the

---

[30]Davis, *Challenging the Boundaries of Slavery*, p. 42.

[31]Newspaper clipping enclosed in letter to Rufus King from Charleston, South Carolina, along with drawing of gallows, from which dangles the name "R. King," received Aug. 14, 1822, collection of the New-York Historical Society, New York, N.Y.

nation's slaves, convinced some South Carolinians that the state's continued existence within the Union—or, at least, within a Union that had power over the states—represented an intolerable threat to slavery or, in other words, to life as they knew it. From as early as 1822, these men worked to provoke confrontations with the federal government over slavery, designed to undermine South Carolina's citizens' confidence in the federal state, and to neutralize, as much as possible, the government's power to restrict slavery or the power of slaveholders.

In December 1822, at the instigation of antinationalist planters, the South Carolina legislature passed the Negro Seamen's Act, a law designed to restrict contact between local slaves and free black seamen in order to prevent "the moral contagion of their pernicious principles and opinions."[32] The law called for the jailing of any black sailors on ships in South Carolina harbors while in port and required the ships' captains to pay the jailers' expenses—the seamen to be sold into slavery to cover these costs if payment were not forthcoming. It is hard to view the law as seriously intended to accomplish its avowed object, since the mariners would be incarcerated among the most rebellious and recalcitrant slaves—the very ones most likely to foment revolt and to be susceptible to the free black seamen's "pernicious principles." Whatever its stated aim, the act had a more strategic purpose as well, as the well-planned response to its court challenge demonstrated.

The Negro Seamen's Act constituted a direct and, I believe, a deliberate challenge to federal authority and to international and interstate commerce. Indeed, it would be hard to design a law with greater constitutional and diplomatic ramifications. By imprisoning citizens of other states, the South Carolina authorities would be violating the privileges and immunities clause of the Constitution—the same provision that had embroiled Congress in a second year of controversy over the admission of Missouri. If the seamen were citizens of Great Britain, their detention would represent a violation of maritime law and the recently adopted Commercial Convention with Great Britain, which guaranteed free access of British and American seamen to the ports of the other nation. In either case, the act could be regarded as an infringement of the Constitution's commerce clause.

---

[32]Thomas Cooper and David J. McCord, eds., *The Statutes at Large of South Carolina*, 10 vols. (Columbia, 1838–41), 7:461–62; Alan F. January, "The South Carolina Association: An Agency for Race Control in Antebellum Charleston," *South Carolina Historical Magazine* 78 (1977):195.

The evidence suggests that these conflicts with federal authority were no accident. Almost immediately after the act's passage, the authorities began seizing and jailing free persons of color on vessels in Charleston harbor. Blacks made up perhaps 20 percent of the Atlantic maritime fleet and often more on a given vessel; some ships were left at anchor virtually crewless. British and American ship captains protested against the act to Supreme Court Justice William Johnson, sitting as judge of the Charleston Circuit Court. Johnson, the maverick South Carolinian who had defended the constitutionality of internal improvements to President Monroe, urged the state courts to overturn the hastily drafted act and defuse the mounting national and international confrontation. Not surprisingly, however, the South Carolina courts affirmed the law's constitutionality, and Congress, for its part, took no action on the complaints of American shipmasters.

The international conflicts over the Negro Seamen's Act were not as easy to ignore. British ships, sailing out of West Indian as well as English ports, frequently had black crew members. In February 1823, after Charleston authorities imprisoned four black British subjects from a Bahamian ship, the British government protested to Secretary of State John Quincy Adams. Adams handled the affair discreetly, bringing the problem to the attention of two levelheaded South Carolina congressmen, relaying the British concerns, and evidently suggesting that the offending statute might remain on the books but not be enforced—a common phenomenon in the regulation of slavery. Evidently Adams's suggestion bore fruit, since within a few weeks black seamen were again commonplace on the streets of Charleston.

What happened next was both peculiar and momentous. A new organization of private citizens, calling itself the South Carolina Association and including among its roster of officers many of the most distinguished names in the low country, announced its formation. The association avowed its purpose as "to aid the execution of the laws founded upon the *local and peculiar policy of South Carolina*, by giving to the Civil Magistrate, through its agents . . . information of their infringement" and described itself as "perhaps the most important association that ever has been, or ever can be formed, in the Southern States."[33] This unofficial group proceeded to press the state government to enforce the Negro Seamen's Act, with full understanding of its

[33]January, "South Carolina Association," pp. 192–93. The South's restrictive laws concerning blacks were apparently rarely enforced to the letter, and such enforcement, when it occurred, often took place in the context of competing political factions within the white elite.

implications for South Carolina's relations with the federal government and in international law. It deliberately sought to place the state on a collision course with both.

The principal goal of the South Carolina Association does not seem to have been to break up the Union. Indeed, its rather cosmopolitan leadership included Revolutionary War veterans, transplants from the North, and graduates of Yale and Harvard. Several of them would have no patience with the coercive tactics of the nullifiers a decade later. Rather, the association sought to accomplish two related ends, both of which had momentous effects on American politics and society long after the Civil War.

The association's first objective was to render the federal government impotent to threaten slavery, by demonstrating the government's incapacity and unwillingness to uphold basic constitutional principles that conflicted with the security of the institution. Their second goal was to neutralize the threat to slavery posed by free blacks—who had the greatest opportunity to foment rebellion, as the Vesey conspiracy demonstrated, and who, by their very existence, embodied an alternative to enslavement. By passing and enforcing a patently unconstitutional law that gutted the rights of free blacks, South Carolina Association leaders sought to accomplish both ends simultaneously.

We can now see that South Carolinian proslavery strategists set about building an additional line of defense on the anomalous constitutional position of free blacks created—or revealed—by the second Missouri Compromise, which had ambiguously held that Missouri's ban on blacks entering the state should not be interpreted as a violation of the U.S. Constitution.[34] The Negro Seamen's Act and its successors in South Carolina and other states of the Deep South represented a bold first move. Shortly thereafter, Thomas Cooper, the president of South Carolina College and a close associate of the leaders of the South Carolina Association, published a scholarly and seemingly dispassionate essay in the Charleston *Courier* under the title "Coloured Marriages," which asserted that "people of colour are, in every part of the United States, considered, not merely by the populace, but by the law, as a permanently degraded people; not participating as by right of

---

[34]The question of black citizenship remained a fundamental source of sectional discord. In 1844, the Commonwealth of Massachusetts dispatched a special envoy, Samuel Hoar, to Charleston to protest the unjust treatment of black citizens of the Bay State in South Carolina. When his mission was reported to the South Carolina legislature, Hoar barely escaped the state with his life.

the civil privileges belonging to every white man, but enjoying what civil privileges they possess, as a right and grant, as a matter of favour conceded by the law, and revocable by the law."[35] A protégé of Thomas Jefferson, Cooper drew upon colonial and state law, the Missouri debates, and South Carolina's Negro Seamen's Act itself to lay down a paper trail designed to provide legal precedent for regarding free blacks as indistinguishable from slaves in terms of civil rights. Cooper's essay, reprinted in the first volume of the *Carolina Law Journal* in 1830 at the outset of the nullification crisis, formed an important link in the chain of formal racism that connects Thomas Jefferson's *Notes on the State of Virginia* with Chief Justice Roger Taney's decision in *Dred Scott v. Sandford*, holding that the African "had no rights which the white man was bound to respect; and . . . might justly and lawfully be reduced to slavery for his benefit." The same decision, of course, found Congress's imposition of a barrier to slavery expansion at 36° 30' to be unconstitutional, and struck it down.[36]

In institutional terms, then, slavery's defenders won the sectional conflict set in motion by the Missouri debates; the second compromise's invalidation of black citizenship, one might say, trumped the first compromise's limit on the spread of slavery. The Monrovian attempt to contain the political influence of slavery failed; and the Jacksonian coalition of "Southern planters and plain Republicans of the North" rolled back the fragile gains of nationalism. Over the course of the 1840s, the Monrovian effort to contain slavery geographically also appeared to falter after the annexation of Texas and the huge territorial gains of the Mexican War. By that time, however, the principle of the Missouri Compromise, initially interpreted as a victory for slaveholders, had become sacrosanct to the North. In the long run, then, the Monroe administration's policy of containment provided the crucial underpinning of Northerners' determination to hold the line on slavery and to ensure that the Monrovian goal of eventual free state control of Congress would not be overthrown. The solid Northern coalition that had mobilized against the spread of slavery in 1820 was reborn in the presidential campaign of 1860, and the war that compromise averted then was finally fought in bloody earnest. The Thirteenth Amendment to the Constitution brought the curtain down on slavery, while the Fourteenth formally erased any ambiguities about the national citizenship of blacks.

---

[35] *Charleston Courier*, Oct. 29, 1823.
[36] *Scott v. Sandford*, 60 U.S. (19 How.) 393 (1857).

And yet, the sectional conflict bequeathed by the Missouri conflict was not so easily or completely overcome. The automatic presumption of most Americans not directly involved in the institution—and many who were—that slavery was wrong, gave way to a sense that its presence or absence could best be understood as a reflection of sectional political power. The powerful nationalizing impulse of the administrations of Monroe and Adams, their determination to harness the country's wealth to the goals of national integration and growth, was plowed under by Southern politicians who rightly viewed the exercise of federal power—and the accumulation of federal revenues—as subversive to their unchecked dominion over their homes and state houses, an outlook that persists in some quarters to the present day. The question of race as a condition of citizenship, which a nearly united North had rejected in the face of overwhelming pressure in 1820–21, was written into the fabric of the Constitution, bestowing a new level of formal reality upon the offensive concept even while ostensibly undoing its effects, thus seeming to substantiate the poignant query of the folk singer Ferron: "Do we have to live inside its walls to identify the cage?"[37]

The sectional legacies of the Missouri contest, it can be said, live on. By understanding their origins in conflicts that have for the most part been resolved or abandoned, we may perhaps be permitted to hope that the habits of sectionalism that emerged from that struggle of almost two centuries ago can finally be laid to rest.

---

[37]Ferron, "It Won't Take Long," *Shadows on a Dime*, Lucy Records, 1984.

Tim Alan Garrison

United States Indian Policy
in Sectional Crisis

Georgia's Exploitation of the Compact of 1802

O N MAY 17, 1830, Wilson Lumpkin, a congressman from Georgia, rose
to speak in support of a bill in the House of Representatives that
would endow President Andrew Jackson with the authority to relocate the
Indian tribes residing in the organized United States to a territory beyond
the Mississippi River. In his lengthy defense of what would come to be
known as the Indian Removal Act of 1830, Lumpkin issued blistering attacks against opponents of the resettlement plan. He condemned Jackson's
political antagonists and the Cherokee Nation, which doggedly refused to
surrender the territory it possessed within the borders of the congressman's
state. Lumpkin reserved his greatest anger, however, for the philanthropists
and "leading religionists" from the Northeast who were providing material
and political support to the Cherokee resistance and "going up and down in
the land" spreading opposition to removal. Lumpkin complained that "intermeddlers and disturbers of the peace and harmony of society" publicized
the Cherokees as "the most prosperous, enlightened, and religious nation
on earth—except, indeed, the nation of New England," while they depicted
his constituents, the people of Georgia, as "Atheists, Deists, Infidels, and
Sabbath-breakers, laboring under the curse of slavery." He stated that he
did not blame the Indians for their reluctance to relocate; rather, it was "the
wicked influence of designing men, veiled in the garb of philanthropy and
Christian benevolence" who had induced the Cherokees to oppose removal.

Georgia, Lumpkin added, could not accept responsibility for the sectional antagonisms that had gripped the nation during the removal crisis. "Let it be remembered," he declared, that it was "the fruit of *cant and fanaticism*, emanating from the land of steady habits; from the boasted progeny of the Pilgrims and Puritans."[1]

Lumpkin's address reminds us that if the United States became "a house divided," as Abraham Lincoln described it in 1858, then it was a structure fractured by an accumulation of disparate fissures. Of course, the issue that almost brought the nation crumbling down upon itself was slavery; and regardless of how many other forces existed or developed to divide the Northern and Southern states, it was the South's acceptance of slavery, its perceived economic need to perpetuate it, and the desire of some to extend bonded labor to the territories that ultimately provoked the catastrophe of the Civil War. That being said, other issues and disagreements, some only vaguely proximate to slavery, helped undermine national unity and corroded feelings between Northerners and Southerners in the antebellum era. In the 1820s, the question of how the United States would treat its indigenous population produced another sectional crack in the Union's foundation. The debate over the future of Native Americans—that is, whether the United States would allow the eastern tribes to remain in their homelands or force them to relocate west of the Mississippi River, as many white Southerners wished—became so divisive that by the late 1820s, several politicians in the South raised the specters of secession and civil war.[2]

The awful consequences of the sectionalization of federal Indian policy —the removal of the American Indian nations from the East and the acceleration of discord between North and South—might not have occurred but for the Compact of 1802, in which Georgia ceded its claim to lands between the Chattahoochee and Mississippi rivers to the United States in exchange for a promise from the federal government that it would extinguish the Indian title in the remainder of the state as soon as it could acquire the right "peaceably" and "on reasonable terms." The evidence for this argument is found in the public rhetoric of political leaders from Georgia. For

---

[1]Wilson Lumpkin, *The Removal of the Cherokee Indians from Georgia, 1827–1841* (1907; reprint ed., New York, 1971), pp. 57–88.

[2]Michael P. Johnson, *Abraham Lincoln, Slavery, and the Civil War: Selected Writings and Speeches* (Boston, 2001), p. 63.

instance, in his speech and in his autobiography, Lumpkin attributed his animosity against the "Northern fanatics" to their part in obstructing the federal government's completion of the compact; and throughout the 1820s, as we will see, removal proponents from Georgia—in Congress and in the state general assembly and governor's office in Milledgeville—called on the federal government over and over again to fulfill the pledge it had made in the compact.[3]

The Compact of 1802 has never received the attention it deserves for the role it played in moving the United States from a policy objective of accelerated assimilation in the East to one of removal and racial separation. Granted, the causes for the resettlement of the eastern tribes are many and complex, and the state possessed and applied other arguments in support of its removal demands. Andrew Jackson's election in 1828, moreover, was a pivotal point in the national government's transition to removal as official policy. However, by that point Georgia had already bullied Congress and Jackson's predecessors in office into accepting removal in theory and into a very real quandary over how to satisfy the compact's promise. This chapter, therefore, will hew solely and strictly to Georgia's determined, if not pathological, efforts to bring the compact's conditions to the attention of the president and the Congress and, to a lesser extent, the impact of the state's campaign on sectional relations between North and South.

Before approximately 1817 (the date Andrew Jackson began calling on President James Monroe to remove the eastern tribes), the Indian policy of the United States was, if not a subject of national consensus, at least an area relatively untainted by sectional anxiety. Although some politicians and many of their constituents on the nation's western frontier often challenged specific principles and programs devised during George Washington's administration, most prominent figures in the national government generally agreed on objectives, strategies, and application of resources. In the late 1780s, Henry Knox, Washington's secretary of war, persuaded the president that the United States should consider the Indian tribes as sovereign nations, recognize that they possessed title to their territories, and pay for, rather than simply seize, their lands. He convinced the president to follow the British

---

[3]Thomas Jefferson to Congress, Apr. 26, 1802, in *American State Papers: Public Lands*, ed. Walter Lowrie and Walter S. Franklin, 8 vols. (Washington, D.C., 1832–61), 1:114 (hereafter *ASPPL*); Lumpkin, *Removal of the Cherokee Indians*, pp. 43, 63.

colonial practice of managing Indian relations through treaties, and Washington established the precedent of sending treaties with the Indian nations to the Senate for approval and ratification.[4]

Washington and Knox also persuaded Congress to implement a "civilization program" to prepare American Indians for social and political assimilation. The national legislature appropriated funds for agencies and model farms to teach Indians to live like Anglo-American yeoman families. Knox argued that the acculturation of Native Americans would facilitate his ambitious plan to transfer Indian land into the hands of white Americans. In theory, as Indians adopted the Anglo-American way of life, they would no longer need their vast hunting grounds. The United States would acquire these unneeded lands by treaty and parcel them out to American citizens as the nation expanded westward. Once Native Americans abandoned their customary way of life, Knox theorized, their tribal ties would fray and they would integrate, socially and politically, with the Americans that moved among them. Knox predicted that within fifty years all Indians east of the Mississippi would be assimilated by the American republic. Many Indians embraced the civilization program with gusto, and acculturated minorities among the Choctaws, Chickasaws, Creeks, and Cherokees quickly proved the feasibility of the federal plan.[5]

Two developments, one within the southeastern Indian community and the other within the American political class, began to threaten the future envisioned by the civilization theorists. First, many of the Native American disciples of civilization accepted the idea of social acculturation but rejected the proposed path toward political assimilation. For instance, although its leadership and population divided bitterly over the question of removal at signal points between 1808 and 1835, the Cherokee Nation, as a political entity, attempted to preserve its sovereignty and land base during that period. By the 1820s, the Cherokee government was consistently refusing to surrender national territory. Second, the United States began to divide between those in the Northeast and New England who wanted to continue with the goal of accelerated assimilation and those in the South who wanted to move

---

[4]Henry Knox to George Washington, June 15, 1789, July 7, 1789, and Jan. 4, 1790, in *American State Papers: Indian Affairs,* ed. Walter Lowrie and Walter S. Franklin, 2 vols. (Washington, D.C., 1832–61), 1:13, 52–54, 61 (hereafter *ASPIA*); Francis Paul Prucha, *The Great Father: The United States Government and the American Indian* (Lincoln, Neb., 1984), pp. 49–55.

[5]*ASPIA,* 1:13–14, 53–54.

the United States toward a new policy that came to be commonly identified as removal.[6]

If Henry Knox was the primary architect behind the assimilation plan, then Thomas Jefferson was the father of removal. In 1776, Jefferson wrote a letter to Edmund Pendleton suggesting that the Cherokees, who had attacked settlers intruding into their territory, "be driven beyond the Mississippi." When he was elected president, Jefferson returned to the idea of relocating the eastern tribes beyond that great continental divide. Removal would not only eliminate hostilities between whites and Native Americans, he argued, but also protect the Indians from the trespasses of settlers and the deceitful manipulations and alcohol peddling of unscrupulous white traders. More important, it would open up all of the land between the Appalachians and the Mississippi to white settlement. In 1803, Jefferson completed the Louisiana Purchase, which offered, in his view, a perfect destination for the eastern tribes.[7]

What stood in the way of a general removal, however, was the United States' policy of recognizing the sovereign rights of the tribes, its determination to provide the Indian nations with the right to consent to or reject any cession or exchange proposal, and its tradition of reducing those precedents to writing in treaties with the tribes. However, just a few months before the Louisiana Purchase, Jefferson's administration signed the Compact of 1802, which eventually forced a national retreat from those commitments. The compact was part of Jefferson's effort to resolve the tangled land titles of the Mississippi Territory that Congress had established in 1798. Titles to the parcels in the region were not only clouded by those claiming rights as bona fide purchasers under the fraudulent Yazoo grants from Georgia, but they were also roiled by those holding titles tracing back to charters from the European imperial powers, those who had simply declared squatters' rights, and those Native American peoples who pointed out that their ancestors

---

[6]William G. McLoughlin, *Cherokee Renascence in the New Republic* (Princeton, N.J., 1986); Theda Perdue, "The Conflict Within: Cherokees and Removal," in *Cherokee Removal: Before and After,* ed. William L. Anderson (Athens, Ga., 1991), pp. 55–74; Tim Alan Garrison, *The Legal Ideology of Removal: The Southern Judiciary and the Sovereignty of Native American Nations* (Athens, Ga., 2002), pp. 51–57.

[7]Thomas Jefferson to Edmund Pendleton, Aug. 13, 1776, in *The Papers of Thomas Jefferson,* ed. Julian P. Boyd et al., 33 vols. to date (Princeton, N.J., 1950–), 1:494; Bernard W. Sheehan, *Seeds of Extinction: Jeffersonian Philanthropy and the American Indian* (Chapel Hill, N.C., 1973), pp. 244–45; Anthony F. C. Wallace, *Jefferson and the Indians: The Tragic Fate of the First Americans* (Cambridge, Mass., 1999), pp. 223–26.

had lived there for centuries. Jefferson, the faithful benefactor of the aspiring yeoman farmer, worked with Congress to clear the titles and open the region to settlement. The government established commissions to hear and rule on conflicting claims, set up a distribution mechanism for unclaimed sections, and worked methodically to acquire cessions from the Indian nations —the Choctaws, Chickasaws, Creeks, and Cherokees—that occupied large portions of the territory.[8]

Jefferson's agents—James Madison, the secretary of state; Albert Gallatin, the secretary of the treasury; and Levi Lincoln, the attorney general— persuaded Georgia to relinquish "all the right, title, and claim" over land south of Tennessee and west of specific points along the Chattahoochee River. (Georgia's royal charter purported to provide the state with title westward to the "South Sea.") In return, the United States government promised to pay the state $1,250,000 of the net proceeds from the sales of the ceded territory; the remainder of the proceeds obtained from the sale of the territory would be considered a common fund "for the use and benefit of the United States, Georgia included." The agreement set aside five million acres of the ceded region to satisfy any private claims that predated the agreement and provided that the territory would be admitted into the Union as a new state as soon as its population reached sixty thousand "free inhabitants," or earlier if Congress thought it expedient. The states of Mississippi and Alabama were subsequently carved out of the compact cession and entered the Union in 1817 and 1819, respectively. While the compact did not end the Yazoo controversy, which dragged on until Congress passed a final compensation act in 1814, it did finally terminate Georgia's claims to the territory.[9]

The fourth article of the Compact of 1802, however, sowed the seeds for another protracted and eventually tragic contestation. In that provision, the United States promised that it would, at its "own expense, extinguish, for the use of Georgia, as early as the same can be peaceably obtained, on reasonable terms, the Indian title." The agreement not only listed specific territories

---

[8]R. S. Cotterill, "The National Land System in the South, 1803–1812," *Mississippi Valley Historical Review* 16 (1930):495–506; Peter C. Magrath, *Yazoo: Law and Politics in the New Republic* (Providence, R.I., 1966), pp. 8–16.

[9]Thomas Jefferson to Congress, Apr. 26, 1802, *ASPPL,* 1:113–14; Magrath, *Yazoo,* pp. 35–36, 93–100. Georgia commissioned its own formidable negotiating team: Rep. John Milledge, Sen. Abraham Baldwin, and Sen. James Jackson, the man who dominated the state's politics during this era and the force behind the state's repeal of the Yazoo enabling act (Dumas Malone, *Jefferson and His Time* [Boston, Mass., 1970], vol. 4, *Jefferson the President, First Term, 1801–1805,* p. 246).

in the state subject to extinguishment but also added the general promise "that the United States shall, in the same manner, also extinguish the Indian title to all the other lands within the State of Georgia."[10]

Georgia did not pursue its claims under the compact for many years. For a considerable period, the state acknowledged that the promise to extinguish the Indian title was subject to the territorial rights of the Creeks and Cherokees, as guaranteed in treaties between the tribes and the United States. The state also accepted the federal government's exclusive authority to extinguish the Indians' title. For example, as late as 1819, the state legislature, in a memorial to President James Monroe, had declared that Georgia had the right to extend its jurisdiction to its territorial limits. It had admitted, however, that the right was "inchoate—remaining to be perfected by the United States." Georgia could not honestly deny, as it tried to do throughout the 1820s, that it had customarily recognized the legitimate treaty rights of the Indians and acknowledged federal jurisdiction over Indian affairs. The simple fact that the state had entered into the Compact of 1802 was compelling evidence that the state had, at the time of its conclusion, accepted the premise that the federal government's promise to extinguish was subject to the rights of the Indian nations.[11]

Georgia became more assertive in pursuing its claims under the compact after the War of 1812. There were several reasons for the state's renewed interest. First, the explosion of the Southern cotton economy increased the value of land in western Georgia. Second, the population of Georgia doubled between 1800 and 1820, and state leaders felt compelled to acquire room to expand. Third, Andrew Jackson's destruction of the Redstick Creek forces at Horseshoe Bend and his subsequent triumph in New Orleans greatly diminished respect for Indian military power in the Southeast. After the war, Jackson urged President James Monroe to end what he called the "absurdity" of treating the Indian tribes as sovereign nations. It was time, he said, to begin "legislating for, rather than treating with, the Indians." Jackson

---

[10]*ASPPL*, 1:114. The agreement stated that the United States would clear the Indian title to "the country of Talassee, to the lands left out by the line drawn with the Creeks, in the year one thousand seven hundred and ninety-eight, which had been previously granted by the State of Georgia, both which tracts had formally been yielded to the Indians; and to the lands within the forks of the Oconee and Ocmulgee rivers; for which several objects the President of the United States has directed that a treaty should be immediately held with the Creeks" (114).

[11]In *Worcester v. Georgia,* John McLean, associate justice of the United States Supreme Court, provided a long list of instances where Georgia had acknowledged Indian treaty rights, both before and after the compact (31 U.S. [6 Pet.] 515, 584–595 [1832]).

argued that the federal government's policy of recognizing the rights of the Indian tribes was obstructing the expansion of the country, preventing white Americans from exploiting valuable agricultural land, and endangering the security of the nation. He advised the president to remove the Indians beyond the Mississippi River or subject them to state jurisdiction. The general's public repudiation of Indian rights encouraged Georgia to abandon its submission to existing federal policies, and the state's officials quickly added their support to Jackson's recommendations.[12]

In 1817, John C. Calhoun, Monroe's secretary of war, directed Jackson and Joseph McMinn, the Tennessee governor, to begin removal negotiations with the Cherokees. When the Cherokee council refused to negotiate, Jackson obtained cessions in Tennessee and Georgia from a group of dissident towns. The Cherokees living on the ceded lands were told that they could either accept an allotment of 640 acres and fall under the jurisdiction of the state in which they resided or emigrate to the West. Several hundred families agreed to resettle in the Arkansas River valley. An optimistic Calhoun, apparently anticipating a wholesale relocation of the Cherokees, wrote that he hoped that the recent negotiations would also "lead ultimately to the removal of the Creeks, Chickasaws, and Choctaws," and he worked diligently to convince the rest of the Cherokees to remove to Arkansas in the winter of 1818–19. The Cherokees, however, grew more unified and determined in their opposition to future cessions. After McMinn asked Cherokee chief Path Killer to persuade the national council to surrender the rest of its territory and remove, he received a resolute rejection signed or marked by more than seventy chiefs and prominent men.[13]

The determined refusal of the Cherokees to abandon Georgia incited the state to escalate its campaign, and it was around this time that state officials began using the Compact of 1802 as public leverage to force the federal government to go back to the tribe repeatedly with removal proposals. On December 22, 1819, the Georgia legislature sent a memorial to Monroe. The legislators noted that Georgia had concluded the compact to settle

---

[12]McLoughlin, *Cherokee Renascence*, pp. 206–9; Garrison, *Legal Ideology of Removal*, pp. 21–22; Bureau of the Census, 1800 and 1820; Robert V. Remini, *Andrew Jackson and His Indian Wars* (New York, 2001), pp. 118–20.

[13]J. C. Calhoun to Gov. Joseph McMinn, Mar. 16, 1818; McMinn to Path Killer, Nov. 15, 1818; Path Killer to McMinn, Nov. 17, 1818; McMinn to the Cherokee chiefs, in council, Nov. 18, 1818; Cherokee chiefs to McMinn, Nov. 21, 1818; McMinn to Calhoun, Nov. 29, 1818; all in *ASPIA*, 2:478, 481–87. See also McLoughlin, *Cherokee Renascence*, pp. 221–38, and Duane Champagne, *Social Order and Political Change: Constitutional Governments among the Cherokee, the Choctaw, the Chickasaw, and the Creek* (Stanford, Calif., 1992), pp. 131–32.

boundary disputes and establish a more defensible border. They complained
that the state had waited seventeen years for the federal government to complete its end of the bargain. The legislators called on Monroe to fulfill the
agreement and declared that the promise to extinguish had "assumed the
more definite and substantial shape of positive right." The Georgia congressional delegation presented its own memorial declaring the federal government in breach of the compact. By failing to extinguish the title of the
Creeks and Cherokees in Georgia, they wrote, the United States had violated the state's territorial rights. With these memorials, the state transformed removal from an attractive panacea to its Indian dilemma into a
mechanism to shame the federal government into atoning for its purported
national slight.[14]

Monroe was not unmoved by Georgia's protests. On March 17, 1820,
he asked Congress to consider the feasibility of completing the Compact of
1802. In January 1822, a House of Representatives subcommittee chaired
by George Gilmer, a leading removal advocate from Georgia, called for
Congress to extinguish the titles of the Creeks and Cherokees. The committee agreed with Georgia that the federal government had possessed several opportunities to clear the Indians out of the state in recent treaties but
had instead chosen to accept lands outside the state's borders. This had the
effect of concentrating Creeks and Cherokees who had moved from ceded
lands into tribal territories in Georgia. Gilmer also criticized the federal
government's policy of guaranteeing Indian titles in previous cession treaties;
he pointed out that the guarantees and the Compact of 1802 created "very
opposite and conflicting obligations." Gilmer referred to the allotment plan in
the Cherokee Treaty of 1817 as a "direct violation of the rights" of Georgia.
Gilmer warned that if the federal government was going to comply with
the compact, it would have to abandon its goal of civilizing and assimilating the Creeks and Cherokees in the state. The compact did not simply call
for the extinguishment of the Indian title, Gilmer implied, it required the
eradication of every Indian community in the state.[15]

---

[14]Quoted in Edward J. Harden, *The Life of George M. Troup* (Savannah, Ga., 1859), p. 196;
House Journal, 16th Cong., 1st sess., Mar. 27, 1820, p. 338; Lumpkin, *Removal of the Cherokee Indians*, pp. 54, 86.

[15]*Senate Journal*, 16th Cong., 1st sess., Mar. 17, 1820, pp. 243–44; *House Journal*, 16th Cong.,
1st sess., Mar. 17, 1820, pp. 315; *House Journal*, 17th Cong., 1st sess., Dec. 15, 17, 1821, pp. 58–59,
63; "Extinguishment of the Indian Title to Land in Georgia," Jan. 7, 1822, *ASPIA*, 2:259–60.
The committee was composed of Gideon Barstow (Massachusetts), James Blair (South Carolina), Gilmer, James McSherry (Pennsylvania), John Jordan Morgan (New York), John Randolph (Virginia), and Samuel Swan (New Jersey).

On January 23, the full House responded to the committee's call and passed a resolution urging Monroe to extinguish the tribal claims of the Cherokees and Creeks as well as the titles of individual Indians in Georgia. On June 15, Calhoun, at Monroe's direction, appointed two congressmen from Georgia, Duncan G. Campbell and James Meriwether, as federal commissioners to acquire all remaining Indian territory in the state. In their negotiations at the Cherokee capital of New Echota, the federal commissioners reminded the Cherokees of the existence and specific terms of the Compact of 1802. The commissioners' mission was to see that "the rights of Georgia and the obligations of the United States" were fulfilled, they said. As required by the compact, the national government was making an offer to purchase the Cherokees' territory in a peaceable fashion and on reasonable terms; they offered a territory "embracing great variety of soil and climate" in the West and "such other advantages, as may be agreed upon." Campbell and Meriwether then explained Georgia's interests in relocating the Cherokees: "[The president's] white people are becoming so much crowded, that they are driven from friends and connexions to foreign lands. Others are confined to a scanty piece of soil, without timber for fencing or fuel." They noted that the population of the state had increased from 252,433 in 1810 to 344,773 in 1820, while only 12,000 Cherokees resided in the state. The commissioners asserted that "this difference is too great ever to have been intended by the Great Father of the Universe, who must have given the earth *equally* to be the inheritance of his white and red children."[16]

Path Killer, the principal chief; Major Ridge, speaker of the national council; and John Ross, president of the national committee, responded for the Cherokees and brusquely deflected the commissioners' arguments. The Cherokee Nation, they wrote, had agreed to "cession after cession" to "gratify the wishes of our neighboring brethren" until "our limits have become circumscribed." Therefore, the Cherokees declared, "It is the fixed and unalterable determination of this nation never again to cede *one foot* more of land." The Cherokees' position did not waver, despite several more days of pressure from the federal commissioners. Before they left New Echota,

---

[16]*House Journal*, 17th Cong., 1st sess., Jan. 23, 1822, p. 190; See also "Excerpt of a letter from the Secretary of War to the commissioners appointed to hold a treaty with the Cherokee Indians," June 15, 1822; "Copy of a correspondence between Commissioners on the part of the United States, and the Council of the Cherokee nation," Oct. 4, 1823; Duncan G. Campbell and James Meriwether to the Council of the Cherokee Nation, Oct. 16, 1823; all in *ASPIA*, 2:204–5, 465, 467–68.

Campbell and Meriwether warned the Cherokees about the dangers inherent in ignoring the obligations pending under the Compact of 1802: "The General Government is bound to Georgia, and we doubt not but that she will fulfill her engagements." The commissioners reported to Calhoun that the Cherokees had demonstrated a "determined resistance" to future cessions and recommended that the government refrain from further negotiations in the near future.[17]

The Cherokees and Georgia attempted to pull the president in their direction over the following winter. In December, George M. Troup, the governor of Georgia, suggested that the state legislature send another memorial to Monroe urging his administration to fulfill the compact. It was now time to complete the bargain, Troup declared: "The words, 'as soon as may be'" in the compact, "will no longer avail the United States anything; the operation of these has been long since estopped by time." Neither party, the governor added, ever contemplated at the time of the compact that "twenty years should elapse, and that Georgia should find herself in possession of only one half of her reserved territory." "Further procrastination," Troup said, "can subserve no useful purposes to the United States, or to the Indians themselves. . . . [S]oon, very soon, Georgia must have what is her own." Troup also sent a letter to the Georgia congressional delegation, urging them to put pressure on the president and the national legislature. Congressman John Forsyth, another vocal proponent of removal in Congress, visited the president for the express purpose of ensuring that he had received the state's memorial.[18]

In January 1823, a Cherokee delegation traveled to Washington to clarify their nation's position on land cessions and the Compact of 1802. On the nineteenth, the Cherokees informed President Monroe: "The Cherokee nation have now come to a decisive and unalterable conclusion not to cede away any more lands." They noted that their own population was increasing and that "it is an incumbent duty on the nation to preserve, unimpaired, the rights of posterity to the lands of their ancestors." They asked the president to find a way to persuade Congress to "authorize an adjustment between

---

[17]Path Killer, Major Ridge, and John Ross in answer for the Cherokee council, Oct. 20, 1823; Duncan G. Campbell and James Meriwether to the council, Oct. 25, 1823; Path Killer, Ridge, and Ross to the commissioners, Oct. 27, 1823; Campbell to J. C. Calhoun, Nov. 28, 1823; all in *ASPIA*, 2:464, 468–69.

[18]G. M. Troup to the legislature, Dec. 15, 1823, quoted in Harden, *Life of George M. Troup*, pp. 197–201; Alvin Laroy Duckett, *John Forsyth: Political Tactician* (Athens, Ga., 1962), p. 106.

the United States and the State of Georgia, so that the former may be released from the existing compact, so far as it respects the extinguishment of
the Cherokee title to lands within the chartered limits of Georgia."[19]

On January 30, Calhoun responded for Monroe. He reminded the Cherokee delegation of the terms of the compact and told them that "the Legislature and Executive of Georgia now press the fulfilment of that stipulation,
with the utmost possible earnestness." The president was anxious to fulfill
the compact, he said, if it could be done in a manner "satisfactory to the
Indians." Calhoun appealed to the "good sense and to the interest of the
nation" and asked the Cherokees to reconsider their refusal to cede their
lands and remove to the West. He warned: "You must either cease to be a
distinct community, and become, at no distant period, a part of the State
within whose limits you are, or remove beyond the limits of any State." The
Cherokees responded that they acknowledged the difficulties the Compact
of 1802 created for the federal government but reminded Calhoun that the
agreement was a "conditional one" that could not be accomplished "without the free and voluntary consent of the Cherokee nation." The United
States should find an alternative means to satisfy Georgia, the Cherokees
said. "The United States now possess an extensive territory in the Floridas,"
they suggested—"[W]hy not extend the limits of Georgia in that section of
country, if her present bounds be considered too small?"[20]

Calhoun had the unfortunate job of forwarding the record of these negotiations to Troup and the state's rabid-for-removal congressional delegation. Troup replied that he had expected the Cherokees to refuse the offer
of the federal commissioners. The word "no," Troup suggested, had been
"put into [the Cherokees' mind] by the white men," apparently referring to
the missionaries and philanthropists in New England who were beginning
to urge the Cherokees to resist the state's pressure. The right to refuse had,
however, "ceased to be available to the Indians" at the signing of the Compact of 1802. "No" was not an appropriate answer "to the people of Georgia,
who have endured so long and so patiently; who have parted with an empire for a song."[21]

---

[19]"Extract of a letter from the Cherokee Delegation to the President of the United States,"
Jan. 19, 1824, *ASPIA*, 2:473.

[20]J. C. Calhoun to John Ross, George Lowrey, Major Ridge, and Elijah Hicks, Jan. 30, 1824;
Ross, Lowrey, Ridge, and Hicks to Calhoun, Feb. 11, 1824; both in *ASPIA*, 2:473–74.

[21]J. C. Calhoun to George M. Troup, Feb. 17, 1824; Calhoun to John Elliott and John
Forsyth, and the Georgia delegation in Congress, Feb. 19, 1824; Troup to Calhoun, Feb. 28,
1824; all in *ASPIA*, 2:475–76.

Troup then tried to instruct Calhoun on how to deal with the Cherokees: their leaders had to understand that the United States would negotiate only with "councils strictly Indian in character and composition." This statement was a product of Troup's obsessive belief, spread by Georgia removal advocates over the subsequent years, that the real Cherokees wished to remove but were being intimidated and controlled by a nefarious, self-interested, half-breed leadership. Troup told Calhoun that he needed to inform the Cherokees that the Compact of 1802 was "a very different instrument from that which it has been represented to them." Tell them, he said, that "the word of the United States is passed, and that nothing can redeem it but the cession of all the lands within [Georgia's] limits." Postponing the completion of the compact, Troup added, would be a "breach of faith, of which the United States will never permit herself to be suspected." (Troup apparently did not believe that welching on agreements to an Indian nation diminished the national honor.) At the end of his instructions, he told Calhoun to tell the Cherokees that if they continued to refuse to relocate, they would face the inevitable consequences of the federal government assisting Georgia's people in the occupation of "the country which is their own, and which is unjustly withheld from them." If they continued to resist, the combined forces of the federal and state governments would "make war upon, and shed the blood of your brothers and friends."

The governor turned to the existing federal alternative for the allotment of Cherokee land and the proposed integration of the Cherokee people into the Georgia population. Troup declared that the people of Georgia would never assent to the solution: "If such a scheme were practicable at all, the utmost of rights and privileges which public opinion would concede to Indians, would fix them in a middle station, between the negro and the white man." If "they survived this degradation," he said, the Indians "would gradually sink to the condition of the former—a point of degeneracy below which they could not fall." Georgia's rejection of any allotment program signified that, for all practical purposes, the federal objective of in situ assimilation was a dead letter in the state.[22]

Ten days later, the Georgia congressional delegation offered its own bombastic response to Monroe. John Forsyth, writing for the group, condemned the federal policy of recognizing the tribes as sovereign nations. If the United

---

[22]The quotes in this paragraph and the preceding paragraph are from George M. Troup to John C. Calhoun, Feb. 28, 1824, *ASPIA*, 2:475–76.

States was going to treat the Cherokees as "an independent nation," he wrote, then jurisdiction over Indian affairs should be transferred to the state department, which could then consider who held the legitimate authority to speak for the tribe. Georgia's congressional delegation had embraced Troup's suspicions that tribal affairs were being controlled by acculturated men like John Ross. Forsyth then turned specifically to the compact and offered a new, sinister threat. The Cherokees were claiming lands that belonged to Georgia and "should be taught by the General Government that there is no alternative between their removal beyond the limits of the State of Georgia and their extinction." The United States "will deceive them grossly," he added, if the Cherokees were led to believe that they had the right to consent to the completion of the Compact of 1802.

Forsyth placed partial blame for the controversy on the federal government's civilization program: "What has created the strong desire of the Cherokee Indians to remain where they are? The policy of the General Government; the pretended guaranties of their possessions; the attempted changes in the nature of their titles to them; the lessons received from their masters in the arts of civilized life." Existing federal Indian policy was "just and generous to the Indians," Forsyth wrote, "but solely at the expense of a member of the Union." If the Cherokees were "unwilling to remove," he concluded, "the causes of that unwillingness are to be traced to the United States," and the president needed to be alerted to the possibility that he would be accountable if he did not complete the bargain. The only solution for the president was "to order their removal to a designated territory, beyond the limits of Georgia."[23]

On March 29, 1824, Calhoun provided Monroe with the War Department's history of its efforts to fulfill the compact. The secretary included a detailed analysis, prepared by the bureau of topographical engineers, delineating the cessions acquired by the government from the Creeks and Cherokees, the amounts paid, and the Indian lands remaining within Georgia's borders. Since the signing of the compact, the United States had acquired seven cessions from the Creeks and Cherokees comprising 15,744,000 acres. Including the original payments made under the compact, the United States had expended $7,735,243 to clear Indian title in the state. Calhoun argued that the list of acquisitions demonstrated that the United States had

---

[23]J. Elliott, N. Ware, et al. (Georgia congressional delegation) to the president of the United States, Mar. 10, 1824, *ASPIA*, 2:476–77; Duckett, *John Forsyth*, p. 107.

"ever been solicitous to fulfill, at the earliest period, the obligation of the convention." "In fact," he added, "little regard has been had to the price, whenever it has been found possible to obtain a cession of lands to the State"; in addition, the prices paid for the cessions within Georgia's borders far exceeded the amounts paid for acquisitions from other tribes beyond the state. Calhoun declared that he could maintain "with confidence, that no opportunity of extinguishing the Indian titles, 'on reasonable terms,' has been neglected to be embraced by the United States."

Calhoun then briefly described the futile efforts made by his commissioners to acquire Cherokee land since the treaties of 1817 and 1819. Calhoun blamed the Cherokees' reluctance to part with their territory on "their growing civilization and knowledge, by which they have learned to place a higher value upon their lands than more rude and savage tribes." He suggested that, "lying in large masses, they do not feel that depression which is invariably felt by small and detached tribes in the neighborhood of whites." The climate, the fertility of the soil, and the profitability of cotton, he added, made the Cherokees reluctant to abandon their homeland. Calhoun then rejected the allegations that the federal proponents of the civilization program had encouraged the Indians to resist removal. "In performing the high duties of humanity to the wretched aborigines of our country," he said, it had never been the intention of the government to abdicate its responsibilities under the Compact of 1802.[24]

Monroe quickly reported to Congress on his efforts to complete the compact. He included with his message copies of recent correspondence between the Cherokees and the treaty commissioners. Monroe said that the exhibits demonstrated his efforts to fulfill the federal government's responsibilities under the compact and showed that the question "now rests with the Cherokees." He added that he had been "animated . . . with an anxious desire" to "meet the wishes of the State." His efforts to complete the compact and negotiate a removal of the Cherokees, however, had received an "unqualified refusal" from the tribe. "In their present temper," he said, "they can be removed only by force; to which, should it be deemed proper, the power of the Executive is incompetent." Monroe warned that any unilateral effort to expel the Cherokees would violate the rights of the tribe. "The Indian title," he wrote, "was not affected in the slightest circumstance by the

[24]J. C. Calhoun to the president of the United States, Mar. 29, 1824, *ASPIA*, 2:461–63.

compact with Georgia." The agreement, moreover, did not oblige the United States to remove the Indians by force. "The express stipulation of the compact, that their title should be extinguished at the expense of the United States, when it may be done *peaceably* and on *reasonable* conditions," Monroe said, "is a full proof" that the Indian tribes were regarded as free agents when it came to their right to accept or reject any cession. Monroe closed by saying that the compact gave Georgia a claim "which ought to be executed, in all its conditions, with perfect good faith." At the same time, though, the United States should construe it strictly and "make no sacrifice of [the Indians'] interest not called for by the compact, nor contemplated by either of the parties when it was entered into." The United States should not "commit any breach of right or of humanity, in regard to the Indians, repugnant to the judgment and revolting to the feelings of the whole American people."[25]

On April 24, Troup responded to these vacillating statements with a sarcastic letter to the secretary of war. He declared that it assumed "principles which I controvert" and asserted "facts which I cannot permit myself to admit." Troup said that he had a duty to protest Monroe's conclusion, which "involves the destruction of the compact, . . . makes it null and void, and leaves no alternative to Georgia but acquiescence or resistance." If the federal government nullified the compact, Troup continued, Georgia then had the right to return the situation to the status quo ante: "Give us back our lands; we give you back your money; and, without making war upon the States of Alabama and Mississippi, we will run the risk of concluding with them the best bargain we can." He asked if the compact was "all a dream, a vision, a phantasma, with which the deluded people of Georgia have been plaguing themselves for twenty years." Troup protested that in his reading of the compact the president had construed the "peaceably" and "on reasonable terms" conditions "into a stipulation, to do in this respect whatever it might please the Indians at any time to do." Georgia had not asked the federal government to violate the rights of the tribes, Troup said, it had "only asked of the United States to do for her what she has done for herself; acquire Indian lands whensoever and wheresoever she wanted them." "Employ the same means for us in the fulfillment of [the compact's] obligation," Troup pleaded, "which you habitually employ for yourselves without any such ob-

---

[25]President James Monroe to the Senate of the United States, Mar. 30, 1824, *ASPIA*, 2:460.

ligation." He flatly rejected Monroe's assertion that he had done all that was possible to fulfill the compact. It was not fair to Georgia, Troup added, for the United States to decide at this point in its history to respect the treaty rights of Native Americans. If Georgia had to surrender its claims under the compact, then for the sake of fairness the federal government should have to compensate every wrong back to the "landing on the rock of Plymouth." "Not even the Puritans and the Quakers will consent to give up now," Troup asked. "[W]hy is Georgia to be selected as the propitiary offering?"[26]

In his annual message to the state legislature in 1824, Troup offered a unique interpretation of Calhoun's report on the history of Indian cessions in the state. He suggested that if the United States had sold the territory released by Georgia in the compact at the same price at which the War Department assessed the remaining Indian lands in the state, then the federal government would owe the state more than 150 million dollars. Troup argued that it would take seven years of federal revenues to pay this debt; if the national government endeavored to retire it in one year, the expenditure would "leave the mass of the population of the United States in infinite distress." The interest from those proceeds, Troup calculated, could have "enabled Georgia to dispense with taxes—to educate all her citizens at the public expense—to have armed and equipped her militia—to have made a garden of the face of the country, intersected everywhere by turnpikes and canals, and studded with the monuments of art." In agreeing to the Compact of 1802, Georgia had abandoned these "advantages for the benefit of the United States," the governor said. Troup also publicly raised the threat of armed conflict in this address. He warned that the state "in the last resort" might be "forced to draw the sword against her own flesh and blood." The United States would be responsible, Troup argued, for "fomenting civil war."[27]

When John Quincy Adams inherited the Compact of 1802 dilemma, he adopted Monroe's position: he would applaud a general removal, but the federal government would maintain assimilation as its objective and continue

---

[26]George M. Troup to the secretary of war, Apr. 24, 1824, in Harden, *Life of George M. Troup*, pp. 210–16.

[27]"His First Annual Message," Nov. 2, 1824, in Harden, *Life of George Troup*, pp. 232–34. Troup subsequently denied that he had threatened to initiate a war against the United States: "It was never my intention to resist the civil process by a military force, unless they resorted to a military force to enforce it" (G. M. Troup to Dr. Daniell, Feb. 24, 1827, in Harden, *Life of George Troup*, p. 492).

its policy of respecting the right of the tribes to consent to any cession or relocation proposal. Georgia's congressional delegation, already angered by the so-called corrupt bargain that had produced Adams's election, quickly went on the attack as soon as the new president was sworn in. On March 9, 1825, John Forsyth visited Adams and asked him to address the state's rights under the compact. Adams referred Forsyth to his secretary of war, James Barbour. That same afternoon, Forsyth pointed out to Barbour that a delegation from the Cherokee Nation was in Washington, and he suggested that Barbour tell them "that the United States will, sooner or later, *insist* upon the surrender of the lands in Georgia." Barbour assured Forsyth that the Adams administration would do all it could to satisfy the state's request.[28]

On March 12, Thomas L. McKenney, the new director of Indian affairs, wrote to the Cherokee delegation and asked them to once again consider a cession of their nation's lands. The Cherokees referred McKenney to their letter of February 11, 1824, which included the defiant refusal to consider any cession proposal. "We have full authority in saying," the Cherokees wrote, "that those sentiments remain the same, and are unchangeable." The Cherokees also sent a note congratulating Adams on his inauguration. They told the new president that though they were "ever ready to comply with the views and wishes of the Government, they cannot consent to yield another foot of land." They urged Adams to find a way to complete the Compact of 1802 without forcing the Cherokee Nation to yield territory and encouraged him to maintain the United States' commitment to the objectives of acculturation and assimilation.[29]

On March 23, Barbour reported on these conversations and summarized Adams's views on the compact to Troup. He wrote that Adams was inclined "as a sense of duty" to complete the compact with Georgia, "whenever that can be done consistently with its provisions" and that he would try to persuade the Cherokees to embrace removal "on every suitable occasion." Barbour warned, however, that the Cherokees continued to exert "determined opposition" to all removal entreaties.[30]

---

[28]Lynn Hudson Parsons, "'A Perpetual Harrow upon My Feelings': John Quincy Adams and the American Indian," *New England Quarterly* 46 (1973):339–79; E. Merton Coulter, *Georgia: A Short History* (1933; reprint ed., Chapel Hill, N.C., 1960), pp. 247–48; John Forsyth to James Barbour, Mar. 9, 1825, *ASPIA*, 2:774; Duckett, *John Forsyth*, p. 110.

[29]Thomas L. McKenney to John Ross, George Lowrey, and Elijah Hicks, Mar. 12, 1825; "Extract of a letter from the Cherokee Delegation to Thomas L. McKenney," Mar. 14, 1825; John Ross, George Lowrey, and Elijah Hicks to John Q. Adams, Mar. 12, 1825; all in *ASPIA*, 2:775–76.

[30]James Barbour to John Forsyth, Mar. 23, 1825, *ASPIA*, 2:775.

This last letter exasperated Troup. On April 6, the governor revealed his feelings about the Cherokees and the new administration's position to Forsyth. Troup said that he had tried to avoid a "painful altercation" with the federal government and had previously been optimistic that it would satisfy the conditions of the compact. His confidence in a peaceful settlement, however, was waning. Troup told Forsyth: "The Cherokees must be told, in plain language, that the lands they occupy belong to Georgia, that, sooner or later, the Georgians must have them; that every day, nay, every hour of postponement of the rights of Georgia, makes the [case] more strongly for Georgia, and against both the United States and the Cherokees."[31]

Troup and Georgia's removal advocates became more and more frustrated as the Cherokees continued to parry their maneuvers in Washington. Troup revealed the depths of the conspiratorial tendencies and self-doubts harbored by some removal proponents. It was suspicious, he said, "that, of all the various tribes of aborigines dispersed over the vast country, . . . two of them, within the limits of Georgia, have been specially selected as most fit subjects for the operation of this great scheme of reclamation." The civilization of the Cherokees, Troup despaired, was "held up to us as . . . a mirror in which we are invited to see at once our own deformity and the moral beauty of its authors."[32]

Despite these rather obvious doubts about the morality of its campaign, Georgia's governor, legislature, and congressional delegation continued to pursue vigorously the state's claim under the Compact of 1802 during the remainder of Adams's administration. Troup asked the Georgia legislature to pass a law prohibiting whites from entering or living in Cherokee territory; this measure, he hoped, would deter the missionaries from New England who he believed were moving into the Cherokee Nation to stir up resistance to removal. (The general assembly adopted a law along these lines in 1830.) He also urged the assembly to extend the state's jurisdiction over the Cherokees residing within Georgia's borders. Troup renewed his threats against the federal government, as well. The state "had not demanded justice of the Federal Government in her day of tribulation," he declared, "but at a moment when, with an ample treasury, at peace with all nations, and prosperous beyond example, she had her option to do us justice." If it did not, Troup threatened, the federal government might have to "present a military

---

[31]G. M. Troup to John Forsyth, Apr. 6, 1825, *ASPIA*, 2:776.
[32]"Governor's Message to the General Assembly of the State of Georgia," Nov. 7, 1825, *ASPIA*, 2:779–81.

chest and armed men" to prevent his state from exerting its rights. Georgia was no longer willing to stand by and see the state's sovereignty reduced to "the power of a municipal corporation."[33]

Though the Cherokees continued to infuriate Troup for the rest of his gubernatorial administration, he could claim one victory for his removal agenda: he was able to push the federal government to extinguish the title of the Creeks. After constant pressure from federal and Georgia officials, William McIntosh, a prominent Creek chief, persuaded several towns under his influence to accept the Treaty of Indian Springs (1825). The agreement required the Creeks to exchange the remainder of their territory in Georgia for a tract of equal size west of the Mississippi River. Adams, just days into his presidency, signed the treaty and sent it to the Senate for ratification. However, after he received reports that the treaty negotiations had been marked by fraud, he ordered an investigation. Troup and the state's legislature and congressional delegation were outraged at Adams's reversal, and relations between Georgia and the federal government deteriorated dramatically from that point. The Treaty of Indian Springs provoked serious criticism from missionaries and newspapers in the Northeast. As George Gilmer put it, the treaty "became the subject of . . . much altercation in Congress and violent opposition on the part of the northern people." When Troup sent surveyors into the Creek territory against Adams's advice, the president threatened to use force to evict the trespassers, if necessary. Adams ordered a revision of the treaty, and on January 24, 1826, the Creek Nation signed the Treaty of Washington. While the agreement nullified and replaced the Treaty of Indian Springs, it still included the cession of all Creek lands in Georgia, except for a small tract. In a subsequent agreement on November 15, 1827, the Creeks surrendered this last remaining parcel. Georgia had successfully used the Compact of 1802 to clear the Creeks out of the state and could now focus all of its attention on the Cherokee Nation.[34]

In his annual message of 1826, Troup told his state legislature that it had a choice: it could either take the initiative and extend the laws of the state over the Cherokees or "abide by the result of future negotiations by the

---

[33]Ibid., pp. 780, 783–84; Jeremiah Evarts, *Cherokee Removal: The "William Penn" Essays and Other Writings*, ed. Francis Paul Prucha (Knoxville, Tenn., 1981), pp. 265–66; 1830 Ga. Laws 114.

[34]Michael D. Green, *The Politics of Indian Removal: Creek Government and Society in Crisis* (Lincoln, Neb., 1981), pp. 69–139; Gilmer, *Sketches*, pp. 163–64; Duckett, *John Forsyth*, pp. 108–13; James W. Silver, "General Gaines Meets Governor Troup: A State-Federal Clash in 1825," *Georgia Historical Quarterly* 43 (1943):248–70.

United States to extinguish [the Cherokees'] claims, in virtue of the compact of 1802." The men of the Georgia General Assembly, Troup said, would have to decide if they would continue to accept "a state of things so unnatural and so fruitful of evil, as an independent Government of a semi-barbarous people co-existing within the same limits." Troup added that the failure of the federal government to address Georgia's claims under the Compact had "given rise to the unhappy differences subsisting between the Federal Government and us." "Wrong has been done to Georgia; her views misrepresented, and her character traduced," he said. "[B]ut wrong will come to right, and what prejudice has misrepresented, history will correct."[35]

In July 1827, the Cherokees adopted a republican constitution and declared their people a sovereign nation beyond the reach of Georgia's jurisdiction. The Cherokees' declaration completely unnerved the removal leaders in the state. Troup demanded that President Adams repudiate the Cherokees' constitution. The Georgia legislature "solemnly warn[ed]" the Cherokees that they would suffer the consequences of their actions and issued a resolution stating that it "had the power and the right to possess herself, by any means she might choose, of the lands in dispute." On May 21, 1828, John Forsyth, Troup's successor, declared that the Cherokees would be "inevitably subjected to the State laws if the compact made in 1802 is not speedily executed by the U. States." Congress and Adams were now stuck between two subordinate polities that claimed to be sovereign. For the rest of Adams's term, his cabinet and federal Indian policy were paralyzed by the compact, trapped between Georgia's demands for removal and the traditional national commitment to assimilation in the East. Existing treaties with the Cherokees inhibited Adams from satisfying the former; the compact prevented him from holding fast to the latter.[36]

Andrew Jackson's election as president in 1828 augured a change in the federal government's attitude toward a general relocation of the tribes, and Georgia removal proponents sensed that their efforts to force the federal government to complete the compact were finally to come to fruition. In December, the Georgia legislature followed the advice of Troup and Forsyth

---

[35]"Annual Message of 1826," in Harden, *Life of George Troup*, pp. 469–71.

[36]McLoughlin, *Cherokee Renascence*, pp. 394–401; "Resolutions," in *New American State Papers: Indian Affairs*, ed. Loring B. Priest, 13 vols. (Wilmington, Del., 1972), 9:52–62; John Forsyth to Hugh Montgomery, May 21, 1828, quoted in Duckett, *John Forsyth*, pp. 114–15; Garrison, *Legal Ideology of Removal*, p. 25.

and annexed the Cherokees' land in Georgia. The state also purported to abolish the Cherokee Nation's courts and legislature and declared its laws null and void. (Alabama, Mississippi, and Tennessee subsequently followed Georgia's lead and extended state jurisdiction over the Native Americans within their borders.) When Governor Forsyth learned that the new president had written to the Cherokees, informing them that they would either have to remove or fall under Georgia's jurisdiction, he wrote to John Eaton, the new secretary of war, and told him that "rigid adherence to the principles developed" would finally "enable the President to execute the Compact of 1802."[37]

Jackson, however, still had to build a majority for removal in Congress. He found only mixed support, even among his partisans, in the Northeast. The removal pressures that Georgia brought to bear on the Cherokees had ignited widespread outrage, particularly in New England. Churches and missionary societies in the region published pamphlets and newspapers criticizing Georgia's actions. The *Missionary Herald* of Boston called upon "every Christian, every philanthropist, and every patriot . . . to save a persecuted and defenseless people from ruin." College students arranged public protests. The abolitionist and reformer, George Cheever, then a student at Andover Seminary, wrote that the Cherokees would be better off to "stand to their arms and be exterminated" than to "remain to be trampled as the serfs of Georgia." Cheever also declared that "we would rather have a civil war, were there no other alternative, than avoid it by taking shelter in crime" and that "we would take up arms for the Indians, in such a war." Women's groups and abolitionists also joined the opposition. Catherine and Harriet Beecher led the first national women's petition campaign against removal. William Lloyd Garrison published articles condemning Georgia in the *Liberator*. In 1829, Jeremiah Evarts, the New England missionary and lawyer, began publishing lengthy attacks on Georgia under the pseudonym William Penn in the *National Intelligencer*. His articles persuaded hundreds of people to send memorials to Congress protesting the state's actions. Evarts painstakingly analyzed the history of Georgia's claims under the compact in the essays. He wrote that the "original right of the Cherokees, confirmed and guaranteed by so many treaties, was not, and could not be, affected by the compact

---

[37] Quoted in Duckett, *John Forsyth*, pp. 116–17; 1828 Ga. Laws 87; Garrison, *Legal Ideology of Removal*, pp. 103–5, 152–53, 204–5; Sidney J. Harring, *Crow Dog's Case: American Indian Sovereignty, Tribal Law, and United States Law in the Nineteenth Century* (New York, 1944), p. 39.

of 1802." Evarts added that Georgia's legislature had recognized that fact for "a quarter of a century after the year 1802."[38]

The criticism raining down from the Northeast produced an exaggerated defensiveness among Georgia's removal advocates. Wilson Lumpkin pointed out that the "William Penn" essays were "published in Boston" and described them as having "more savage, superstitious, and diabolical spirit than was ever possessed by the authors of the pow-wow, scalping, slave, and dog laws." A judge in Georgia noted that several states in the North had already extended their jurisdiction over the Indian tribes within their borders without editorial comment. "So soon as the State of Georgia pursues the same course," he complained, "a hue and cry is raised against her." In looking back on his actions during the removal crisis, George Gilmer wrote that "sensible, well informed and good men, had viewed my conduct through the same prejudiced medium as the ignorant." The reason many outside of the South were so critical of the state, Gilmer said, was that "the organs for diffusing information at the North, and in the Middle States, had refused or neglected to publish any of the official documents, or other matters, tending to set public opinion upon the subject." Southern partisans like Gilmer believed that the common people of the North would have been reassured of Georgia's intentions regarding the compact if newspapers simply printed copies of their lengthy documents and memoranda justifying removal; Gilmer reasoned that the refusal to allocate print space to their rationalizations was indicative of sectional prejudice.[39]

The removal crisis revealed distinctive sectional attitudes about the human nature of Native Americans. Many in the Northeast continued to cling to the Enlightenment-inspired belief in the inherent equality of whites and Indians and to the objective of an accelerated assimilation. Most removal advocates, on the other hand, maintained that blood and race determined an individual's fate, and the party line among removers was that the real Cherokees were not really civilized, could not be improved, and were incapable of orchestrating the intelligent resistance that confronted their campaign. Wilson Lumpkin maintained that the "naive people of New England"

---

[38]Cheever and the *Missionary Herald* quoted in Mary Hershberger, "Mobilizing Women, Anticipating Abolition: The Struggle against Indian Removal," *Journal of American History* 86 (1999):15–40; Evarts, *Cherokee Removal*, pp. 146, 155–59.

[39]Lumpkin, *Removal of the Cherokee Indians*, pp. 71–76; Gilmer, *Sketches*, p. 332; *Georgia v. Tassels*, 1 Dud. 229, 234 (1830).

who opposed relocation had been duped by the Cherokees' missionary bene-
factors. While there were some Cherokees who enjoyed "the common com-
forts of civil and domestic life," he said, "the principle part of these enjoy-
ments [were] confined to the blood of the white man, either in whole or in
part." "Few, very few, of the real Indians," Lumpkin declared, "participate
largely in these blessings. A large portion of the full-blooded Cherokees still
remain a poor degraded race of human beings." George Gilmer, who asked
for reports on the exact blood quantum of Cherokee leaders, surmised: "The
whites and half-breeds, who are most capable of understanding and valuing
the benefits of civil government, are the most active in opposing the jurisdiction of the States." Later, Gilmer maintained that a class of "white men
with Indian families, and the half-breeds" possessing "wealth and intelligence" controlled the Cherokee Nation."[40]

Georgia's manipulation of the compact, its ability to stigmatize the leaders of the removal opposition as self-interested half-breeds or Puritan cant-
ing fanatics, and its success at depicting its white citizens as innocent victims
of a national welching helped drive the United States out of its policy paraly-
sis toward a new regime of racial separation. In 1830, after more than a
decade of lobbying and threats by the state, Congress provided the president with broad authority to remove the eastern tribes beyond the Mississippi River. Hostility and distrust between the sections marked the long debates over the Indian removal bill. Lumpkin's address was perhaps the best
representative both of the animosity that the Georgia delegation harbored
toward the Northeast and that region's members of Congress and of the
sense of victimization the state had assumed in its campaign to complete
the compact. Lumpkin declared that Georgia was "one of the good old
thirteen States; she entered the Union upon an equal footing with any of
her sisters." By denying Georgia's right to extend its jurisdiction over the
Cherokees, he charged, critics in the North were attempting to reduce the
state to an inferior status in the Union. Lumpkin also rejected the notion
that the people of Georgia were greedily seizing the land of the Cherokees:
"If you want any evidence of the generous spirit and liberality of Georgia,
turn your eye to the maps which adorn your walls; look upon the two flour-
ishing states of Alabama and Mississippi; for these States may, to a considerable extent, be considered a donation on the part of Georgia to this con-

---

[40]Lumpkin, *Removal of the Cherokee Indians*, p. 77; Gilmer, *Sketches*, pp. 263, 287, 312, 313.

federation of states." "From the signing of the compact of 1802," Lumpkin continued, "Georgia had a right to expect . . . a speedy, reasonable, and peaceable relief from all Indian claims to lands within her borders." The federal government had "been wanting in good faith to Georgia," and the state had been "the subject of unremitted and unmerited abuse." Lumpkin then raised the threat of secession: "We have no supplications to make. We deny your right of jurisdiction. Our right of sovereignty will not be yielded. If you do not perform your duty . . . and fulfill the conditions of your contract of twenty-eight years standing, I would then advise you to let us alone, and leave us to manage our own affairs in our own way. . . . The Cherokees, as well as the Georgians, are tired of suspense. A crisis has arrived which calls for action."[41]

Northern senators and representatives, including Asher Robbins of Rhode Island, Peleg Sprague and George Evans of Maine, Edward Everett and Isaac Bates of Massachusetts, Henry Storrs of New York, and Theodore Frelinghuysen of New Jersey, delivered powerful speeches against the removal bill. They also attempted to block or leaven it with amendments that offered significant protections for tribal rights. All of the proposals, however, were defeated by united opposition from the South and West. Consequently, though the Indian Removal Act of 1830 implied that the Indian tribes held the right of consent to any relocation proposal (the law stated that the president could establish a territory west of the Mississippi River for those tribes that "may choose to exchange the lands where they now reside"), it did not deter Jackson's treaty commissioners from using fraud, deceit, and coercion to secure removal treaties under the authority of the new law.[42]

The final votes on the Indian Removal Act revealed a fairly rigid sectional division between the Northeast and the South. Southern members in the House voted for the removal bill by a 60 to 15 margin, while representatives from the Northeast voted against it by a 79 to 42 count. The swing section was the Northwest; those states abutting the northern territorial frontier favored the bill by a 27 to 17 margin. The same sectional division

---

[41]Lumpkin, *Removal of the Cherokee Indians*, pp. 69–70, 88.

[42]Prucha, *Great Father*, pp. 200–208; Ronald N. Satz, *American Indian Policy in the Jacksonian Era* (Lincoln, Neb., 1976), pp. 19–31; Remini, *Andrew Jackson and His Indian Wars*, pp. 231–38; Jason Meyers, "No Idle Past: Uses of History in the 1830 Indian Removal Debates," *Historian* 63 (2000):53–65; *Register of Debates*, 21st Cong., 1st sess., Apr. 9, 1830, pp. 309–20, May 18, 1830, pp. 1132–33.

marked the vote in the Senate. Southern senators voted 14 to 3 in favor of removal; 13 of 18 from the Northeast voted against it. The Northwest again provided the difference (9 to 3). George Gilmer recognized that the question of Indian removal had been marked by regional discord, although he did not apportion any of the responsibility for the division to his state. The votes against the Removal Act, he later wrote, were a consequence of "the sectional interests of the Northern and Middle States, and the partisan opposition to the Administration."[43]

The Indian Removal Act did not, however, resolve the struggle between Georgia and the Cherokees; the president still had to procure a removal agreement from the Cherokee Nation. The Cherokees, led by their principal chief, John Ross, continued to refuse all removal overtures. In addition, the Cherokee government challenged Georgia's extension laws in the federal courts (where it won a Pyrrhic victory from the U.S. Supreme Court in *Worcester v. Georgia*)[44] and hoped that the next general election in the United States would produce a government more amenable to Cherokee rights. Politicians in Georgia, for their part, continued to use the compact to push the federal government to conclude a removal treaty with the Cherokees. In 1831, Lumpkin looked toward the day when the Cherokees' "claims to the territory thus occupied by Georgia will be extinguished by the Federal Government, in compliance with the compact of 1802." Gilmer, now the governor, wrote on several occasions to Jackson and John H. Eaton, the secretary of war, urging them to turn their attention to the compact. Georgia's congressional delegation continued to introduce resolutions calling for the completion of the agreement. The Cherokee Nation consistently refused to yield to the pressure. Only in late December 1835, when a disaffected and frustrated minority of Cherokees signed a removal agreement with a federal representative at New Echota, did the state secure the extinguishment it had so long desired.[45]

The completion of the Compact of 1802 was ruinous for the Cherokees and the American Indian nations east of the Mississippi River. Between the

---

[43]Alfred A. Cave, "Abuse of Power: Andrew Jackson and the Indian Removal Act of 1830," *Historian* 65 (2003):1336–37, 1351; Gilmer, *Sketches*, p. 266.

[44]See note 11, above.

[45]Garrison, *Legal Ideology of Removal*, pp. 169–97; Lumpkin, *Removal of the Cherokee Indians*, pp. 101–2; George R. Gilmer to the president of the United States, Dec. 29, 1829; Gilmer to John H. Eaton, May 14, 1831; Gilmer to Lewis Cass, Aug. 20, 1831; all in Gilmer, *Sketches*, pp. 260, 308, 314–18, 320; Thurman Wilkins, *Cherokee Tragedy: The Ridge Family and the Decimation of a People* (1970; reprint ed., Norman, Okla., 1986), pp. 254–78; Francis Paul Prucha, *American Indian Treaties: The History of a Political Anomaly* (Berkeley, Calif., 1994), pp. 177–81.

passage of the Indian Removal Act and 1843, when the Seminoles were finally expelled from Florida, the United States relocated almost every major tribe in the East. According to a report prepared by the U.S. Army, about ninety thousand Native Americans, roughly three-quarters of the Indian population in the East, were removed in that period. The so-called civilized Indian nations of the South were all relocated in a series of infamous and deadly long walks. The total number of casualties from the removal is unknown, but scholars have provided some startling estimates. Perhaps one-quarter to one-half of the Cherokees, Creeks, and Seminoles, for instance, died as a direct consequence of their removal. The southeastern tribes were not the only victims. The Delawares, Menominees, Miamis, Ojibwas, Oneidas, Potawatomis, Sacs, Foxes, and Winnebagos, among many other nations in the Northwest, were all forced off of their lands and pushed across the Mississippi. The Indian removal, and the spread of white racial determinism throughout the United States, also almost destroyed the national commitment to assimilation. In the 1840s, the federal government, lacking a territory to exile the tribes west of the Mississippi River, adopted the reservation as its mechanism to separate and isolate Native Americans from white Americans. The whole notion of the racial separation of Indians and whites driven by Georgia partisans in the 1820s, in other words, not only created national momentum toward removal but also helped produce the reservation solution that followed.[46]

The removal crisis, which resulted in the death, demoralization, and relocation of so many American Indians, also left the United States a more divided society. The campaign initiated by Georgia, and joined rather quickly by its Southern neighbors, prompted discussions of a general sectional insurrection in the late 1820s. Georgia's removal campaign and South Carolina's nullification movement helped make the alternative of secession more palatable for the succeeding generation of Southerners. Removal was, at its most fundamental level, an attack on federal authority. The campaign constituted an attempt to deny the federal government jurisdiction over Indian affairs, an attack on the accepted national program for the assimilation of Native Americans, and a repudiation of the Founders' recognition of American Indian political and territorial rights. By 1836, when the South felt so besieged by Northern abolitionists that it instituted the gag rule on slavery

---

[46]Russell Thornton, *The Cherokees: A Population History* (Lincoln, Neb., 1990), pp. 73–76; Prucha, *Great Father*, pp. 214–69; Reginald Horsman, *Race and Manifest Destiny: The Origins of American Racial Anglo-Saxonism* (Cambridge, Mass., 1981).

petitions in the House of Representatives, the region had already held considerable discussions on what it would mean to repudiate federal authority and abandon the Union. One of those occasions was the Indian removal crisis. As John Ross suggested during the controversy, Georgia's campaign to exile his people beyond the Mississippi was as much of an effort to nullify federal law and political authority as South Carolina's attack on the tariff. It is difficult to imagine how Georgia could have brought about such a revolutionary transformation of federal Indian policy without the claims it possessed under the Compact of 1802.[47]

---

[47]David C. Frederick, "John Quincy Adams, Slavery, and the Disappearance of the Right of Petition," *Law and History Review* 9 (1991):113–55; John Ross to the General Council, May 13, 1833, in *The Papers of John Ross*, ed. Gary E. Moulton, 2 vols. (Norman, Okla., 1985), 1:268.

BORN TO COMMAND.

OF VETO MEMORY.

HAD I BEEN CONSULTED.

KING ANDREW THE FIRST.

President Andrew Jackson's veto of the congressional bill to recharter the Bank of the United States in 1832 led to this caricature of him as "King Andrew the First." He holds a veto in his left hand, and the Constitution lies in tatters at his feet. *(Courtesy Library of Congress.)*

THE DOCTORS PUZZLED OR THE DESPERATE CASE OF MOTHER U.S BANK.

"The Doctors Puzzled or the Desperate Case of Mother U.S. Bank." Henry Clay, Daniel Webster, and John C. Calhoun ponder how to save the Bank from Jackson's September 1833 order withdrawing federal funds in this satirical lithograph depicting the Bank as a sick patient vomiting coins. Clay suggests "my Patent American System," Webster counters with "a few grains of Common Sense," and Calhoun offers "the leaden pills of Nullification." *(Courtesy Library of Congress.)*

An 1834 pro-Jackson cartoon depicts a satisfied president watching as his opponents Nicholas Biddle, Daniel Webster, Henry Clay, and John C. Calhoun are blown away. *(Courtesy Library of Congress.)*

Sen. Henry Clay sews shut Jackson's mouth in this 1834 caricature, "Symptoms of a Locked Jaw," possibly in reference to the Senate's censure of Jackson on March 28, 1834. *(Courtesy Library of Congress.)*

Sen. Thomas Hart Benton appears as the "great tumble bug" rolling the "expunging resolution" ball uphill toward the Capitol in this 1837 print. *(Courtesy Library of Congress.)*

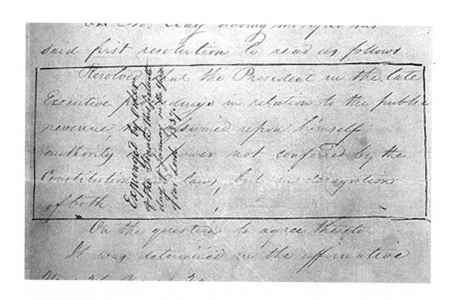

On January 16, 1837, the Senate voted to expunge its 1834 censure of President Jackson. The Senate Legislative Journal was brought into the chamber, where the secretary of the Senate drew a black border around the censure resolution and wrote across it, "Expunged by order of the Senate this Sixteenth day of January in the year of our Lord, 1837." *(Courtesy National Archives and Records Administration.)*

2: Congress in the Age of Jackson

William W. Freehling

Andrew Jackson, Great President (?)

A NDREW JACKSON was undeniably a monumental president. But was this
monument to his age a great president? The puzzle illuminates more
than presidential evaluations, indeed more than political history. Jackson's
several presidential falterings—and his one unqualified triumph—personify
central aspects of the American travail.[1]

ONE WORD SUMS up the Jackson puzzle: *egalitarianism.* The Tennessee frontiersman was the first offspring of the impoverished to attain the presidency.
Old Hickory was the first chief executive with a nickname. He was the first
to marry a pipe-smoking divorced frontier wife. He was the first to rise to
power west of the original thirteen colonies, the first to mix Irish (or any
non–Anglo-Saxon strains) with English origins, the first to proclaim that any
Tom, Dick, or Harry could administer any governmental post, the first to
thunder that by the heavens he would hang anyone who defied his populist
missions—in short, the first to strike commoner voters as their peer, their
comrade, even their buddy. His admirers danced on his White House sofas
to celebrate his presidential inauguration. His detractors trembled at the
prospect that his mob would level more than his furniture.

---

[1]For a skillful summary of the Jackson era and the most balanced interpretation of the
Jacksonian phenomenon, see Harry L. Watson, *Liberty and Power: The Politics of Jacksonian America*
(New York, 1990).

His partisans had already leveled one treasure of the Founding Fathers: aristocratic republicanism. While previous presidents had affirmed that citizens must choose their rulers, they had presumed that the chosen few must determine public policy and that voters must defer. Jacksonians scorned this paternalistic viewpoint. Their egalitarian republicanism celebrated white male commoners as determiners of policies no less than leaders. Their revolt against deference invited two national parties' crass electioneering to replace upper-class paternalists as suppliers of republican wisdom. Their hero proved that the poorest white could rise above the richest, without any patronizing aid from the advantaged.

Jackson discerned unacceptable airs inside the financial temples no less than inside the political halls. Just as Jacksonians swept to victory in 1828 by damning John Quincy Adams as a haughty political elitist, so they reelected Jackson in 1832 by denouncing the Bank of the United States as an overweening economic meddler. After his successful veto of the Bank's recharter in 1832, Jackson summoned his folk to slay the latest antiegalitarian monster.

To call a bank a monster may seem a stretch. But nineteenth-century banks possessed a potentially malign power (long since lost). They alone issued paper dollars and guaranteed this currency's worth. The alternative nineteenth-century money, gold or silver coins (alias "specie"), required no guarantee. This hard money's raw material had its own market value.

In contrast to specie, paper dollars (alias "soft money") came printed on a sheet that cost a proverbial halfpenny. In modern times, governments print and shower vast worth on almost worthless paper by guaranteeing that rag dollars shall be legal tender for all private and public debt. But before governments provided this boon to economic order, banks provided the service, and in a potentially disorderly manner. Banks printed paper dollars stamped with a face value. The issuing bank then promised to pay their paper's face value in gold or silver coin on demand. So long as banks fulfilled their promises, rag dollars possessed sterling value.

This paper substitute for sterling silver lent the economy a lithe, light, and easily transported currency. Crushingly heavy specie, unable to provide that benefit, also could not multiply the nation's money supply beyond the amount of gold and silver extant. Banks, in contrast, routinely printed two, three, four, and sometimes ten times more paper dollars than their gold and silver reserves justified.

The gambit allowed banks to lend and earn interest on more dollars than their specie covered. Bankers' inflationary maneuvers also allowed borrowers more cash for development than their possessions justified. The boost to an undeveloped economy, however, exacted a price. Since banks possessed less specie than their notes guaranteed, suspicious customers sometimes demanded precious coin for paper promise.

As suspicions mounted, demands for gold and silver increased. As specie reserves dwindled, panic ensued. As banks suspended their promises to trade printed paper for precious coin, rag dollars became worthless, and the whole economy (to say nothing of the banks) plunged toward ruin.

Atop this Jacksonian-era house of cards sat the nation's largest bank, the Bank of the United States (alias the BUS), chartered by the federal government. The government deposited all its specie in this economic colossus. The BUS used the government gold and silver to redeem its paper money issues. The BUS also used its government-boosted power to discourage other banks' excessive issuance of rag dollars. When suspicious that some bank had issued too much soft money, the BUS demanded precious coin in exchange for the suspect institution's printed stuff. The threat led local banks to curtail promises. Nicholas Biddle, president of the BUS, saw his regulatory banking practices as the natural lid on a paper money system that must not boil over.[2]

Jackson scorned Biddle's paternalistic regulation. This banker, despite his government-granted power over all other bankers, was himself unanswerable to the government. Biddle was responsible only to his shareholders, who wanted to maximize their investment. The potentially irresponsible private tycoon as national economic czar—how better to define a republican monster?

Even if the republic could control the demon, Jackson saw pernicious inequalities in Biddle's government-inflated power. The government's deposited hard money gave this one corporation unequalled power to loan out soft money. Moreover, the people's specie could increase the people's risks. Biddle's paper dollars could feed the national cycles of booms and busts; and the busts, Jacksonians argued, disproportionately endangered the poor. Laborers could ill afford to have wages, paid in paper dollars, turn worthless or to have jobs, endangered by banking panics, turn scarce. The rich, in contrast, had resources to ride out the storms. Or as Jackson exclaimed in

---

[2]For the best explanation of the paper money system and of Nicholas Biddle's statecraft, see Bray Hammond, *Banks and Politics from the Revolution to the Civil War* (Princeton, N.J., 1957). Hammond, however, overstates the soft-money intentions of the Bank War initiators. Unintended consequences are unusually important in understanding this Jacksonian episode.

the critical passage of his Bank veto message, "When the laws . . . grant . . . exclusive privileges, to make the rich richer and the potent more powerful, the humble members of society—the farmers, mechanics, and laborers— who have neither the time nor the means of securing like favors to them- selves, have a right to complain of the injustice of their Government."

In 1832, the supposed egalitarian who employed this class war rhetoric would not settle for killing the Bank's recharter. The old charter still gave the monster four more years to savage the people's equality. So Jackson ordered his secretary of the Treasury to remove the federal government's specie from the BUS. When two secretaries refused to seize the specie, Jackson fired them and found a third who would comply. Thus did Nicholas Biddle lose his un- equal power.

And thus did Jackson begin his unintentional augmentation of inequal- ity. The president needed to put the government's specie somewhere. He could hand the treasure to a revised national bank, this time responsible to the government instead of to the shareholders. But Jackson hated all banks and all paper money, particularly because he had lost one fortune (before garnering another) in a paper money banking panic on the southwestern frontier. He also disdained to give one new national bank, however respon- sible, a monopoly over the people's specie.

Alternatively, Jackson might secure a new arm of the Treasury Depart- ment, charged with using the government's gold and silver to regulate local banks' paper money issues. But the president, chary of paternalism in white politics, instinctively distrusted regulation of whites from above. His suc- cessor, Martin Van Buren, nicely expressed the antipaternalist instinct: "All communities are apt to look to governments too much."

Looking away from Big Brother Washington's paternalistic control, Jackson opted to scatter the former BUS deposits among several dozen local banks. This supposedly egalitarian "pet bank" scheme only traded multiple unequal pets for one unequal favorite. Moreover, none of the newly favored few banks harbored Biddle's ambition to police other bankers. The pet be- neficiaries of the government's unequal largesse coveted only the opportunity to issue more soft money with their new hard-money jackpot. The president, despite his conviction that paper dollars eventually would devastate the poor, had helped rain soft money on the economy.

Nicholas Biddle may have been more the rainmaker. After Jackson re- moved the public's deposits (and thus relieved the BUS, so Biddle sniffed, of public responsibility to control paper money inflation), the BUS's president maximized his expiring bank's own inflation. A worldwide increase of silver had increased his and other bankers' speculative appetites. Why not feast on rag money more than ever, with ever more silver coin behind ever larger multiples of paper dollars?

Jackson, horrified by the soft-money flood that his pet banks, in part, had let loose, tried to dam the surge. His secretary of the Treasury, although armed with too little authority, lamely tried to restrain the pets. Then the president's Specie Circular of 1836, requiring payments for public lands in gold or silver coin, more effectively jammed on the brakes. Jackson's deflationary circular may have been too abrupt, for British bankers' simultaneous new demands for specie also pressed on overextended American banks.[3]

The ensuing Panic of 1837, the nation's worst yet, provided the country's headline story immediately after Jackson departed the White House. Like many subsequent presidents, Jackson caught too much of the blame; forces beyond his control had done more to generate the boom and bust. But his pet bank scheme had contributed to the boom; his Specie Circular had contributed to the bust; and, as he had predicted, the paper money disaster particularly devastated the poor. His supposedly egalitarian Bank War had helped heap more inequality on his folk.

AFTER JACKSON'S PRESIDENCY, Jacksonians' substitute institution for national and pet banks came somewhat closer to achieving the former president's hard-money objectives. Jacksonians labeled their substitute the Subtreasury, or the Independent Treasury system. This concoction retained the federal government's specie in the government's own vaults, removed from benefiting any bank or from guaranteeing a single paper dollar. The new regime also required payment of all federal taxes and debts in specie. That requirement somewhat discouraged local banks' paper money issues. Bankers knew that customers would demand specie to pay the government, even if the citizenry trusted the paper notes.

Still, the government's gold and silver lay dormant in the Treasury Department. If the government had instead issued paper money on the basis

---

[3]All aspects of this economic crisis are expertly detailed in Peter Temin, *The Jacksonian Economy* (New York, 1969), although Professor Temin understates, I think, the importance of the Specie Circular. See Richard H. Timberlake, Jr., "The Specie Circular and the Distribution of the Surplus," *Journal of Political Economy* 68 (1980):109–17.

of one dollar circulated for one dollar of gold and silver retained, the under-developed economy would have gained what it usually desperately needed: a trustworthy source of credit. Nor could specie buried in the Treasury Department be used when the inflationary cycle needed additional curbs. The Jacksonians' Subtreasury solution left the private banking system largely unregulated, free to boom and bust as its internal dynamics dictated.

This triumph less of equality than of laissez-faire—of leaving private individuals at liberty to produce profits and inequities—emerged most clearly not in Jackson's stab at banking regulation but in his renunciation of regulating any entrepreneurs except bankers. The president sharply distinguished between artificial and natural inequality. Artificial inequality came from economic activities that produced no hard, useful product. Culprits included paper money bankers and government handouts to the wealthy. Natural inequality, in contrast, came from entrepreneurial ventures that produced a substance to feed or clothe or shelter or transport the folk. Its heroes included manufacturers, miners, and farmers.

Jackson declared war only on the artificial. In the very bank charter veto wherein he urged the poor to mass against rich capitalists' unnatural inequalities, he promised legal protection for natural inequalities stemming from the "fruits of superior industry, economy, and virtue." But "when the laws undertake to add to these natural advantages artificial distinctions," he drew the line.

His line placed most of the American economy off limits to government regulation. Only paper money bankers faced whatever (slim) interference his bias against governmental regulation allowed. No inequality of wages, prices, profits, inheritance—of the basic structure of American capitalism —had to fear Jackson's egalitarian scorn.

This blinkered disapproval of economic inequality characterized American mainstream liberalism for generations after Jackson's presidency. While some Jacksonian theorists transcended Jackson, deploying his egalitarian rhetoric against some of the wider economic inequalities that he had called natural, Jacksonian economic hatred continued to focus on banks. So, too, while some later American reformers railed against trusts, railroads, and robber barons, the American instinct for reform usually targeted political corruption, manipulated money, and monster banks for a century after 1832. The American political mainstream long continued to consider the basic business of America sound and only government corruption and a gyrating currency unsound. William Jennings Bryan derided a cross of gold; Woodrow Wilson erected a Federal Reserve System; and Franklin Delano Roosevelt started his presidency with a bank holiday. Thus did Andrew Jackson's blinkered war against white men's social inequality continue to prevail, until FDR's New Deal began to tear off the blinkers.

SOUTHERN UNREGULATED CAPITALISM, and especially the unregulated slaveholder, fared particularly comfortably in Jacksonian celebrations of natural inequality. Jackson's popular majority in the South swelled far beyond his percentages of victory in the North. His majorities in the deepest South set records never since approached in any American region. Although Jackson also won a slight majority of Northern popular votes in 1828, John Quincy Adams held a one-vote majority among Northern electors in the Electoral College. But while Adams would have been reelected in an exclusively free-labor state Electoral College, the slave-labor states' electors turned the Age of Adams into the Age of Jackson.

Victorious Southern Jacksonians soon sought two slaveholder prizes: no Indians and no abolitionists. Southern capitalists wanted the removal of Indians from the South to open landed opportunities and the silencing of abolitionists in the North to perpetuate slaveholders' profits. Both of these natural economic goals also served Southerners' supposedly natural racial goals. The allegedly superior white race, Southerners argued, could better direct and control the supposedly inferior black and red races. Jacksonian faith that unfettered capitalists (except for banking capitalists) would generate only natural inequality here received a racist twist.

Racism turned the Jacksonian laissez-faire bias 180 degrees. On white men's economic issues, the Jackson party shied away from a paternalistic federal state, even to secure hard money. But when race compounded capitalism, Jacksonians inclined toward using the state actively to clear the way for the supposedly paternalistic racist capitalist.

Andrew Jackson was the ideal Southerner to further the racist twist. Jackson's 161 slaves at the time of his death put him in the top 1 percent of Southern slaveholders.[4] None of the other towering slaveholding presidents —not Washington or Jefferson or Madison or Monroe or Polk or Tyler—

---

[4]Robert Remini, *Andrew Jackson and the Cause of American Democracy, 1833–1845* (New York, 1984), p. 602 n. 63. I am indebted to Henry Wiencek for information about the other slaveholding presidents' estates.

died with so many slaves in their estates. All the previous slaveholding chief executives had inherited a large portion of their slaves. In contrast, Jackson's hard-driving entrepreneurship had acquired every one of his bondsmen. His hard-driving army career had also often cleared reds out of whites' land-hungry way.

On Jackson's southwestern frontier, his heroes included the sturdy yeomen, who raised crops to sustain white men's independence; and the resourceful capitalists, who massed the slaves to produce the profits that enabled pater-nalists and wards to forge smiling social orders. His villains included the Indians, who allegedly savaged the peace; the abolitionists, who supposedly fed happy darkies murderous ideas; and the paper money bankers, who purportedly stole white yeomen's and patriarchs' well-earned fortunes. To sustain the heroes and annihilate the villains was the essential purpose of the good state. To separate the Jacksonian political wars into anti-Indian, antiabolitionist, and anti–soft money crusades is to miss Southern Jacksoni-ans' integrated assault on all the unnatural demons that threatened white farmers' natural enterprise.[5]

Much recent historical debate has focused on whether the West or the East most defined the Jackson movement. The debate blurs Southern Jacksonians' predominance. Jackson defined his own policies, including and especially his Bank War. His crude, rude Southwest supplied his largest majorities, as well as his conviction that each white frontiersman was equal to every other in political intelligence, his animus against paper money bankers, his Indian removals, and the proslavery impetus that soon dominated his movement.

True, eastern industrial dislocations generated intellectuals and laborers who favored hard money as much as Jackson did.[6] The more radical of these Northern Jacksonians sought to push economic egalitarianism beyond hard money, to secure inheritance taxes and shorter workdays. They scorned their Southern allies' anti-Indian and proslavery impulses.

---

[5]The problem is one of the several difficulties in Sean Wilentz's effort to resurrect an older "democratic" interpretation of the Jacksonian movement. While Professor Wilentz sees the Indian and slavery problems with that interpretation, he seeks to push these alleged Southern exceptions to the margins. But nothing was marginal about the undemocratic racism at the center of Jackson's view of the world. See Sean Wilentz, *The Rise of American Democracy: Jefferson to Lincoln* (New York, 2005).

[6]This side of Jacksonian democracy is wonderfully explained and detailed in Arthur M. Schlesinger, Jr., *The Age of Jackson* (New York, 1945). Schlesinger has suffered much criticism from those who think that a soft-money animus informed Jackson's Bank War. These critics miss the point. Although the Bank War, as they say, played into the hands of Jacksonians who favored uninhibited paper currency and unregulated economic development, that blow to hard money was an unintended consequence of Jackson's fumbling Bank War efforts. The real entrepreneurial triumph of Jacksonian statecraft came in its *non*banking economic politics,

They did not prevail. Jackson's statecraft everywhere yielded far more soft money than hard and no prolabor laws at all. Even Northern Jacksonians' attempts to abolish small paper bills, of the five-dollar variety, usually failed at the state level. In contrast, Southern Jacksonians swept Indians and abolitionists no less than Nicholas Biddle out of white capitalists' way.

By 1828, Indian removal served mostly Southern whites' economic advancement. Southern capitalists wanted powerful Creeks, Cherokees, and Seminoles out of their sight. Their man in the White House furthered their area's version of federal ethnic cleansing with his Indian Removal Act of 1830. This law authorized the president to trade land beyond the Mississippi River for Indian lands in eastern states and to pay for the departure of all tribes who agreed to leave. When the Cherokee majority rejected exile, Jacksonian officials cynically arranged a removal agreement with a rump minority in the 1835 Treaty of New Echota.

In 1838, when the Cherokee majority still refused exile, the U.S. Army collected the dissidents and dispatched them on a Trail of Tears to Oklahoma. Eighteen thousand Cherokees dragged along the trail. Four thousand of them perished. The survivors received only one acre of cheap Oklahoma land for every three acres of expensive eastern land expropriated from them.[7]

In his slavery policies as well, Jackson served Southern whites' ambitions. The main abolitionist attack on slavery emerged during Jackson's first administration, as the slaveholding president screeched at the supposed fanatics. Abolitionists' mailings to the South climaxed at the end of his second administration, as the president proposed federal censorship of the mails. Simultaneously, gag rules against abolitionists' petitions infested Jackson's last Congress: the Jackson party passed the silencers, and Northern anti-Jacksonians led the opposition (as Jackson's Yankee foes had led the opposition to Indian removal).[8]

Jackson's racial statecraft, like his economic statecraft, long survived his presidency. The Jackson policy of segregating Indians on reservations

---

involving a retreat from governmental intervention that Schlesinger too much ignores. For a more successful attempt to see Jacksonian hard-money bank reforms in the context of the nonbanking entrepreneurial activity that most Jacksonians placed beyond reformers' grasp (including and especially slaveholder capitalism), see Charles Sellers, *The Market Revolution: Jacksonian America, 1815–1846* (New York, 1991).

[7]On Jackson and Indians, see Michael Paul Rogin, *Fathers and Children* (New York, 1975), and Ronald N. Satz, *American Indian Policy in the Jacksonian Era* (Lincoln, Neb., 1975). For a more benign view on these matters than mine, see Robert Remini, *The Legacy of Andrew Jackson: Essays on Democracy, Indian Removal, and Slavery* (Baton Rouge, 1988).

[8]On the proslavery side of Jacksonian endeavor, see William W. Freehling, *The Road to Disunion*, 2 vols. (New York, 1990–2007).

continued for a century; the old reservations still remain a major habitat of American reds. Jackson's policy of using the federal government to contain the abolitionists spread like a weed in the 1845–60 period, replacing bank reform as the main thrust of Democratic party policy. Democrats provided the congressional majorities for proslavery legislation during the years before the Civil War, and Jackson's old Whig opponents provided most of the Republican opposition. Some Northern Jacksonians, inspired by his rhetoric of egalitarianism, moved beyond his proslavery policies to help the Republicans' anti–Slave Power appeal, just as some Northern Jacksonians had moved beyond his distinction between natural and artificial economic inequality in Bank War times. But once again, his majority disproportionately massed behind his limited version of *social* egalitarianism (so unlike his unlimited version of white men's *political* equality).

Jackson meant racial superiority to generate kindness. The Tennessee planter honestly thought himself the benevolent friend of his 161 slaves. He conceived that "his people" would starve without his paternalistic direction and that whites would annihilate reds without his merciful removals. The paternalist even adopted and raised an Indian son. The Great White Father here proudly acted not as the equal of the folk but as the patriarch of the inferiors.

If his paternalistic dominion represented exactly the aristocratic republican posture that he despised in white politics (and in Nicholas Biddle), his statecraft presumed that reds and blacks were different from whites. When Jackson asserted that "the humble members of society . . . have a right to complain" when "laws . . . make the rich richer," he did not include nonwhites in the humble folks who could complain. Nor did humble whites have a right to complain when the laws allowed natural entrepreneurs to further economic inequality. Poorer whites had only the right to try for Jackson's own rise from rags to riches, with no paper money bankers blocking their path and no government handouts favoring richer competitors. Because empowerment of natural capitalism was a central outcome of Jacksonian governance, the rich (except the rich bankers) had nothing to fear from Jackson's occasional class war polemic or from his voters who danced on his sofas.

What then can be salvaged of the case for Jackson's presidential greatness, based on his cry for egalitarianism? There remains his completion of the governmental shift from white men's aristocratic republicanism to white men's egalitarian republicanism, his dismantling of Nicholas Biddle's unequal and irresponsible power, his demonstration that regulators of the national economy must be responsible to the national state, and his efforts to curtail currency inequities. Perhaps some will think that these egalitarian crusades outweigh his 1832–36 banking wanderings, his narrow definition of white economic inequities, and his expansive consolidation of racial inequality. But others will wonder how his once formidable presidential reputation can ever be resurrected.

A PARTIAL RESURRECTION must look past his bank crisis to his nullification crisis, past the impure egalitarianism that limited his economic crusades to the pure Unionism that drove his unlimited antinullification heroics. Jackson's antinullification performance featured all the elements that define presidential greatness (and were missing in his banking performance): a major crisis, fully resolved; superb tactics, perfectly designed to achieve pristine goals; a disinterested initiative, risking trouble for his class and party; and a long-term impact, bolstering the best of his civilization.

South Carolina nullifiers, led by John C. Calhoun, provoked Jackson's greatest moment.[9] Enraged by a high protective tariff on which they blamed their severe economic travail and distressed by the abolitionist crusade that they spied before other Southerners, South Carolinians deployed a clever variation on Americans' unique theory of sovereignty. What branch of republican government, English republicans asked, was the ultimate sovereign, the final arbitrator? Americans replied that no government was sovereign. Sovereignty lay in the people, in their act of consenting to government.

South Carolinians pointed out that the people of each state, in state conventions or in state referendums, had initially consented to the federal Constitution. It followed, arguably, that the people of each state must continue to act as ultimate sovereigns on constitutional questions. Most Americans retorted that the U.S. Supreme Court must be the final constitutional arbiter. Yet the Court, pointed out the nullifiers, was but a branch of the agency. Only the creator of all governmental branches could properly judge what it had created. So the sovereign people of any state could declare any law of the federal agency unconstitutional and thus null and void in their locale.

---

[9] On the origins of nullification and the nature and tactics of Jackson's inspired opposition to the nullifiers, see William W. Freehling, *Prelude to Civil War: The Nullification Controversy in South Carolina* (New York, 1966).

Nullifiers conceded that three-fourths of the other sovereigns, in their state conventions assembled, could nullify the nullification by passing a constitutional amendment. The addition to the Constitution would grant the federal agency the late nullified power. The late nullifying state could then entirely withdraw its consent to be governed by legally seceding from the agency's governance. At no time in this nullification/secession process could governmental agents coercively overturn the sovereign's judgment.

In November 1832, the South Carolina nullifying convention put theory into action. The alleged sovereign declared that it had given its federal agency no constitutional right to pass tariffs protecting one portion of the people's economic activity at the expense of another's. Thus the federal protective tariffs of 1828 and 1832 were unconstitutional. If the agency coercively enforced the nullified laws in South Carolina, threatened the sovereign, the state would secede.

The rulers of this tiniest Lower South state had not sought, much less secured, any advance promise that even one Southern state would support their defiant stand. Once out on the limb, they found that all the slave states rejected the principle that a state (or any minority) could reject a national (or any majority) law and still stay in the Union (or any democratic government).

Jackson shared Southerners' outrage at nullification. He threatened to hang Calhoun and the nullifiers from a higher tree than Biddle and the Bank. He believed in the Union as a shining example of majority rule. If minority veto destroyed majority rule, the Union would lose its holy purpose. His anti-nullification propositions won such widespread applause in the South that the president had the power to isolate the South Carolinians if he affirmed only that no minority could veto a majority and still remain in a majoritarian government.

But South Carolina could break free from isolation if Jackson also challenged nullifiers' claimed right to secede. Most Southerners distinguished between a right to withdraw consent from one law and a right to withdraw consent from all laws. They saw themselves as sons of 1776. They claimed as much right to withdraw their consent from an unjust federal union as their forebears had to withdraw consent from an unjust British Empire. They saw their natural right to consent to a different government as a slaveholder's inalienable escape valve, forever preserving internal order against external meddlers. They also saw consent to governance as the crucial right that distinguished free citizens from unconsenting slaves. They would not allow

Jackson's coercion to enslave whites who withdrew consent. They urged the president to ignore South Carolina's threat of secession, defy the nullifiers' present deployment of state veto, and hope that mauled nullifiers would shrink from the next step.[10]

Many of Jackson's advisers, including Martin Van Buren, urged this politic evasion of South Carolina's secession threat. But the president scorned evasion. He believed that the Union provided every protection that a slaveholder would ever need. He conceived that a minority could no more withdraw consent from all the majority's laws than from any one decree. Either way, republican government meant no government. He must throw his full force at the full nullification/secession threat at its first moment, so that the entire monster would be annihilated, for his South's sake no less than his nation's. Thus he went indiscreetly out of his way in his December 1832 nullification proclamation to thunder against secession as well as against nullification.

His outburst somewhat leveled the Southern playing field, lately massively tilted in his favor. A minority of Southern Jacksonians, despising his cries against a state's right to depart the Union, deserted to the Whigs. The deserters, now calling themselves States' Rights Whigs, gave Jackson's opponents their first chance to win in the farthest South. The hemorrhage of Jacksonians away from Jackson could intensify—and could become a disaster to the Union no less than to the Jackson party's Southern power base— if the president's law enforcers slaughtered nullifiers and thus provoked a withdrawal from the Union. Jackson's verbal war against secession could sway Southern public opinion most effectively if no physical war occurred on nullification or if nullifiers fired discreditable first shots.

Jackson accordingly enforced the tariffs so cleverly that nullifiers stood barred from nullification, even if outcasts wished to put themselves obviously in the wrong. The president first asked South Carolina's opponents of nullification to enforce the nullified tariff. If South Carolinians negated each other, federal officials could stand above the fray.

Although South Carolina Unionists eventually shrank from enforcing Jackson's laws, the president still quarantined the nullifiers. He ordered the tariffs of 1828 and 1832 collected far off shore, using naval vessels outside

---

[10]On the formidable Southern resistance to and partial revolt against Jackson's stand on disunion, see Richard E. Ellis, *The Union at Risk: Jacksonian Democracy, States' Rights, and the Nullification Crisis* (New York, 1987).

Charleston's inner harbor. South Carolinians, lacking a navy, possessed no way to stop this tariff enforcement.

Meanwhile, Jackson shrewdly implicated Congress in his antinullification stratagems. His Whig opponents called him King Andrew, a non-American monarch who ruled by dictation. Jackson had in fact disrupted the balance of power between the presidency and Congress. He had seized control of the Bank by his own decrees, first vetoing the Bank recharter, then removing the deposits, then establishing the pet bank system, then issuing the Specie Circular, all without consulting Congress. His nullification proclamation threatened to put down nullification and secession by force, whatever Congress desired. This reestablishment of King Andrew's fiat could intensify the Southern revolt against the president. If the issue became despotic executive rule, the right to withdraw consent could become more precious.

Jackson would not allow the crisis to focus on alleged executive tyranny, just as he would not allow nullifiers to provoke a fight on the mainland. He invited Congress back into the political game. He asked congressional approval for whatever force might be necessary to enforce the tariff, although he believed he had adequate authority. He also asked Congress to lower the tariff to nonprotective levels. Then nullifiers, lacking the ships to nullify, would also lack any protective tariff to veto. His tariff plea to Congress further mollified restive Southerners, who wanted lower rates almost as much as the South Carolinians did.

Not only did King Andrew's bow to congressional power recalibrate the balance of executive-congressional authority, but his plea for congressional action also yielded a lesson in congressional decision making. As would happen during the Compromise of 1850, the congressional stars of the opposition to the Democratic party, this time Henry Clay and John C. Calhoun, seized the public limelight. Calhoun and Clay gave the historic orations and drafted the so-called Compromise Tariff, lowering the rates more slowly than Jackson had proposed.

But they could not deliver the votes. Clay's Northern Whig supporters opposed his lower rates, however compromised the reduction. Northern Jacksonians, in contrast, split almost evenly on the settlement, while 95 percent of Southern congressmen voted aye. The same coalition of half the Northern Jacksonians and almost all the Southerners (most of them Jacksonians) would pass almost all the proslavery legislation before the Civil War. The moral of this important story is that congressional analysts must watch who collects the votes in back rooms, a phenomenon often different than who makes speeches in the open air.

When Congress passed not only the Compromise Tariff but also the so-called Force Bill, endorsing presidential coercion of the nullifiers, Jackson's victory was complete. The isolated nullifiers accepted the Compromise Tariff but nullified the Force Bill. Yet they could no more enforce their newest nullification than carry out their original veto. Never again would a Southern state try nullification. Jackson had pulled off his provocative defiance of secession while still peaceably cornering the nullifiers.

LIKE HIS ECONOMIC philosophy, Jackson's unionist mandates remained crucial long after he retired to Tennessee. Antebellum South Carolinians remained the faction of the Southern upper class most pressing for a purely slaveholder nation. Yet the would-be rebels came away from their nullification debacle with a crippling fear of starting a revolution. They must never again go out alone on a limb, while all Southern states allowed them to spin in the wind. The memory of Jackson's isolating tactics prevented edgy South Carolinians from attempting disunion in 1850–52. Again in 1860, nervous South Carolina extremists shrank from precipitating the revolution, until they received reassurances that other states would follow.[11]

When they at last dared strike for a new nation on December 20, 1860, two successive presidents sought the mantle of Jackson's unionism. Once again, the outcome of the crisis hinged on whether Southerners would mass behind the first rebels. Once again, South Carolinians could best be cornered if no war occurred or if rebels fired the first shots against pacific federal law enforcers.

President James Buchanan purportedly shuddered to play Andrew Jackson in late December 1860, after U.S. Army Col. Robert Anderson occupied Fort Sumter, located inside Charleston's harbor. Actually, President Buchanan only briefly delayed. Colonel Anderson occupied Fort Sumter six days after South Carolina seceded. Buchanan ordered a reinforcing ship to sail for Charleston harbor less than six days later.

Buchanan played Jackson well by acting promptly, but badly, by dispatching military force provocatively. Jackson had enforced the nullified tariff laws

---

[11]On the importance of the memory of 1832 in the secession crises of 1850–52 and 1860–61, see Freehling, *Road to Disunion*, 1:528–33, 2:81–84, 352–426.

offshore, where no South Carolina guns could begin a civil war. Buchanan, in contrast, sent his *Star of the West* into the teeth of Charleston's defenses. True, his reinforcing soldiers hid beneath the *Star*'s deck. The deceit, however, could not match Jackson's cunning, not least because the *Star* flaunted its U.S. flag as the ship churned into Charleston's harbor, toward Fort Sumter's little island. The ensuing barrage of cannonballs would have started the Civil War then and there if the *Star*'s commanders had not turned her around toward the safe and open sea.

Buchanan's military intrusion helped precipitate more secessions. The six Lower South states beyond South Carolina, still deciding on disunion, found Buchanan's coercion outrageous. Their outrage helped to tip their decision on secession to the South Carolina side. By early February 1861, the seven southernmost states had all departed the Union.[12]

The eight Upper South states still clung to their nation. Buchanan, fearful of another false step, decided to stall. He would hand the status quo over to the recently elected Abraham Lincoln on Inauguration Day, March 4, 1861. Then the new president could try his hand at playing Jackson's high-stakes game.

Lincoln, unlike Buchanan, understood Jackson's game at least as well as had Jackson. The new president knew that to contain the erosion of Southern support for Union, he must enforce the Union's laws as peacefully as possible, allowing the rebels to fire any first shot. At first, Lincoln toyed with the Jacksonian gambit of enforcing the laws offshore. Then Lincoln decided on another strategy of peaceable law enforcement that exuded Jackson-style finesse. The commander in chief delayed a decision on whether to reinforce Fort Sumter. He meanwhile ordered the reinforcement of the only other major Lower South fort in federal possession, Fort Pickens near Pensacola, Florida (map 1).[13]

Unlike Fort Sumter, Fort Pickens's geographic situation made a peaceable reinforcement plausible. Reinforcing ships could approach the Pensacola island fort on its open Gulf side. The rebels' cannon, situated on the fort's mainland side, could not reach the rescuing federal vessels. Nor could the Florida militia easily reduce the reinforced fort. Mainland troops would have to cross the harbor waters to capture the fort. They possessed no vessels

---

[12]Ibid., 2:476–89.

[13]I will detail the largely untold and underappreciated Fort Pickens story in my forthcoming *Lincoln's Room for Growth: A Great President's Early Presidential Stumbles*.

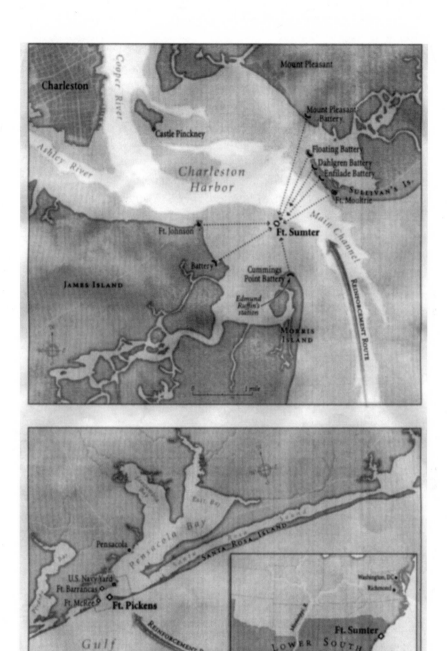

MAP 1. Forts Sumter and Pickens

remotely as powerful as the U.S. naval squadron that patrolled the area. Their plight could add up to 1832 revisited. Once again, federal law could be enforced beyond the range of rebels who lacked adequate ships to interfere. If the ploy allowed Lincoln to enforce the law peaceably at Fort Pickens, he could consider abandoning Fort Sumter.

The gambit fell victim to the irresponsibility of Lincoln's subordinates. His army and navy botched his Fort Pickens orders. Lincoln heard of the "fizzle" (his word) in late March, too late to correct the mistakes before a decision had to be made on Fort Sumter. There, Colonel Anderson and his men had little left to eat.

The president responded with yet another version of Jackson's clever moment.[14] Lincoln dispatched an early April messenger to South Carolina's governor, bearing the notice that U.S. vessels were en route to Fort Sumter. The ships would land only food for hungry men, promised Lincoln, unless rebels attacked the mercy expedition.

The rebels thus had to decide whether to fire guns against bread or whether to allow Captain Anderson's troops to be fed. If the federal soldiers were peaceably nourished, secession would be discredited. If rebels annihilated the Fort Sumter remnant of federal authority, they would be discredited aggressors. Then the Southern hemorrhage from the Union might be partially stemmed.

The Confederacy chose to reduce Fort Sumter before Lincoln's ships arrived. The rebels' successful bombardment smashed one Jackson objective but sustained another. While peace had been shattered, lawbreakers had fired the first shot. The president escaped much of the blame for the gunfire, and the northernmost Border South states tilted against the Confederacy. Their ultimate decision to remain in the Union provided Lincoln's army with crucial men, material, and geographic advantage. Thus did the legacy of Jackson's great presidential moment help save the Union almost three decades later.

DURING HIS OTHER epic presidential moments, Jackson's saved white men's egalitarian Union had usually sustained antiegalitarian social orders. His egalitarian shortfall emulated the American mainstream's. His political be-

---

[14]Lincoln's Fort Sumter strategies are detailed from different angles in Richard Current, *Lincoln and the First Shot* (Philadelphia, 1963); David Potter, *Lincoln and His Party in the Secession Crisis* (New Haven, 1942); and Kenneth M. Stampp, *And the War Came: The North and the Secession Crisis, 1860–1861* (Baton Rouge, 1950).

liefs, like his nation's, took *white* men's egalitarian *government* to its (racial) limits and far beyond the (class) limits of the Founding Fathers' aristocratic republicanism. His occasional class warfare rhetoric, like that of America's most radical reformers, swept egalitarianism beyond politics to society, promising to wither unnatural social inequality.

But his constricted definition of the unnatural excluded almost all of American social inequality from governmental assault. His limited banking reforms left Northern manufacturers and Southern slaveholders untouched. His racial agenda sanctioned governmental consolidation of reds' and blacks' natural inferiority. His persona, featuring the risen Horatio Alger as untrammeled hero, celebrated the independent cowboy on an uncontrolled range, a range stripped of Indians and peopled with slaves. This monument to American individualism had slaughtered the Bank, crushed the nullifiers, and impeded the secessionists. But that unacknowledged monster, his unimpeded racist capitalism, would haunt egalitarians for generations.

Bank War - unnatural inequality
racist capitalism - Indian removal & protecting
nullification - Unionism - J's greatest moment

Michael Les Benedict

States' Rights, State Sovereignty, and Nullification

THE CONFERENCE THAT led to the publication of this book was held at an opportune time and touched on two themes of growing importance in the historical study of American constitutionalism. First, the revival of conservative constitutionalism has reinvigorated debate over federalism—the nature of the relationship between the central government and those of the states.[1] Second, reacting to the Supreme Court's sweeping claim of final authority to declare the meaning of the Constitution,[2] constitutional scholars have begun to stress the role of other governmental institutions and the people themselves in determining how to interpret our fundamental law.[3] Orthodox American constitutional history teaches that in the first three decades of the nineteenth century, the Marshall Court, led by the great chief

---

[1]There is as yet no objective scholarly history of the revival of conservative constitutionalism. For an overview, see chapters 18 and 19 of my textbook, *The Blessings of Liberty: A Concise History of the United States*, 2d ed. (Lexington, Mass., 2005). For conservative constitutionalism's commitment to states' rights doctrines of federalism, see ibid. and David B. Walker, *The Rebirth of Federalism: Slouching toward Washington*, 2d ed. (New York, 2000), pp. 141–71. For overviews of the Supreme Court's revival of aspects of states' rights federalism, see Walker, *Rebirth of Federalism*, pp. 175–211; William E. Leuchtenburg, "The Tenth Amendment over Two Centuries: More than a Truism," in *The Tenth Amendment and State Sovereignty: Constitutional History and Contemporary Issues*, ed. Robert J. Kaczorowski (Lanham, Md., 2002), pp. 41–105, esp. pp. 51–105; or Mark V. Tushnet, "The Federalism Revolution," in *A Court Divided: The Rehnquist Court and the Future of Constitutional Law* (New York, 2005), pp. 249–78.

[2]See especially *City of Boerne v. Flores*, 521 U.S. 507 (1997).

[3]For example, Larry D. Kramer, *The People Themselves: Popular Constitutionalism and Judicial Review* (New York, 2004); Wayne D. Moore, *Constitutional Rights and Powers of the People* (Princeton, N.J., 1996); Mark V. Tushnet, *Taking the Constitution Away from the Courts* (Princeton, N.J.,

justice and his close associate Joseph Story, established the principle of national supremacy in American constitutional law. The casebooks assigned in
constitutional law courses reproduce the great nationalist decisions *McCulloch
v. Maryland,*[4] *Cohens v. Virginia,*[5] and *Gibbons v. Ogden,*[6] but with few exceptions
they ignore the debates over the nature of the federal Union that fill the
records of Congress.[7] Yet nationalist Supreme Court decisions were only a
part—and not the most important part—of the larger struggle to define
American federalism. Americans learned of the different interpretations of
federalism not only from the opinions of the Supreme Court but also from
congressional debates (which were reprinted in newspapers and circulated
as political pamphlets), presidential messages, and a wide-ranging polemical
literature. It was in the Jacksonian era, and during the nullification crisis,
that these arguments culminated in the articulation of three discrete understandings of the nature of the American Union: the nationalist, states' rights,
and state sovereignty doctrines of federalism.[8]

1999); and Keith E. Whittington, *Constitutional Construction: Divided Powers and Constitutional
Meaning* (Cambridge, Mass., 1999). See also "Symposium: Theories of Taking the Constitution Seriously Outside the Courts," *Fordham Law Review* 73 (2005):1341–476. In an essay of special relevance to the subject of this article, Gerald Leonard argues that the Jacksonian Democratic party was organized and conceived as a vehicle through which the American people
would reimpose what Jacksonians saw as the correct, states'-rights-oriented interpretation of
the Constitution, despite the Supreme Court's misguided nationalism. See Gerald Leonard,
"Party as a 'Political Safeguard of Federalism': Martin Van Buren and the Constitutional
Theory of Party Politics," *Rutgers Law Review* 54 (2001):221–81.

[4] *McCulloch v. Maryland,* 17 U.S. (4 Wheat.) 316 (1819).
[5] *Cohens v. Virginia,* 9 U.S. (6 Wheat.) 264 (1821).
[6] *Gibbons v. Ogden,* 22 U.S. (9 Wheat.) 1 (1824).
[7] See, for example, Jesse H. Choper et al., *The American Constitution: Cases, Comments, Questions,* 9th ed. (St. Paul, Minn., 2001); and Lee Epstein and Thomas G. Walker, *Constitutional
Law for a Changing America: Institutional Powers and Constraints,* 4th ed. (Washington, D.C., 2001).

[8] Amazingly, there is no in-depth scholarly history of federalism in the United States. In
American Theories of Federalism (University, Ala., 1964), Walter Hartwell Bennett devotes 176 of his
220 pages to pre–Civil War developments, barely touching on the twentieth century. Forrest
McDonald's *States' Rights and the Union: Imperium in Imperio, 1776–1876* (Lawrence, Kans., 2000)
takes the story only through the Civil War era and barely attends to coherent constitutional theory at all. The best historical overview is David B. Walker, *Rebirth of Federalism,* noted above.
   Historians began to attend to issues of federalism in the early nineteenth century. Andrew
C. Lenner's *The Federal Principle in American Politics, 1790–1833* (Lanham, Md., 2001) recognizes
that Americans divided over three theories of federalism but eschews careful theoretical
analysis of the difference, painting in broad strokes instead. John Lauritz Larson discusses the
constitutional issues surrounding internal improvements in the early republic in *Internal Improvement: National Public Works and the Promise of Popular Government in the Early United States*
(Chapel Hill, N.C., 2001). Richard Ellis attends to theories of federalism in his classic *The
Union at Risk: Jacksonian Democracy, States' Rights, and the Nullification Crisis* (New York, 1987).

Understanding Federalism

A federal system is one in which separate and interdependent governments have responsibility for different aspects of public policy. The state or provincial governments are not subordinate to the central government but have independent authority, which in some areas is final and beyond the power of the central government to countermand. The central government has final authority in other areas. In the United States, those areas are specified in the Constitution, which also provides that where state and federal authority overlap, the central government's power is supreme. Thus, American federalism is essentially about where democratic decisions regarding public policy on different subjects will be made. Will they be made by state governments, or local governments if the states have delegated authority to them, or will they be made by the federal government? The governments of the United States, state and federal, are democracies. Majorities will make the decisions (although of course the system is more complex than that—we rarely have direct democratic decision making). But which majority? Will a particular decision be made by government agencies responsible only to the citizens of a locality or a state? Or will it be made by government agencies responsible to a national majority—Congress, the president, the federal bureaucracy?

This is more than a theoretical issue. Where decisions are made can critically affect the outcome of a particular issue. Federalism gives a right to both the people of each state and individual Americans to have decisions affecting public policy made in the appropriate forum. A state's interests are more likely to be served by making as many decisions as possible within the state. For example, my state of Ohio once had a thriving coal-mining industry, which supplied electric power generating plants in Ohio and neighboring states. Unfortunately, Ohio's coal has a high sulfur content. The resulting pollution affects our own people, but our prevailing winds blow from west to east, affecting New Yorkers and New Englanders as well. Given the importance of the coal industry to the state's economy, Ohioans may be willing to bear the burden of its attendant pollution. New Yorkers and New Englanders do not get as much of the economic benefit and consequently are less happy to suffer the acid rain and health-damaging pollutants. However, our suffering neighbors have little input into our decision making. Besides just asking us to be considerate, at the expense of thousands of jobs, there is little they can do to influence our legislators.

But of course they can ask Congress to pass antipollution laws. New awareness of how automobile emissions contribute to pollution led to the passage, by overwhelming majorities, of the Clean Air Act of 1970, which amended earlier clean air acts. That law and later amendments authorized the Environmental Protection Agency to specify levels of allowable pollutants far beyond those produced by vehicles. When the agency acted to protect the environment from acid rain, it devastated Ohio's coal industry.[9] Not realizing the potential consequences of the law, Ohio's congressional delegation had joined the almost unanimous support for it. Had they been more prescient, Ohio's representatives might have argued that how to deal with industrial pollution is not a decision to be made by the federal government but one that the Constitution reserves to the states. Whether to make such an argument would have depended upon a number of things:

1. How much are *Ohioans* affected by things that *other* states do that we want to have a say in through our influence in the federal government?

2. How much would we benefit in other ways by conceding broad authority to the federal government? Would it help pay for things we could not ourselves afford?[10]

3. Have we already taken a firm position on similar questions in the past? Do we have an intellectual and emotional stake in one or another theory of federal power based on past conflicts?

4. Is there already a clear rule established in this case or similar cases? Is there much of a chance of convincing others that our view of federal power over pollution is constitutionally correct? Would we be undermining the rule of law by changing or evading the dominant rule? And do we care?

If Ohioans were going to challenge the constitutional authority of the federal government to regulate the emission of pollution in Ohio, where would they go to make the argument? We often think of constitutional issues as *legal* issues to be settled in courts, but the first place Ohio's representatives would

---

[9]Coal production in Ohio peaked in 1970. Since the passage of the Clean Air Act of 1970 and its successor amendments, production has plunged 51 percent. Douglas L. Crowell, "History of Coal Mining in Ohio," *GeoFacts No. 14*, posted by the Ohio Department of Natural Resources, http://www.ohiodnr.com/geosurvey/geo_fact/geo_f14.htm. For an account of the devastation, see "Coal Mines Cling to Hope That Mines Will Reopen," *Columbus Dispatch*, Oct. 20, 1985.

[10]For example, in 1985 Ohio representatives worked to earmark five hundred million federal dollars to support research in cleaning high-sulfur coal (*Columbus Dispatch*, Aug. 1, 1985; Dec. 17, 1985).

consider making the argument would be in the bodies considering the leg-islation. They would have to argue that decisions about how to fuel power plants were within the jurisdiction of the state and not that of the federal government—that it was a state's right to make that decision and not Con-gress's. To sustain that position, they would have to make arguments that sound rather legal. They would point out previous decisions in Congress to abstain from analogous legislation. They would distinguish prior examples in which Congress did act from the present proposition. If the courts had ruled on a similar question, they would cite the case if it sustained the states' rights position. If a decision seemed to support the other side, they would try to distinguish the circumstances. If Ohio lost the struggle in Congress, somebody affected by the new antipollution law could challenge it in court, no doubt using many of the same legal arguments articulated in Congress. But if Ohioans won in Congress, the issue would never get to court, and a precedent would have been established outside the judicial system. It would not be a legal precedent binding on the courts. But it ought to be what courts call "persuasive."[11]

The foregoing has described what can be called "constitutional politics" —the reliance on fundamental constitutional principles to secure a particu-lar interest—a notion well-developed among scholars and analysts outside the United States.[12] It involves more than making arguments in courts and

---

[11]The foregoing account of federalism issues in making public policy differs somewhat from others. Martha Derthick, a prolific analyst of federalism in public policy, treats Congress and the states more as discrete entities, Congress having the power to determine what role the states will play in the administration of public policy. See her survey chapter, "Enduring Fea-tures," in *Keeping the Compound Republic: Essays on American Federalism* (Washington, D.C., 2001), pp. 35–42. For her thoughtful overview of American federalism in historical context, see "How Many Communities?" ibid., pp. 9–32. My own stress on how the people of the states utilize the federal government to affect the conduct of the people of other states bears more resemblance to Jesse H. Choper's account in *Judicial Review and the National Political Process: A Functional Re-consideration of the Role of the Supreme Court* (Chicago, 1980).

[12]For the application of the idea to the United States, see G. Alan Tarr, ed., *Constitutional Politics in the States: Contemporary Controversies and Historical Patterns* (Westport, Conn., 1996); Peter W. Schramm and Bradford P. Wilson, eds., *American Political Parties and Constitutional Poli-tics* (Lanham, Md., 1993); Wayne D. Moore, "Constitutional Citizenship," in *Constitutional Poli-tics: Essays on Constitution Making, Maintenance, and Change*, ed. Sotirios A. Barber and Robert P. George (Princeton, N.J., 2001), pp. 238–60. A main focus of those analyzing "constitutional politics" is how interests are secured through programmatic litigation. See, for example, Alec Stone Sweet, *Governing with Judges: Constitutional Politics in Europe* (Oxford, 2000). By constitu-tional politics I mean something broader—efforts to secure interests by claiming them as fundamental rights before the public and before all varieties of government institutions. Courts are only one forum for constitutional politics so conceived.

Congress. It involves creating a public opinion, bringing the debate to the public sphere in general. Newspapers take editorial stands, people write books and articles. And in the example outlined above, when appealing to the public beyond the states whose immediate interests are involved, asserting a general principle about where decisions ought to be made is a lot more attractive than defending pollution. In response, supporters of federal legislation will point to the number of situations in which residents of any state might need to turn to the federal government to protect themselves from decisions of neighboring states.

In reality, Congress considered the Clean Air Act of 1970 at a time when doctrines of states' rights were largely discredited outside the South. They were identified with racial segregation and opposition to the general-welfare legislation of the New Deal. It hardly seems to have occurred to doubters to raise federalism issues (even though the first clean air acts of the 1960s applied to automobile emissions at least in part because they implicated interstate commerce, an area over which the federal government has broad authority).[13] Indeed, no one seems to have objected that the 1970 law took the unusual step of ordering the states to establish antipollution rules and agencies. Opposition to the law developed as its disparate effects became apparent: the division between midwesterners and New Englanders over sulfur and acid rain was especially sharp.[14] But critics stressed other constitutional issues.[15] As states' rights notions of federalism have revived in recent decades, however, Ohio's members of Congress, especially Sen. George Voinovich, have come to stress the benefits of letting states deal with their own pollution problems, in what observers call "Ohio's 30-year war with the Clean Air Act."[16] Moreover, opponents have launched legal challenges on the grounds

[13]Christopher J. Bailey, *Congress and Air Pollution: Environmental Policies in the USA* (Manchester, Eng., 1998).

[14]Ibid., pp. 220–26; Gary C. Bryner, *Blue Skies, Green Politics: The Clean Air Act of 1990* (Washington, D.C., 1993), pp. 91–93.

[15]Rather than appeal to states' rights, Ohio and other opponents of the Clean Air Act argued that Congress had violated the Constitution by delegating the Environmental Protection Agency too much unconstrained authority to administer the law, succeeding in the lower courts but losing in the Supreme Court. For a partisan account, see Frank O'Donnell, "Special Report: Clean Air Act under Siege," September 18, 2000, Clean Air Trust, http://www.cleanairtrust.org/villain.0400.html. See *Whitman v. American Trucking Associations*, 531 U.S. 457 (2001).

[16]Margaret Newkirk and Bob Downing, "Power to Pollute—Clearing the Air," *Akron Beacon Journal*, Jan. 7, 2001, posted by Environmental Health Watch, http://www.ehw.org/Air_Pollution/AIR_AkronBeaconJournal.htm. See the summary of the Clean Air Act hearings of May 20, 1999, and June 24, 1999, posted by the Government Affairs Program of the American Geological Institute, http://www.agiweb.org/gap/legis106/cleanair_hearings.html.

that the Clean Air Act unconstitutionally commandeers the agencies of the sovereign states to carry out federal programs, in violation of the Tenth Amendment and general principles of federalism.[17]

Constitutional Politics in the Early Republic and the Jacksonian Era

While constitutional issues of federal power were raised far less often in Congress after the New Deal than they had been before that watershed era, the description of how different notions of federalism might affect efforts to secure national antipollution legislation reflects the reality of public policy in the nineteenth century. Americans' intense constitutionalism encouraged advocates and opponents of almost any public policy to make constitutional arguments. As Alexis de Tocqueville famously observed, parties to political controversies "borrow . . . the ideas, and even the language, peculiar to judicial proceedings." He thought that the reason was that "scarcely any political question arises in the United States that is not resolved, sooner or later, into a judicial question."[18] But the Frenchman got it backwards. In the nineteenth century, political questions resolved into judicial ones because Americans thought in constitutional terms, and they more and more conceived constitutional issues to be legal issues. That being so, it was natural to turn to the courts as well as to the other institutions of government to secure one's goals. Still, it was true that framing the issues in legal and constitutional terms gave the courts a special influence in the process. Judges were conceded special knowledge of the law, and they staked a special claim to its interpretation. As Chief Justice Marshall averred in his claim that courts were obligated to consider the constitutionality of the legislation they were asked to enforce, "It is emphatically the province and duty of the judicial

---

[17]*Friends of the Earth v. Carey*, 552 F.2d 25 (2d Cir. 1977); *Virginia v. Browner*, 80 F.3d 869 (4th Cir. 1996); *Virginia v. EPA*, 108 F.3d 1397 (D.C. Cir. 1997). For the rise and legal effect of federalism concerns about the Clean Air Act and other environmental regulation, see Richard J. Lazarus, *The Making of Environmental Law* (Chicago, 2004), pp. 91–94, 135–37, 204–6. See David D. Salmon, "The Federalist Principle: The Interaction of the Commerce Clause and the Tenth Amendment in the Clean Air Act," *Columbia Journal of Environmental Law* 2 (1976):290–367, for an early argument that the Clean Air Act violated Tenth Amendment limits on federal power and a reference to some early cases raising the issue.

[18]Alexis de Tocqueville, *Democracy in America*, 2 vols. (New York, 1946), 2:280.

department to say what the law is."[19] At the height of the Marshall Court's power, its authority seemed formidable indeed. "The peace, prosperity, and the very existence of the Union is vested in the hands of seven Federal judges," Tocqueville told his readers. "Without them the Constitution would be a dead letter."[20]

But that was a great exaggeration, reflecting the concerns of conservative lawyers worried by the growing criticism of the Court's nationalism that had helped to propel Jackson into the White House. In fact, constitutional debates over public policy were wide ranging. They went far beyond Congress and the courts. Newspapers took editorial stands. Advocates wrote pamphlets. Newspapers reprinted congressional speeches. Congressmen had their speeches printed up in pamphlet form and circulated, especially to their constituents, aided by the congressional "franking privilege"—the right of congressmen to send mail on public issues without paying postage. By the 1840s, political parties supported and paid for the printing and the circulation of partisan newspapers that promoted their constitutional principles. The very first Democratic party platform began by affirming "that the federal government is one of limited powers, derived solely from the constitution, and the grants of power shown therein, ought to be strictly construed." The following two planks both began with "the Constitution does not confer upon the general government the power to . . . ." The resolutions were repeated verbatim for the next sixteen years.[21] This sort of constitutional politics was the rule throughout the nineteenth century. Sobered by the Jacksonian reaction, the courts acted with restraint, rarely challenging predominant popular notions of constitutionalism. The one great exception —the Court's ill-considered effort to settle the constitutionality of legislation

---

[19]*Marbury v. Madison*, 5 U.S. (1 Cranch.) 137, 177 (1803). Nowadays, *Marbury v. Madison* is often held to mean that the Supreme Court has the primary, and even final, responsibility for assessing the constitutionality of legislation. A considered reading demonstrates that the Court's claim was more modest—that it was not obligated to enforce a law even though the justices believed it to be unconstitutional. In other words, the Court was claiming that it had the same obligation to observe constitutional limits as the other branches of government. Of course, the justices knew that this would give them great authority, both because of their special claim to legal knowledge and as the last expositor of the law in terms of its practical application.

[20]Tocqueville, *Democracy in America*, 2:151.

[21]Democratic platforms of 1840, 1844, 1848, and 1856. The platforms may be found online at the American Presidency Project, University of Santa Barbara, http://www.presidency .ucsb.edu/platforms.php, or in *National Party Platforms, 1840–1872*, comp. Donald Bruce Johnson and Kirk H. Porter, (Urbana, Ill., 1973), or earlier editions.

to ban slavery in the territories in the Dred Scott case—demonstrated the limits of its authority.[22] Not until late in the century did courts, especially the U.S. Supreme Court, even begin to play the role that it does today in determining constitutional rules.

It was in this general environment that the major Jacksonian-era developments in theories of federalism took place. Jackson's election as president was directly related to bitter struggles over the nature of the Union and the extent of federal power that had roiled politics over the previous decades. These struggles related to fundamental social and economic issues. Most of them had taken place in Congress and in the public sphere. By the time Jackson campaigned for the presidency in 1824 and 1828, they had led to the crystallization of two competing doctrines of American federalism.[23]

Perhaps the best known of the controversies is the conflict over the establishment of a national bank, a debate that had already been going on for nearly forty years and that would continue for decades more. In a decision directly related to the encouragement of modern commercial capitalism, Congress established the first national bank in 1791, with a charter to run for twenty years. It was because constitutional objections had been raised to establishing the Bank in the first Congress that President George Washington had asked the members of his cabinet for their opinions.[24] The letters that Secretary of the Treasury Alexander Hamilton and Secretary of State

---

[22]*Scott v. Sandford*, 60 U.S. (19 How.) 393 (1857). Earlier cases creating constitutional bulwarks for slavery, such as *Prigg v. Pennsylvania*, 41 U.S. (16 Pet.) 539 (1842), which upheld the constitutionality of the Fugitive Slave Act and ruled inconsistent state legislation unconstitutional, reflected dominant opinion. See generally Don E. Fehrenbacher, *The Slaveholding Republic: An Account of the United States Government's Relations to Slavery*, completed and edited by Ward M. McAfee (New York, 2001); Robert M. Cover, *Slavery Accused: Antislavery and the Judicial Process* (New Haven, Conn., 1975).

[23]In his *Federal Principle in American Politics*, Andrew C. Lenner discerns divisions among those who focused on states' rights and sovereignty in the federal system. While such nuances did exist, Americans generally perceived two positions until the Jacksonian era—one nationalistic and one that exalted the states. The nullification controversy precipitated a clear break in states' rights/state sovereignty ranks; looking back from that event, one can see the origins of the Jacksonian position in what Lenner identifies as the moderate Republican position.

[24]A number of congressmen challenged the constitutionality of the proposed bank. Madison offered a detailed constitutional critique that prefigured the objections that Jefferson articulated in his more famous opinion in response to Washington's query (*Annals of Congress*, 1st Cong., 3d sess., Feb. 2, 1791, 1944–52). The whole debate is in the *Annals* from February 1 through February 8. M[atthew] St. Clair Clarke and D. A. Hall compiled a *Legislative and Documentary History of the Bank of the United States* (Washington, D.C., 1832), which was republished by Augustus M. Kelly Publishers of New York in 1967. It is a handy compendium of materials. The original publication itself is a tribute to the popular constitutionalism of the times.

Thomas Jefferson wrote in response even today remain founding documents of nationalist and states' rights constitutionalism respectively.

Hamilton argued that the Constitution delegated complete and sovereign powers to the central government of the United States and that the explicit delegation of "all powers necessary and proper" to carry out the enumerated substantive powers (Article I, Section 8) made this clear. Thus the only question was whether a power was delegated. If it were, the central government could exercise it to the same extent as any sovereign government.[25]

Jefferson saw Hamilton's plans to promote commercial development as duplicating the corrupt British system in which government guaranteed the privileged few the power to live off the exploited many. Like other enlightened radicals of the age, he wanted to prevent government from granting special privileges that deprived ordinary people of the opportunity to harness their own energies for their own advancement. So he argued that the reference to "all powers necessary and proper" to carrying out the substantive powers was a *restriction* on the government's power, not a further delegation of it. To bolster that interpretation he quoted what became the Tenth Amendment. "I consider the foundation of the Constitution as laid on this ground: that 'all powers not delegated to the United States, by the Constitution . . . are reserved to the states or to the people.' To take a single step beyond the boundaries thus specially drawn around the powers of Congress, is to take possession of a boundless field of power, no longer susceptible to any definition." Hamilton's latitudinarian construction would permit Congress "to break down the most ancient and fundamental laws of the several states."[26]

So as early as 1791, three years after the Constitution was ratified, Jefferson at least implicitly articulated two of the main tenets of what became the state sovereignty and states' rights doctrines of federalism: (1) that there be "strict construction" of the powers of Congress and (2) that the powers delegated to Congress be interpreted in light of the jurisdiction of the states, as mandated by the Tenth Amendment.

Washington agreed with Hamilton and signed the bill, making it law and a powerful precedent for nationalist constitutionalism. That precedent was

---

[25]Henry Cabot Lodge, ed., *The Works of Alexander Hamilton*, 9 vols. (New York, 1904), 3:445–94.

[26]Paul Leicester Ford, ed., *The Writings of Thomas Jefferson*, 10 vols. (New York, 1892–99), 5:145–53.

vitiated by congressional refusal to continue the Bank when its original charter lapsed in 1811. But note that throughout the Bank's twenty-year existence,
the issue of the its constitutionality was never tested in the Supreme Court.
Rather it was fought out in Congress in the recharter fight in 1811 and then
from 1815 to 1816 when Congress considered and finally chartered a second
national bank, in another affirmation of nationalist constitutionalism made
that much more objectionable to states' rights–oriented opponents because
it was passed by a Congress dominated by Jeffersonian Republicans, the
party originally dedicated to states' rights.[27]

Issues of federalism continued to be contested through constitutional politics, not through the courts. States' rights versus broad national power was
a key issue separating Federalists from Jefferson's Republicans in the 1790s.
The Republicans further developed the states' rights doctrine in their response to the Alien and Sedition Acts, passed in 1798 to counteract their
efforts to displace the Federalists in the elections of 1800. Republican leader
Albert Gallatin stressed the importance of the Tenth Amendment (referring to it as the Twelfth, its original number among the Bill of Rights Congress sent to the states for ratification). That amendment reserved to the
states or people all powers not delegated to the federal government. The
Constitution nowhere expressly delegated control over friendly aliens to the
federal government (as distinct from "enemy aliens," the subjects of states
with which the nation was at war), nor was the exercise of such control
"necessary and proper" to carry out expressly delegated powers. Thus the
amendment reserved them to the states. "The amendment to the Constitution above cited was positively introduced to prevent the General Government from assuming powers which were never intended to be given to it."[28]
That the federal government had no power over seditious libel was even
clearer; it was explicitly denied the power to infringe freedom of speech by
the First Amendment.[29] According to the Tenth Amendment, that power
too was reserved to the states.

---

[27]The extensive arguments over the constitutionality of rechartering the first bank, and of
later efforts to reestablish a national bank, are reprinted in Clarke and Hall, *Legislative and Documentary History of the United States Bank*, pp. 138–471, 472–713.

[28]*Annals*, 5th Cong, 2d sess., June 16, 1798, 1956.

[29]David P. Currie briefly, and rather superficially, describes the constitutional debates over
the Alien and Sedition Acts in *The Constitution in Congress: The Federalist Period, 1789–1801*
(Chicago, 1997), pp. 254–62. Better but ranging beyond the congressional debates is Lenner,
Federal Principle in American Politics, pp. 62–72.

In resolutions passed by the Kentucky and Virginia state legislatures in 1798 and 1799 and in Madison's report on the resolutions in 1800, Republicans articulated the proposition that the Constitution was a compact among the sovereign states to which the states were parties, adding a third component to the states' rights understanding of federalism. Taking their ideas a step further, Jefferson, Madison, and their allies in the Kentucky and Virginia legislatures claimed that the states had an ill-defined obligation to "interpose" to protect the liberties of their citizens against central government usurpations.[30]

The Kentucky and Virginia Resolutions themselves were a manifestation of constitutional politics—the "Principles of '98," as Jeffersonian Republicans would refer to them for another generation—and they elicited an appropriately political response from Federalist-dominated state legislatures. Defending both the policy and the constitutionality of the Alien and Sedition Acts, the Massachusetts state legislature denied the proposition that the states had created the Union. It was "the people themselves" who "by a solemn compact, have exclusively committed their national concerns" to the government of the United States.[31] Pennsylvania warned Virginia that "no portion of the people can assume the province of the whole, nor resist the expression of its combined will"—assuming that the American people constituted a whole of which Virginians were merely a part.[32] Most of the responding legislatures resolved that the courts (staffed, of course, by good Federalists) rather than the state legislatures were the appropriate body to rule on the constitutionality of legislation.[33]

The congressional and presidential elections of 1800 turned on the constitutional issues raised in the 1790s. When Republicans won these and

---

[30]Kentucky Resolutions, in Julian P. Boyd et al., eds., *The Papers of Thomas Jefferson*, 31 vols. to date (Princeton, N.J., 1950–), 30:550–55; Virginia Resolutions of 1798, in William T. Hutchinson et al., eds., *Papers of James Madison* 17 vols. (Chicago, 1962–91), 17:185–91; Report of 1800, ibid., 17:303–51. See, alternatively, *The Virginia Report of 1799–1800: Touching the Alien and Sedition Laws, Together with the Virginia Resolutions of December 21, 1798 . . .* (1850; reprint ed., New York, 1970), which reprints the Kentucky Resolutions as well as debates on the resolutions in the Virginia state legislature.

[31]Herman V. Ames, ed., *State Documents on Federal Relations: The States and The United States* (1906; reprint ed., New York, 1970), p. 18.

[32]Ibid., p. 21.

[33]Rhode Island, Massachusetts, Pennsylvania, New York, New Hampshire, and Vermont joined Massachusetts in asserting that the responsibility for declaring laws unconstitutional lay with the judiciary rather than the state legislatures. Ibid., pp. 17, 18, 20, 23, 25, 26.

subsequent elections, they saw their victories as vindications of the Principles of '98.[34] Although presidents Jefferson and Madison, as well as Gallatin, who served as secretary of the Treasury through both administrations, advocated federal programs that dismayed more purist allies, the nationalistic constitutionalism of the Federalists was checked. Nothing made this clearer than the refusal to renew a revised national bank charter in 1811, despite Gallatin's endorsement. Pennsylvania paraphrased Jefferson's Kentucky Resolutions in sending its protest to Congress. Having ventilated the issue thoroughly twenty years earlier, Virginia's resolution was terse: the proposal was "a dangerous encroachment on the sovereignty of the states."[35] Rep. William A. Burwell of Virginia warned, "In the administration of this Government, two things alone are necessary to ensure its durability. You must, 1st, avoid every measure which will produce uneasiness among the States; or, 2d, that will extend the jurisdiction of the United States Government to subjects purely local."[36] "The Federal Government . . . is, *imperium in imperio,* a government within a government," Rep. Peter B. Porter of New York observed, "and the misfortune is, that there exists no friendly third power to decide the controversies which may arise between these two great, independent, and, in may respects, rival authorities." (Note the casual rejection of the Federalist notion that questions of constitutionality were reserved to the federal judiciary, articulated in the war of state legislative resolutions over the Alien and Sedition Acts.) Like Burwell, Porter warned that peace could be kept between the federal and state governments only "by the conciliatory dispositions of the parties themselves." Congress "ought to act with great circumspection and delicacy, in the assumption of powers which do not clearly belong to us."[37]

Not only was it necessary to construe federal powers strictly, but even if one also conceded that the authority to charter a bank could be implied from the expressly delegated powers, there were insuperable constitutional objections: "There are certain powers which may be said to belong peculiarly and exclusively to the State Governments; and certain other powers

[34]See Michael Les Benedict, "The Jeffersonian Republicans and American Liberty," in *Essays on the History of Liberty: Seaver Institute Lectures at the Huntington Library* (San Marino, Calif., 1988), pp. 23–41.

[35]Ames, *State Documents on Federal Relations,* pp. 52–54 (Pennsylvania), 54 (Virginia).

[36]*Annals,* 11th Cong., 3d sess., Jan. 16, 1811, 585.

[37]Ibid., Jan. 18, 1811, pp. 628–29.

which may be said to belong peculiarly and exclusively to the Federal Government." Erecting banking corporations were among the former, "connected immediately, necessarily and inseparably with the internal political economy of the State."[38] Thus Porter made clear what had been implicit in the Kentucky and Virginia Resolutions—that the constitutional reservation of powers to the states, explicitly articulated in the Tenth Amendment, limited the exercise even of powers that the Constitution did delegate to the federal government—the heart of what constitutional scholars would come to call "dual federalism." He especially urged his more latitudinarian Republican colleagues "to beware how they familiarize themselves with the doctrine of constructive power. It is a creed at war with the vital principles of political liberty."[39]

Futilely, Federalists repeated the arguments Hamilton had made in defense of the original bank charter. Republican supporters of the recharter worried about "extremes on this subject." Affirming their commitment to states' rights, they worried, "Whilst we are guarding against *Scylla*, with care and solicitude, is there no danger of falling on *Charybdis?* Are not the power and influence of some of the States now almost paramount to the power and influence of the General Government?"[40] Congress's refusal to renew the bank charter reflected the dominant popular interpretation of the Constitution, a public opinion that sustained states' rights–oriented Republicans with votes. It was the people's interpretation, "whatever may be the opinion of the gentlemen of the *long robe*," as Porter put it, and as practically effective as any Supreme Court decision.[41]

To the dismay of states' rights purists, Republicans' commitment to the Principles of '98 eroded. The difficulties of financing and fighting the War of 1812 clearly affected many. By the mid-1810s a new generation of Republicans, represented by Henry Clay of Kentucky, John C. Calhoun of South Carolina, and John Quincy Adams of Massachusetts, advocated government promotion of a vibrant commercial economy free of English influence. As part of their program, in 1816 they established a second national bank.

---

[38]Ibid., pp. 645–46.

[39]Ibid., p. 646.

[40]Ibid., Jan. 24, 1811, p. 822.

[41]Ibid., Jan. 18, 1811, p. 642. The congressional debate over rechartering the national bank is reprinted conveniently in Clarke and Hall, *Legislative and Documentary History of the Bank of the United States*, pp. 115–471.

Although a number of congressmen indicated that they opposed reestablishing a bank on constitutional grounds, the House quickly and overwhelmingly agreed to a resolution affirming the expediency of creating a national bank with branches in the states.[42] After that, debate turned primarily to the exact contours the bank would take. When opponents again tried to derail the project on constitutional grounds, they were amazed by "the apathy which pervaded the House" as it prepared to vote the objections down with hardly any debate.[43]

Although President James Madison vetoed the bill, he waived his constitutional objections in light of "repeated recognitions under varied circumstances of the validity of such an institution in acts of the legislative, executive, and judicial branches of the government."[44] Even John Taylor, the Republican purist who blasted the national bank in his *Inquiry into the Principles and Policy of the Government of the United States,* objected to it as a massive transfer of wealth from the people to a moneyed aristocracy rather than as a violation of states' rights.[45] When Calhoun brought forward a bill designed to meet Madison's practical objections, he eschewed constitutional arguments. "To discuss these questions . . . would be a useless consumption of time."[46] Those who remained doubtful conceded that the question of constitutionality "which has heretofore been the occasion of so much heated controversy . . . is now at rest."[47]

Dismissing the importance of constitutional issues in the bank debates, nationalist Republicans could avoid acknowledging that they had in practice adopted the constitutional position of their old Federalist opponents. But the financial crisis and resulting depression of 1819 revived opposition to the Bank. States like Ohio, Kentucky, and Maryland determined to use their own sovereign powers to frustrate its operations within their boundaries by levying taxes on its local branches and arresting bank officers if they refused to comply. Within their own boundaries, states had a sovereign

---

[42]*Annals,* 13th Cong., 3d sess., Oct. 28, 1814, 498–99.

[43]Ibid., Dec. 14, 1814, p. 987. The *Annals* report makes almost no allusion to the constitutionality of the measure in the Senate. The course of debates in Congress is followed most easily in Clarke and Hall, *Legislative and Documentary History of the Bank of the United States,* pp. 472–585.

[44]James D. Richardson, comp., *A Compilation of Messages and Papers of the Presidents,* 20 vols. (New York, 1897), 2:540 (hereafter *Messages and Papers of the Presidents*).

[45]John Taylor, *An Inquiry into the Principles and Policy of the Government of the United States* (Fredericksburg, Va., 1814), pp. 253–342.

[46]*Annals,* 14th Cong., 1st sess., Feb. 26, 1816, 1460.

[47]Sen. William H. Wells, ibid., Apr. 1, 1816, p. 259.

power to tax and an equally sovereign "police power" to regulate, state officials insisted. The Tenth Amendment, reserving nondelegated powers to
the states, signified the intention to maintain these powers unimpaired under
the Constitution, to maintain a dual system of federalism. As Maryland's
counsel put it, "The exercise of one sovereign power cannot be controlled
by the exercise of another."[48] Federal laws and their enforcement must be
tailored to avoid collisions with these sovereign state powers.[49]

Conflicts over other nationalist public policies led to similar articulations of the two alternative theories of federalism. Nationalist Republicans
urged internal improvements to develop a national transportation network.
Emblematic was construction of the Cumberland Road—the National Road
—from Cumberland, Maryland (already connected to Baltimore), to the
West. It, like similar proposals, elicited hundreds of pages of constitutional
debate in Congress, as well as vetoes from two presidents.[50] Nationalist Republicans revised customs duties to encourage the development of American
industry and agriculture free of British influence. At first conceding the constitutionality, if not the wisdom, of a protective tariff,[51] by 1823 its opponents were arguing for strict construction of Congress's power to collect duties. "The power granted . . . is a power to raise revenue for the purpose of

---

[48]*McCulloch v. Maryland*, 17 U.S. (4 Wheat.) 316, 370 (1819).

[49]See generally the arguments on behalf of Maryland, ibid., pp. 337–52, 369–70, 374–77.
For the context, see Bray Hammond, *Banks and Politics in America: From the Revolution to the Civil
War* (Princeton, N.J., 1957), pp. 279–85; Charles Warren, *The Supreme Court in United States His-
tory*, 3 vols. (Boston, Mass., 1924), 1:499–540; Marion A. Brown, *The Second Bank of the United
States and Ohio (1803–1860): A Collision of Interests* (Lewiston, N.Y., 1998), pp. 103–22.

[50]Larson, *Internal Improvement*, pp. 54–57, 137–40, 163–64; Harry N. Scheiber, "The Transportation Revolution and American Law: Constitutionalism and Public Policy," in *Transportation and the Early Nation: Papers Presented at an Indiana American Revolution Bicentennial Symposium:
Allen County–Fort Wayne Historical Society Museum, Fort Wayne, Indiana, April 24–26, 1981* (Indianapolis, Ind., 1982), pp. 1–29; Douglas E. Clanin, "Internal Improvements in National Politics,
1816–1830," ibid., pp. 30–42.

[51]Few constitutional objections were raised to the first proposals for protective tariffs. South
Carolina legislators advocated a state sovereignty–based protest in 1829, but the committee to
which the proposal was referred recommended against it. "When they advert to the consequences likely to result from the practice, unfortunately become too common, of arraying upon
the questions of national policy, the states as distinct and independent sovereignties in opposition to, or, (what is much the same thing) with a view to exercise a control over the general
government—Your committee feel it to be their indispensable duty to protest against a
measure, of which they conceive the tendency so mischievous" (Ames, *State Documents on Federal Relations*, p. 135). Note that at this time South Carolina's leading politician, John C.
Calhoun, serving as secretary of war in President James Monroe's cabinet, was still identified
with nationalistic policies.

executing your granted powers; not a power to impose taxes to diminish the revenue, thereby to encourage and protect domestic manufactures."[52] Congress could not utilize a delegated power as a means to accomplish an undelegated end, they insisted.[53]

At the same time, federal judges interpreted the clause of the Constitution prohibiting states from impairing the obligation of contracts to negate state policies concerning allocation of property, the regulation of corporate privileges, and laws governing the collection of debts. Angry westerners and southerners blasted such federal usurpation of states' rights.[54] Closely linked and particularly bitterly disputed were claims by Tennessee, North Carolina, Alabama, Georgia, and other states to jurisdiction over land that federal treaties reserved to Indian nations.[55] Finally, there were disputes related to slavery. Of these, the most divisive had been the Missouri crisis. The controversy at first involved the scope of federal power to set conditions for the admission of new states. When antislavery congressmen abandoned the effort to bar slavery in the new state, Missouri's ban on African American immigration precipitated a second conflict—over Congress's responsibility to secure to citizens of each state the privileges and immunities of citizens of the several states, as mandated by Article IV of the Constitution.[56]

---

[52]Virginia Rep. Alexander Smyth, *Annals*, 17th Cong., 2d sess., Jan. 30, 1823, 760.

[53]See, for examples, the Resolution of South Carolina on Internal Improvements and the Tariff, December 16, 1825, in Ames, *State Documents on Federal Relations*, p. 139; Resolutions of Virginia, Mar. 4, 1826, ibid., p. 142; Resolution of Virginia, Mar. 6, 1827, ibid., p. 143.

[54]Warren, *Supreme Court in United States History*, 1:474–98, 2:93–111; Charles Grove Haines, *The Role of the Supreme Court in American Government and Politics, 1789–1835* (New York, 1959), pp. 285–310; F. Thornton Miller, *Juries and Judges versus the Law: Virginia's Provincial Legal Perspective, 1783–1828* (Charlottesville, Va., 1994). See generally Dwight Wiley Jessup, *Reaction and Accommodation: The United States Supreme Court and Political Conflict, 1809–1835* (New York, 1987), pp. 140–243.

[55]Warren, *Supreme Court in United States History*, 2:189–239; Tim Alan Garrison, *The Legal Ideology of Removal: The Southern Judiciary and the Sovereignty of Native American Nations* (Athens, Ga., 2002); James Taylor Carson, "State Rights and Indian Removal in Mississippi, 1817–1835," *Journal of Mississippi History* 57 (1995):25–41; Ulrich B. Phillips, *Georgia and State Rights: A Study of the Political History of Georgia from the Revolution to the Civil War, with Particular Regard to Federal Relations*, vol. 2 of *Annual Report of the American Historical Association for the Year 1901* (Washington, D.C., 1902), pp. 39–86; Mary Young, "The Exercise of Sovereignty in Cherokee Georgia," *Journal of the Early Republic* 10 (1990):43–64.

[56]Congress compromised this dispute by requiring Missouri to pledge that it would not deny the privileges and immunities of citizens of the United States. Its legislature did so, tacitly assuming that black citizens of other states were not citizens of the United States, a position the Supreme Court ultimately endorsed in the Dred Scott decision. See Glover Moore, *The Missouri Controversy, 1819–1821* (Lexington, Ky., 1953); Don E. Fehrenbacher, "The Missouri Controversy and the Sources of Southern Sectionalism," in *The South and Three Sectional Crises* (Baton Rouge, La., 1980), pp. 9–23.

When Porter had lamented the lack of a neutral arbiter to adjudicate disputes over state and federal jurisdiction in 1811, the Supreme Court had not yet staked its claim to that position, and as a Republican, Porter would hardly have been likely to have welcomed it if the Court had. By the 1820s, the Supreme Court's role in disputes over federalism had become a matter of intense controversy. In a series of powerful decisions, the Court had repudiated the Principles of '98. Sustaining the constitutionality of the activist program promoted by nationalist Republicans like Clay and Calhoun, the Court endorsed the broad exercise of national powers; such powers were "complete and plenary" and not subject to constraint simply because they trenched on what would otherwise be state jurisdiction. At the same time that it sustained a broad interpretation of national powers, it limited the powers of the states, vigorously enforcing an expansive interpretation of constitutional prohibitions on state actions affecting property rights. A look at these famous decisions—the Yazoo Land Case (*Fletcher v. Peck*), the Virginia Land Cases (*Fairfax's Devisee v. Hunter's Lessee, Martin v. Hunter's Lessee*), the Kentucky Land Cases (*Green v. Biddle*), the Bankruptcy Case (*Sturges v. Crowninshield*), the Dartmouth College Case (*Dartmouth College v. Woodward*), *McCulloch v. Maryland, Gibbons v. Ogden*—demonstrates the Court's engagement in constitutional politics on the side of nationalist Republicanism.[57] Written in grand style, they eschewed lawyerly precedents, citations, and technicalities. They were powerful rhetorical statements written to affect public opinion.[58]

Those opposed to the Court's decisions might deny its authority, claiming along with Ohio's state legislature that "the majority of the American people" had "recognized and adopted" the doctrines of the Kentucky and Virginia Resolutions as to the relative powers of the state and federal governments.[59] But the American understanding of constitutionalism, forged

---

[57] *Fletcher v. Peck* 10 U.S. (6 Cranch.) 878 (1810); *Fairfax's Devisee v. Hunter's Lessee* 11 U.S. (7 Cranch.) 603 (1813); *Martin v. Hunter's Lessee*, 14 U.S. (1 Wheat.) 304 (1816); *Green v. Biddle*, 21 U.S. (8 Wheat.) 1 (1823); *Sturges v. Crowninshield*, 17 U.S. (4 Wheat.) 122 (1819); *Dartmouth College v. Woodward*, 17 U.S. (4 Wheat.) 518 (1819); *McCulloch v. Maryland*, 17 U.S. (4 Wheat.) 316 (1819); *Gibbons v. Ogden*, 22 U.S. (9 Wheat.) 1 (1824).

[58] Mark A. Graber explains the relationship between the Marshall Court's nationalist decisions and the programs promoted by the nationalist wing of the Jeffersonian Republican party in "Federalist or Friend of Adams: The Marshall Court and Party Politics," *Studies in American Political Development* 12 (1998):229–66.

[59] Resolutions of Ohio, in Ames, *State Documents on Federal Relations*, p. 43. The resolutions were in defense of the state's right to tax branches of the Bank of the United States after the Supreme Court's decision in the *McCulloch* case ruling such taxes unconstitutional.

during the conflict that led to the Revolution, was that a constitution embodied fundamental law. Enactments that violated constitutional limitations
were legally void. The courts had claimed, and Americans generally had
conceded, that in cases of conflict between constitutional limitations and
legislative enactments, judges were bound to enforce the Constitution and
disregard the enactment. This understanding underlay John Marshall's great
accomplishment as chief justice, which was to claim that law was distinct
from and superior to politics and that it was the peculiar province of the judiciary to interpret what the law was. From that perspective, Supreme Court
decisions regarding constitutional *law* appeared to foreclose the people's right
to define the fundamental law through constitutional *politics*.[60] "Thus, the
Constitution was legalized," legal scholar Stephen M. Griffin observed. "It
was made enforceable in ordinary courts of law and interpreted as any other
legal document." The development was consistent with the deeply held view
that the Constitution was legally binding. "But this legalization was not without costs. The legalization of the Constitution was based on denying the
importance of the differences between the Constitution and ordinary law."
It "warped the original idea of constitutionalism."[61]

Despite the tension between legal and popular constitutionalism, even
opponents of broad national power conceded the obligation of the judiciary
to disregard unconstitutional laws. But they denied that the Constitution
made the *United States* Supreme Court the court of last resort. In the course
of their arguments, they further refined states' rights theory. As the Marshall Court justified nationalist Republican programs with nationalist
constitutionalism, opponents responded with refinements of states' rights
theory that challenged the Court's jurisdiction. The most effective challenge
emanated from the Virginia Court of Appeals, whose decisions were among
those the justices had overturned. In a series of battles with the federal
justices, surrounded by newspaper and pamphlet wars over the issue, the
Virginia judges denied that the federal Supreme Court could hear appeals
of Virginia decisions construing the Constitution.[62] Building on Jefferson's

[60]See Kent Newmyer, *John Marshall and the Heroic Age of the Supreme Court* (Baton Rouge, La.,
2001), pp. 378–79.

[61]See also Stephen M. Griffin, *American Constitutionalism: From Theory to Politics* (Princeton,
N.J., 1996), p. 16.

[62]Newmyer, *John Marshall and the Heroic Age of the Supreme Court*, pp. 322–75; Newmyer, "John
Marshall, *McCulloch v. Maryland*, and the Southern States' Rights Tradition," *John Marshall
Law Review* 33 (2000):875–934; Gerald Gunther, ed., *John Marshall's Defense of* McCulloch v.

Kentucky Resolutions, Spencer Roane, the chief justice of the Virginia high court, avowed, "The constitution of the United States was not adopted by the people of the United States, as one people. It was adopted by the several states, in their highest sovereign character, that is by the people of the said states, respectively." They, and not a single "people of the United States," were the parties to the compact that created the Union. "Our general government . . . is as much a federal government, or a 'league' as was the former confederation," he insisted.[63] Fellow Virginian John Taylor averred, "In the creation of the federal government, the states exercised the highest act of sovereignty, and they may, if they please, repeat the proof of their sovereignty, by its annihilation. But the union possesses no innate sovereignty. . . . It is . . . subordinate to the sovereignties by which it was created."[64] The states' rights doctrine of federalism had evolved into the doctrine of "state sovereignty."

If the states were sovereign, the claim of the Supreme Court—a mere department of the central government—that it had the ultimate authority to interpret the Constitution was unsustainable. In Article VI, the Constitution itself indicated that in a conflict between state and federal law, the *state* judges were to give precedence to laws passed "pursuant to the Constitution." As the judicial arm of the sovereign powers, they were the proper forum for legal interpretation of the Constitution. Section 25 of the Judiciary Act of 1789, which provided for appeals of such decisions from the highest state courts to the U.S. Supreme Court, was an unconstitutional usurpation of power. Virginia acted on this conviction by refusing to honor the Supreme Court's demands for records and papers and refusing to appear as party to appeals. These arguments were republished, repeated, and echoed wherever people opposed national banking policies, sought to deprive Native Americans of rights guaranteed by federal treaties, worried about the potential of federal decisions regarding slavery, or resented federal court decisions overturning important state policies. They became the new staple of the state-focused theory of federalism.

Maryland (Stanford, Calif., 1969); Bennet, *American Theories of Federalism*, pp. 108–25; W. Ray Luce, Cohens v. Virginia *(1821): The Supreme Court and State Rights; A Reevaluation of Influences and Impacts* (New York, 1990); Richard E. Ellis, "The Path Not Taken—Virginia and the Supreme Court, 1789–1821," in *Virginia and the Constitution*, ed. A. E. Dick Howard and Melvin I. Urofsky (Charlottesville, Va., 1992), pp. 24–52.

[63]Gunther, *John Marshall's Defense*, pp. 139–46 (quoted material pp. 140, 146).

[64]John Taylor, *New Views of the Constitution of the United States* (Washington, D.C., 1823).

In response to this state sovereignty onslaught, the Supreme Court articulated its most forceful statement of the nationalist theory of federalism. The notion that the United States was merely a league of sovereign states and separate peoples was grossly wrong, the justices expostulated in *Cohens v. Virginia.* "The United States form, for many and for most important purposes, a single nation. . . . In war we are one people, in making peace, we are one people. In all commercial regulations, we are one and the same people. In many other respects, the American people are one. . . . America has chosen to be, in many respects, and to many purposes, a nation; and for all these purposes her government is complete; to all these objects, it is competent." With regard to those objects the federal government could control even the states, which were "members of one great empire—for some purposes sovereign, for some purposes subordinate."[65] Again the Court's opinion eschewed mere legalisms; it was a broadside in a political war over the nature of the Union.

Proponents of state sovereignty reacted with utter fury. "It is a fatal heresy to suppose that either our state governments are superior to the federal, or the federal to the state; neither is authorized literally to decide which belongs to itself or its copartner in government," Jefferson expostulated to Roane. And he suggested a new idea that would be picked up by advocates of state sovereignty a few years later: "In differences of opinion, between their different sets of public servants, the appeal is to neither, but to their employers peaceably assembled by their representatives in convention."[66] Advocates of state sovereignty issued a new fusillade of pamphlets and formal letters in newspapers. They blasted away at the idea that the Supreme Court could overturn state high court decisions. In Congress, they proposed a number of bills to curb the Court and alter its membership.[67]

Desultory proposals in Congress to repeal section 25 of the Judiciary Act went nowhere, a significant if negative victory for nationalist constitutionalism. Nonetheless, the highest courts of Virginia, Georgia, and other states continued to dispute the Supreme Court's jurisdiction on state sovereignty grounds, refusing to forward case materials. State officials declined to appear to make arguments. However, the federal courts had their own law-enforcement machinery. They could make their writs effective as long as

---

[65]*Cohens v. Virginia,* 19 U.S. (6 Wheat.) 264, 294 (1821).

[66]Thomas Jefferson to Spencer Roane, June 27, 1821, in *The Writings of Jefferson,* ed. Thomas Ellery Bergh, 20 vols. (Washington, D.C., 1903–4), 15:328–29.

[67]Warren, *Supreme Court in United States History,* 2:112–45.

TABLE I
Nationalism versus State Sovereignty in the 1820s

	Nationalism	*State Sovereignty*
Who created the government? Who is sovereign?	People of the U.S.	States or people of the several states
What is the Constitution?	Constitution	Compact
What is the U.S. government?	Nation	League or confederacy
What is the measure of federal power; how broad?	Broad construction; supreme/plenary power	Strict construction; limited by state power —"dual federalism" or "dual sovereignty"
What is the measure of state power?	Strictly limited by the Constitution; overlapping powers with federal supremacy	Broad, sovereign power; dual federalism
Who judges constitutionality?	Supreme Court	State courts

they were sustained by the president, who appointed U.S. attorneys and marshals and who would, if necessary, call forth the militia to enforce court orders. By the mid-1820s, states like Georgia, worried about Supreme Court intervention on behalf of the Cherokees, longed for a president firmly committed to state sovereignty, like their own Virginia-born senator William H. Crawford, the leading candidate as the election of 1824 approached.

So as Andrew Jackson campaigned for the presidency in 1824 and 1828, there were two well-developed theories of American federalism. Advocates of each disagreed about who created the Union, where sovereignty was located, the nature of the Constitution, the measure of federal and state power, and what institution had final authority to interpret the Constitution's meaning.

Andrew Jackson and Federalism

Andrew Jackson was not the candidate most strongly identified with resistance to nationalist constitutionalism when he first ran for the presidency in 1824. That distinction belonged to the Georgian Crawford, who was supported by the self-denominated radical faction of purist Republicans led by the New Yorker, Sen. Martin Van Buren, among others, that had come to predominate in Congress.[68] It was a Virginia-Georgia-New York axis bitterly opposed to the national Republicanism of western candidate Henry Clay, New Englander John Quincy Adams, and Southerner John C. Calhoun, whose constitutional views at that time, Van Buren recalled, were still "latitudinarian in the extreme."[69] Jackson, too, denounced consolidation and spoke up for states' rights. But he worried about going too far. "To keep the sovereignty of the States and the general government properly and harmoniously poised is the pivot on which must rest the freedom and happiness of this Country," he wrote in 1824.[70] It was a carefully studied statement specifying that the states were sovereign but ambiguous as to whether the United States was sovereign as well. He endorsed a version of the Principles of '98, maintaining that "the State governments hold in check the federal." Nor did he see the Supreme Court as the ultimate arbiter of the system. "The virtue of the people supported by the sovereign States, must prevent consolidations," he said. But he did not clearly endorse the doctrines that Virginians had developed over the previous five years.[71]

Jackson's congressional partisans had supported internal improvements that they identified as clearly national in scope. As senator from Tennessee, Jackson had voted for the protective tariff, enabling him to wrest the support of Pennsylvania's dominant Republican factions from John C. Calhoun, who decided to aim for the vice presidency instead. (Indeed, Jackson's supporters would be the prime movers behind the higher protective tariff of 1828—the so-called Tariff of Abominations.)[72] But he was known as a hardline advocate of Indian removal, which led many Southerners and Southwesterners to assume he agreed with Georgia and Alabama's state sovereignty claims to authority over Indian lands.[73]

When Crawford's candidacy deflated after a stroke incapacitated him, it was Jackson who acquired much of his former support.[74] In 1824, he received

---

[68]See Robert V. Remini, *Martin Van Buren and the Making of the Democratic Party* (New York, 1959), pp. 36–42.

[69]John C. Fitzpatrick, ed., *The Autobiography of Martin Van Buren*, vol. 2 of the *Annual Report of the American Historical Association for the Year 1918* (Washington, D.C., 1920), p. 513.

[70]Jackson to James W. Lanier, May 15 [?], 1824, quoted in Robert V. Remini, *Andrew Jackson and the Course of American Freedom, 1822–1832* (New York, 1981), p. 31.

[71]Jackson to James Hamilton, Jr., June 29, 1828, ibid.

[72]Remini, *Andrew Jackson and the Course of American Freedom*, pp. 67–71, 136–38; David Lindsey, *Andrew Jackson and John C. Calhoun* (Woodbury, N.Y., 1973), p. 59.

[73]Robert V. Remini, *Andrew Jackson and His Indian Wars* (New York, 2001).

[74]The standard account of Jackson's rise to the presidency is Remini, *Jackson and the Course of American Freedom*, pp. 1–155.

a plurality of the popular and electoral vote but not a majority, throwing the election into the House of Representatives. There the nationalists Adams and Clay allied to win the presidency for Adams, who named Clay secretary of state and heir apparent, to the dismay of Calhoun, whose positions had been ambiguous enough to make him the vice presidential candidate of both Adams's supporters and Jackson's.

By 1828, proponents of state sovereignty theories of federalism, led by Van Buren, had rallied behind Jackson in opposition to the more nationalistic Clay and Adams. So, too, did Calhoun's influential Washington supporters as he moved in the state sovereignty direction along with his South Carolina constituents. Thus, despite the ambiguity of some of Jackson's positions, his election was taken to mark the triumph of purist Republicanism and the Principles of '98. It was no accident that Georgia immediately passed legislation (to take effect in six months) extending its jurisdiction over Cherokee Indian lands.

Encouraged by Van Buren, who aspired to restore constitutional purity by converting Jackson's loose personal following into a disciplined political party dedicated to the Principles of '98, Jackson made a respect for states' rights a major commitment of his administration.[75] "That this was intended to be a government of limited and specific, and not general, powers must be admitted by all, and it is our duty to preserve for it the character intended by its framers," he wrote in his first message to Congress. "Let us . . . not undermine the whole system by a resort to overstrained constructions. . . . The great mass of legislation relating to our internal affairs was intended to be left where the federal convention found it—in the state governments. . . . I cannot, therefore, too strongly or too earnestly, for my own sense of its importance, warn you against all encroachments upon the legitimate sphere of state sovereignty."[76]

Although his own supporters had fashioned the highly protective tariff of 1828 to win support from every economic interest in every region, he now indicated a need for revision to respond to complaints, voiced most forcefully in South Carolina and other Southern states, that it bore unequally on different sections of the country.[77] Likewise, he acknowledged the doubts that many of his supporters had about the constitutionality of applying

---

[75]For Van Buren's conception of the Jacksonian Democratic party as a vehicle for constitutional politics, see Remini, *Martin Van Buren and the Making of the Democratic Party,* esp. pp. 123–25, and Leonard, "Party as a 'Political Safeguard of Federalism.'"

[76]Richardson, *Messages and Papers of the Presidents,* 3:1015.

[77]Ibid., 3:1012–13.

government money to internal improvements. Echoing Van Buren, he noted "the difficulties which have hitherto attended appropriations" for that purpose, which seemed inevitable "whenever power over such subjects may be exercised by the General Government."[78]

Jackson's opponents determined to put him on the spot by passing bills extending the national road system into ever more localities clamoring for access to waterways and markets. Even Jackson's strongest supporters, like Sen. Richard M. Johnson of Kentucky, backed them, especially when their own constituencies were involved.[79] Jackson chose to make a stand on a bill funding a road entirely within Clay's (and Johnson's) state of Kentucky. The Maysville Road veto set the pattern for the rest of Jackson's administration, ending most direct federal support for internal improvements within the states. Instead, Congress responded to state petitions, turning money over to them to undertake their own internal improvements.[80]

Jackson used Georgia's decision to extend state jurisdiction over the treaty land guaranteed to the Cherokees to pressure them and other Native Americans to sign new treaties surrendering their lands and to move west. When the Supreme Court denied that Georgia could in effect nullify federal treaties with Native Americans, Jackson made it clear that the justices could not count on him to enforce any consequent court order directed to the state's defiant officials. The Cherokees and other tribes gave up the fight and signed the new treaties. It was a tremendous victory for claims of state sovereignty.[81] In these circumstances, it is no wonder that observers assumed that Jackson would sympathize with efforts to strengthen the state sovereignty constitutional argument.

These efforts centered around Southern opposition to the 1828 Tariff of Abominations, in which South Carolinian and Vice President John C. Calhoun, the former nationalist, took the lead with the zeal of a convert.

---

[78]Ibid., 3:1014.

[79]For example, Jacksonian senators Thomas Hart Benton (Missouri) and Edward Livingston (Louisiana), as well as Johnson, all voted for the Maysville Road, which would become the touchstone issue of internal improvements (Remini, *Andrew Jackson and the Course of American Freedom*, p. 252).

[80]Ibid., pp. 253–56; Naomi Wulf, "'The Greatest General Good': Broad Construction, National Interest, and Federal Funding in Jacksonian America," in *Federalism, Citizenship, and Collective Identities in U.S. History*, ed. Cornelius A. Van Minnen and Sylvia L. Hilton (Amsterdam, Netherlands, 2000), pp. 53–72.

[81]Garrison, *Legal Ideology of Removal*; Jill Norgren, *The Cherokee Cases: The Confrontation of Law and Politics* (New York, 1996).

The problem for advocates of state sovereignty constitutionalism was that the nationalist Supreme Court's claim of superior authority to interpret the Constitution, sustained by the failure of Congress to repeal its power to hear appeals from state court decisions, severely weakened claims that state sovereignty was the law of the land. Calhoun and his allies aimed to establish the states' authority to override unconstitutional federal action even when sustained by the federal courts. The vehicle was nullification.

Nullification built upon the proposition that the people of the individual states had established the Constitution. They had exercised that sovereign prerogative through state ratifying conventions that represented them in their highest, sovereign capacity. In the same capacity, they could terminate their connection to the Union. Likewise, the sovereign people must be the ultimate authority for resolving disputes about constitutional interpretations. As Jefferson and Madison had indicated in the Kentucky and Virginia Resolutions, states might interpose to protect the liberty of their citizens by rendering judgments on the constitutionality of federal actions. But, Calhoun posited, it was not the state legislature that exercised this power on their behalf. It must be exercised by an organic act of the people of the state through a specially called convention—the same medium through which they had ratified the Constitution in the first place. As advocates of nullification conceived it, the constitutional judgment of the people of one state could be subject to reversal only by the people of the other states, through the Constitution's amendment process. Nullification was, its advocates insisted, the ultimate articulation of the Principles of '98.[82]

Calhoun had begun to develop his nullification ideas in the "South Carolina Exposition and Protest" that he secretly prepared for the state legislature in 1828 as he ran for vice president on the Jackson ticket. A protective tariff was unconstitutional, the exposition asserted. "The Constitution grants to Congress the power of imposing a duty on imports for revenue; which power is abused by being converted into an instrument for rearing up the industry of one section of the country on the ruins of another. The violation then consists in using a power, granted for one object, to advance another." The exposition expressed confidence in a "great political revolution

---

[82]See Bennett, *American Theories of Federalism*, pp. 128–51. Lacy K. Ford, Jr., describes Calhoun's theory of federalism in the context of his notion that liberty required government by "concurrent majorities" representing different social interests. See Ford, "Inventing the Concurrent Majority: Madison, Calhoun, and the Problem of Majoritarianism in American Thought," *Journal of Southern History* 60 (1994):19–58.

which will . . . bring in[to the presidency] an eminent citizen, distinguished for his services to his country and his justice and patriotism." But it affirmed the states' power to interpose if Jackson's ascendance were not followed by "a complete restoration of the pure principles of our government."[83]

The articulation of South Carolina's nullification doctrine led to one of the greatest and most influential constitutional debates of American history —a debate that took place not before the justices of the Supreme Court but in the halls of Congress. In January 1830, as Daniel Webster responded to a speech by Sen. Robert Y. Hayne of South Carolina on the sale of western lands, he alluded in passing to the tendency of some in the South to disparage the Union. Hayne replied with a forceful defense of states' rights/state sovereignty constitutionalism. "Who . . . are the true friends of the Union?" he asked. They were "[t]hose who would confine the federal government strictly within the limits prescribed by the Constitution; who would preserve to the States and the people all powers not expressly delegated; who would make this a federal and not a national Union, and who, administering the government in spirit of equal justice, would make it a blessing, and not a curse." "And who are its enemies?" he continued. "Those who are in favor of consolidation; who are constantly stealing power from the States, and adding strength to the federal government; who, assuming an unwarrantable jurisdiction over the States and the people, undertake to regulate the whole industry and capital of the country."[84]

Hayne scorned claims that Webster and his allies were "National Republicans" and thus heirs of Jefferson. "The National Republicans of the present day were the Federalists of '98. . . . They have always been animated by the same principles, and have kept steadily in view a common object, the consolidation of the government."[85] "The South Carolina doctrine" of interposing state authority against unconstitutional federal action was "the good old Republican doctrine of '98—the doctrine of the celebrated 'Virginia Resolutions' of that year, and of 'Madison's Report' of '99."[86] Stressing the hints of interposition in the resolutions, he defended nullification as having

---

[83][John C. Calhoun], "Exposition and Protest," [Dec. 19, 1828], in *The Papers of John C. Calhoun*, ed. Clyde N. Wilson and W. Edwin Hemphill, 28 vols. (Columbia, S.C., 1959–2003), 10:445–46, 531.

[84]Lindsay Swift, ed., *The Great Debate between Robert Young Hayne of South Carolina and Daniel Webster of Massachusetts* (Boston, Mass., 1898), pp. 89–90.

[85]Ibid., p. 91.

[86]Ibid.

been "promulgated by the fathers of the faith." In contrast, "the doctrine that the federal government is the exclusive judge of the extent as well as the limitations of its powers . . . [is] utterly subversive of the sovereignty and independence of the States."

It made no difference whether one lodged that power in Congress or the Supreme Court: "If the federal government, in all, or any, of its departments, is to prescribe the limits of its own authority, and the States are bound to submit to the decision, and are not to be allowed to examine and decide for themselves, when the barriers of the Constitution shall be overleaped, this is practically government without limitation of powers."[87]

Hayne's articulation of the state sovereignty doctrine provided the occasion of Webster's famous second reply to the South Carolina senator, the most powerful antebellum statement of nationalist theory. Although Webster was responding to Hayne, in reality he was directing his remarks to Calhoun, who as vice president was presiding over the Senate, and the floor and gallery filled to overflowing with expectant congressmen and visitors. Indeed, the convention of the Senate was that, in debate, all remarks were directed to the presiding officer. When Webster interjected "Sir" in his remarks, Calhoun was the "Sir" being addressed.

Whose agent is the federal government? "Is it the creature of the State legislatures, or the creature of the people?" Webster asked, ignoring Calhoun's creative recurrence to the sovereignty of the people in state conventions. And he answered unequivocally, "It is, Sir, the people's Constitution, the people's government, made for the people, made by the people, and answerable to the people." The people were sovereign over both the state and federal governments. "We are all agents of the same supreme power. . . . So far as the people have restrained State sovereignty, by . . . the Constitution of the United States, so far . . . State sovereignty is effectually controlled."[88] They did that by declaring the Constitution and laws passed in pursuance of it the supreme law of the land and creating a judiciary to decide all cases arising under it. "These two provisions . . . are, in truth, the keystone of the arch! With these it is a government; without them it is a confederation."[89]

Webster's great oration marked a turning point in the history of nationalist constitutionalism. Advocates of state sovereignty had possessed the

---

[87]Ibid., p. 100.

[88]Ibid., pp.187–88.

[89]Ibid., pp. 204–6 (quotation at p. 206).

advantage of arguing for liberty against government usurpation. After all, the Principles of '98 had been a response to the Sedition Act. Federalists, the apostles of nationalist constitutionalism, had been identified with the suppression of free speech, the persecution of aliens, support of religious establishments, and special privileges for the rich and powerful. Republicans had tied states' rights and state sovereignty to their defense of liberty and equal rights.[90] Webster challenged this identification. He scorned those words "of delusion and folly, 'Liberty first and Union afterwards.'" Rather, he closed his great oration, let Americans' motto be "Liberty *and* Union, now and for ever, one and inseparable!"[91] It was an address aimed at the multitudes. Circulated throughout the Union, it provided a moral justification for nationalist constitutionalism that enabled it to compete in the public forum, where Americans still believed constitutional controversies would be settled.

Calhoun expected Jackson's support. After all, at that very moment Jackson was at least countenancing Georgia's similar defiance of federal law with regard to the Cherokees. "I thought the president professed to be a state rights' man, placed at the head of a state rights' party; that he believed the people of these states were united in a constitutional compact, as forming distinct and sovereign communities," he would later reflect bitterly.[92]

In April 1830, Calhoun's powerful Washington allies arranged the program of toasts at the Jefferson birthday dinner that purist Republicans had sponsored annually for more than a decade. They invited Jackson to attend and to follow the prepared toasts with a "volunteer toast" of his own. It would be followed by a responding toast from Calhoun. The lead-up toasts prepared by the organizers were carefully worded to identify nullification with the Principles of '98, reflecting the South Carolinians' effort to establish nullification as a tenet of Republicans' state sovereignty ideology. Jackson and Van Buren had worded the president's toast equally carefully. When the time came, Jackson lifted his glass to "Our federal Union: *it must be preserved.*"

The report of Jackson's toast electrified the nation; all knew it was a repudiation of Calhoun's doctrines. Probably with some exaggeration, Van Buren remembered that the color drained from the vice president's face. His hand shook as he rose to respond: "The Union. Next to our liberty, the

---

[90]See Benedict, "Jeffersonian Republicans and American Liberty."
[91]Ibid., pp. 216–17.
[92]*Register of Debates*, 23d Cong., 1st sess., 1645 (May 6, 1834).

most dear." It was exactly the sentiment Webster had denounced some ten weeks before.[93]

After Congress enacted only minor changes to the tariff in 1832, Calhoun found his influence in the administration to be nil and decided to force the issue. The result was the nullification crisis.[94] South Carolina's legislature called a convention of the people in November 1832, a few weeks after Jackson's triumphant reelection. The convention declared the protective tariff unconstitutional, "null, void, and no law," and instructed the legislature to prevent its enforcement in the state. It barred any appeal of a state court decision on the constitutionality of nullification to the U.S. Supreme Court.[95] Calhoun resigned the vice presidency to return to the Senate to defend his state's course, replacing Hayne, who took over the governorship in preparation for the showdown.

This time, Calhoun could not have been surprised at Jackson's reaction. The president's proclamation denounced the ordinance, which "prescribes to the people of South Carolina a course of conduct in direct violation of their duty as citizens of the United States, contrary to the laws of their country, subversive of its Constitution, and having for its object the destruction of the Union."[96] No state backed South Carolina. Jackson's supporters and opponents alike voted to authorize the use of force to overcome resistance, if necessary, to enforce federal laws.[97]

Although prepared to resort to force, Jackson also supported Henry Clay's effort to avoid violence by securing a reduction in the tariff. Upon passage of a new, reduced tariff, the South Carolina convention reassembled, repealing its nullification. But the South Carolinians hardly surrendered their convictions. Repealing the nullification ordinance, it nullified the Force Act instead. Because the tariff was scheduled to decline to a level that eliminated its protective aspects, Calhoun had some justification for claiming victory, despite the lack of support from other states.[98]

---

[93]Remini, *Andrew Jackson and the Course of American Freedom*, pp. 233–36.

[94]The standard constitutional account of the nullification crisis is Richard E. Ellis, *The Union at Risk: Jacksonian Democracy, States' Rights, and the Nullification Crisis* (New York, 1987).

[95]Ames, *State Documents on Federal Relations*, pp. 37–41.

[96]Richardson, *Messages and Papers of the Presidents*, 3:1203.

[97]4 Stat. 632 (1833).

[98]Ellis, *Union at Risk*, pp. 158–77; Merrill D. Peterson, *Olive Branch and Sword: The Compromise of 1833* (Baton Rouge, La., 1982).

Jackson, the Bank War, and States' Rights

As Richard E. Ellis has observed, "The nullification crisis was not simply, and perhaps not even mainly, a struggle between the proponents of nationalism and states' rights." Rather, it "involved a struggle between advocates of different kinds of states' rights thought."[99] The division had been foreshadowed by past, nuanced disagreements among Republicans, but it was not until Jackson's repudiation of the state sovereignty doctrine that they became clear.[100] While Jackson repudiated state sovereignty, he did not repudiate states' rights. He and the Democratic party that Van Buren and others organized under his banner continued to stress that commitment and to blast away at the consolidationism of their nationalist opponents.

Even as the nullification storm was gathering, Jackson vetoed the bill rechartering the Second Bank of the United States, long a target of Republican purists. The fact that the Supreme Court had held the Bank to be constitutional did not preclude Congress and the president from reaching the opposite conclusion. Jackson interpreted *McCulloch v. Maryland* to indicate merely that the Court would defer to the judgment of Congress and the president that a measure was a necessary and proper means to carry out a constitutionally delegated power. Thus it was up to them "to decide whether the particular features of this act are *necessary* and *proper* . . . and therefore constitutional, or *unnecessary* and *improper,* and therefore unconstitutional."[101] Among the factors making the Bank unconstitutional were the various ways in which it trenched upon powers the Constitution reserved to the states. "If our power over means is so absolute that the Supreme Court will not call in question the constitutionality of an act the subject of which . . . is 'not prohibited, and is really calculated to effect any of the objects intrusted to the Government,' . . . it becomes us to proceed in our legislation with utmost caution," lest "the rights of the states . . . be indirectly legislated away in the use of means to execute substantive powers."[102] In other words, the existence of state jurisdiction itself operates as a limitation of delegated federal powers. The Union would not be preserved "by invasions of the rights and

---

[99]Ellis, *Union at Risk,* p. 178.

[100]See Lenner, *Federalist Principle in American Politics,* for close attention to earlier signs of division.

[101]Richardson, *Messages and Papers of the Presidents,* 3:1146.

[102]Ibid., p. 1151.

powers of the several States." Its real strength lay "not in binding the States more closely to the center, but [in] leaving each to move unobstructed in its proper orbit."[103]

As noted above, the very first plank of the first Democratic party platform, promulgated in 1840, would resolve "that the federal government is one of limited powers, derived solely from the Constitution, and the grants of power shown therein, ought to be strictly construed by all the departments and agents of the government." The second denied that the government had the constitutional power to assume the costs of state internal improvements. They remained the first two planks of every national Democratic platform until 1860. The sixth plank denied the constitutionality of a national bank. Democratic platforms retained that plank until 1860 as well.[104]

In his proclamation to the people of South Carolina, Jackson repudiated the old states' rights proposition that the Constitution was a compact creating a confederacy of sovereign states. "The Constitution . . . forms a *government*, not a league, and whether it be formed by compact between the States or in any other manner, its character is the same." Each state had "expressly parted with so many powers as to constitute, jointly with the other States, a single nation." That precluded the idea that a still-sovereign state might secede. "Such secession does not break a league, but destroys the unity of a nation."[105]

Jackson referred to the president as "the direct representative of the American people."[106] His language echoed that of constitutional nationalism in assuming that the people of the United States were not merely the people of the individual United States but an entity transcending such localism. Such a claim was incompatible with the state sovereignty view of the Union as a confederation. "The very idea of an American People, as constituting a single community, is a mere chimera," Calhoun wrote in the draft of yet another report adopted by the South Carolina legislature in 1831.

---

[103]Ibid., p. 1153.

[104]See the Democratic party platforms of 1840, 1844, 1848, 1852, and 1856 in Johnson and Porter, *National Party Platforms*. The platforms can be found conveniently as compiled and posted online by the American Presidency Project, University of California Santa Barbara, at http://www.presidency.ucsb .edu/platforms.php.

[105]Richardson, *Messages and Papers of the Presidents*, 3:1211.

[106]Jackson, Protest [of the Senate Resolution of Censure], in Richardson, *Messages and Papers of the Presidents*, 3:1309.

"Such a community never, for a single moment, existed."[107] It was Jackson's claim to represent "the American people" that had led Calhoun to blast Jackson's pretension to be a supporter of states' rights. "He the immediate representative of the American people!" he exclaimed. Calhoun had thought that as a states' rights man, elected as the head of a states' rights party, Jackson must have "believed the people of these States . . . form[ed] distinct and sovereign communities; and that no such community or people as the American people, taken in the aggregate, existed." How could Jackson be "the immediate representative" of something called "the American people"? He had been selected "by the electors chosen either by the people of the States or by their legislatures." "The immediate representative!" he scoffed. "Why he never received a vote from the American people."[108]

Rejecting state sovereignty, what Jackson and most Democrats stressed was the Constitution's strict division of jurisdiction between the state and federal governments, what constitutional scholars call "dual sovereignty" or "dual federalism." Downplaying the hints of interposition in Jefferson's philosophy, they emphasized the belief, articulated to Roane in 1821, that "the people . . . have divided the powers of government into two distinct departments," which they "made coordinate, checking and balancing each other, . . . each equally supreme as to the powers delegated to itself . . . , [a]s independent, in fact, as different nations." In such a system, "each party should prudently shrink from all approach to the line of demarcation, instead of rashly overleaping it."[109]

In his message to Congress on the crisis and in his proclamation to the people of South Carolina, Jackson made clear that the Supreme Court, and not the states, had the authority to define the boundaries between state and federal jurisdiction.[110] In this he echoed the Federalist response to the Kentucky and Virginia Resolutions. But Jackson did not mean this recognition of the legitimacy of judicial review to imply that the courts had the sole, or even the primary, power to interpret the Constitution. Judicial review was but one of several checks to federal usurpation. "The veto of the Executive and the authority of the judiciary . . . are the obvious checks" upon the

---

[107]Calhoun, Draft Report on Federal Relations, in Wilson, *Papers of John C. Calhoun*, 11:495.
[108]*Register of Debates*, 23d Cong., 1st sess., 1645–46 (May 6, 1834).
[109]Jefferson to Roane, June 27, 1821, in Bergh, *Writings of Jefferson*, 15:328.
[110]Proclamation, Dec. 10, 1832, in Richardson, *Messages and Papers of the Presidents*, 3:1205; [Message to Congress], Jan. 16, 1833, ibid., p. 1186.

abuse of congressional power, while "the sound action of public opinion, with the ultimate power of amendment, are the salutary and only limitation upon the powers of the whole."[111] Thus after the nullification crisis, there were two rival state-oriented theories of federalism to compete with the heritage of constitutional nationalism expounded by the Marshall Court (and accepted by many leaders of the Whig party that organized to oppose Jackson's Democrats).

Although Calhoun and other adherents of state sovereignty returned to the Democratic party between 1837 and 1844, they continued to develop their own theory, particularly as a bulwark to promote the interests of slavery. State sovereignty doctrines gained more and more support among Southern Democrats. As early as 1832, Calhoun was speaking of the federal government as the agent of the sovereign states. But he did so primarily to reinforce his argument for nullification. As the agent of the states, the federal government could not impose its construction of the constitutional compact against one of the principals.[112] By 1837, he had carried the idea further, using it to limit the purposes for which the federal government could carry out even its delegated powers. The federal government, far from being separate and independent of the states, as both nationalists and Jacksonian states' rights advocates insisted, had been created by the states "as a common agent, in order to carry into effect the powers which they had delegated by the Constitution for their mutual security and prosperity." In fulfilling that responsibility, it was bound to promote the interests of all the states, slave and free, equally and without discrimination. Therefore, even where its authority was undoubted, the federal government could not discriminate against the citizens of slave states by taking actions hostile to slavery. It was precluded from using its delegated powers in ways that would undermine the states' domestic institutions. Thus the federal government was obligated to assure Southerners the right to carry their slaves into the territories and Washington, D.C.[113]

The federal government thus being required to act on behalf of the slave states, there was no longer any reason for proslavery advocates of state sovereignty to insist on strict construction of federal powers. More and more,

---

[111]Ibid., pp. 1185–86.

[112]Calhoun to James Hamilton, Jr., August 28, 1832, in Wilson, *Papers of John C. Calhoun,* 11:619.

[113]*Congressional Globe,* 25th Cong., 3d sess., 55 (Dec. 27, 1837).

TABLE 2
Three Theories of Federalism

	Nationalist Constitutionalism	*State-Sovereignty Constitutionalism*	*States' Rights Constitutionalism*
Who created government? Who is sovereign?	People of the U.S.	States or people of the several states	States or people of the several states
What is the Constitution?	Constitution	Compact	Constitution
What is the U.S. government?	Nation	League or confederacy	Nation
What is the measure of power; how broad?	Broad/supreme/ sovereign/plenary	Broad but must act as the agent for all the states	Strict construction; dual sovereignty
Who judges Constitution?	Supreme Court	States—nullification	Supreme Court
Union perpetual?	Yes	Secession	Yes

Southerners would demand that the federal government exercise expansive powers to protect the interests of slavery, finding state sovereignty doctrines of federalism more congenial than either nationalism or Jacksonian states' rights. The draconian Fugitive Slave Act of 1850, which projected federal power on behalf of slavery into the heart of Northern states' jurisdiction, denying them the ability to protect their own citizens from kidnapping, would be a case in point.[114]

By the 1850s, state sovereignty theory and states' rights theory were as radically different from each other as both were from nationalist theory. Advocates of state sovereignty and of states' rights might coexist uneasily in the Democratic party, but they disagreed fundamentally about the nature and permanence of the Union, the scope of federal power, and who had authority to interpret the Constitution.

By 1860, under the pressure of Northerners' desire to restrict the spread of slavery into the territories, the party would prove unable to contain the conflict. States' rights Democrats argued that the spirit of the Constitution required that a territory's settlers themselves decide whether to permit slavery

---

[114]Arthur Bestor, "State Sovereignty and Slavery: A Reinterpretation of Proslavery Constitutional Doctrine, 1846–1860," *Journal of the Illinois State Historical Society* 54 (1961):117–80.

—what they called popular sovereignty. State sovereignty Democrats insisted that, as the agent of the states, the federal government was obligated to establish a slave code for the territories. The divisions exploded the party, leading to the nomination of rival Democratic candidates for the presidency and the election of the antislavery Republican (and constitutional nationalist) Abraham Lincoln to the presidency.[115]

When Southerners cited state sovereignty to justify secession, Northern Democrats rallied to the flag of the Union, defending the nation whose sovereignty Jackson's brand of states' rights affirmed.

---

[115]The classic narrative is Roy F. Nichols, *The Disruption of American Democracy* (New York, 1948).

Jenny B. Wahl

He Broke the Bank, but Did
Andrew Jackson also Father the Fed?

D ID ANDREW JACKSON's destruction of the Second Bank of the United
States cause the financial crises of the 1830s? A 1994 survey revealed
that 92 percent of American economic historians say no.[1] Yet recent empirical work indicates that Jackson may not have been quite as blameless as
once believed. By weakening public confidence in paper currency at a time
when the United States practiced fractional reserve banking, adhered to an
international gold standard, curtailed branching by state-chartered banks,
and lacked a national lender of last resort, Jackson's war against the Bank
generated more casualties than just the institution itself.

But does this mean that a healthy Bank could have prevented the financial chaos of the latter half of the 1830s? Would it have? What is more, should
it have? In the following sections, I attempt to answer these questions. In
short, I believe that the Bank could have forestalled the Panic of 1837 but
probably not the crisis of 1839. Whether the Bank would have acted effectively had it existed as a national entity is unclear, however.

---

[1] Robert Whaples, "Where Is There Consensus among American Economic Historians?
The Results of a Survey on Forty Propositions," *Journal of Economic History* 55 (1995):139–54.
Thirty-three economists and twenty-seven historians agreed with the statement "The inflation
and financial crisis of the 1830s had their origin in events largely beyond President Jackson's
control and would have taken place whether or not he had acted as he did vis-à-vis the Second Bank of the U.S." Seven economists and eleven historians agreed with provisos; six econo-

What remains a controversial question is whether centralized financial institutions that prevent panic make people better off than market-directed systems that permit failures. Regardless of the answer, Americans have chosen centralization. I suggest that Andrew Jackson's decision to do away with the Second Bank of the United States helped lead us to that choice.

Financial Intermediation, Fractional Reserves, and the Money Supply

Understanding the events of the 1830s requires a firm grasp of the institutional structures involved. Certain features of Jacksonian finance are common to any modern banking system, namely financial intermediation and fractional reserves. Banks serve as middlemen for those who have extra funds on hand and those who need ready cash. By streamlining the matching process for lenders and borrowers, banks can create a win-win situation.

The practice of fractional reserves potentially makes things even better for everyone. Today, as in the nineteenth century, no bank puts all its deposits in vaults. Instead, it keeps a portion ready in case someone wants to make a withdrawal, but it lends the rest out to make a profit. Prudence or regulation can dictate the amount banks hold in reserve, and the accepted standard determines the composition of that reserve—for instance, gold, silver, or paper. Likewise, prudence or regulation can govern the types and terms of loans made. Both borrowers and depositors can benefit from fractional reserves: by reducing the amount of money lying idle, banks may simultaneously decrease interest rates charged to borrowers and increase rates paid to depositors.

Fractional-reserve banking also ties intimately to the amount of money circulating in the economy and the profits earned by banks. Bank loans could be made in the form of registered or personalized notes (which could conceivably be endorsed over to someone else), but they acquire greater transferability if they simply promise to pay the holder. Banknotes are an

---

mists and one historian disagreed. A survey conducted by David Whitten yielded somewhat different results on a similar but more narrowly focused question about specific causes (ibid., p. 148 n. 23).

example. Nineteenth-century banks essentially made loans by exchanging zero-coupon bearer bonds for the borrower's IOU. These bearer bonds then circulated freely as currency among the public.[2] Ceteris paribus, more bank deposits imply a bigger money supply. By the same token, a lower reserve ratio (and thus a greater quantity of loans based on a given amount of deposits) yields a larger money supply. More money—due to more deposits and more loans—means bigger profits for banks.

This is not the end of the story, of course. Because fractional-reserve banking is built on a fiction, it works only as long as ordinary people have faith in it. As one influential scholar put it, "[Deposit banking's] essence is that a very large number of persons agree to trust a very few persons."[3] If I suddenly want to withdraw my deposits, and so does everyone else, banks must scramble to find sufficient funds. Some banks may fail. At a lesser extreme, a public lacking confidence in the banking system will hold more assets outside the system. More assets outside banks mean fewer deposits against which banks can lend and, therefore, a smaller amount of money in circulation and reduced bank profits. Banks of the 1830s, just like banks today, faced a trade-off of profit and liquidity as they tried to satisfy customers, compete with rivals, and comply with authorities.

Salient Differences between the Bank and Today's Federal Reserve System

Three features of the Second Bank of the United States set it apart from today's Federal Reserve structure. It existed in a commodity-money world, it engaged in private lending and deposit taking, and it acted as a creditor toward other banks rather than a debtor.

---

[2]Whether the market value of nineteenth-century banknotes equaled their face value is a separate issue. Banks that defaulted on their notes could pass on some of the costs of the default to note holders who did not correctly anticipate the probability of default. An interesting empirical question is how well people forecast the failure of a particular bank with outstanding notes. If markets work well, banks may need little regulation because the market value of notes accurately reflects the default probability. Forecasting failure rates still takes real resources, of course, so a regime with defaults is not costless regardless of people's ability to anticipate them. If markets work poorly, policy makers might want to require a minimum amount of capital for prospective banks and limit the number of loans offered and banknotes issued. Rolnick and Weber take up this topic for the free-banking era, as I discuss later. Arthur Rolnick and Warren Weber, "New Evidence on the Free Banking Era," *American Economic Review* 73 (1983):1080–91.

[3]Walter Bagehot, *Lombard Street: A Description of the Money Market* (London, 1873), p. 78. Walter Bagehot was the leading nineteenth-century authority on central banking. His influential work is featured in later sections of this paper.

The first feature meant that banks generally had to redeem their notes for specie (gold and silver) upon demand.[4] If I received payment for my merchandise in notes issued by the Suffolk Bank, I could insist that the Suffolk Bank exchange those notes for specie whenever I wished. Today, all I could get for my Federal Reserve note is another easily printable Federal Reserve note.

Specie also serves as an international medium of exchange in a commodity-money world. Consequently, countries that commit to a specie standard and trade with one another cannot undertake monetary policy in isolation. Take the United States and Great Britain in the Jackson era, for example. An increase in the British money supply would initially raise prices there—more money would chase the same amount of goods, thus bidding up the price of each good. British imports would increase relative to exports because imports would be relatively cheaper. Specie would then flow out of Britain to pay for the increase in net imports. This would in turn reduce British money stock and prices. This process is commonly termed "Hume's price-specie flow mechanism," named after eighteenth-century philosopher David Hume.

In sum, a monetary system based on commodity money means that the amount of specie held in a given location matters quite a lot. What is more, policies—both domestic and foreign—that affect the geographical distribution of gold and silver could have profound economic consequences. If a policy pulled specie out of a region just when local depositors wished to withdraw it, for instance, a bank in the region could find itself in trouble.

The Second Bank's private activities, coupled with its need to adhere to a specie standard, meant that it had to worry about its own liquidity and profitability. A true central bank could simply trade liquid assets (specie or its own notes) for less liquid assets (other banks' notes) in times of financial crisis. But the Bank did not have this luxury: if it disbursed large amounts of specie to other banks in exchange for their notes, it might encounter major liquidity problems as its own depositors clamored for payment. Holding notes issued by other banks also effectively meant an interest-free loan made to rivals and thus lost profits.

---

[4]The Coinage Act of 1792 put the mint ratio of gold to silver at 15 to 1 when France had a ratio of 15.5 to 1. In 1834, the United States increased its ratio to 16 to 1. Therefore, although the United States was officially on a bimetallic standard, the country effectively enjoyed a silver standard for the first third of the nineteenth century, then switched to gold. For details, see Michael Bordo and Finn Kydland, "The Gold Standard as a Commitment Mechanism," in *Modern Perspectives on the Gold Standard*, ed. Tamim Bayoumi, Barry Eichengreen, and Mark Taylor (Cambridge, 1996), pp. 55–100, and Barry Eichengreen, *Globalizing Capital: A History of the International Monetary System* (Princeton, N.J., 1996).

Why not simply exchange Second Bank notes for the notes of other banks in the event of financial panic, then? Here is where the third feature of the Bank—its creditor status—comes into play. The main reason for chartering the Bank was to regain control over the money supply after the financial upheavals following the expiration of the charter for the First Bank of the United States and the War of 1812.[5] The only way the Bank retained power over the nation's money supply was to remain a net creditor of other banks.

How did the Second Bank keep this control? As a repository of the federal government, the Bank received funds collected from customs and land-office administrators, mostly in the form of notes issued by state banks. Other banks, knowing that the Second Bank could at any time require them to redeem these notes for specie, had to keep a lid on the number of notes they issued. The Bank's creditor position made this a credible threat. But if, in trying to stem a panic, the Bank exchanged enough of its own notes for others' notes to become a net debtor, it relinquished its policing power over those other banks.

Today's Fed can influence the money supply in a much different way—by requiring member banks to hold a given proportion of reserves against their liabilities. These reserves, denominated in Federal Reserve notes and held in Federal Reserve banks, make the Fed a net debtor to other banks. The Fed's chief policy instruments are its power to change the required reserve ratio, manipulate the rate at which member banks borrow and lend funds, and conduct open-market purchases and sales of Treasury securities.[6]

The Fed therefore has a greater ability to interact with other banks in times of financial crisis. For example, the Fed can relieve liquidity stresses on member banks by acting as a true lender of last resort, a role made easier

---

[5]When Congress chartered the First Bank of the United States in 1791, half of its $10 million capital was owned by the federal government. Like the Second Bank, the First Bank was a repository for government receipts, operated branches in many states, and acted as net creditor to other banks. State-chartered banks, which could not branch across state lines and rarely could branch within a state, vehemently opposed the First Bank. Thomas Jefferson disliked the size of the Bank and the concentration of British stock ownership. As a consequence, the First Bank's charter was not renewed in 1811. For greater detail, see Richard Sylla, "U.S. Securities Markets and the Banking System, 1790–1840," *Federal Reserve Bank of St. Louis Quarterly Review* 80 (1998):83–98. The period following the demise of the First Bank was chaotic financially, featuring a huge increase in the number of state-chartered banks, a doubling of banknotes in circulation, a reduction in specie held by banks, and eventually a run on banks and suspensions of specie payment.

[6]To increase the money supply, for example, the Fed can purchase Treasury notes in the open market and put more dollars into the hands of the public. The main Fed tool used today is a targeted federal funds rate.

if a central bank has no private depositors to worry about and if a country is not on a specie standard.

One other notable difference between banking in the 1830s and banking today is branching. Although the First and Second Banks of the United States had branches in a number of cities across the country, their state-bank contemporaries could not branch across state lines and could branch only within some states, typically in contiguous counties. Branching restrictions continued well into the twentieth century but have since been relaxed significantly.

The Bank from Charter to Veto

When the Second Bank of the United States was chartered in 1816 with capital of $35 million—80 percent privately funded and paid in specie, the rest paid in federal bonds—the entire nation held less than $50 million in specie.[7] This was a big bank. Yet it was also part of a sophisticated financial network. Richard Sylla notes that, as early as 1825, the United States had more than twice the banking capital of England and Wales.[8] State banks in that year held $93.7 million in capital.

The inept leadership of the Bank's first president, William Jones, soon gave way to that of the more savvy Langdon Cheves and then of Philadelphian Nicholas Biddle. Biddle was regarded as a financial wizard by some, an evil megalomaniac by others, including Andrew Jackson. Leery of the Bank's size, wealth, and power, Jackson also mistrusted any form of money other than gold or silver.[9] Among Jackson's staunch supporters was Roger Taney, later infamous for his opinion in the Dred Scott case. Other allies included some strange bedfellows—on one hand, the Locofoco hard-money

[7]Peter Temin, *The Jacksonian Economy* (New York, 1969); J. Van Fenstermaker, *The Development of American Commercial Banking, 1782–1837* (Kent, Ohio, 1965); Raymond Walters, Jr., "Origin of the Second Bank of the U.S.," *Journal of Political Economy* 53 (1945):115–31.

[8]Sylla, "U.S. Securities Markets."

[9]As a young man, Jackson suffered a major financial loss when he accepted banknotes that turned out to be worthless. Later, he and his business partners considered themselves fleeced by banks. He also was horrified by the role the Second Bank may have played in triggering the panic of 1819. For more information, see Robert Remini, *The Life of Andrew Jackson* (New York, 1988), pp. 33–34, 51, 143; Arthur Schlesinger, Jr., *The Age of Jackson* (Boston, 1945); and Claude Campbell, *The Development of Banking in Tennessee* (self-published, 1932). Taylor contains a history of the struggle between Jackson and Biddle (George Taylor, ed., *Jackson and Biddle: The Struggle over the Second Bank of the United States* [Boston, 1949]). See also Edward Green, "Economic Perspective on the Political History of the Second Bank of the United States," *Federal Reserve Bank of Chicago Economic Perspectives* (2003):59–67.

zealots,[10] on the other, the jealous state-chartered banks who resented restrictions imposed by the creditor Bank and who wanted a chance at the profits associated with lending out federal deposits.[11] Both Locofocos and state banks hated the Bank of the United States but wanted to replace it with very different monetary systems.

Jackson announced his goal of torpedoing the Bank early in his first term of office. Biddle brought matters to a head shortly before Jackson stood for reelection, when he had congressional allies pass a recharter bill four years early. Jackson's veto spelled the death of the Bank as a national institution. In an eerie foreshadowing, Biddle's brother, a director of the Bank's St. Louis branch, lost his life in a September 1831 duel over the recharter.

Jackson's Trilogy of Financial Reforms and the Aftermath

In swift succession, three events changed the face of the U.S. financial system. Although the Second Bank remained in operation under a Pennsylvania charter, Jackson withdrew its federal deposits and placed them in several state banks (known as pet banks) starting in 1833.[12] He retired the entire federal debt by the end of 1834; Congress then authorized redistribution (the Distribution Act) to the states of federal surpluses created by land-sale revenues.[13] In the midst of all this, hard-money advocate Jackson issued an

---

[10]The Locofocos derived their name from a self-igniting match. At a gathering of the Democratic party at New York's Tammany Hall, one faction doused the lights in an attempt to adjourn the meeting. In response, the hard-money men took out their locofocos, struck them, and created enough light to proceed.

[11]The famous case of *McCulloch v. Maryland* (1819) wrestled with whether a state could tax notes issued by the Second Bank—a cleverly indirect way of scooping off part of the Bank's profits. Dangerfield offers a clear, brief description of *McCulloch* (George Dangerfield, *The Era of Good Feelings* [New York, 1952], pp. 166–74).

[12]Although the Senate voted to censure Jackson in 1834 for this action, it expunged the censure three years later.

[13]Scheiber and Rousseau contain good discussions of this episode. Harry Scheiber, "The Pet Banks in Jacksonian Politics and Finance, 1833–1841," *Journal of Economic History* 33 (1963):196–214, and Peter Rousseau, "Jacksonian Monetary Policy, Specie Flows, and the Panic of 1837," *Journal of Economic History* 62 (2002):457–88. See also Edward Bourne, *The History of the Surplus Revenue of 1837* (New York, 1885). The land sale booms in 1835 and 1836 led to a huge increase in federal government deposits at the so-called pet banks. By the end of 1835, these deposits amounted to more than $22 million. The official Distribution Act passed in late June 1836; under it, about $37 million was to go to the states in proportion to their population. Each state designated its own deposit banks, and Treasury Secretary Levi Woodbury kept busy moving the money around, as no bank could hold federal funds in excess of 75 percent of its capital.

executive order (the Specie Circular) requiring specie payments for every purchase of public land.[14]

What happened in the financial sector during this time? Perhaps not surprisingly, the number of commercial banks exploded, from 220 in 1830 to 506 in 1834 and to 729 in 1837.[15] Chartering banks, taxing banks, and investing in banks were ways for states to build in financial and budgetary flexibility when they could not issue their own money.[16]

Richard Sylla, John Legler, and John Wallis show that the percentage of state revenue derived from banks became quite significant, meaning that the fortunes of the states were tied closely to those of their banks.[17] In the latter half of the 1830s, for example, Georgia received 61 percent of its revenue from banks; Maine, 47 percent; and Pennsylvania, 35 percent. The money supply—specie and banknotes—swelled by 64 percent from 1833 to 1836. Over the same period, prices rose by 28 percent, with large upsurges in the prices of land, cotton, and slaves.[18] States embarked on ambitious new canal and rail construction, working closely with their respective state banks to finance these operations.[19] This atmosphere contrasted sharply with the previous decade's stable prices, money supply, and specie stock.

Panic Sets In

Then came the upheaval. Starting in September 1836, specie flooded away from eastern financial centers as the federal surplus traveled to the state depository banks and as land purchasers in the West clamored for hard money. In early May 1837, New York banks suspended the redemption of banknotes for gold. Nearly every other bank in the nation quickly followed.

---

[14]Jackson signed this in July 1836, to take effect the following month.

[15]J. Van Fenstermaker, *Development of American Commercial Banking,* cited in Rousseau, "Jacksonian Monetary Policy." By contrast, Hammond reports that only thirty-one banks existed in 1801 (Bray Hammond, "Jackson, Biddle, and the Bank of the United States," *Journal of Economic History* 7 [1947]:1–23). These numbers do not correct for bank size, of course, and many of the new banks were quite small relative to the older banks.

[16]States agreed to this as part of the Constitutional Convention. For detail, see Sylla, "U.S. Securities Markets."

[17]Richard Sylla, John Legler, and John Wallis, "Banks and State Public Finance in the New Republic: The United States, 1790–1860," *Journal of Economic History* 47 (1987):391–403.

[18]Temin, *Jacksonian Economy;* Hugh Rockoff, "Money, Prices, and Banks in the Jacksonian Era," in *The Reinterpretation of American Economic History,* ed. Robert Fogel and Stanley Engerman (New York, 1971), pp. 448–58.

[19]John Wallis, "What Caused the Crisis of 1839?" *NBER Historical Working Paper* 133 (Cambridge, 2001); Sylla, Legler, and Wallis, "Banks and State Public Finance"; and H. Jerome Cranmer, "Canal Investment, 1815–1860," in *Studies in Income and Wealth, vol. 24: Trends in the American Economy in the Nineteenth Century* (Princeton, N.J., 1960), pp. 547–72.

The 1837 panic subsided within a few months, only to be followed by a second wave of suspensions starting in Philadelphia on October 9, 1839. Although this wave was less widespread—New Jersey, New York, and New England (except for Rhode Island) banks did not stop specie payments—the crisis lasted much longer and had more profound effects. Numerous banks failed, state transportation projects languished, stock prices halved between May 1835 and January 1843, nonfinancial business incorporations fell by more than 80 percent from 1837 to 1843, and real per capita imports during that period were only half the level they had reached in 1836.[20] Land sales in many places came to a dead halt.[21] The money supply fell by 34 percent from 1838 to 1842; prices fell 33 percent from 1839 to 1843. Failures and loan losses reduced the book assets of state banks by 45 percent, and 194 of the 729 state-chartered banks closed their doors.[22] The percentage of state revenue from banks fell to 14 percent in Georgia, 7 percent in Maine, and 5 percent in Pennsylvania between 1841 and 1845, contrasting sharply with the figures for the previous five years.[23] Recovery took most of a decade.

Connections between Real and Financial Sectors

The data on per capita real GDP over this period are revealing. Although these figures are hard to estimate, Louis Johnston and Samuel Williamson have put together a coherent annual series that reflects the work of several scholars.[24] As table 1 shows, real per capita GDP grew by an average of 3.16

---

[20]Sylla, Legler, and Wallis, "Banks and State Public Finance"; Sylla, "American Banking and Growth"; George Evans, *Business Incorporations in the United States, 1800–1943* (New York, 1948); and Douglass North, *The Economic Growth of the United States, 1790–1860* (Englewood Cliffs, N.J., 1961).

[21]Lakeshore land sales in Manitowoc, Wisconsin, went to zero in the early 1840s, for example. William Melton, "A History of the Veblens," unpublished manuscript, 2005.

[22]Joseph Martin, *Seventy-Three Years' History of the Boston Stock Market* (self-published, 1871); Fenstermaker, *Development of American Commercial Banking.*

[23]Sylla, Legler, and Wallis, "Banks and State Public Finance."

[24]Louis Johnston and Samuel Williamson, "The Annual Real and Nominal GDP for the United States, 1789–Present," *Economic History Services,* http://www.eh.net/hmit/gdp/ (March 2004). See also Angus Maddison, *Monitoring the World Economy, 1820–1992* (Paris, 1995); Thomas Berry, *Production and Population since 1789: Revised GNP Series in Constant Dollars* (Richmond, Va., 1988); Robert Gallman, "Gross National Product in the United States, 1834–1909," in *Studies in Income and Wealth, vol. 30: Output Employment, and Productivity in the United States after 1800* (New York, 1966); and North, *Economic Growth.*

TABLE I

Real Per Capita GDP in the United States, 1830–47

Year	Real per capita GDP	Real per capita GDP as percentage of 1847 real per capita GDP	Period	Annualized growth rate over the period
1830	1660	81.4		
1831	1680	82.4		
1832	1730	84.8		
1833	1820	89.2		
1834	1880	92.2	1830–34	3.16
1835	1790	87.7		
1836	1740	85.3	1834–36	-3.80
1837	1840	90.2		
1838	1800	88.2		
1839	1920	94.1	1836–39	3.34
1840	1860	91.1		
1841	1850	90.7		
1842	1770	86.8	1839–42	-2.68
1843	1900	93.1		
1844	1920	94.1		
1845	1930	94.6		
1846	1920	94.1		
1847	2040	100.0	1842–47	2.88

Source: Louis Johnston and Samuel Williamson, "The Annual Real and Nominal GDP for the United States, 1789–Present," *Economic History Services,* http://www.eh.net/hmit/gdp/ (March 2004).

percent annually from 1830 to 1834. It then fell an average 3.8 percent annually from 1834 to 1836. The annual average change was +3.34 percent from 1836 to 1839, -2.68 percent from 1839 to 1842, and +2.88 percent from 1842 to 1847.

Much of this variability is linked to agricultural cycles, of course, so we must be cautious in making inferences. But the data suggest that the ups and downs in financial markets corresponded to real movements in the economy. What these figures do not reveal is the direction of causality, and this is part of what we need to explore to determine Andrew Jackson's responsibility for the events of the late 1830s.

The Classical View: The Panic of 1837 Was Jackson's Fault

The classical explanation for the financial crises of the late 1830s places blame squarely on Andrew Jackson's shoulders. Scholars like Bray Hammond, Fritz Redlich, Reginald McGrane, and Richard Timberlake—who shares his surname with Peggy Eaton's first husband[25]—laud the Bank of the United States for providing a stable financial foundation.[26] The veto of the Bank and the dispersal of federal deposits meant that unsophisticated (or dishonest) state banks could engage in unrestrained lending without supervision, making them vulnerable to a liquidity crisis. Instead of satisfying the Locofoco demand for hard money, Jackson opened the way for a proliferation of paper. As Hammond colorfully puts it, "[Jackson] professed to be the deliverer of his people from the oppressions of the mammoth—but instead he delivered the private banks from federal control and his people to speculation. No more striking example could be found of a leader fostering the very evil he was angrily wishing out of the way."[27] Add the Specie Circular, which increased public demand for gold in the West, and the distribution of federal surplus, which drained reserves from the East, and conditions were ripe for bank runs.

Hammond also places some responsibility for the disaster upon Nicholas Biddle, who arrogantly proclaimed his bank's capacity to destroy state banks if it so chose. Between Biddle and Jackson, "the fury and folly of these two

---

[25]John Timberlake reportedly committed suicide after he defrauded the government to cover his wife's debts. Her subsequent relationship with John Eaton gave rise to rumors of inappropriate behavior. When Jackson appointed Eaton to his cabinet, he angrily defended Mrs. Eaton's chastity, perhaps recalling similar gossip about his own wife (Remini, *Life of Jackson*).

[26]See, for example, Bray Hammond, *Banks and Politics in America from the Revolution to the Civil War* (Princeton, N.J., 1957); idem, "Jackson, Biddle, and the Bank of the United States"; Fritz Redlich, *The Molding of American Banking: Men and Ideas* (New York, 1951); Reginald McGrane, *The Panic of 1837: Some Financial Problems of the Jacksonian Era* (Chicago, 1924); Richard Timberlake, Jr., "The Specie Circular and the Distribution of the Surplus," *Journal of Political Economy* 68 (1960):109–17; and idem, *The Origins of Central Banking in the United States* (Cambridge, Mass., 1978). Another useful early source is Ralph Catterall, *The Second Bank of the United States* (Chicago, 1903). See also Arthur Fraas, "The Second Bank of the United States: An Instrument for an Interregional Monetary Union," *Journal of Economic History* 34 (1974):447–67.

[27]Hammond, "Jackson, Biddle, and the Bank of the United States," p. 9. Tocqueville also considered Jackson to have made himself an instrument of private banks (reported in Phillips Bradley, ed., *Democracy in America: Part I of the writings of Alexis de Tocqueville* [New York, 1945], p. 409).

ruined an excellent monetary system—as good as any the country has ever possessed—and left a reckless, booming anarchy."[28]

The Revisionists: Jackson Was Not to Blame

Set against this traditional school of thought are revisionist cliometricians, including George Macesich, Hugh Rockoff, and Peter Temin.[29] These men ascribe the early run-up in money supply and prices to an inflow of specie from abroad and the 1837 panic to an outflow of specie due to Britain's increased interest rates and a reduction in the price of cotton, an important U.S. commodity export. In this view, the United States is cast as a small open economy that has little control over its monetary system. Because specie served as both bank reserves and international money, the United States easily fell victim to international shifts in specie demand and supply.[30]

The revisionists use detailed data to evaluate the traditional approach. Suppose the Bank War had unleashed wildcat banks that printed notes with abandon and lent with little regard for reserves. We would expect to find the ratio of specie reserves to bank liabilities falling over time. This did not happen, as table 2 shows. Instead, the money supply increased because specie flowed into the United States, not because profit-hungry banks overextended loans.

From where did the additional specie originate? Some came from Mexico, seeking a safe haven and paying for imported commodities. Some was an

---

[28]Hammond, "Jackson, Biddle, and the Bank of the United States," p. 20. Jackson may have been open to some form of central bank that was more responsive to the government and to western interests. But the clash between Jackson and Biddle put an end to any possibility of compromise (Edwin Perkins, "Lost Opportunities for Compromise in the Bank War: A Reassessment of Jackson's Veto Message," *Business and Economic History*, 2d ser., 14 [1985]: 53–56). I thank Hugh Rockoff for pointing me to this source.

[29]See, for instance, George Macesich, "Sources of Monetary Disturbances in the U.S., 1834–1845," *Journal of Economic History* 20 (1960):407–34; idem, *Money and Monetary Regimes: Struggle for Monetary Supremacy* (Westport, Conn., 2002); Rockoff, "Money, Prices, and Banks"; Peter Temin, "The Economic Consequences of the Bank War," *Journal of Political Economy* 76 (1968):257–74; and idem, *Jacksonian Economy.*

[30]Huffman and Lothian ran a series of Granger causality tests that suggest that the contractions of 1836, 1839, 1845, and 1857 started in England and spread to the United States (Wallace Huffman and James Lothian, "Money in the United Kingdom, 1830–1880," *Journal of Money, Credit, and Banking* 12 [1980]:155–74). Granger causality is not causality, however. As I argue later, the evidence persuades me that domestic policy generated much of the U.S. financial upheaval in the 1830s.

TABLE 2

U.S. Prices, Money Stock, Specie, and Reserves during the 1830s

Year	Prices	Annualized rate of change	Money ($mil)	Annualized rate of change	Specie ($mil)	Annualized rate of change	Bank specie reserves as percentage of bank liabilities	Percentage of specie held by the public
1831	89		155		30		15	5
1832	91		150		31		16	5
1833	95		168		41		18	8
1834	90		172		51		27	4
1835	108		246		65		18	10
1836	122		276		73		16	13
1837	111		232		88		20	23
1838	106		240		87		23	18
1839	115	2.6	215	7.2	83	9.2	20	23

Sources: Hugh Rockoff, "Money, Prices, and Banks in the Jacksonian Era," in *The Reinterpretation of American Economic History,* ed. Robert Fogel and Stanley Engerman (New York, 1971); Peter Temin, *The Jacksonian Economy* (New York, 1969).

indemnity payment by France for shipping losses suffered during the French Revolution and the Napoleonic Wars. London sent specie to pay for American securities, especially canal stock. And part of the inflow was really reduced outflow of specie to China. The United States ran a trade deficit with China, initially paying for it in silver. China wanted to import more opium from British India. The two countries came to a mutually satisfying arrangement—Americans began to pay for Chinese imports with London bills of exchange instead of silver; the Chinese then used these bills to pay for opium.

So Jackson was not responsible for the inflation after the demise of the Second Bank, according to the revisionists. Nor was he to blame for the panics and crises that followed. Instead, when the Bank of England raised interest rates for the first time in fifteen years to stem Britain's specie outflows and, simultaneously, cotton prices fell, specie left the United States. As a consequence, banknote holders changed their view of the security of their assets. The revisionists found little evidence of specie flowing from the East to the West, so they determined that the New York bank failures in May 1837 had no domestic trigger.

The Critics: Putting Jackson Back in the Hot Seat

One of the first to question these findings was Stanley Engerman.[31] As he notes, the revisionist accounts do not adequately discuss the public's role in determining the amount of money circulating and the quantity of specie held by banks. As table 2 shows, the proportion of specie held by the public in 1837 and 1839 increased substantially, a practice that contributed to a drop in the money supply.[32] Recall that the supply of money depends directly upon the amount of bank deposits made by the public. If people want to hold specie instead of banknotes, banks must call in loans—effectively, the fractional-reserve system works in reverse. Engerman suggests that public confidence in banks was shaken after the Bank War, so Jackson's actions may have made the financial system more vulnerable to outside shocks.

Engerman also emphasizes that paper money yields a social savings over commodity money, because the latter has intrinsic value. When we use gold coins, we forgo the use of gold in jewelry, machinery, and the like. Substituting paper for gold releases it for use elsewhere. What is more, paper is easier to transport than specie. Engerman observes that the greatest economizing on specie in antebellum years occurred during the heyday of the Second Bank. When we lost the Bank, we lost faith in paper and thus lost the social benefits associated with its use as currency.

Marie Sushka reiterates this point, using a rigorous theoretical framework and close empirical analysis.[33] Members of the public increased specie holdings in the 1830s as they lost confidence in the banking system. This practice, along with a greater demand for specie by banks themselves, is what caused the contraction in the money supply. Sushka agrees with the revisionists that banks, far from engaging in speculative lending, wanted greater amounts of specie to hold in reserve against deposits. Although the total amount of specie in the United States escalated throughout the period, individuals and institutions wanted even more. But, because the price–specie

---

[31]Stanley Engerman, "A Note on the Consequences of the Second Bank of the United States," *Journal of Political Economy* 78 (1970):725–28.

[32]Because large amounts of specie flowed into the United States during the first part of the decade, the initial increase in public holdings could reflect a disequilibrium situation rather than a change in desired holdings. The substantial upsurge in the last part of the decade more clearly indicates an elevated desire to hold hard money.

[33]Marie Sushka, "The Antebellum Money Market and the Economic Impacts of the Bank War," *Journal of Economic History* 36 (1976):809–35.

flow mechanism should have caused specie to flow *out* of the country if international events had caused the 1837 and 1839 crises, Sushka rejects revisionist arguments. Instead, she attributes the financial chaos to the absence of a national bank and a national currency. Essentially, she believes that a lender of last resort could have stemmed panics by reassuring the public that the banking system was sound.

Peter Rousseau has most recently added his voice to the discussion.[34] Drawing upon detailed accounting records from individual banks, he discovered a missing piece: specie did indeed flood out of New York to the West in the 1830s.

Why did the outflow occur? Supplemental interbank transfers made in preparation for the official distribution of the federal surplus required large interstate movements of specie. Also, people needed specie to pay for land, which was still selling at a brisk pace even after the Specie Circular took effect.[35] What is more, public land offices that took in specie payment took their time in sending it back to the East. Consequently, New York City banks lost 61 percent of their specie ($4.4 million) between August 1836 and March 1837, yet loans fell by only 14.7 percent ($5.6 million). Specie reserves fell even further before suspension occurred: New York depository banks held $2.8 million on March 1 but only $1.5 million on May 1. Because New York was the nation's financial center, it was left vulnerable to British calls for specie. At the same time, faltering trust in banknotes in this country led individuals to clamor for more specie of their own. Given the paltry amount of reserves, when $600,000 in specie left New York banks on May 8 and even more on May 9, the suspension of convertibility on May 10, 1837, is no surprise.

Like Engerman and Sushka, Rousseau attributes the financial chaos to a decline in public confidence in the banking system. If branch banking had been permitted, it would have mitigated the need for so much movement of specie associated with the distribution of the surplus. Because branches would have had access to internal banking records, they could easily have ascertained the value of their own notes. Thus they might have been less likely than unrelated banks to demand specie transfers.[36]

---

[34]Rousseau, "Jacksonian Monetary Policy."

[35]Ibid. See also Sylla, "U.S. Securities Markets."

[36]More generally, Calomiris has suggested that legislation prohibiting statewide branching is a necessary, though not sufficient, condition for financial panics (Charles Calomiris, "Regulation, Industrial Structure, and Instability in U.S. Banking: A Historical Perspective," in

Rousseau rejects the revisionists, noting that timing does not support the argument that the U.S. financial panic had its roots in international affairs. For example, increases in the Bank of England discount rate occurred a full eight months before the May suspension of convertibility.

What about 1839?

The studies mentioned thus far feature the Panic of 1837. John Wallis focuses on the financial crisis beginning in 1839. He determines that domestic forces clearly generated it. To explain why, he illuminates the strong ties among federal land policy, states, and state depository banks.[37]

Many states in the late 1830s undertook massive canal and railroad projects. Some of the funds came from the distribution of the federal surplus, but much was borrowed. This borrowing was a rational response to federal policy: every public-land state entering the Union after Ohio had to agree to a five-year moratorium on taxation of land sold by the federal government. After that time, property was fair game for taxation. In essence, then, states borrowed against the expected increase in their future income.

Particularly in the South and the West, states used banks as intermediaries. States sold bonds on credit to banks in exchange for a stream of future payments. In turn, banks sold the bonds to other parties, often in land transactions in which the banks ended up with mortgages as assets, collateralized by the land. Notorious for these sorts of credit sales was the Morris Canal and Banking Company of New Jersey, which took credit advances from the state of Indiana of $3 million in 1838 and 1839. Morris overextended itself, as did many other banks, and then defaulted in July 1839. Other banks followed suit, states began repudiating their own bonds, transportation projects halted, and land values plummeted. Southern and western banks suspended specie payments, and these regions were mired in a mess.[38]

Structural Change in Banking, ed. Michael Klausner and Lawrence White [Homewood, Ill., 1993], pp. 1–92).

[37]Wallis, "What Caused the Crisis of 1839?"; Sylla, Legler, and Wallis, "Banks and State Public Finance," also discuss this point.

[38]The reorganized Pennsylvania-chartered Bank of the United States was one of the casualties. After speculating on cotton, it had to suspend specie payments and was eventually liquidated.

Could the Bank Have Prevented the Crises of the 1830s?

Suppose the Bank of the United States had continued to exist in the latter half of the 1830s. Could it have prevented the Panic of 1837? The data suggest that the answer may be yes.[39]

The nation was on a specie standard, so the location of bank reserves held as specie mattered. Because of the Distribution Act and the Specie Circular, and because state banks took the place of the Second Bank as depositories, a substantial amount of specie moved quickly away from the financial centers —particularly New York—and into regional banks. Loans could not shrink nearly as fast as specie fled. Consequently, New York banks were extremely vulnerable even to small changes in demand for specie by depositors.

Let's look at the data. Table 3 offers a month-by-month breakdown of specie balances at the banks holding federal government deposits (indicated as "pets"). Not only did the specie balance in New York depository banks decline precipitously from September 1836 to May 1837, when the panic began, but their specie-to-loan ratio also fell to one-fourth of its former value —from nearly 20 percent to just 5 percent. During the same period, the aggregate specie-to-loan ratio for depository banks stayed fairly constant.

Why the difference between the New York and aggregate ratios? Two reasons seem likely. Specie flowed into the non–New York banks from public land sales: nearly $2 million in specie was deposited by land offices as late as April 1837. The Specie Circular changed the composition of deposits drastically—total deposits ranged from $2 to $3 million every two months from August 1836 to April 1837, but the proportion deposited in specie increased dramatically. Banks outside New York also increased their specie holdings relative to New York banks because of the Distribution Act. Table 3 indicates the total (specie plus nonspecie) net interstate transfers from New York banks. Although the portion transferred as specie is not recorded, logic suggests that, as government deposits left the East coast, western banks would have wanted at least some fraction—maybe a large fraction—in specie.

---

[39]Many scholars have suggested that the Bank probably helped stabilize financial markets and that its disappearance left a gaping hole. See, for example, Richard Sylla, Jack Wilson, and Charles Jones, "U.S. Financial Markets and Long-Term Economic Growth, 1790–1989," in *American Economic Development in Historical Perspective*, ed. Thomas Weiss and Donald Schaefer (Stanford, Calif., 1994), pp. 28–52.

TABLE 3

Specie-Holding Information for the Public and for Pet Banks in New York and Overall
(dollar amounts in thousands)

Month	NYC pets' specie balance	All pets' specie balance	Specie-to-loan ratio, NYC pets	Specie-to-loan ratio, all pets	Estimated percentage nation's specie in NYC pets	Estimated percentage nation's specie in all pets	Estimated percentage nation's specie in pets +public	NYC pet net transfers to non-NYC pets (specie+ non specie)	Specie transfers from land offices to non-NYC pets
September 1836	7191.9	16343.7	0.194	0.113	0.102	0.231	0.651	1709	
October	5142.4	15465.0	0.140	0.100	0.072	0.216	0.636	1991	980.5
November	3804.3	14593.3	0.110	0.092	0.053	0.202	0.622	430	
December	3810.5	15212.5	0.110	0.095	0.052	0.208	0.628	100	1147.9
January 1837								2392	
February								125	1513.5
March	2780.5	14987.4	0.085	0.092	0.038	0.204	0.664	670	
April								892	1974.6
May	1473.1	12150.1	0.050	0.113	0.020	0.165	0.651	0	731.6
June								0	47.6
July	1768.4	10728.0	0.067	0.100	0.024	0.145	0.645	740	106.6

Sources: Peter Rousseau, "Jacksonian Monetary Policy, Specie Flows, and the Panic of 1837," *Journal of Economic History* 62 (2002):457–88; Peter Temin, *The Jacksonian Economy* (New York, 1969); Jack Rutner, "Money in the Antebellum Economy," Ph.D. diss., University of Chicago, 1974.

If the Bank of the United States had remained in existence as the federal depository, the Distribution Act and the Specie Circular would likely have caused much less movement of specie and thus far less stress upon regional financial markets. Distribution of the federal surplus could have gone to the national bank branches scattered about the country. Internal distributions could have taken place without the sort of specie drainage from financial centers required when unrelated banks transferred deposits.[40] Internal channels also could have facilitated the quick movement of specie from land offices

---

[40]Banks certainly had correspondent relations, as Bodenhorn discusses (Howard Bodenhorn, *A History of Banking in Antebellum America: Financial Markets and Economic Development in an Era of Nation-Building* [Cambridge, 2000]). Yet, the amount of monitoring required for separate entities is higher than for internal relationships. No matter how much banks might want to trust their correspondents, the very fact that they do not have access to internal accounting records means that they would request a higher proportion of transferred deposits to arrive in specie than would branches of the same bank.

to where it was most needed. In short, the Panic of 1837 might never have happened had the Bank survived.

What effect might the Bank have had in 1839? Any conclusion about later events is much more tentative because this crisis was related to the close ties between state government and state banks. If the national bank had continued to exist past 1836, the speculative excesses that Wallis describes might not have occurred. State government probably would not have had the cozy relationship with a branch of the Bank that it did with its own chartered banks. Still, one cannot say for sure—the reincarnated state-chartered Second Bank was just as eager to deal in state bonds as any other bank. Wallis reports that, when the Bank went belly-up, more than a third of its assets were state bonds. What its balance sheet as a full-fledged national bank might have looked like is hard to guess. I will address more fully the question of the Bank's possible role in post-1838 events later on.

Would the Bank Have Prevented the Crises of the 1830s?

Suppose the Second Bank had had the resources to stem the financial crises of the 1830s. Would it have done so? Here a look at the Bank's own history and the history of other centralized financial authorities—including those that followed the Bank—is instructive.[41]

Evaluating performance is always easier with the benefit of hindsight. Still, trying to ascertain what might have happened with and without intervention is difficult because, when central banks or other official financial entities exist, they rarely do nothing. Instead, they take an active role doing something at some time during a crisis. Those who judge these actions tend to put them in one of three categories: just right, too little too late, or too much too early. Let's add another complication, however: even when central authorities seem to behave optimally in a particular circumstance, their very existence creates costs that can be quite large. In other words, the best financial framework for an economy might be no central authority at all.

Putting aside this institutional issue until the next section, when have central banks acted appropriately to stop financial panic? Charles Kindleberger speaks admiringly of the actions of the Bank of France in 1810, 1818, and

---

[41]A nice summary of financial panics of the later nineteenth century appears in Elmus Wicker, *Banking Panics of the Gilded Age* (Cambridge, 2000).

1826, although he laments its behavior in 1831.[42] Michael Bordo applauds the efforts of the Bank of England in 1866.[43] Bordo and Anna Schwartz contend that maintaining a specie standard with a contingent rule of wartime escape clauses but recommitment soon after peace arrived worked well for the United States, the United Kingdom, and France in the nineteenth and early twentieth centuries.[44] Jeffrey A. Miron, Bordo, and Charles Goodhart argue that central banks generally reduce the frequency of financial crises.[45] V. V. Chari notes that Fed actions, along with deposit insurance and close regulation, prevented U.S. bank panics after 1933.[46] Some commentators have extolled the Fed's quick action to encourage bank lending after the 1970 Penn Central bankruptcy and after the October 1987 stock market crash.[47]

Yet central authorities sometimes do exactly the wrong thing. The Second Bank itself sold off bonds during the 1825 crisis instead of using specie reserves to buy securities and pump reserves into other banks. This was because of its desire to protect its own profits and liquidity, at least in part.[48]

---

[42]Charles Kindleberger, *Manias, Panics, and Crashes: A History of Financial Crises* (New York, 1978).

[43]Michael Bordo, "Financial Crises, Banking Crises, Stock Market Crashes, and the Money Supply: Some International Evidence, 1870–1933," in *Financial Crises and the World Banking System*, ed. Forrest Capie and Geoffrey Wood (London, 1986), pp. 190–248; and idem, *The Gold Standard and Related Regimes* (Cambridge, 1999).

[44]Michael Bordo and Anna Schwartz, "The Operation of the Specie Standard—Evidence for Core and Peripheral Countries, 1880–1990," in *Currency Convertibility*, ed. Jorge Braga de Macedo, Barry Eichengreen, and Jaime Reis (London, 1996), pp. 238–317.

[45]Jeffrey A. Miron, "Financial Panics, the Seasonality of the Nominal Interest Rate, and the Founding of the Fed," *American Economic Review* 76 (1986):125–40; Bordo, "Financial Crises"; and Charles Goodhart, *The Evolution of Central Banks* (Cambridge, Mass., 1988).

[46]V. V. Chari, "Banking without Deposit Insurance or Bank Panics: Lessons from a Model of the U.S. National Banking System," *Federal Reserve Bank of Minneapolis Quarterly Review* 13 (1989):3–19. Chari's model further suggests that effective reserve requirements, wise use of the discount window, and occasional restrictions of cash payments could eliminate panics without deposit insurance. Mishkin has also raised questions about the effectiveness of deposit insurance, noting that the United Kingdom has not suffered a banking panic since the 1860s, despite having insurance only since 1979 (Frederic Mishkin, "Financial Consolidation: Dangers and Opportunities," *Journal of Banking and Finance* 23 [1999]:675–91). As I note later, the way we have handled deposit insurance in this country may have caused more harm than good.

[47]Franklin Edwards, "Hedge Funds and the Collapse of Long-Term Capital Management," *Journal of Economic Perspectives* 13 (1999):189–210, contains a discussion.

[48]The Bank's actions also may have been attributable to its relative lack of reserves. Although the Bank held some 30 percent of all specie in the country in 1834, it held only about 14 percent in 1825 (Milton Friedman and Anna Schwartz, *Monetary Statistics of the United States* [New York, 1970]). One might also consider banks to have been in a learning phase in 1825—this was a global crisis year, and the Bank of England stalled for a long time before it finally plunged in with reserves too late to prevent massive bank failures (Michael Bordo, "Commentary," *Federal Reserve Bank of St. Louis Review* [1998]:77–82).

Stephen Quinn and Michael Bordo note that the failure of the Bank of England to perform well in 1825 and the 1830s caused authorities to split it into an Issue Department and a Banking Department in 1844.[49] Even Charles Kindleberger, a big fan of a lender of last resort, declares that the U.S. Treasury acted too slowly in 1873 but came to the rescue too early in 1857.[50]

Among the more vocal critics of central-bank policy are Milton Friedman and Anna Schwartz. In their magisterial *Monetary History of the United States*, they note that the Fed presided over the more than doubling of prices during and after World War I and that its subsequent overreaction led to a sharp depression in 1920 and 1921.[51] The number of bank failures went from 63 in 1919 to 155 in 1920 and to 506 in 1921. Less than a decade later, the Fed's refusal to follow its New York branch's lead to lend and to conduct open-market purchases of Treasury securities spurred a flurry of bank failures. Of the more than nine thousand banks that suspended operations at some point between 1930 and 1933, more than one-third failed after March 15, 1933. Had the Fed simply bought $1 billion in securities, it could have satisfied public and bank demands for currency and stemmed the tide. Instead, banks inundated by depositors wanting their money had to dump assets on the market at fire-sale prices.

In more recent history, government actions surrounding banks have sometimes created perverse incentives. Instead of calming financial markets, official policies can stir them up. One need only recall the financial disasters of the 1980s. The failure rate for U.S. banks was 2 per year in the 1970s and 130 per year from 1982 to 1991. By the end of 1982, the Federal Deposit Insurance Corporation (FDIC) listed 863 banks with combined assets of $464 billion as problem institutions.[52] Savings and loan institutions were in even worse shape.

As we realize now, deregulating the industry without modifying deposit insurance requirements meant that financial institutions could take risks with

[49]Stephen Quinn, "Money, Finance, and Capital Markets," in *The Economic History of Britain since 1700*, ed. Roderick Floud and Donald McCloskey (Cambridge, 1994), and Bordo, *Gold Standard*. Other useful sources include Arthur Gayer, Walter Rostow, and Anna Schwartz, *The Growth and Fluctuation of the British Economy, 1790–1850* (Oxford, 1953), and Larry Neal, "The Financial Crisis of 1825 and the Restructuring of the British Financial System," *Federal Reserve Bank of St. Louis Review* 80 (1998):53–76.

[50]Kindleberger, *Manias*; Charles Kindleberger and Jean-Pierre Laffargue, eds., *Financial Crises* (Cambridge, 1982).

[51]Milton Friedman and Anna Schwartz, *A Monetary History of the United States, 1867–1960* (Princeton, N.J., 1963).

[52]John Boyd and Mark Gertler, "The Role of Large Banks in the Recent U.S. Banking Crisis," *Federal Reserve Bank of Minneapolis Quarterly Review* 18 (1994):2–21.

depositor money without worrying about failed gambles. John Kareken succinctly viewed this as the financial version of putting the cart before the horse.[53] John Boyd and Mark Gertler observed that large banks were mainly responsible for poor performance because they were considered too big to fail—the combination of deposit insurance and a central authority that refused to permit failure allowed them to speculate to their hearts' content.[54]

Where does this leave us in thinking about whether the Bank of the United States would have forestalled financial panics if it had existed after 1836? The answer is not clear. History tells us that the track record of central-bank behavior is mixed. Even if the Bank could have acted to prevent the financial turmoil of the 1830s and 1840s, it might not have.

What Role Should Centralization Play in the Financial Sector?

As the last section suggests, the heart of an ongoing debate in banking is the role of government in preventing financial panics. At one extreme are those who believe that markets are efficient enough and that monetary crises should be left to sort themselves out. Milton Friedman, for instance, has paraphrased Georges Clemenceau by saying, "Money is too important to be left to the central bankers."[55] At the other end of the spectrum are those who think that the government should take an active part in regulating the establishment and administration of financial intermediaries and should step in as lender of last resort when needed.[56]

---

[53]John Kareken, "Deposit Insurance Reform; or, Deregulation Is the Cart, Not the Horse," *Federal Reserve Bank of Minneapolis Quarterly Review* 7 (1983):1–9.

[54]Boyd and Gertler, "Role of Large Banks."

[55]Milton Friedman, *The Essence of Friedman* (Stanford, Calif., 1987), p. 429. See also Anna Schwartz, "Real and Pseudo-Financial Crises," in *Financial Crises and the World Banking System*, ed. Forrest Capie and Geoffrey Wood (London, 1986), pp. 1–10. Disagreeing with Charles Kindleberger, Schwartz suggests that markets are better able to discriminate between a firm or city in financial distress and one in sound condition. For a related point, see Finn Kydland and Edward Prescott, "Rules Rather Than Discretion," *Journal of Political Economy* 85 (1977):473–92.

[56]Among these people are Charles Kindleberger, *The International Economic Order: Essays on Financial Crisis and International Public Goods* (Cambridge, Mass., 1988), who has suggested that the lack of a lender of last resort increases timidity among lenders, which can stagnate growth. As evidence, he cites the experience of London after the strengthening of the Bubble Act in 1734 to forbid short sales. Fischer has defended the notion of having an international as well as a domestic lender of last resort (Stanley Fischer, "On the Need for an International Lender of Last Resort," *Journal of Economic Perspectives* 13 [1999]:85–104). See also Alan Blinder, "Central-Bank Credibility: Why Do We Care? How Do We Build It?" *American Economic Review* 90 (2000):1421–31, and Xavier Freixas, Curzio Giannini, Glenn Hoggarth, and Farouk Soussa, "Lender of Last Resort," *Financial Stability Review* (November 1999):151–67.

The Case for an Active Central Bank
in Times of Financial Panic

Walter Bagehot's *Lombard Street,* published twenty-eight years after Andrew Jackson's death, has become the classic source of advice for central bankers.[57] Most people remember it for Bagehot's adage that, to prevent financial panics, a central authority should lend freely against solid assets but at a high interest rate. Because the essential element of financial panics is the depyramiding of reserves, which leads to frantic loan calls, contraction of the money supply, and possible bank failures, something that prevents the initial kindling of the panic—namely, quick provision of reserves where and when necessary—will avert the panic.

The leading theoretical model supporting this view is set forth in Peter Diamond and Philip Dybvig.[58] In their model, random withdrawals generate the possibility of panic in a world in which depositors are served on a first-come, first-served basis. A surge in the demand for funds occurs for some reason, perhaps related to the agricultural cycle.[59] The combination of sequential service and fractional reserves means that the first to demand their funds from the bank will get them but that later arrivals may not. Essentially, then, the panic arises from a self-fulfilling set of beliefs. If this model accurately describes the real world, even prudent banks can fail in the absence of a lender of last resort or some other scheme that helps stabilize the system.

A different theory centers on asymmetric information between banks and their creditors. This alternative models a financial panic starting when depositors and holders of banknotes—who have imperfect information about a particular bank's asset portfolio—revise their perception of the risk associated with banks when they receive bad news about the macroeconomy. Because people cannot immediately distinguish among banks, they might withdraw their deposits from all banks. This seems to call for a lender of last resort or a stabilizing external influence, just as in the random-withdrawal model.

As we shall see later, however, the asymmetric-information model does not necessarily support the notion that providing emergency liquidity via a centralized governmental authority will halt a panic. In fact, a panic may be

---

[57]An earlier, though less cited, source is Henry Thornton, *An Enquiry into the Nature and Effects of the Paper Credit of Great Britain* (1802; reprint ed., Fairfield, Conn., 1978).

[58]Peter Diamond and Philip Dybvig, "Bank Runs, Deposit Insurance, and Liquidity," *Journal of Political Economy* 91 (1983):401–19.

[59]Chari, "Banking without Deposit Insurance," suggests this possibility.

just what is needed to separate the wheat from the chaff, as it tends to drive out poorly managed banks.

Problems with Central Bank Activism

Despite its potentially stabilizing influence during a crisis, the very existence of an institutional lender of last resort can lead to a special sort of trouble, as the financial troubles of the 1980s revealed. If banks know they will be rescued with reserves, they may have an incentive to take risks they otherwise would have avoided. This is the problem of moral hazard. Bank bailouts mean that uninsured creditors have no incentive to monitor the behavior of banks.[60] Although constructive ambiguity about the circumstances in which a lender of last resort will step in could mitigate this problem, it is unlikely to erase it. Where one stands on the efficacy of a lender of last resort depends in part on how well one believes such an entity can employ constructive ambiguity.[61]

Hugh Rockoff points out that Walter Bagehot was aware of this issue.[62] In fact, the advice in *Lombard Street* is more complicated than typically represented. Bagehot suggested lending freely at a high interest rate in times of panic but protecting reserves when the market is only apprehensive. This recommendation recognized the delicate balance between defending the integrity of the currency in an international marketplace and preserving liquidity within a country. According to Bagehot, lenders of last resort should not always show up eagerly brandishing loans to worried bankers. The problem is that Bagehot did not tell us how to distinguish panic from apprehension.[63]

---

[60]Kaufman discusses this point, for example. G. Kaufman, "Lender of Last Resort: A Contemporary Perspective," *Journal of Financial Services Research* 5 (1991):95–110.

[61]Xavier Freixas, "Optimal Bailout Policy, Conditionality, and Creative Ambiguity," in *Financial Markets Group Discussion Paper* (London, 1999), p. 327, develops a theoretical case for constructive ambiguity.

[62]Hugh Rockoff, "Walter Bagehot and the Theory of Central Banking," in *Financial Crises and the World Banking System*, ed. Forrest Capie and Geoffrey Wood (London, 1986), pp. 160–80.

[63]Does this still matter in a fiat-money world, as we now have? In "Walter Bagehot," Rockoff points out that a central bank would never run out of reserves when it prints its own money, yet it might have other goals that would conflict with its role as a lender of last resort. So the tension still exists.

Some lament the demise of the gold standard and fixed exchange rates. Bordo and Kydland, "The Gold Standard," suggest that we have not really developed a better commitment

So here is the question: how well can a central bank psychoanalyze the market, and does it do so better than anyone else? Rockoff notes that central banks find it hard to resist the pressure to lend even when they are not sure whether a panic exists. If they do lend at some times but not at others, they leave themselves open to criticisms of cronyism. For instance, the Bank of France did not save Crédit Mobilier in 1868 or Union Générale in 1882, but it did rescue the Comptoir d'Escompte de Paris in 1889; these actions generated charges of favoritism.[64]

Here is another problem: rather than constructive ambiguity, destructive ambiguity could be the path chosen if an authority fails to step in when everyone thinks it will. Jack Guttentag and Richard Herring describe the worst possible scenario as one in which a lender of last resort is expected to take action but does not.[65] Russia's failure to intervene in August 1998 is a historical example. Although the market anticipated that the Russians would act to prevent devaluation of the ruble, the country instead declared a moratorium on the equivalent of $13.5 billion of treasury debt. Financial chaos ensued.

Alternative Approaches to Resolving Financial Panic

Let's add some wrinkles to the asymmetric-information model that may circumvent the problems of moral hazard and central-bank behavioral uncertainty, at least theoretically. One is to assume that at least some depositors

---

mechanism to price stability than the gold standard. See also Michael Bordo and Hugh Rockoff, "The Gold Standard as a 'Good Housekeeping Seal of Approval,'" *Journal of Economic History* 56 (1996):389–428, and Michael Bordo and Anna Schwartz, eds., *A Retrospective on the Classical Gold Standard, 1821–1931* (Chicago, 1984). Bordo, Eichenberg, and Kim find it disheartening that the current international monetary system is no better than the gold standard at handling international financial crises (Michael Bordo, Barry Eichengreen, and Jongwoo Kim, "Was There Really an Earlier Period of Financial Integration Comparable to Today?" *NBER Working Paper* 6738 [Cambridge, 1998]). DeLong suggests that fixed exchange rates helped speed worldwide recovery before World War I, although he recognizes the impossibility of returning to such a system (J. Bradford Delong, "Financial Crises in the 1890s and the 1990s: Must History Repeat?" *Brookings Papers on Economic Activity* [1999]:253–94). But are we worse off today? Not necessarily: Frankel has concluded, in fact, that no single currency regime is best for all countries or even for a given country at all times (Jeffrey Frankel, *No Single Currency Is Right for All Countries or at All Times*, Princeton Essays in International Finance 215 [Princeton, N.J., 1999]).

[64]Kindleberger, *Manias*, pp. 150ff.

[65]Jack Guttentag and Richard Herring, *The Lender of Last Resort Function in an International Context*, Princeton University Essays in International Finance 151(Princeton, N.J., 1983).

and note holders are well informed about particular banks.[66] These people are more likely to line up for their money at problem banks, signaling something about soundness to everyone else. Consequently, a panic works to cull the weak banks, leaving the system stronger as a result.

Another possible solution is a privately operated clearinghouse. Instead of having a central bank or well-informed individuals as monitors, the banks monitor themselves—when a panic starts, the clearinghouse issues temporary certificates that expire when it sorts out which banks are problems. Again, a panic simply flushes bad banks from the system.

History tells us that private arrangements have had some success in warding off extensive financial panic. Arthur Rolnick, Bruce Smith, and Warren Weber, along with Charles Calomiris and Charles Kahn, attribute the stability of the New England region during the 1839 crisis years to the presence of the Suffolk Bank, which was chartered by the state but privately owned.[67] This Boston bank essentially acted like a central bank: it required members to keep deposits there, then it would clear notes and provide overdraft protection so that member banks could hold and transfer relatively less specie. Suffolk also took notes of nonparticipating banks and sent them immediately for redemption. Banks trusted Suffolk because of its quick turnaround and because it kept a high ratio of specie relative to net liabilities. The wide-ranging membership of the system meant that any particular bank could count on getting its own notes back in a clearing, so that loan contraction upon deposit withdrawal was less than it would have been without the centralized clearing process. Something to note is that the only New England banks that failed in the late 1830s and early 1840s were Rhode Island banks, which were not part of the Suffolk system.

Other private successes exist as well. Iftekhar Hasan and Gerald Dwyer found evidence that Indiana and Wisconsin banks capably sorted out solvent and failed institutions during the free banking period (1837–63), when no central bank existed.[68] Rolnick and Weber likewise discovered that losses

---

[66]Gorton uses this assumption, for instance. Gary Gorton, "Clearinghouses and the Origin of Central Banking in the U.S.," *Journal of Economic History* 45 (1985):277–83.

[67]Arthur Rolnick, Bruce Smith, and Warren Weber, "The Suffolk Bank and the Panic of 1837," *Federal Reserve Bank of Minnesota Quarterly Review* 24 (2000):3–13; "Lessons from a Laissez-Faire Payments System: The Suffolk Banking System (1825–58)," *Federal Reserve Bank of St. Louis Review* (1998):105–16; Charles Calomiris and Charles Kahn, "The Efficiency of Self-Regulated Payment Systems: Learning from the Suffolk System," *Journal of Money, Credit, and Banking* 28 (1996):767–96.

[68]Iftekhar Hasan and Gerald Dwyer, "Bank Runs in the Free Banking Period," *Journal of Money, Credit, and Banking* 26 (1994):271–88.

to note holders from failed banks during this time were much less than had been thought.[69] That is, banknotes circulated at less than par value: their market value reflected the probability of bank failure.

The rise of demand deposits relative to banknotes in the latter part of the free-banking era made private clearinghouses even more attractive, and New York City banks began such arrangements in the 1850s.[70] At the start of a panic, a member bank could submit part of its portfolio as collateral. The clearinghouse then issued certificates equal to a percentage of an approved portfolio's value. The certificates had a fixed term (usually one to three months), carried an interest charge, and initially came in large denominations. Member banks could then use these in the clearing process instead of currency, freeing currency to pay off depositors. The clearinghouse also suppressed all bank-specific information so that the public could not tell which banks had applied for certificates. Banks retained membership in the clearinghouse throughout a financial upheaval, but they were expelled if they did not pay off certificates in a timely fashion.

What if a member bank failed? If its collateral was smaller in value than its outstanding loan certificates, remaining members shared the loss in proportion to their capital. In short, banks created a form of self-insurance that protected against widespread financial panic.

As the clearinghouse arrangement grew to dominate the New York banking scene, certificates in small denominations were even issued directly to the public—$100 million in 1893 (about 2.5 percent of the money stock) and $500 million in 1907 (4.5 percent of the money stock). A secondary market in these soon developed, meaning that the public effectively adopted them as currency.

Chari has suggested that the end of the national bank era (1863–1907) heralded increasingly difficult times for clearinghouses.[71] Trust companies and other financial innovations existed outside the system, posing potentially destabilizing forces. In fact, the failure of outsider Knickerbocker Trust sparked the panic of 1907.

Does this mean that the private clearinghouse method eventually failed? Scholars disagree on the answer to this question. Milton Friedman believes

---

[69]Rolnick and Weber, "New Evidence."

[70]The following discussion relies heavily on Gorton, "Clearinghouses." See also Richard Timberlake, Jr., "The Central Banking Role of Clearinghouse Associations," *Journal of Money, Credit, and Banking* 16 (1984):1–15, and Gerald Dwyer and R. Alton Gilbert, "Bank Runs and Private Remedies," *Federal Reserve Bank of St. Louis Review* 71 (1989):43–61.

[71]Chari, "Banking without Deposit Insurance."

that the bad banks would have disappeared but the solvent ones survived if the panic had simply run its course.[72] O.M.W. Sprague, a renowned academic authority on banking who wrote just after the 1907 panic, did not see how a central bank would improve upon existing clearinghouses.[73] But most people at the turn of the twentieth century tended away from Friedman's and Sprague's views, and our current Federal Reserve System came into being as a consequence.

Yet the Fed alone certainly did not ward off financial crisis: witness the Great Depression. Not until the introduction of deposit insurance did bank runs become a thing of the past. This raises an interesting question: might deposit insurance, rather than a central banking authority, be the best way to organize financial markets? Insurance could not be complete; otherwise, the problem of moral hazard would again arise. But partial insurance might be enough to stop runs on healthy banks—it solves Diamond and Dybvig's problem of self-fulfilling expectations—yet still to allow bad banks to fail. Even Milton Friedman approves of partial insurance for small depositors.[74] Because our financial system has taken a very different path, however, we cannot investigate this matter empirically.

What Does All of This Mean for the 1830s?

Both the theoretical models developed long after the 1830s and real-world events help us think about a counterfactual: What would the world have been like had the Second Bank remained in place? In particular, what models seem to fit conditions of the time and what reactions and outcomes might have been most likely?

For the 1837 panic, I suggest that the random-withdrawal model seems apt.[75] Certainly a mismatch of supply and demand occurred—not because of sharp increases in demand for specie in a particular location but because

---

[72]Milton Friedman, *Money Mischief* (Orlando, 1992), and idem, *Essence.*

[73]O.M.W. Sprague, "The Proposal for a Central Bank in the United States: A Critical View," *Quarterly Journal of Economics* 23 (1909):363–415. Gorton, "Clearinghouses," notes that the Fed as originally conceived was simply an institutionalized version of the New York clearinghouses.

[74]Milton Friedman and Anna Schwartz, "Has Government Any Role in Money?" *Journal of Monetary Economics* 17 (1986):37–62.

[75]Others suggest that this model accurately describes the early nineteenth-century banking system. See, for instance, Sudipto Bhattacharya and Douglas Gale, "Preference Shocks, Liquidity, and Central Bank Policy," *New Approaches to Monetary Economics: Proceedings of the Second International Symposium in Economic Theory and Econometrics* (1987):69–88, and Chari, "Banking

of a large and sudden decrease in supply on the East Coast generated by the Distribution Act and the Specie Circular. If the bank and its branches had remained in place, the conditions giving rise to the 1837 panic would not have existed. Absent Jackson's financial policies, moreover, real GDP per capita (reported in table 1) might have continued its steady upward trend after 1834. In short, financial disorder yielded real consequences.

The crisis that began in 1839 is a different animal. This crisis seems rooted more in the intimacy among state treasuries, public works projects, and state banks than in mismatched demand for and supply of funds. Charles Calomiris and Gary Gorton find that the asymmetric-information model more accurately portrayed the economic situation in the United States during the national-banking period than did the random-withdrawal model; it seems reasonable to think that this model might also apply to the years 1839 and following.[76] What started the panic was risky behavior by some banks and naiveté by state governments, not some sudden divergence between specie supply and demand. Once individuals realized what was happening, they had to act quickly to protect themselves, unless a mechanism existed to shield them. In New England, it was the Suffolk system: its presence put the burden on banks to prove themselves sound and protected people whose assets were held by unsound banks. Depositors and note holders in the South and West had no such luxury.

If the Bank had continued to exist in 1839, the conditions for panic may or may not have arisen—that depends upon how the federal surplus would have been redistributed and how states would have undertaken and financed operations using Bank branches rather than state-chartered banks. Trying to construct such a scenario relies on a number of "what ifs?"

Still, suppose the 1839 panic had occurred in the presence of a Bank of the United States. The Bank might well have reacted as it did in 1825, pulling back to protect its own profits rather than acting as a lender of last resort. The power of the Bank might then have dissipated, leaving the field open to private concerns. For example, the success of the Suffolk system might

---

without Deposit Insurance." Spatial separation of banks and transport difficulties could be reasons for a lack of coordination among depositors and thus the failure to overcome the first-come, first-served problem. If depositors could have cheaply formed coalitions, bank assets could have been disbursed on a pro rata basis, which would have blunted the contagious impact.

[76]Charles Calomiris and Gary Gorton, "The Origins of Banking Panics: Models, Fact, and Bank Regulation," in *Financial Markets and Financial Crises*, ed. Glenn Hubbard (Chicago, 1991), pp. 107–73.

have encouraged other regions to form clearinghouses and reserve reposi-
tories of their own more quickly than they did, as bankers would have seen
that a central authority would not necessarily bail them out. Insurance markets might have arisen to provide ex ante protection for small depositors,
particularly if people had evidence that the central bank in their midst failed
to act as an ex post lender of last resort.

This is certainly plausible: Americans have proven themselves adept at
financial innovation throughout the nation's history. Richard Sylla details
exactly how active early-nineteenth-century Americans were at creating and
running a complex financial system. We had an active securities market as
early as the 1790s, far more developed than similar markets in other countries.
Sylla, among many others, has suggested that our nimbleness in financial-
market innovation may even have facilitated our phenomenal economic
growth during the nineteenth century.[77] Sylla has also warned that any
conclusions about the effects of the Bank War may be misleading because
scholars have not appropriately accounted for the presence of private, non-
state-chartered banks.[78]

The Current State of Affairs

Central banks offer one way of organizing a nation's financial system. They
can potentially stave off financial crisis, although two things are clear: central
banks do not always prevent panic, and mechanisms other than central banks
can also manage crisis effectively. History has taught us, however, that the
absence of a central bank can lead to an emphasis on its potential benefits
—and a downplaying of its detrimental effects—particularly in times of
transition. Had the Second Bank renewed its charter, we might well have seen
a different financial history for the United States. Instead, what we have now
is a set of centralized institutions, including the Fed, which generally replaces
the market in coping with financial panics.

A clear-eyed view of the current system must acknowledge its costs. One
looming concern is that the simple presence of a central bank can prevent

---

[77]Sylla, "U.S. Securities Markets." See also Bodenhorn, *History,* and Hugh Rockoff, "Banking and Finance, 1789–1914," in *The Cambridge Economic History of the United States,* vol. 2, *The Long
Nineteenth Century,* ed. Stanley Engerman and Robert Gallman (New York, 2000), pp. 643–84.

[78]Richard Sylla, "American Banking and Growth in the 19th Century: A Partial View of
the Terrain," *Explorations in Economic History* 9 (1972–73):197–227.

an efficient solution to financial problems. The classic recent example is Continental Illinois, emblematic of the too-big-to-fail (TBTF) doctrine. When Continental's risky and aggressive style brought it to the brink of bankruptcy in May 1984, the Fed and the FDIC came to the rescue with a multibillion-dollar assistance package. All depositors and general creditors received full protection (despite the $100,000 stated limit on deposit insurance) courtesy of U.S. taxpayers. Those who benefited from the upside of risk successfully shifted the costs of the downside to someone else.

Could Continental happen again? The FDIC Improvement Act of 1991 addressed many of the issues surrounding TBTF, but regulators and central bankers have yet to confront another Continental-type bank. One recent occurrence suggests they would not stand by idly, however. The collapse of the ruble in 1998 spelled disaster for the U.S.-based Long Term Capital Management (LTCM) hedge fund. A day before a Fed-organized consortium rescued the fund, the lead partner of LTCM refused a $4 billion cash offer from Warren Buffett, Goldman Sachs, and American International Group. Why? Because the top management at LTCM benefited far more under the Fed-brokered bailout than they would have with the cash offer.[79]

Certainly, an LTCM failure could have caused a serious disturbance in financial markets. Yet the salient fact is that private agents alone could have averted the disaster. The possibility of a better deal for LTCM management forestalled the purely private solution. LTCM investors knew exactly what they were getting into—this was a very risky fund, with a required minimum investment of $10 million, a prohibition on withdrawals for three years, and high fees on assets and profits. But what ultimately happened meant that someone else paid for the risks undertaken by LTCM investors and managers, just as taxpayers bore the cost of bailing out Continental. Moral hazard is alive and well in U.S. financial markets today.

Last Remarks

Andrew Jackson's personal history formed his attitude toward banks. Seared by his experience with worthless paper currency and wary of powerful aristocrats, he believed in hard money and decentralization.

---

[79]For more information, see Edwards, "Hedge Funds."

In much the same way, our nation's history has shaped its financial policies and institutions. The First Bank of the United States arose to help bankroll debts arising from the American Revolution and to stabilize the monetary system. Its demise resulted from animosity toward its power, sparked in part by Jeffersonian influence and in part by antagonism toward Albert Gallatin. In a similar cycle, the Second Bank came into being in response to the chaos created by war and financial turmoil; Jackson and other enemies of the Second Bank distrusted—and finally destroyed—blueblood Biddle and the influence he wielded.

The cycle has continued since Jackson's time. The death of the Second Bank gave birth to the freewheeling free-banking era, which allowed anyone with enough capital the privilege of setting up a bank but which also generated more than nine thousand types of banknotes by 1860.[80] Ironically, Jackson's success at ridding the nation of the hated Bank also led it far away from hard money.

As a consequence, the country took another turn Jackson would have despised—back toward centralization. The National Bank Act of 1863 was enacted partly to help unify the country's currency. Although individuals and privately owned banks had some success in coping with the panics of the late nineteenth century, the panic of 1907 convinced enough people that a central bank was the solution. But the bank failures of the 1930s demonstrated that the Fed was fallible, and the Federal Deposit Insurance Corporation and the Federal Savings and Loan Insurance Corporation entered the picture. Ill-advised deregulation then failed to account for moral hazard problems; the result was the financial debacles of the 1980s and yet more centralized control.

Where are we today? Financial markets are global in nature, and large amounts of capital flow across national borders every day. Some see this as reason for celebration and call for even fewer restrictions; others want capital controls and suggest establishing a strong international financial authority.

One thing is certain: Andrew Jackson would be stunned by what he has wrought. He never understood the benefits of financial intermediation and fractional reserves, nor his countrymen's desire for credit to help fund their entrepreneurial schemes. Free banking surely was not in his forecast of the

---

[80]For details, see E. Stevens, "Composition of the Money Stock Prior to the Civil War," *Journal of Money, Credit, and Banking* 3 (1971):84–101, and Rolnick and Weber, "New Evidence."

post–Second Bank era. That states would charter ever-greater numbers of banks, then use them to finance industry and transportation projects, must have shocked him in his later years.

Jackson's ideal of a simple agrarian society was obsolete in his own lifetime; today's world would be incomprehensible to him. What he would make of fiat money, floating exchange rates, investment banking, hedge funds, and Alan Greenspan is almost amusing to contemplate.

But the worst blow of all? No doubt it would be finding his face on the front of the most widely circulated paper bill in the nation.[81]

[81] Why Andrew Jackson's visage has appeared on the twenty dollar bill since 1929 is not clear from Treasury Department records. But I like to think it is because the monetary authorities consider him to be, at least indirectly, a founding father of the Fed.

Tim Alan Garrison

The Devil and Andrew Jackson

Historians and Jackson's Role in the Indian Removal Crisis

T HE HISTORICAL REPUTATION of an American president evolves, appropriately, with changes in perspective, focus, and illumination of evidence. The legacy of Andrew Jackson has not fared well from our professional tendency toward cautious revision. Until relatively recently, students of presidential administrations regarded Jackson as one of the United States' most successful chief executives. In 1948, Arthur Schlesinger, one of the first to conduct such a poll, surveyed fifty-five historians and other scholars and asked them to rank the presidents as "great," "near great," "average," "below average," or "failure." Jackson polled out as one of the "great" presidents, trailing only Abraham Lincoln, George Washington, Franklin D. Roosevelt, Woodrow Wilson, and Thomas Jefferson.[1] Jackson remained popular among historians and the public for the subsequent quarter century.[2] In the 1970s, however, Jackson's status began to decline; this trend was noticeable in a 1982 Siena College Research Institute poll. Recent surveys of historians by both C-SPAN (2000) and Siena (2002) placed Jackson at a mere thirteenth in the rankings, while C-SPAN's poll of viewers placed him even lower, at fourteenth.[3] Only one compelling reason explains this rather rapid fall from

---

[1] Arthur M. Schlesinger, "Historians Rate U.S. Presidents," *Life* 1 (1948):65–66, 68, 73–74.

[2] Arthur M. Schlesinger, Jr., "Rating the Presidents: Washington to Clinton," *Political Science Quarterly* 112 (1997):179–90.

[3] Jackson had already fallen to thirteenth by the time of the 1982 Siena poll. His position fluctuated between ninth and thirteenth in surveys conducted in 1982, 1990, 1994, and 2002.

such a lofty perch: increasing disapprobation of Jackson's role in the re-moval of the tribal nations of the eastern United States.[4]

Not only has Jackson's reputation diminished, but the man himself has become a figure vehemently despised by many. Condemnations of Jackson appear regularly in newspapers and magazines and on the Internet. For ex-ample, in an article on a museum exhibit on Cherokee women in Cleveland, Tennessee, curator R. Michael Abram offered an opinion that has become quite commonplace in the public discourse. Abram explained why material on Jackson was included in the exhibit: "I want the public to know who the real Andy was, not the Tennessee Andy. . . . He was a racist and an ethnic cleanser."[5] On a Web site criticizing Wichita North High School's use of "Redskins" as its nickname, the producers call for Jackson to be "tried for his crimes against humanity." They add, "By having Jackson glorified in history the United States declares that it is honorable to hate a redskin. The history books do not speak well of Adolf Hitler, likewise, we are demanding that Andrew Jackson's name be explained as the man who is responsible for the death of 4,000 Cherokees."[6] Any simple Nexis or Google search will produce dozens of expressions of this sentiment. Jackson critics even walk into my office from time to time. As I worked on this essay one afternoon, one of my students dropped by with her bright three-year-old son. She asked me what I

See Siena Research Institute of Siena College, Londonville, New York, http://www.siena.edu/sri/results/2002/02AugPresidentsSurvey.htm. The 2000 C-SPAN survey questioned fifty-eight historians. Jackson ranked thirteenth in that study; not only had he been surpassed by men who had held office since Schlesinger's poll (Eisenhower, Truman, Kennedy, Johnson, and Reagan), but he had also dropped behind Theodore Roosevelt and James K. Polk. Among C-SPAN viewers surveyed, Jackson had fallen to fourteenth, trailing Lincoln, Washington, Theodore Roosevelt, Franklin Roosevelt, Jefferson, Reagan, Truman, Eisenhower, Monroe, Madison, John Adams, Kennedy, and Wilson. "C-SPAN Survey of Presidential Leadership: How Did the Presidents Rate?" http://www.americanpresidents.org/survey.

[4]Despite the general decline in the surveys described above, those historians and other scholars deemed "conservative," by either self-identification or by those polling them, con-tinue to hold Jackson in high regard. In a recent presidential ratings survey conducted by the *Wall Street Journal* and the Federalist Society that purported to include scholars in history, po-litical science, and law "from both liberal and conservative ideological camps," Jackson rated sixth, the same slot he held in the first Schlesinger poll. One could hypothesize from these re-sults that Indian removal may remain less significant to Jackson's legacy for historians of a conservative political bent than the historical profession at large (Federalist Society–Wall Street Journal Survey on Presidents, http://www.opinionjournal.com/hail/rankings.html).

[5]Associated Press, "Cherokee Women Exhibit Opens at Southeast Tennessee Museum," May 31, 2005.

[6]American Comments: A Web Magazine, http://www.iwchildren.org/genocide/shame9.htm.

was working on. When I replied that I was investigating why so many people hate Andrew Jackson, she turned to her young son and asked, "Is Andrew Jackson good or bad?" "He's baaaaaaad," replied the precocious boy. Apparently, evaluating presidents starts at an early age in my student's household.

Jackson is especially reviled by the descendants of those Native Americans who were removed from the Southeast. One commentator has suggested that eastern Oklahoma, the area to which the five major southeastern tribes were removed, tends to vote Republican because its residents "still remember Andrew Jackson."[7] The Cherokees are perhaps Jackson's most vocal detractors, despite the fact that it was technically Martin Van Buren who pushed their ancestors onto the Trail of Tears. According to the All Things Cherokee Web site, Andrew Jackson was "The Worst President the Cherokee Ever Met." "Some Cherokees," the site declares, "would rather carry two ten-dollar bills or twenty one-dollar bills than carry a single twenty dollar bill."[8] Jackson's image on the currency is a sore point for many. Carrie McLachlan, a Ph.D. student at the University of California–Riverside at the time I wrote these words, hosts a Web site that considers the question of whether the U.S. government should remove Jackson's image from the currency.[9] If he is replaced by Ronald Wilson Reagan, whose admirers are on their own expansionist movement to rename federal properties in the United States, it will be because of Jackson's participation in the exile of the eastern tribes.[10]

Ironically, Jackson has fallen in esteem despite the publication of several works during the past few decades that have tended to exonerate him from harboring malicious intent toward the people he helped remove. Condemnations of Jackson are so vehement and so common that Robert V. Remini, Jackson's preeminent biographer, was moved to conclude his study, *Andrew Jackson and His Indian Wars*, with this bitter comment: "To his dying day on June 8, 1845, Andrew Jackson genuinely believed that what he had accomplished rescued these people from inevitable annihilation. And although that

---

[7] Jim Adams, "Kerry's Election Hopes Hinge on Native Vote," *Indian Country Today*, Oct. 5, 2004.

[8] All Things Cherokee, http://www.allthingscherokee.com/atc_sub-culture_feat_events_020201.html.

[9] American Indian Nations, http://www.americanindian.ucr.edu/discussions/jackson/index.shtml.

[10] Rebecca Adamson has suggested just such a change, albeit with tongue in cheek ("Redeeming the National Landscape," *Indian Country Today*, Feb. 4, 2005). For an alternative portrait for the twenty, see "Put Martin Luther King, Jr. on the Twenty Dollar Bill," http://putkingonthe20.com/index.php.

statement sounds monstrous, and although no one in the modern world wishes to accept or believe it, that is exactly what he did. He saved the Five Civilized Nations from probable extinction."[11]

The emotion evinced in Remini's comment suggests another point: the removal has come to replace the issues, such as nullification, the Bank of the United States, internal improvements, and the nature of democracy, that historians once regarded as the polarizing interpretive questions of Jackson's presidency. This is a rather remarkable phenomenon, considering that his biographers essentially ignored the subject of Indian removal until the late 1960s. This transformation of intellectual and emotional investment was evident at the U.S. Capitol Historical Society's 2005 symposium "Congress in the Age of Jackson." At the end of a series of illuminating papers on a variety of subjects about Jackson and his era, the audience was invited to engage in an open-ended discussion with the speakers. The patrons did not ask a single question about the old disagreements that used to divide students of Jackson. Rather, every query pertained to Jackson's attitudes about, and policies regarding, American Indians. The scholars who had presented papers on a variety of issues during the day, moreover, appeared at their most animated while offering their own views on the subject.

The event confirmed my suspicion that it was time, once again, to reflect on the gap between the contemptuous view of Jackson held by many today and the triumphalist interpretation that dominated for so long. This essay is an effort to provide some historiographical context to a debate that has accumulated unique emotional overtones, one in which the collective American conscience has bound up all of its guilt over the nation's treatment of American Indians and dumped it onto one man. My purpose, I should explain, is not to offer a unique interpretation of Jackson's Indian policy as president. I tender this piece, instead, as a broad overview of the literature on the subject. I mean to remind readers that condemnations of Jackson's Indian policy are relatively new, to suggest that some of the depictions of Jackson are a product more of the political and ideological projections of the author than

---

[11]Robert V. Remini, *Andrew Jackson and His Indian Wars* (New York, 2001), p. 281. Remini's sense of isolation is somewhat misplaced, however; as we will see, several historians have embraced aspects of his interpretation of Jackson's motives during the removal crisis. See, for instance, Philip Weeks, *Farewell, My Nation: The American Indian and the United States in the Nineteenth Century* (Wheeling, Ill., 1990), pp. 41–42 (quotes and page references to 2001 edition); and H. W. Brands, *Andrew Jackson: His Life and Times* (New York, 2005), pp. 490–91.

of any distinctive exercise in evidentiary analysis, and to point out that there have been thoughtful efforts to get beyond the old hero/devil castings offered by most biographers.[12] Let me make this clear: This is not a defense of Jackson; to some extent, it is another call on my part to bring those who aided and abetted the removal under the light of historical scrutiny. I suggest that we, historians and members of a reading citizenry that relish scrutinizing presidencies, be more willing to spread the culpability heaped on Jackson to a broader class of eighteenth- and nineteenth-century Americans.[13]

While almost all biographies of Jackson described, in detail, his exploits against the Redstick Creeks in 1813–14 and his punitive action against the Seminoles and Creeks in Florida, nearly all of them, until the last forty years, completely ignored his Indian policy as president or treated it as merely a peripheral matter. Jackson's most significant biographers hardly touched the subject. James Parton, whose work has influenced Jacksonian scholars since its publication, expended a perfunctory one paragraph on the removal in his three-volume biography. Writing in the late 1850s, he explained that he did not need to "revive the sad details of a measure which, hard and cruel as it was then thought, is now universally felt to have been as kind as it was necessary."[14] John Spencer Bassett, another of Jackson's most prominent biographers, briefly discussed the removal in a chapter entitled "Minor Problems of the Two Administrations."[15] Arthur Schlesinger, Jr.'s, *The Age of Jackson*, which

---

[12]I focused almost exclusively on the biographies and historical studies of Jackson and his era. I do not address the remarks or interpretations of Jackson's contemporaries, unless they offered them as historical or biographical works. Many scholars have examined their words, and that exercise would really take us beyond the scope and goal of this paper. For a recent discussion, see Mary Hershberger, "Mobilizing Women, Anticipating Abolition: The Struggle against Indian Removal in the 1830s," *Journal of American History* 86 (1999):15–40. For a more complete bibliography of publications dealing with contemporaneous praise and criticism of Jackson's actions, see Ronald N. Satz, "Rhetoric versus Reality: The Indian Policy of Andrew Jackson," in *Cherokee Removal: Before and After*, ed. William L. Anderson (Athens, Ga., 1991), pp. 45–46 n. 8–11. Because of the awe-inspiring quantity of commentary on Jackson, I was forced to place some rational parameters on my research. For the most part, I hewed rather closely to an analysis of the development of historical writing about Jackson's removal policy. Procedurally, I examined every relevant or material title listed under Remini's bibliographical headings of "biographies" and "Indian affairs" (Robert V. Remini, *Andrew Jackson: A Bibliography* [Westport, Conn., 1991)]. I also reviewed the works noted in the following bibliographical essays: F. P. Prucha, "Andrew Jackson's Indian Policy: A Reassessment," *Journal of American History* 56 (1969):527–39, and Satz, "Rhetoric versus Reality," pp. 29–54.

[13]For my effort to implicate Southern judges, see Tim Alan Garrison, *The Legal Ideology of Removal: The Southern Judiciary and the Sovereignty of Native American Nations* (Athens, Ga., 2002).

[14]James Parton, *Life of Andrew Jackson*, 3 vols. (Boston, 1860), 3:279–80.

[15]John Spencer Bassett, *The Life of Andrew Jackson* (New York, 1916).

won the Pulitzer Prize and was considered for years the gold standard of Jacksonian biographies, barely hints at the removal controversy.[16] This dearth of historical consideration was so patently obvious that in 1967, Arthur H. DeRosier, Jr., could write that Jackson's removal policy was "the most neglected chapter in the study of this fascinating era."[17]

Public awareness of the removal, and Jackson's part in it, spiked dramatically with the emergence of the modern Indian rights movement in the late 1960s. Interest also escalated with the development of Native American history as a dynamic field of inquiry. After this transitional period, scholars began to fix their gaze more carefully on Jackson's relationships with Native Americans; as we will see, a spate of studies written since DeRosier's lament have offered much-needed depth to the conversation. That being said, we are nowhere near a consensus on what motivated Jackson to bring the long-discussed plan of Indian removal to fruition or whether his expressed concern for the removed Indians was cynical or sincere.

This is not surprising. Jackson is a subject who has always fomented controversy and disagreement. Parton warned long ago that perceptions of Jackson were often so contradictory that they nearly thwarted useful evaluations of his life:

---

[16]Arthur M. Schlesinger, Jr., *The Age of Jackson* (Boston, 1945), p. 350.

[17]Arthur H. DeRosier, Jr., "Andrew Jackson and Negotiation for the Removal of the Choctaw Indians," *Historian* 29 (1967):362. The following biographies do not mention Jackson's Indian policies as president: "Andrew Jackson," *Harpers New Monthly* 10 (1855):145–72; Alexander Walker, *The Life of Andrew Jackson* (New York, 1858); John Frost and Harry W. French, "Andrew Jackson," in *The Presidents of the United States from Washington to Cleveland* (New York, 1888); James Morgan, "Andrew Jackson," in *Our Presidents: Brief Biographies of Our Chief Magistrates* (1924; rev. ed., New York, 1946); Helen Nicolay, *Andrew Jackson: The Fighting President* (New York, 1929); Clifford Smyth, *Andrew Jackson: The Man Who Preserved Union and Democracy* (New York, 1931).

The following works offer barely minimal discussions of Jackson's policies: J. T. Headly, *The Lives of Winfield Scott and Andrew Jackson* (New York, 1852), p. 328; John S. Jenkins, *Life and Public Services of Gen. Andrew Jackson* (Buffalo, N.Y., 1853), p. 177; William O. Stoddard, *Andrew Jackson and Martin Van Buren* (New York, 1887), pp. 214–15; Oliver Dyer, *General Andrew Jackson: Hero of New Orleans and Seventh President of the United States* (New York, 1891), pp. 325, 356; William Garrott Brown, *Andrew Jackson* (Boston, 1900), p. 131; Alfred Henry Lewis, *When Men Grew Tall or the Story of Andrew Jackson* (New York, 1907), pp. 283, 392–94; Thomas E. Watson, *The Life and Times of Andrew Jackson* (Thomson, Ga., 1917). Perhaps Augustus C. Buell spoke for those who wrote so little of Indian affairs: "The minute details of his Indian conferences, councils and negotiations; of their speeches and his own replies; of their demands and his concessions would fill this volume. They would, however, be more interesting to the student of aboriginal character than to the reader of history in these times" (Augustus C. Buell, *History of Andrew Jackson: Pioneer, Patriot, Soldier, Politician, President* [New York, 1904], 2:105).

If any one, at the end of a year even, had asked what I had yet discovered respecting General Jackson, I might have answered thus: "Andrew Jackson, I am given to understand, was a patriot and a traitor. He was one of the greatest of generals, and wholly ignorant of the art of war. A writer brilliant, elegant, eloquent, without being able to compose a correct sentence, or spell words of four syllables. The first of statesmen, he never devised, he never framed a measure. He was the most candid of men, and was capable of the profoundest dissimulation. A most law-defying, law-obeying citizen. A stickler for discipline, he never hesitated to disobey his superior. A democratic autocrat. An urbane savage. An atrocious saint."[18]

Charles Grier Sellers, Jr., in an essay on Jacksonian scholarship, noted Parton's frustration and suggested that Jackson could not be understood by simply "splitting the difference." Sellers concluded that "Parton and all who followed him on this difficult terrain have been forced pretty substantially either into the Jackson camp or into the camp of Jackson's enemies." While this characterization does hold true to many superficial commentaries on Jackson's relations with Indians, the scholars who have delved into the general's words and actions with rigor have offered intriguing and complex explanations in an effort to move beyond the simple Manichean approach. Getting to that point, however, took quite a bit of time.[19]

The earliest biographers attempted to capitalize on Jackson's victory at New Orleans or promote his political career.[20] While these works predated the removal crisis, the authors did agree upon the nature of Jackson's relations with Indians up until the point of his arrival on the national stage. They consistently portrayed Native Americans as violent and treacherous obstacles to American security and Jackson as the man uniquely qualified to overcome them. They glorified Jackson's service against the Redsticks in the Creek Civil

---

[18]Parton, *Life of Andrew Jackson*, 1:vii. Parton did go on, after investigating Jackson in greater depth, to provide a character study that was less conflicted than this first blush expression of despair.

[19]Charles Grier Sellers, Jr., "Andrew Jackson versus the Historians," *Mississippi Valley Historical Review* 44 (1958):615. Ronald N. Satz has called for historians to "avoid thinking about the Jacksonian Indian policy in dualistic terms" (Satz, "Rhetoric and Reality," p. 44).

[20]Jackson authorized his own biography in 1815 to satisfy those who wanted to know more about the new American hero. His loyal aide John Reid initiated the work. Reid died, however, from a fever in 1816, and John H. Eaton, who would become an instrumental and controversial figure in Jackson's career, completed the volume. John Henry Eaton, *The Life of Andrew Jackson, Major General in the Service of the United States: Comprising a History of the War in the South, from the Commencement of the Creek Campaign* (Philadelphia, 1817).

War, minimized the brutality and insubordination of his actions in Florida, and glossed over the unscrupulous negotiating tactics he used during his stints as federal treaty commissioner in the South. Most biographers in the century and a quarter after Jackson left office followed the lead of the campaign propagandists.[21] For the most part, these histories typically depicted Jackson as a fearless military leader who used courage and dash to defeat the savages who were terrorizing heroic and innocent frontier families.[22] Jackson's biographers were less than critical in analyzing the tactics that he used to expropriate Indian land. In the Treaty of Fort Jackson, the general imposed a draconian settlement on the Creeks. Although most of the Creeks had remained neutral in the Redstick uprising, Jackson forced their government to surrender roughly half of their national territory, some of which actually belonged to the Cherokees and Chickasaws. In 1887, William O. Stoddard offered a typical interpretation of the Fort Jackson dictated peace: "The treaty . . . was a good piece of work. He tried to deal justly with the savages whom he had been fighting, and they quickly understand [*sic*] that he was their friend."[23]

Biographers in the first age of Jacksonian historiography also tended to denigrate the intelligence and character of Native Americans and failed to appreciate any semblance of agency on their part. John S. Jenkins, in an 1853 biography, argued that the Redsticks were simply treacherous savages in the pay of the British government.[24] At the outset of a discussion of Tecumseh and his part in the provocation of the Redstick war, Parton offered the following comments:

> The Indian is a creature who does not improve upon acquaintance. Living near a tribe dispels so much of the romance which novelists and poets have thrown around the dusky race, as to induce considerable incredulity with re-

[21]See, for instance, Isaac Hill, *Brief Sketch of the Life, Character and Services of Major General Andrew Jackson* (Concord, N.H., 1828), pp. 11–13; and William Cobbett, *Life of Andrew Jackson: President of the United States of America* (New York, 1834), pp. iv, vi, 33.

[22]See, for example, Amos Kendall, *The Life of General Andrew Jackson* (New York, 1844); *Sketch of the Life of Gen. Andrew Jackson, Late President of the United States* (Worcester, Mass., 1845), pp. 9–12; J. T. Headly, *The Lives of Winfield Scott and Andrew Jackson* (New York, 1852), pp. 289–91; Walker, *Life of Andrew Jackson*, pp. xli–lxxix; Stoddard, *Jackson and Van Buren*, pp. 100–122; William Graham Sumner, *Andrew Jackson* (Boston, 1899), pp. 38–40 (Sumner, one of the first American sociologists, was otherwise quite critical of Jackson in this work); John Fiske, "Andrew Jackson," in *The Presidents of the United States, 1780–1914*, ed. James Grant Wilson (New York, 1914), pp. 266–69; Samuel M. Wilson, *Andrew Jackson: An Address* (Louisville, Ky., 1915), pp. 7–8; Smyth, *Andrew Jackson*, pp. 66–73.

[23]Stoddard, *Andrew Jackson and Martin Van Buren*, p. 121.

[24]Jenkins, *Life and Public Services of Gen. Andrew Jackson*, p. 55.

gard to the tales they have told of Indian valor and generosity. As he *now* appears upon our western border, the Indian is a filthy, idle, cruel, lying coward, wholly a cumberer of the ground, incapable of any of the white man's virtues, while exaggerating all his vices; respecting whom the thrifty pioneer finds it hard to cherish any desire but this—to exterminate him.[25]

These racist sentiments continued to corrupt Jackson biographies into the next century. In 1907, for example, Alfred Henry Lewis, in *When Men Grew Tall or The Story of Andrew Jackson,* referred to the Creeks as "fatuous savages." Of the exile, Lewis wrote: "He removes the Creeks and Cherokees from Florida and Georgia, and thereby guarantees the scalp on many an innocent head." It is little wonder that Parton, Lewis, and other biographers who held these views refrained from criticizing Jackson's removal policy.[26] The few who did recognize the legal and moral questions raised by the policy rationalized Jackson's actions. In 1906, William McDonald concluded, for instance, that the removal was "at least humanely conceived, so far as Jackson was concerned, and represented an earnest effort to deal justly with the difficult problem of the relations between superior and inferior races."[27]

William Joseph Snelling, a journalist and abolitionist from Boston, was one of the few biographers to dissent from the view that removal was "humanely conceived." Snelling began his brief discussion of the issue by stating that he was turning, "with regret, with shame, with mortification," to "the darkest page of American annals." "Gladly would we pass it in silence," Snelling wrote, "but as our hero had a prominent share in the affairs, . . . we cannot do so." At the same time, Snelling understood better than many subsequent biographers that the responsibility for the "great iniquity," which was only coming to fruition at the time of his work's publication (1832), was widespread. Snelling wrote that the Southern states "showed themselves avaricious and cruel" in their efforts to expel the tribes and that the United States, as a whole, had "looked coolly on while the faith of treaties was violated."[28] This was rare criticism of Jackson's Indian policy, and it did not reappear

---

[25]Parton, *Life of Andrew Jackson,* 1:401.

[26]Lewis described the Creek delegates at the Treaty of Fort Jackson as "blanketed to the ears" and "feathered to the eyes." He also offered his own observations on Native American character. "The Indian is terrible only when he is winning," he wrote, "he is not upholstered, whether mentally or morally, for an uphill, losing war" (Lewis, *When Men Grew Tall,* pp. 98, 102, 113–15, 283).

[27]William McDonald, *Jacksonian Democracy, 1829–1837* (New York, 1906), pp. 172–73, 178.

[28]A Free Man [William Joseph Snelling], *A Brief and Impartial History of the Life and Actions of Andrew Jackson, President of the United States* (Boston, 1831), pp. 179–87.

again regularly in biographical form for another dozen decades. A few writers in the latter part of the nineteenth century did cast a sorrowful glance back toward the removal. Helen Hunt Jackson, for example, condemned the relocations as a collective American sin in *A Century of Dishonor*: "In the whole history of our Government's dealings with the Indian tribes, there is no record so black as the record of its perfidy to this nation." She added, prophetically, "There will come a time in the remote future when, to the student of American history, it will seem well-nigh incredible."[29]

The taint of the removal, however, did not stain Jackson's legacy for his admirers. Rather, they constructed defenses for the policy and their hero's part in its implementation. Their most enduring contribution was the lesser-of-evils argument. In 1911, John Spencer Bassett argued that the United States held limited alternatives when it came to dealing with its "Indian problem" in the Southeast:

> They could not be pushed gradually back as in the Northwest: they must be exterminated or induced by one means or another to remove to the plains, where the problem of contact with the whites would be postponed to a remote generation. The other alternative, peaceful residence among the whites, was not considered possible for any large body of Indians, North or South. The only thing which people thought feasible was to remove them bodily: and as this was a task for the national government its execution devolved on the President.[30]

Many scholars since Bassett's explication of this rationalization, including Francis Paul Prucha, Remini, Ronald N. Satz, and Robert F. Berkhofer, Jr., among the most prominent, have adopted this reasoning.[31]

---

[29]Helen Hunt Jackson, *A Century of Dishonor* (New York, 1881), p. 270.

[30]Bassett, *Life of Andrew Jackson*, pp. 684–85. In 1969, Prucha also argued that the federal government possessed four choices when it came to the eastern tribes: (1) it could have allowed or facilitated the Indians' extermination or expulsion and simply seized their lands; (2) it could have continued its objective of assimilating the Indian population in situ, a possibility that he says was not feasible; (3) it could have defended and protected the tribes in the East from state intimidation and settler encroachment, an alternative that he said was "infeasible, given the political and military conditions at the time"; and (4) it could remove the tribes beyond the reach of unscrupulous traders and white trespassers. Jackson's "only answer," Prucha declared, was removal (Prucha, "Andrew Jackson's Indian Policy," pp. 534–35).

[31]The following historians, among others, specifically espoused the "limited alternatives" interpretation: DeRosier, "Andrew Jackson and Negotiation for the Removal of the Choctaw Indians," p. 362: Kenneth Penn Davis, "The Cherokee Removal, 1835–1838," *Tennessee Historical Quarterly* 32 (1973):331; Ronald N. Satz, *American Indian Policy in the Jacksonian Era* (Norman, Okla., 1975); Robert F. Berkhofer, Jr., *The White Man's Indian: Images of the American Indian from Columbus to the Present* (New York, 1978), p. 157.

The catalogue of justifications expanded over the course of the twentieth century. In 1904, Augustus C. Buell wrote that Jackson, as general, treaty commissioner, and president, sought to "tranquilize the Southern frontier and make positive and well-defined boundaries between the lands of the Indians and those available for white settlement." Removal, he maintained, was a policy designed to protect the United States from foreign-Indian intrigue.[32] Some argued that Jackson was prompted by a desire to expand the territorial reach of the United States.[33] James F. Conser, for instance, maintained that Jackson had a "vision of a muscular, expanding American republic, a white society beholden to no foreign power and secure from all domestic threats."[34] Several argued that Jackson supported removal because he was sympathetic to the rights of Georgia and the other Southern states. According to some writers, supporting the removal campaign of the Southern states burnished his bona fides with their partisans in the nullification crisis.[35] DeRosier suggested that Jackson, ironically, took a states' rights position (recognizing the power of a state to extend its jurisdiction over a tribe

---

[32]Buell, *History of Andrew Jackson*, 2:104–5. A half century later, Dorothy Burne Goebel and Julius Goebel, Jr., agreed with Buell's characterization: "To the 'noble red man' school of thinkers the demands have seemed brutal. The general, however, was moved by considerations that do credit to his political sagacity. He had experienced the damage done by British and Spanish incitation of the Indians. He was proposing a treaty that would minimize future trouble" (Dorothy Burne Goebel and Julius Goebel, Jr., "General Jackson," in *Generals in the White House* [Garden City, N.Y., 1952], p. 74).

[33]See, for example, Thomas P. Abernethy, "Andrew Jackson," in *Dictionary of American Biography*, ed. Dumas Malone (New York, 1946), 9:533; Walter L. Williams, "Southeastern Indians before Removal: Prehistory, Contact, Decline," in *Southeastern Indians since the Removal Era*, ed. Walter L. Williams (Athens, Ga., 1979), p. 17; Rickey L. Hendricks, "Henry Clay and Jacksonian Indian Policy: A Political Anachronism," *Filson Club History Quarterly* 60 (1986):219, 238; Clara Sue Kidwell, *Choctaws and Missionaries in Mississippi, 1818–1918* (Norman, Okla., 1995), pp. 36, 129.

[34]James F. Conser, "John Ross and the Cherokee Resistance Campaign, 1833–1838," *Journal of Southern History* 44 (1978):194.

[35]Brown, *Andrew Jackson*, pp. 130–31; U. B. Phillips, "The Expulsion of the Cherokees," in *Georgia and State Rights* (Washington, D.C., 1902), pp. 66–86; Thomas Valentine Parker, *The Cherokee Indians: With Special Reference to Their Relations with the United States Government* (New York, 1907), p. 30; William S. Hoffman, "Andrew Jackson, State Rightist: The Case of the Georgia Indians," *Tennessee Historical Quarterly* 11 (1952):329–30; Grant Foreman, *Indian Removal: The Emigration of the Five Civilized Tribes of Indians* (Norman, Okla., 1953), p. 21; Edward Yarbrough, *Old Hickory: A Biography of Andrew Jackson* (Tyler, Tex., 1953), p. 71; Frank B. Williams, Jr., *Tennessee's Presidents* (Knoxville, Tenn. 1981), p. 27; John R. Finger, *The Eastern Band of Cherokees, 1819–1900* (Knoxville, Tenn., 1984), p. 15; Duane Champagne, *Social Order and Political Change: Constitutional Governments among the Cherokee, the Choctaw, the Chickasaw, and the Creek* (Stanford, Calif., 1992), pp. 125–26; Laurence Armand French, "Native American Reparations: Five Hundred Years and Counting," in *When Sorry Isn't Enough: The Controversy over Apologies and Reparations for Human Injustice*, ed. Roy L. Brooks (New York, 1999), p. 243.

within its borders) to achieve the nationalist goal of expansion.[36] Dorothy Burne Goebel and Julius Goebel, Jr., saw Jackson's Indian policy as a tactic to preserve the separation of powers. His reaction to the *Worcester* decision, they suggested, was an effort to protect the presidency from an encroaching federal judiciary.[37] Several historians, from Annie H. Abel to Remini, argued that Jackson's administration of Indian policy simply represented continuity with that of his predecessors. They pointed out that Jefferson proposed the idea of removal, and that James Monroe and John Quincy Adams agreed with it on the condition that the tribes retained the right to consent to any relocation. As DeRosier put it, "The militancy shown in Indian affairs by the Jackson officials represented the completion of an evolving Indian policy."[38]

The question of Jackson's responsibility for the removal frequently turned to efforts to analyze his heart; critics and admirers bickered over the specific question of whether or not he despised the indigenous peoples. His more vocal and vitriolic critics have always pointed to several rather demeaning statements, some horrific battlefield atrocities, and the removal policy as per se proof of Jackson's animosity toward Indians. His defenders usually cited four arguments to support their contention that Jackson actually possessed noble intentions when it came to dealing with Indian people. First, they noted that Jackson sought the assistance of Indian allies during his military campaigns. Second, they referred to the fact that Jackson maintained cordial relations with many individual Indians. Third, they cited several public speeches that denoted a paternalistic concern for Indian interests. Many, in fact, quoted these documents as evocative of his inner thoughts and gave little consideration to the possibility that Jackson's rhetoric might have been offered as public propaganda. Marquis James, for example, used Jackson's words to portray Jackson as a bulwark against, rather than a symbol of, white rapaciousness. James wrote that "while yielding to the greed of the whites, Jackson endeavored to obtain a measure of practical justice for the Indians. Liberal terms were held out to them to remove peaceably beyond the Mississippi."[39]

---

[36] Arthur H. DeRosier, Jr., *The Removal of the Choctaw Indians* (Knoxville, Tenn., 1970), p. 102.

[37] Goebel and Goebel, "General Jackson," p. 88.

[38] See, for example, Annie H. Abel, "The History of Events Resulting in Indian Consolidation West of the Mississippi River," *Annual Report of the American Historical Association for 1906* (Washington, D.C., 1906), 1:251, 287, 341–44; DeRosier, "Andrew Jackson and Negotiation for the Removal of the Choctaw Indians," p. 362; Satz, *American Indian Policy in the Jacksonian Era*, p. 6; Remini, *Andrew Jackson and His Indian Wars*, p. 115.

[39] For prominent examples of these arguments, see text discussions of Prucha, Satz, and Remini. For the quote, see Marquis James, *Andrew Jackson, Portrait of a President* (Indianapolis, 1937), p. 305.

Finally, they pointed out that Jackson adopted a Creek boy named Lincoya who had been orphaned on the battlefield of Tallushatchee. James Morgan's caricature encapsulated the sentimentalist interpretation of Lincoya's adoption offered by Jackson's admirers: "After one of the battles, a tender pity was awakened in him for an Indian baby, still clasped in the arms of its mother as she lay among the dead on the field. The squaws among his prisoners steadfastly refusing to nurse it, he took the motherless infant to his tent and finally to the Hermitage, where the red boy grew up like a son of the family."[40] William O. Stoddard was perhaps even more romantic: "Perhaps there is in all his life no picture more pleasant to look upon than that of his tent on the Coosa, and of the stern, fiery-tempered leader of rugged frontiersmen holding in his arms and feeding the helpless little relic of that fierce massacre."[41] Samuel G. Heiskell, "a Tennessean," as he declared in his title, noted that "there was another side we rarely read about." "Jackson," he wrote, "was one of the tenderest and most affectionate men that ever lived, and with a strong, romantic strain in his make-up that made him a high-bred, knightly gentlemen always in his contact with women and children, and persons in poverty, sickness or distress." Heiskell then held up Lincoya as evidence of these qualities: "Volumes are expressed in his act of taking the infant Indian boy lying on his dead mother's breast after the battle of Talluschatches, and sending him to the Hermitage, where he was named Lincoya, and there nourished and raised until his death at the age of eighteen; and when President in not neglecting to ask in his letters as to Lincoya's health and how he was getting along."[42] More recent defenders of Jackson have continued to use the adoption to negate charges of racism or anti-Indianism.[43] Other scholars, such as Richard H. Faust, used Lincoya to suggest that Jackson's

---

[40]Morgan, "Andrew Jackson," p. 61.

[41]Stoddard, *Andrew Jackson and Martin Van Buren*, pp. 106–7.

[42]S. G. Heiskell, *Andrew Jackson and Early Tennessee History Illustrated* (Nashville, Tenn., 1920). Heiskell, at least, acknowledged that Jackson's participation in the removal policy was a legitimate subject for criticism: "The treatment by our Government of the American Indian is a closed chapter in history. The tribal governments have been dissolved, and the members have been merged into the general body of the American people. Our Indian chapter being closed, we have every facility for judging of the conduct of the American people of that day toward the red man, and it must be confessed that that conduct produced the same results as in every age of the world where the stronger and the weaker nations met in combat, the weaker were crushed and demolished. While it is true the United States spent many millions of dollars on the red man, it is also true that the Government's policy was not always straight, above board and honorable" (Heiskell, *Andrew Jackson and Early Tennessee History Illustrated*, pp. 1–2, 195).

[43]See, for instance, Prucha, "Andrew Jackson's Indian Policy," p. 531; Donald Barr Chidsey, *Andrew Jackson: Hero* (Nashville, Tenn., 1976), pp. 118–19; Satz, *American Indian Policy in the Jacksonian Era*, p. 9; Remini, *Andrew Jackson and His Indian Wars*, pp. 64–65, 214–15, 228.

attitudes toward Indians were more complex than simple bigotry or irrational antipathy.[44]

Jackson's critics were not impressed with this evidence. They also purported to understand Jackson's soul; and the removal, they argued, was the product of a distinct animus against Native Americans and all things Indian. The idea that Jackson hated Indians and wanted them either exterminated or relocated has a long heritage in the literature and accumulated a foothold in the corners of many American minds in the twentieth century. James Mooney, Merrill Peterson, and Roy Harvey Pearce are just a few of the renowned scholars who referred to Jackson as an "Indian hater."[45] Clement Eaton, James F. Corn, and others wrote that not only was Jackson an Indian hater, but he was also one of those "who believed that the only good Indian was a dead Indian."[46] This latter characterization has become commonplace in the anti-Jackson vernacular in popular culture, in classrooms, and on the World Wide Web.[47]

---

[44]Lincoya's adoption, Faust argued, was only representative of a number of humane or magnanimous acts that Jackson demonstrated to American Indians. Faust also maintained that Jackson was ignorant of most of the battlefield atrocities attributed to his troops and punished those of his men who violated principles of "humanity and proper military conduct" (Richard H. Faust, "Another Look at General Jackson and the Indians of the Mississippi Territory," *Alabama Review* 28 [1975]:209–10, 213).

[45]James Mooney, *James Mooney's History, Myths, and Sacred Formulas of the Cherokees* (Asheville, N.C., 1992, originally published as *The Sacred Formulas of the Cherokees* [1891] and *Myths of the Cherokees* [1900]), p. 117; Merrill D. Peterson, *The Great Triumvirate: Webster, Clay, and Calhoun* (New York, 1987), pp. 91–92. In one work, Pearce described the psyche of the "Indian Hater" that crops up quite often in American literature: "[H]e is a man paradoxically kept by his hatred from falling entirely into the very state which defines it. Moreover, he fights on the side of civilization, not against it. In his life, good is accomplished through evil; for only by living as a savage is he able to destroy savages and thus, consciously or not, to contribute to the advancement of civilization. In his evil life as a savage, he must be destroyed; but since he accomplishes good, his fate and its meaning must be comprehended and celebrated as one of the tragic or pathetic works of progress." Pearce did not make it clear whether this characterization applied to his own conception of Jackson as an "Indian Hater," but it was certainly implicit in his work (Roy Harvey Pearce, *The Savages of America: A Study of the Indian and the Idea of Civilization* [Baltimore, 1953], pp. 55, 70, 225–26). Others who offer blanket assertions that Jackson was an Indian hater or held enmity for Indian peoples or individuals, without any effort to explain such an attitude, include Dale Van Every, *Disinherited: The Lost Birthright of the American Indian* (New York, 1967), pp. 31, 43, 51, 283, and Charles Crowe, "Indians and Blacks in White America," in *Four Centuries of Southern Indians*, ed. Charles M. Hudson (Athens, Ga., 1975), pp. 155, 157. Grace Steele Woodward referred to Jackson as "a well-known Cherokee-hater" in her 1963 tribal history, *The Cherokees* (Norman, Okla., 1963), p. 154.

[46]Clement Eaton, *A History of the Old South* (New York, 1949), p. 292; James F. Corn, "Removal of the Cherokees from the East," *Filson Club of History Quarterly* 27 (1953):40.

[47]See, for example, "When Words Fail: Some Reflections on Holy Week at the Choctaw Singing School," http://pilgrimproduction.org/sacredharp/union/whenwordsfail.html; "Illustrated Stories of Royal Roger Eubanks," Sequoyah Research Center, http://www.anpa

In the late 1960s, Indian activists and historians more suspicious of American colonialist tendencies began to construct a truly critical view of the United States' Indian policy. For instance, in 1967, Reginald Horsman argued that the paternalistic rhetoric of the Founders and the removal policy, specifically, were simply propaganda used to disguise a systematic expropriation of Indian land.[48] Andrew Jackson became the figure held in special contempt by critics of American policy. In describing the Indian Removal Act of 1830, for instance, Peter Farb argued that Jackson had forced Congress to adopt legislation that "in our own time, under the Nuremberg laws, would be branded as genocide." The act, Farb added, "gave the President the right to extirpate all Indians who had managed to survive east of the Mississippi River." In fact, the Indian Removal Act only authorized Jackson to negotiate land exchange treaties with the eastern tribes.[49]

In 1969, Francis Paul Prucha, the prolific student of U.S. Indian policy, responded to the general assaults on the morality of the United States and the specific attacks on Jackson's character with an article entitled "Andrew Jackson's Indian Policy: A Reassessment." Prucha complained that many of his contemporaries had embraced what he called a "devil theory" of United States Indian policy, and he despaired that Jackson held "first place" in "their demonic hierarchy." Prucha declared that this construction of federal policy was "unacceptable"; he maintained that most of the disastrous consequences of federal policy for Indians resulted unintentionally from the government's paternalist tendencies. He then set out to defend Jackson from what he thought were unjust attacks: "In his direct dealings with the Indians, Jackson insisted on justice toward both hostile and peaceful Indians. Those who committed outrages against the whites were to be summarily punished, but the rights of friendly Indians were to be protected. Too much of Jackson's reputation in Indian matters has been based on the first of these positions." Prucha added that though Jackson was brutal in enforcing a "no-nonsense policy toward hostile Indians," he was "not oblivious to Indian rights," that "he matched this attitude with one of justice and fairness," and

---

.ualr.edu/digital_library/WeaRoya.html; Kurt Albert Mayer, Seminar WS 2000, Rewriting the West, Protocol of Summer Session 1, Notions of the West, http://angam.ang.univie.ac.at/western2000/protocols/Protokoll1Schedl.htm.

[48]Reginald Horsman, *The Frontier in the Formative Years, 1783–1812* (East Lansing, Mich., 1967), pp. 109–11, 116–17, 140. Years later, Horsman suggested that "Jackson spent no sleepless nights over Indian Removal" (idem, *Race and Manifest Destiny: The Origins of American Racial Anglo-Saxonism* [Cambridge, Mass., 1981], p. 202).

[49]Peter Farb, *Man's Rise to Civilization as Shown by the Indians of North America from Primeval Times to the Coming of the Industrial State* (New York, 1968), p. 250.

that he was "firm in upholding the rights of the Indians who lived peaceably in friendship with the Americans." As evidence for this equanimity, Prucha noted that Jackson adopted Lincoya, embraced Indian allies, and "personally liked and respected individual Indian chiefs." According to Prucha, Jackson was sincere in his paternalism and "was genuinely concerned for the well-being of the Indians and for their civilization."[50]

Prucha's plea for evenhanded judgment, however, was ground down by powerful waves of sentiment pouring from the pens and typewriters of avowed anti-Jacksonians in the 1970s. Some of the denunciations descended into caricature. Alice Marriott and Carol K. Rachlin sneered that "Old Hickory Andrew Jackson, mumbling his false teeth in the White House while he brooded over insults gratuitously offered his wife, was an inveterate Indian fighter. If he did not himself say that the only good Indian was a dead one, he certainly would have agreed with the later general who did."[51] Other critics addressed the question in a less capricious way; as a result, their analyses were that much more devastating. Edward Pessen, for example, wrote that

---

[50]Prucha, "Andrew Jackson's Indian Policy: A Reassessment," pp. 527–39. In the same year that Prucha published his article, Bernard Sheehan bemoaned the demonization of U.S. Indian policy in general. See his "Indian-White Relations in Early America: A Review Essay," *William and Mary Quarterly*, 3rd ser., 26 (1969):267–86. Many authors have concentrated on Jackson's paternalism. In addition to those discussed in the text, see Cole, *Presidency of Andrew Jackson*, pp. 68–70, and John William Ward, *Andrew Jackson: Symbol for an Age* (New York, 1962), pp. 40–41.

[51]Alice Marriott and Carol K. Rachlin, *American Epic: The Story of the American Indian* (New York, 1969), pp. 142–43. Charges that Jackson was a racist infuriated one apologist. Donald Barr Chidsey wrote that "the goggle-eyed *wunderkinder* who cackle so smoothly at our cocktail parties these days have a new word of unspeakable contempt to replace the worn-out 'communist.' Anybody they don't like they call a racist. And the worst kind of racist—at least, the latest worst kind, perhaps because he is never at hand to defend himself—is the hater of Indians." Jackson was "not a racist," Chidsey declared, "he was a realist." Chidsey complained that "these reinterpreters of history would have us believe that all federal dealings with the Indians were fraught with fraud, that no treaty ever was made that was not immediately broken, and that the reason for all this villainy lay in the color of the victim's skin. Posing as sophisticates, they are the most gullible of the gullible." The critics of Jackson, he added, thought of the Indian as "the 'noble savage' who can do no wrong." They believed that "the complex story of race relations in the United States, as far as it pertains to the American Indian, is that of evil, avaricious men using guile, whiskey, false promises, and Iagoesque planted clues to bamboozle and degrade the innocent, unresting aborigine." They did not appreciate the "real" Jackson. According to Chidsey, Jackson was a man who truly understood the Indians; they, in turn, trusted him and enjoyed his company. Chidsey pointed to the trump card of the Jackson loyalists: "But race hatred in the White House? That is a recent theory, originated and promulgated by the *wunderkinder* of the cocktail parties, who seemingly never heard of Lincoyer. . . . Lincoyer was pure Creek, no half-breed. He went to school with the other three boys and ate with them and their parents. When he died of tuberculosis at the age of sixteen, he was buried in the family plot. Surely not racism" (Chidsey, *Andrew Jackson: Hero*, pp. 111–14, 118–19).

"Jacksonian Indian policy was a blending of hypocrisy, cant, and rapaciousness, seemingly shot through with contradictions." Pessen argued that Jackson's rhetoric of progress, paternalism, and humanitarianism was "sheer
rationale for policy based on much more mundane considerations" and that
there was "every reason to think that the Jacksonians were fully aware" that
they were misleading the public by portraying the Eastern Indians as no-
madic savages who did not cultivate their land. "If cunning, bribery, and guile
were the main tactics used to assure Indian prior agreement to removal,"
Pessen added, "brute force and cruelty were employed to execute the policy."
Pessen concluded that Jackson's "performance was not that of a responsible
government official deferring to the will of constituents but rather that of a
zealot who fully shared their biases and rapacity."[52]

Andrew Jackson had devolved into the archfiend of removal for many,
and some historians began to assign him full responsibility for the exile in
an offhanded fashion. Dale Van Every, for instance, described Jackson as
the "chief adversary" of the Indian.[53] In an article on the reemergence of
the Cherokee national government, Albert L. Wahrhaftig and Jane Lukens-
Wahrhaftig wrote that "Cherokee settlements have maintained their integrity
since long before Andrew Jackson had the tribe removed from its southeastern homelands."[54] Critics offered pithy characterizations to explain the
kind of depraved personality that could drive entire communities of decent
people from their homes. Some described Jackson as a malignant hypocrite.
Leonard L. Richards, for example, charged that "the President's words were
merely words" when it came to his justifications for Indian removal.[55] Burke
Davis concluded that Jackson "offered rather specious reasoning to justify
the removal of southern Indians beyond the Mississippi." Ronald T. Takaki
wrote that Jackson was a "disguise artist" who "used the techniques of confidence to cover up . . . the crimes and moral absurdities of the market society."[56] Jackson was also described as a monstrously ambitious man who,

[52]Edward Pessen, *Jacksonian America: Society, Personality, and Politics* (Homewood, Ill., 1969),
pp. 317–22.

[53]Dale Van Every, *Disinherited: The Lost Birthright of the American Indian* (New York, 1967), p. 31.

[54]Albert L. Wahrhaftig and Jane Lukens-Wahrhaftig, "New Militants or Resurrected State?
The Five County Northeastern Oklahoma Cherokee Organization," in *The Cherokee Indian
Nation: A Troubled History*, ed. Duane H. King (Knoxville, Tenn., 1979), p. 224. See also, among
many others, Barry M. Pritzker, *A Native American Encyclopedia: History, Culture, and Peoples* (New
York, 2000), pp. 368, 375.

[55]Leonard L. Richards, *The Advent of American Democracy* (Glenview, Ill., 1977), p. 163.

[56]Ronald T. Takaki, *Iron Cages: Race and Culture in Nineteenth-Century America* (New York,
1979), pp. 84, 105–7.

by brute force or chicanery, ruthlessly eliminated obstacles to his political or material objectives.[57] Alfred A. Cave wrote that Jackson ignored laws and treaties respecting Indian property and political rights and "tacitly encourag[ed] the intimidation and dispossession" of Indians.[58] Gloria Jahoda pushed the argument far beyond what any fair reading of the evidence suggests. She wrote that at Horseshoe Bend, "Andrew Jackson silently pledged himself to the policy of Indian Removal." Jackson determined at that point that "any Indian who remained on his ancestral lands affirming his Indian identity would be a criminal."[59]

Ward Churchill has been the most notorious and perhaps the most prolific critic of U.S. Indian policy in recent years, and Jackson has not escaped his disdain. In one essay, Churchill noted Jackson's famous promise to the Creeks in 1829 that if they removed to the West they would keep their lands "as long as the grass grows or the water runs, in peace and plenty." Rather than attempting to explain what happened after this promise or what Jackson intended by the offer, Churchill simply declared, "Jackson was, to put it bluntly, lying through his teeth."[60] In another forum, Churchill wrote: "In heroicizing people like . . . Andrew Jackson . . . society strongly reinforces the notion that their genocidal conduct was/is an appropriate and acceptable manner in which to attain fame and 'immortality.' Conversely, placing them where they belong in the historical lexicon—alongside the likes of Attila the Hun and Heinrich Himmler—would tend to convey the opposite message."[61] Perhaps words like these have encouraged historians who are usually more guarded in their language to cast caution aside when it comes to Jackson specifically. Have the polemical word choices of Jahoda and Churchill, for example, encouraged usually more cautious scholars to write that Jackson adopted removal "as a genocidal national policy"?[62]

---

[57]John Ehle, *Trail of Tears: The Rise and Fall of the Cherokee Nation* (New York, 1988), p. 125.

[58]Alfred A. Cave, "Abuse of Power: Andrew Jackson and the Indian Removal Act of 1830," *Historian* 65 (2003):1353.

[59]Considering the title of this paper, it is probably worthwhile to note that Jahoda pointed out at least twice in her text, unfortunately without attribution, that the Choctaws referred to Jackson as "The Devil" (Gloria Jahoda, *The Trail of Tears* [New York, 1975], pp. 5–6, 12–18, 26–27).

[60]Ward Churchill, "Like Sand in the Wind: The Making of an American Indian Diaspora in the United States," in *From a Native Son: Selected Essays on Indigenism, 1985–1995* (Boston, 1996), p. 199. The Jackson quotation can be found in the *Southern Recorder* (Milledgeville, Ga.), May 30, 1829.

[61]Ward Churchill, *A Little Matter of Genocide: Holocaust and Denial in the Americas, 1492 to the Present* (San Francisco, 1998), p. 251n.

[62]Robert A. Williams, Jr., *Linking Arms Together: American Indian Treaty Visions of Law and Peace, 1600–1800* (New York, 1999), p. 18; Takaki, *Iron Cages*, p. 103.

Fortunately, some moved beyond simple glorification or disapprobation and offered explanations for Jackson's attitudes and actions. Many historians, from Frederick Jackson Turner to scholars as recent as Andrew Burstein, attributed Jackson's attitudes and policies to the fact that he was a "western man" or a "frontier fighter" who viewed Native Americans and their interests through the prism of his own experience with them during his young adulthood and military career.[63] In 1919, for instance, Frederic Austin Ogg wrote that Jackson was "an old frontier soldier, who never doubted that it was part of the natural order of things that conflict between [whites and Indians] should go on until the weaker was dispossessed or exterminated."[64] In 1949, Clement Eaton observed that Jackson's Indian policy was representative of "his sympathy with the point of view of the frontiersmen and of the common people of the South." Jackson "accepted the frontiersman's estimate that the only good Indian was a dead Indian," Eaton wrote, "and he was zealous in robbing Indians of their land by treaties imposed by force or by chicanery."[65]

Some portrayed Jackson as a man of mixed motives. Jill Norgren, in her study of the Cherokee cases, emphasized both Jackson's frontier background and his patriotic desire for national expansion.[66] Arrell Morgan Gibson suggested that Jackson's "patronizing and paternalistic" policies were the product of several factors: his frontier background, his intellectual rejection of tribal sovereignty, and a rather wide "anti-Indian" streak.[67] In *Liberty and Power: The Politics of Jacksonian America*, Harry L. Watson suggested that the Tennessean's

[63]Frederick Jackson Turner, *The Rise of the New West* (New York, 1906), pp. 309–10; Fiske, "Andrew Jackson," p. 292; Theodore H. Jack, "Alabama and the Federal Government: The Creek Indian Controversy," *Mississippi Valley Historical Review* 3 (1916):302; John P. Brown, *Old Frontiers: The Story of the Cherokee Indians from Earliest Times to the Date of the Their Removal to the West* (Kingsport, Tenn., 1938), p. 489; William T. Hagan, *American Indians* (Chicago, 1961), pp. 71–75; David C. Whitney, "Andrew Jackson," in *The American Presidents* (New York, 1967), p. 77; Dee Brown, *Bury My Heart at Wounded Knee: An Indian History of the American West* (New York, 1971), p. 5; Wilcomb E. Washburn, *Red Man's Land/White Man's Law* (Norman, Okla., 1971), p. 67; Catherine Turney, "Sharp Knife: Andrew Jackson and the Indians," *Mankind* 4 (1974):56–63; Brian W. Dippie, *The Vanishing American: White Attitudes and U.S. Indian Policy* (Middletown, Conn., 1982), pp. 60, 182; Richard A. Cook, "Andrew Jackson and American Indian Policy," *Denver Westerners Monthly Roundup* 40 (1984): 3, 5–6; and Andrew Burstein, *The Passions of Andrew Jackson* (New York, 2004), pp. 6–7, 23, 63, 120, 154.

[64]Frederic Austin Ogg, *The Reign of Andrew Jackson: A Chronicle of the Frontier in Politics* (New Haven, 1919), p. 201.

[65]Eaton, *History of the Old South*, p. 292.

[66]Jill Norgren, *The Cherokee Cases: The Confrontation of Law and Politics* (New York, 1996), pp. 72–73.

[67]Arrell Morgan Gibson, *The American Indian: Prehistory to the Present* (Lexington, Mass., 1980), pp. 305–7.

Indian policy was prompted by a concern for personal political ambitions. Watson added that "Jackson's role was one of condescending paternalism— not benevolence—that refused to take the Indians seriously as competent adults. . . . Jackson's professed benevolence to the Indians must . . . be viewed with skepticism as possibly sincere but undoubtedly self-serving."[68]

Some biographers looked for psychological reasons to explain Jackson's insistence on removal. In 1898, William Graham Summer wrote that Jackson possessed an undisciplined, barbaric character that had never been reined in by "high-bred parents and relatives."[69] In suggesting an explanation for why Jackson allowed Georgia free reign against the Cherokees while he faced down South Carolina in the nullification crisis, both William McDonald and Ogg remarked upon the "erratic character" of Jackson's mind, a trait apparent, according to Ogg, in "many such illustrations" in the general's political career.[70]

Michael Paul Rogin was the first to offer a comprehensive psychological explanation for Jackson's behavior. At the outset of *Fathers and Children: Andrew Jackson and the Subjugation of the American Indian,* Rogin declared that Jackson, who "accomplished a giant land grab," was "the single figure most responsible for Indian destruction in pre–Civil War America." Rogin's Jackson was an Indian hater as a young man who was subsequently transformed into a conniving paternalist. Rogin noted that Jackson's father died two months before his birth and that his mother was a strong, independent woman. Unfortunately for Jackson's psyche, she left him with relatives during the Revolutionary War to help nurse sick and injured prisoners of war in Charleston. As a result, Jackson developed a "buried rage against his mother for at once dominating him, abandoning him, and denying him nurture." As a boy, he came to fear "both maternal domination and the forbidden fulfillment of dangerous nurturing and sensual desires." Jackson thus "retreated to a purified paternal authority"; and, according to Rogin, "the struggle to create a reified paternalism, to rescue sons from maternal power, informs

---

[68]Harry L. Watson, *Liberty and Power: The Politics of Jacksonian America* (New York, 1990), pp. 111–12. Although R. David Edmunds acknowledged that Jackson "may have held paternal feelings towards Indians," he concluded that the president was also "receptive" to local politicians and missionaries who wanted Indians removed (R. David Edmunds, *The Potawatomis: Keepers of the Fire* [Norman, Okla., 1978], p. 240).

[69]Sumner, *Andrew Jackson*, pp. 29, 224.

[70]McDonald, *Jacksonian Democracy*, p. 178; Ogg, *Reign of Andrew Jackson*, p. 213. John Frost and Harry W. French put it more benignly. They described Jackson as "occasionally arbitrary" (Frost and French, "Andrew Jackson," p. 256).

Jackson's life." Jackson suffered from "moods of manic omnipotence, paranoid rage, and occasional deep depression," penned "repetitive, incoherent, vengeful letters," and "often expressed himself in metaphors of devouring violence." This behavior was reflective, Rogin contended, of a "problematic oral relationship." Rogin pointed to reports that Jackson occasionally "drooled" and "slobbered" and suggested that the president's dysfunctional relationship to his mother "precipitated" these "early problems with speech, mouth, and aggression." Children of this nature possessed "insecure ego boundaries" and fluctuated between a sense of complete control over their world and feelings of complete helplessness. Because "American culture idealized mothers," Jackson was unable to release his despair from these feelings against his mother (or any other woman). Instead, he projected his rage at "men who oppressed women." As with most whites of his place and time, Jackson feared and despised Native Americans; and his hatred of Indians roared at its most fevered pitch, Rogin argued, when the general received a report alleging warrior atrocities against women.[71]

Rogin also noted that Jackson matured in the post-Revolution era and feared that he would be unable to prove his manhood and live up to the republican legacy of the Founders. His campaign against the Redstick Creeks, however, transformed him; success in battle permitted him to "reexperience his feelings of primitive violence" and enabled him to "destroy lingering fears of feminine domination and grow securely to manhood." Rogin argued that Jackson's paternalism, so often expressed in his removal-era speeches and letters to the tribes, emerged only after the Battle of Horseshoe Bend in 1814. Conquering the Redsticks allowed Jackson to abandon his tendency to view the Indian as a fraternal rival. In Jackson's mind, the Indian was transformed into an inferior being who required protection and guidance. The adoption of Lincoya, Rogin theorized, was a demonstrative act of Jackson's assumption of "paternal authority" over indigenous peoples. Jackson's psychological epiphany in the Redstick conflict thus determined his political future; he evolved from a troubled and violent "frontier particularist" on the make into a more mentally stable nationalist who used the status achieved through his

---

[71]Michael Paul Rogin, *Fathers and Children: Andrew Jackson and the Subjugation of the American Indian* (New York, 1975), pp. 13–15, 30–31, 42–43, 45–47, 171. Ronald T. Takaki, relying on Rogin's analysis, argued a few years later that "as Jackson marched against the Indians, he also waged a private battle against his own body." By disciplining his body and Indians, "Jackson could lay claim to the republican virtue of respectable work, which he could not do as a land speculator" (Takaki, *Iron Cages*, pp. 94–96).

military exploits, his knowledge of Indian negotiating tendencies, and his experience in speculation to achieve his own personal aspirations. Jackson used a vision of national security—cleansing the East of Indians and European interlopers and bringing native lands into the American market—to enrich his friends, extend the strength of his patronage, expand his base of political support, and, according to Rogin, unconsciously salve his own psychological foibles. Rogin's work, if anywhere near accurate, demonstrates, among many other things, that Jackson's paternalistic language during the removal was far more complex and deep-seated than simple misrepresentation, or "lying through his teeth," as Jackson's most ardent detractors have charged.[72]

Rogin also argued, however, that Jackson's paternalist removal rhetoric was indeed motivated by a conscious, disingenuous design. Jackson repeatedly claimed that he was acting in the best interests of the Indian, that he was powerless to prevent the states from extending their laws over the tribes, and that the federal government was unable to restrain trespassers from entering Indian territory. At the same time he was attempting to conciliate the tribes and justify removal to his detractors, Jackson and his minions were actively encouraging whites to move onto tribal lands. According to Rogin, this duplicitous posing as a paternalist enabled Jackson to distinguish himself from the "predatory desires of ordinary whites" and "deprived the Indians of the right to their anger." The Great Father persona also offered Jackson an opportunity to wash his hands of the Indians' fate; their demise was their own responsibility if they ignored his advice to relocate to the West. Rogin's work begs the question of whether Jackson's removal rhetoric was the product of deep psychological scars or simple and malicious contrivance. He tells us to look to the psyche: "Those who see Jackson merely as an acquisitive swindler—a confidence man—badly miss the point. He needed to ground acquisitiveness on moral bedrock. The more egregious the activity, the more he engaged in falsification of memory, denial, militant self-righteousness, and projection of his own motivations onto others."[73]

Some critics of Rogin assailed him for his general decision to use Freudian psychology to explain Jackson; others criticized him for misapplying specific psychological precepts. Detailing their objections would require a separate paper. One fundamental concern deserves mention here, however. Rogin

---

[72]Rogin points out that Jackson did not refer to Lincoya as "his son" in letters until after his campaign in the First Seminole War (Rogin, *Fathers and Children*, pp. 110, 114, 128, 159, 165, 188–89, 198–99, 272).

[73]Ibid., pp. 171–78, 186, 217, 220–26.

offered a comprehensive psychological explanation for Jackson's Indian policy yet condemned him for actions that he, according to these theories, could not control. Though there were obviously profound psychological reasons for Jackson's behavior, the demons troubling the president were apparently not so strong that Rogin could absolve him of the charge that he had subjugated the American Indian. In the end, though, the work is compelling for the simple reason that it offers an explanation for how a man whose own defenders have described as an Indian hater could come to perceive himself as the savior of the eastern tribes.[74]

In the same year that Rogin offered his controversial thesis, Ronald N. Satz published *American Indian Policy in the Jacksonian Era*. The two interpretations could hardly have been more incompatible. Satz examined the philosophy, legislation, and bureaucracy of the removal policy and contended that Jackson was motivated by personal and party political interests and a distinctive, fervent nationalism leavened by a strict philosophical construction of federal power. Satz recited some familiar themes: "The tremendous energy and perseverance Andrew Jackson expended on Indian affairs . . . was not related to any feelings of animosity toward the Indians. Jackson was not the merciless Indian-hater most historians have portrayed. Although he was a ruthless opponent in battle, Old Hickory demonstrated great paternalism in his dealings with the Indians as territorial governor of Florida. He also openly sanctioned Indian-white marriages, adopted an Indian orphan, whom he treated as his own son, and counted hundreds of full-bloods as personal friends." According to Satz, Jackson's "views on Indian policy were not governed so much by any personal negative attitude toward the Indians as by his overwhelming concern for the nation's growth, unity, and security." Jackson's

---

[74]For criticism of Rogin's theories, see, among others, Elizabeth Fox-Genovese, "Psychohistory versus Psychodeterminism: The Case of Rogin's Jackson," *Reviews in American History* 3 (1975):407–18; Lewis Perry, "Fathers and Children: Andrew Jackson and the Subjection of American Indians," *History and Theory* 17 (1977):174–95; William J. Gilmore, "The Individual and the Group in Psychohistory: Rogin's *Fathers and Children* and the Problem of Jackson's Health," *Psychohistory Review* 6 (1977–78):112–26. Many historians have embraced parts of Rogin's analysis, including Takaki, Wallace, James C. Curtis, and even Robert V. Remini. Curtis argued that Jackson's Indian policy was grounded by a "coercive paternalism." To Jackson, "Indians represented disorder, a threat to white family solidarity and community stability." "In reacting to the shock of his mother's death, he tried to disown his troubled childhood, replacing it with aspirations for an orderly life." For Jackson, Indians were "doubly evil, reminding him of a past he was trying to forget and threatening a future he was trying to achieve" (James C. Curtis, *Andrew Jackson and the Search for Vindication* [Boston, 1976], pp. 22–23, 72).

experience as a treaty commissioner in the South had led him to believe that conducting relations with the tribes by diplomatic treaty was an "anachronism," that Indians held only a temporary right to possess their lands, and that this title was subject to extinguishment by the states. The national security of the United States, Jackson believed, demanded that the eastern tribes be relocated; in particular, he wanted to eliminate the potential for foreign and Indian alliances that could threaten trade and settlement of the Mississippi valley. Satz held that Jackson was not being disingenuous when he promised that the tribes would be protected in the West and that he was sincere when he offered federal support toward their cultural advancement. Satz added that every president since Washington had contemplated relocating the Indian tribes beyond the territorial limits of the United States, that Monroe had commented positively on an early Jackson plan for removal, and that John Quincy Adams had come to the conclusion that removal was the only solution to the crisis in the Southeast in the days before he left office. Satz also agreed with several of his predecessors that Jackson conceived of removal as the only alternative that would protect the eastern Indians from annihilation or degradation at the hands of white Americans. According to Satz, Jackson believed, in light of the controversy over the tariff of 1828 and the expectations raised by discussions of removal, that he needed to complete the relocation of the tribes in order to avoid a wholesale rebellion of the states where they resided and, perhaps just as significant to him, a sundering of his party's unity in the region. Satz contends that the death and inhumanity wrought by the actual relocations were a product of bureaucratic confusion, mismanagement at the local level, and poor funding by Congress. He acknowledged that Jackson was accountable for this state of affairs but that the general did not initiate the enterprise with malicious intent: "Old Hickory wanted to accomplish Indian removal quickly, cheaply, and humanely, but his emphasis on speed and economy often undermined efforts to provide adequate care for Indian emigrants."[75]

Satz subsequently moderated these views and called for historians to abandon a dualistic good-versus-evil approach to the question. He argued that Prucha and Rogin, two leading representatives of the hero and devil schools, respectively, concentrated too intently on Jackson's motivations. What historians should do, he wrote, was "follow the old frontier maxim: 'If you want

---

[75]Satz, *American Indian Policy in the Jacksonian Era*, pp. 4, 6, 9–12, 54–56, 64–66, 107.

to know what a politician is up to, watch his feet, not his mouth.'" In applying that principle, Satz backed off of the defense he had offered in his mono-
graph. He noted that although Jackson declaimed paternalistic motivations
in his public addresses, "neither the president nor anyone else in his administration was willing to undertake adequate long-range planning or to commit the federal government to undertake more responsibilities for, or to spend
more money on, the Indians than was absolutely necessary." Satz, in other
words, had moved toward the conclusion that the most egregious act of the
administration was its bungling of the removal plan once Jackson had forced
it through Congress. Historians should worry more about the practical im-
plementations of policies rather than espoused motivations, Satz suggested;
Indian people suffered from what occurred on the ground, not what passed
through Jackson's mind.[76]

Richard H. Faust attempted to synthesize the political interpretation offered by Satz and the psychological thesis devised by Rogin. Faust wrote
that "General Andrew Jackson was not the vindictive man portrayed in the
Indian histories of sentimentalists." To understand Jackson's policies as general and president, he argued, one had to appreciate his "complex motivations." Jackson was genuinely concerned, as he stated in speeches and letters, for the general welfare of indigenous peoples. He was concerned at the
same time, however, for the national security of the United States and his
own political status. Faust suggested that the animosity that Jackson occasionally disseminated about Indians in correspondence was from a man
projecting pent-up rage against a people he truly and consistently hated—
the British, whom the general blamed for the disintegration of his family.[77]
Faust added that Jackson's "military mind" led him to hold that "victory
meant annihilation of the opposition." Jackson did not hate Indians, Faust
concluded; he wanted them eliminated only when they were obstacles to his
personal or national ambitions.[78]

Of course, no paper on the historical scholarship on Andrew Jackson
would be complete without acknowledging the work of Robert V. Remini.

---

[76]Satz, "Rhetoric versus Reality," pp. 36–44.

[77]Faust, "Another Look at General Jackson," pp. 202–71. For another view, see J. Leitch
Wright, Jr., *Creeks and Seminoles* (Lincoln, Neb., 1986), pp. xii–xiii.

[78]Faust wrote that Jackson was also influenced by "the frontiersman's concern for western
financial welfare," a yearning for higher social status, personal political desires for national
expansion, and concerns for national security (Faust, "Another Look at General Jackson and
the Indians of the Mississippi Territory," pp. 202–17).

Remini possesses a reputation as a defender of Jackson's Indian policy. However, while the professor has indeed rationalized Jackson's decision to pursue removal to its conclusion, he has not shied from condemning specific acts committed by his favored subject. And, while Remini does clearly admire Jackson, the historian has never whitewashed the cruelties of the removal policy. In an early biography, for example, he wrote that "the horror of the removal beggars the imagination." He noted that Indians were "tricked into signing away their possessions" and "pressed along 'a trail of tears' to find disease, starvation, and death on the western plains."[79] Years later, Remini added: "The experience of removal is one of the horror stories of the modern era. Beginning with the Choctaws it decimated whole tribes. An entire race of people suffered. What it did to their lives, their culture, their language, their customs is a tragedy of truly staggering proportions."[80]

Remini's first biography (1966) committed only 3 of 188 pages to the issue. He fully embraced in this work the argument that Jackson was a president trapped by limited options, and this explanation became the foundation of the formidable structure of defenses he constructed in subsequent books. Remini added that Jackson's Indian removal policy was demonstrative of his "commitment to the States' rights position." Perhaps, he suggested, Jackson was "trying to maintain one foot in the States' rights camp, at the same time he jammed the other foot into the camp of the nationalists."[81]

By the late 1970s, Remini had developed a more complex interpretation of Jackson's motives. In the first volume of his massive three-volume biography, he contended that Jackson's Indian policy was motivated by a powerful nationalistic desire to expand the United States and to secure its Southwestern flank from the danger of foreign intrigues.[82] Remini summarized the major threads of his expanding defense in the second volume:

> [Jackson's] ideas about the Indians developed from his life on the frontier, his expansionist dreams, his commitment to states' rights, and his intense nationalism. He saw the nation as an indivisible unit whose strength and future

---

[79]Robert V. Remini, *Andrew Jackson* (New York, 1966), pp. 128–30.

[80]He added, perhaps reflexively, that "the irony is that removal was intended to prevent this calamity" (Robert V. Remini, *Andrew Jackson and the Course of American Freedom, 1822–1832* [New York, 1981], p. 275).

[81]Remini, *Andrew Jackson*, pp. 57, 128–30; idem, *Jackson and the Course of American Empire, 1767–1821* (New York, 1977), p. 336; idem, *Jackson and the Course of American Freedom*, p. 263; idem, *Andrew Jackson and his Indian Wars*, pp. 279–80.

[82]Remini, *Jackson and the Course of American Empire*, pp. xi, 305–6, 331–32.

were dependent on its ability to repel outside foes. He wanted all Americans from every state and territory to participate in his dream of empire, but they must acknowledge allegiance to a permanent and indissoluble bond under a federal system. Although devoted to states' rights and limited government in Washington, Jackson rejected any notion that jeopardized the safety of the United States. That included nullification and secession. That also included the Indians. Jackson's nationalism, a partial product of his expansionist ideals, and his states' rights philosophy, a product of his concern for individual liberty, merged to produce his Indian policy.[83]

Remini then added a new element to his defense; removal, he wrote, was a product of Jackson's "reform intentions." By reform, Remini was referring to programs that "focused on a problem the solution of which would 'protect liberty,' [Jackson's words] or 'restore virtue,' or 'guarantee popular suffrage,' or insure 'obedience to the popular will,' or 'eliminate corruption,' or re-establish 'pure republican' principles." Remini argued that Jackson could not abide the principle of tribal sovereignty, for he believed that the United States could not long survive or prosper with independent nations lurking within its borders. Jackson, consequently, "regarded removal as a reform effort because it was designed to protect the liberty and security of the American people."[84]

Remini has struggled mightily with the question of whether Jackson was a racist or harbored a general malice against Indians. On the one hand, he had acknowledged on more than one occasion that Jackson did possess racist or anti-Indian sentiments. In *The Election of Andrew Jackson*, his first work on the president, Remini wrote that Jackson's "affection for the Indian about equaled his affection for Henry Clay."[85] In the first book of his three-volume treatise, he added that Jackson had emerged from his early years "as a fire-breathing frontiersman obsessed with the Indian presence and the need to obliterate it and contemptuous of Congress for failing to help. Jackson railed against the Indians and against Congress. Because of them, innocent settlers were murdered, treaties violated, the frontier splashed with blood."[86] In the second volume, Remini denied that these feelings dominated Jackson's concept of Native Americans: "The key to understanding Jackson's attitude toward the Indian is not hatred but paternalism. He always treated the Indians

---

[83] Ibid., pp. 220, 258.
[84] Ibid., pp. 200–201.
[85] Remini, *Election of Andrew Jackson*, pp. 75, 156.
[86] Remini, *Jackson and the Course of American Freedom*, pp. 70–71.

as children who did not know what was good for them. But *he* knew, and he would tell them, and then they must obey. If they refused, they could expect a fearful punishment from a wrathful parent." Remini then sidestepped again. Though he argued that paternalism was the fundamental mindset controlling Jackson's attitudes toward Indians, he maintained that it was not the intellectual force that produced his position on removal. Rather, he "agreed to it because it was best for the American nation." "Most important of all," Remini wrote, "removal meant the elimination of tribal government, tribal organization, tribal sovereignty from white society." "It was never the Indians *per se* that bothered Jackson," he wrote, "it was their infernal presence as a tribe, as a unit separate and distinct from the rest of the country, as though the Indians as a Nation had a right to the status of a free, independent and sovereign state."[87]

In a passage that confused matters even further, Remini then reversed course and denied that Jackson possessed anti-Indian sentiments:

> It has been asserted that Andrew Jackson hated the Indians and that racial annihilation was his real objective. Nothing could be further from the truth. Jackson neither hated the Indians nor intended genocide. For a slaveowner and Indian fighter he was singularly free of racial bigotry. . . . Moreover, Jackson befriended many Indians; dozens of chiefs visited him regularly at the Hermitage. He adopted an Indian orphan (Lyncoya) and raised him as a son. He sanctioned marriages between whites and Indians. He believed citizenship inevitable for the more civilized Indians, and he argued that Indian life and heritage might be preserved (and should be preserved) through removal.[88]

As Remini evolved his position on Jackson's feelings toward Indians, he clearly moved closer to the argument that removal was a policy motivated, in part, by racist sentiments. Removal, he began, was not an "intentional rape." It was "an exchange of land based on the premise that the two races could not live together, that the Indians occupied more land than they needed or would cultivate, and that the Indians, where they were, endangered the

---

[87]Perhaps Remini was influenced by Rogin's work, for he now saw Jackson's controlling temperament as general in nature. He suggested, for instance, that Jackson exhibited the same paternalism with his troops. "As long as they obeyed him, as long as they demonstrated discipline and loyalty, he praised them without stint," he wrote, "but let them falter in their duty and he could exact the supreme penalty" (Remini, *Jackson and the Course of American Empire*, pp. xii, 305–6, 331–32, 336–37).

[88]Ibid., pp. 336–37.

frontier and menaced not only settlers but the American nation itself." By the end of his three-volume biography, Remini had merged racist, paternalist, and nationalist motivations and ascribed them all to Jackson: "In theory, removal protected everyone: whites, the Indians who stayed, and those who removed. Everyone benefited. Whites obtained the valuable lands relinquished by the departing Indians and thereby strengthened the nation's defenses, particularly near the frontier; the Indians who stayed gave up their wanderings and settled down to civilized life; and the Indians who removed preserved their racial heritage and 'national existence.'"[89]

Remini concluded his discussion of the removal in the biographical set by directing a comment at Jackson's modern critics:

> Andrew Jackson has been saddled with a considerable portion of the blame for this monstrous deed. He makes an easy mark. His objective was not the destruction of Indian life and culture. Quite the contrary. He believed that removal was the Indian's only salvation against certain extinction. . . . The Indian problem posed a terrible dilemma and Jackson had little to gain by attempting to resolve it. He could have imitated his predecessors and done nothing. But that was not Andrew Jackson. He felt he had a duty. And when removal was accomplished he felt he had done the American people a great service. He felt he had followed the "dictates of humanity" and saved the Indians from certain death.[90]

Remini's series left readers with another contradiction. He had determined that Jackson "shares much of the blame for this inhuman deed," for he had been "so anxious to expel the red man from 'civilized society' that he took little account of what his inflexible determination might cost in human life and suffering." That suffering, Remini reminded readers, "was truly horrendous." Despite these awesome words of condemnation, Remini continued to defend Jackson's choice: "Andrew Jackson left office bowed down by the stupefying misery involved in removal, but he left knowing he had accomplished his goal and that thousands of Indians had found what he considered a safe haven west of the Mississippi River. He left believing he had saved the Indians from inevitable doom. And, indeed, he had." Remini has not since moved from this position.[91]

---

[89]Ibid., p. 336.

[90]Ibid., pp. 264–65.

[91]Robert V. Remini, *Andrew Jackson and the Course of American Democracy, 1833–1845* (New York, 1984), pp. 303, 314.

The reactions to Remini's arguments were mixed. Some clearly agreed with his calculation of Jackson's intent. In his study of U.S. Indian policy in the nineteenth century, Philip Weeks complained that "Andrew Jackson's current reputation, shaped by textbooks, teachers, and the media, is that of a scourge to the Indians of the South because of his strong advocacy of their removal to western lands." In reality, Weeks declared, "Jackson viewed himself as a true friend and protector of the Indians, a benevolent advocate acting with paternalistic wisdom in their best interest." Weeks wrote that Jackson truly expected that whites would eventually assimilate Indians on an equal plane.[92]

Remini's thoughts on Jackson also provoked dissent. In 1993, Anthony F. C. Wallace published *The Long Bitter Trail: Andrew Jackson and the Indians*, which revived a materialist critique for a new generation of readers. While he conceded that Jackson never proposed exterminating the Indian population or removing it by force, he did assert that Jackson "was adept at devising conditions that would make those who chose not to remove so miserable that they would emigrate eventually anyway." He noted that Jackson used deceitful and intimidating tactics in cession treaty negotiations with the southeastern tribes between 1815 and 1820 and contended that the general's success in those dealings encouraged him to use the same means when he moved to relocate the tribes as president. Jackson's motivation, according to Wallace, was "some combination of political ambition, financial greed, and philosophical rationalization." Wallace, like many before him, suggested that Jackson was representative of the white frontiersmen of his era in his attitudes about Indians. However, he maintained that Jackson was driven primarily by a desire to accumulate power and position for himself and his clique. Trading and speculating in Indian land, Wallace argued, provided Jackson with the wherewithal to reward "family, friends, and political constituents." Wallace pointed out how ubiquitous John Coffee appeared in the treaty negotiations and surveys of Native American lands. In several cases, Jackson had used influence or pressure to procure commissions for Coffee. As a result, Wallace charged, "Coffee was in a position to know exactly where the most valuable lands were, and he made his fortune by it." Wallace also alleged that Jackson secured specific financial benefits from Coffee's knowledge: "By the time of his death in 1845 (after virtually all the Southern Indians had been removed), he had managed to amass an extensive estate, including the well-furnished mansion at the Hermitage, two plantations, 161

---

[92]Weeks, *Farewell, My Nation*, pp. 41–42.

slaves, a valuable stable of fifty horses, and hundreds of head of livestock." Wallace did not deny that Jackson was partially motivated by a desire to "develop the country by expanding its agriculture and commerce," but it is the Tennessean's pecuniary interests that the author highlights as the most influential in this work. While his charges were not new, Wallace's work ensured that Prucha, Satz, and Remini would not so easily resurrect Jackson's legacy.[93]

But the latter would still try. Almost twenty years after his three-volume biography, Remini returned to the question of Jackson's Indian policy in a book devoted specifically to that subject. Remini had clearly been spurred by the barrage of criticism against Jackson. He began *Andrew Jackson and His Indian Wars* with a broadside aimed at a presentist public looking for simple answers and singular scapegoats: "Today Americans are quite prone to fault Jackson for the removal without understanding the circumstances surrounding the event. They have little appreciation of the mood of Americans at the tail end of the eighteenth and beginning of the nineteenth century. They prefer to single out one culprit for blame, just as King George III is singled out for initiating the American Revolution." Remini then advised his readers to recall how "the so-called greatest generation" interned Japanese Americans during World War II before placing Jackson into the dock of historical judgment. At the same time, he made clear that defending Jackson was not a palatable exercise. He acknowledged throughout the text that Jackson used a variety of nefarious means, including coercion, intimidation, extortion, intoxication, bribery, and what might be characterized as fraud, to expropriate land from the southeastern tribes. He used the phrase "systematic despoliation" to describe the process that Jackson used to secure cessions from the Creeks, Chickasaws, Choctaws, Cherokees, and Seminoles. Remini also finally acknowledged in this work, perhaps in recognition of the arguments offered by Rogin and Wallace, that "there is no doubt that Jackson personally benefited to an extraordinary degree from the land wrenched from Native Americans." However, Remini maintained that financial gain was only a by-product of Jackson's policies rather than a material element in his calculations.[94]

Remini reaffirmed the major lines of defense articulated in his previous work. Jackson viewed Indians as treacherous pawns that could be "used by any foreign power seeking to gain dominance in North America." The

---

[93]Anthony F. C. Wallace, *The Long, Bitter Trail: Andrew Jackson and the Indians* (New York, 1993), pp. 4–6, 50–56, 63.

[94]Remini, *Andrew Jackson and His Indian Wars*, pp. v, 57, 88–89, 93, 99, 107, 163, 171–72, 180, 192–93, 204, 367.

Redstick Campaign, Remini contended, affixed this philosophy in Jackson's mind: "Whether the Indians were friendly or unfriendly, they had to be moved out of any area—but particularly along the Gulf—where they could endanger the safety of the United States. Such a scheme would allow American settlers to occupy this choice land and, at the same time, better protect the nation against foreign invasion." "Security and removal," Remini wrote, "were linked in his mind as the only solution to the problem, and he devoted the rest of his life toward achieving it." Remini also reminded readers that Jackson was not the first to suggest removal as a solution to Indian-white unrest in the East. But "what Jackson did to the Indians as President," he argued, was "end the drift and indecision of previous administrations."[95]

Remini reminded readers that Jackson emerged from a distinct environment: "The white men and women living on the frontier had to maintain a constant vigil against marauding, frequently drunken, and outraged Native Americans. . . . Andrew Jackson learned to fear and hate Indians from an early age—as did most frontier settlers. And they never forgot." As a young man, Remini argued, Jackson "accepted as indisputable fact that Indians had to be shunted to one side or removed to make the land safe for white people to civilize and cultivate." The objective of removal, he added, "became ingrained in the culture" and "lodged securely in Andrew's mind." By the time he was responsible for dealing with the tribes as military commander and treaty commissioner, Jackson believed that "Indians were distinctly inferior to whites, and for them to presume an equality with their 'betters' was offensive and intolerable." Remini continued to maintain that though this set of mind helped determine Jackson's actions as a military commander against the Creeks and Seminoles, and as a negotiator with the Chickasaws and Choctaws in the late 1810s, it did not motivate him directly as president in his removal of the eastern tribes in the 1830s. He did not offer an explanation for how Jackson the Indian hater was transformed into Jackson the paternalist; nor did he explain how a man who believed in the innate inferiority of Indians could say that he looked forward to a future when Native Americans would be assimilated by the white population. Remini repeated the Lincoya example, as he had in previous volumes, to demonstrate that Jackson was not an Indian hater, despite the fact that in his early chapters he had established a rather strong case that Jackson did, in fact, hate Indians. Just a few pages after the first mention of Lincoya, for instance, Remini, in de-

---

[95]Ibid., pp. 17, 27, 33, 53–55, 85, 101, 113, 115–16, 227–28, 279.

scribing the Redstick conflict, stated, "It seems his hatred for the Creeks had become an obsession." Remini had worried in his 1966 biography that "this extraordinary action by Jackson—of brutally killing Indian families on the one hand, and extending kindness to an Indian child on the other—was one of several incidents that kept his contemporaries forever perplexed about the range of contrasts fused within this unusual man." By the end of his long study with Jackson, Remini was also unable to settle on an explanation for this conundrum.[96]

Near the end of the book, Remini returned to the point he had left two decades before. Jackson's offense to humanity was "his insistence on speed and economy in reaching a decision with the several tribes." Jackson "lacked patience, and by his pressure to move things along quickly he caused unspeakable cruelties to innocent people who deserved better from a nation that prided itself on its commitment to justice and equality."[97] Remini even added that it was not unreasonable to hold Jackson accountable for the tragedy of the Cherokees' Trail of Tears: "Although it has been pointed out many times that he was no longer President of the United States when the Trail of Tears occurred and had never intended such a monstrous result of his policy, that hardly excuses him. It was his insistence on the speedy removal of the Cherokees, even after he had left office, that brought about this horror. From his home outside Nashville he regularly badgered Van Buren about enforcing the treaty [of New Echota]." By the time he left office, Remini added, Jackson had become "obsessed" about relocating the eastern tribes.[98]

The source or cause of this obsession remains open for debate. It is difficult for many to believe, considering Jackson's history in broad context, that this anxiousness was the product of benevolent intent. Nor is it clear how a man who viewed Indians as inherently inferior to whites could have, as Remini argued, "fully expected the Indians to thrive in their new surroundings, educate their children, acquire the skills of white civilization so as to improve their living conditions, and become citizens of the United States." In the end, Remini's argument that Jackson was motivated by concerns for national security was compelling; the contention that his paternalistic rhetoric was heartfelt remains open to debate.[99]

---

[96]Remini, *Andrew Jackson*, pp. 128–30.
[97]Remini, *Andrew Jackson and His Indian Wars*, pp. 237–38.
[98]Ibid., pp. 237–38, 270, 276.
[99]Ibid., p. 280.

Recent biographers have recognized that their predecessors had, by depreciating the significance of the removal, failed to tell the whole story of Jackson's life and influence; and they have devoted more attention to the subject. While they have cast their discussions of removal in fuller and more thoughtful ways, it is easy to discern that the residue of the hero/devil interpretations of Jacksonian Indian policy will remain with us for some time. Some biographers continue to see sinister ulterior motives behind Jackson's benevolent words. For example, in *The Passions of Andrew Jackson*, Andrew Burstein argued that Jackson wanted "political control over the tribes" and said that the Tennessean "aimed to be just diplomatic enough to co-opt Indians by a combined show of strength and amity." Burstein wrote that Jackson's policies could be understood only in the light of "his equally anxious speculation and unqualified combativeness" and that his paternalistic rhetoric was essentially a "rationalization" that covered his belief that Indians were innately inferior.[100] In another recent work, a thoughtful history of so-called mixed bloods in North America, Thomas N. Ingersoll contended that removal was essentially an exercise in ethnic cleansing. Jackson and Jacksonians, he argued, viewed Indians as an inferior class of human beings and believed that white Americans would continue to endure the condescension of European elites if the United States allowed whites to interact and intermarry with Indians. These white Americans harbored entrenched anxieties about racial mongrelization, Ingersoll wrote, and Jackson exploited their fears to unite a nation divided by sectional and class interests.[101] Some authors, on the other hand, continue to absolve Jackson for his role in the removal. In the most recent biography of our subject, *Andrew Jackson: His Life and Times*, H. W. Brands embraced much of the Remini interpretation. Brands argued that "from start to finish," Jackson's "foremost concern was the safety of the United States," that the president believed he was saving the Indians from "utter annihilation," and that Jackson meant it when he said that he had the best interests of Indians at heart.[102]

The reassessment of Jackson's legacy will continue, and some clear trends are discernable. Jackson's historical reputation, among the public and among scholars, is becoming more compatible with the opinion held by the de-

---

[100]Burstein, *Passions of Andrew Jackson*, pp. 91, 185–88.

[101]Thomas N. Ingersoll, *To Intermix with Our White Brothers: Indian Mixed Bloods in the United States from Earliest Times to the Indian Removals* (Albuquerque, 2005), pp. 180–216.

[102]Brands, *Andrew Jackson: His Life and Times*, pp. 320–21, 488–93.

scendants of those who were removed. Scholars no longer ignore the fact of Jackson's part in the removal when they evaluate his presidency; the relocations now, consciously and subconsciously, influence individual reactions to his name. This will affect discussions of Jackson's presidency in a broad fashion. The interpretations of Jackson's Indian policy were and will continue to be influenced by the preconceptions that the authors bring to their studies of the subject. Those critical of Jackson's positions on other issues have little difficulty forging a condemnatory description of his role in the removal; they seize upon the evidence that tends to suggest that Jackson was driven by material or racist motives. Those who begin their biographies as admirers of Jackson, whether from respect for his impact on democratization or from simple appreciation of his dramatic life story, seem to want to find ways to excuse or defend their hero. One might predict that in the future, those biographers who enter the study of Jackson with a critical conception of his removal policy will embrace more negative articulations of the other controversial issues that have divided Jacksonian scholars in the past. Bias against Jackson's attitudes and actions regarding Indians, in other words, will bleed back in the opposite direction to interpretations of his personality, his impact on democracy and federalism, and his economic and land policies. Despite best efforts to approach the study of Andrew Jackson and his Indian policy with Olympian objectivity, we will continue to find it difficult to free ourselves of the predilections that we carry into that work.

Remini identified one of the unfortunate prejudices that has obstructed our understanding: a desire for the simple answer. The tendency of many to allocate complete responsibility for the removal to Jackson remains ubiquitous, obtrusive, and historically problematic. It is easy to see, however, why so many have singled out Jackson for condemnation. While he was only one of many who wanted to expel the eastern nations, he had been obsessed with the idea of removal since at least 1817. Moreover, he did force the Indian Removal Act through Congress. He did pressure most of the tribal nations of the East to surrender their lands and retire to the West. He did establish the administrative bureaucracy that implemented the relocations. Perhaps more important, Jackson left evidence of a past that corroborated suspicions of malicious intent. Those who delved into Jackson's life looking for signs of racism or anti-Indianism could find them if they wished. Still, while it might be convenient to equate the removal with Jackson as a shorthand device, it is clearly unfair and illogical to allocate to him complete historical culpability for the relocations. In the past, reductionists, for whatever reasons, deemed it unnecessary to take into account in their narratives the part played by Congress, the U.S. Supreme Court, previous presidents, and Southern state legislators and judges. Most avoided trenchant discussions of the fundamental economic, demographic, and ideological factors that turned the nation toward the removal policy. Rather than trying to explain the roots of the removal, they simply blamed Jackson. In the end, a clear understanding of the removal crisis will remain out of our reach until historians and the reading public accept that the catastrophe was the product of deep and powerful economic and ideological longings on the part of many white Americans.

The real issue, however, is whether we can condemn him, as prosecutors tried to do recently with another Jackson, on evidence of a pattern of prior acts. We have to ask, in other words, whether Jackson's rather violent and bigoted tendencies during his youth and military career, and his occasional inflammatory remarks throughout that period, truly enlighten us as to his intentions and motivations in the late 1820s and 1830s. Personally, I would prefer to rely on evidence closer in time to the act; if we focus on that period, perhaps we will find that the motivations of racism and hatred were superseded to a considerable extent by those of political opportunism, nationalistic dreams of expansion, misguided paternalism, and, to some extent, a natural mellowing produced by age and experience and required by his political ambitions.

The relationship between Jackson's Indian policy and his legacy is complicated by the fundamental dilemma of the documents: the very real evidentiary existence of the man's own words. His public speeches elevate him from the simplistic Indian hater who exiled the eastern tribes out of spite to, at best, a complicated individual with complex motives or, at worst, a conniving hypocrite. Was Jackson, as so many have raged, the self-interested racist who cared not a whit for Indian feelings and callously removed the eastern tribes beyond the Mississippi? Or, was he the man who declared in his second annual message to Congress, "Toward the aborigines of the country no one can indulge a more friendly feeling than myself, or would go further in attempting to reclaim them from their wandering habits and make them a happy, prosperous people"? Was he the man who referred to American Indians during his military career as "cannibals," "savages," and "bloodhounds," or was he the individual who declared in 1831 that he "entertain[ed] the kindest feelings" for American Indians. The discussion remains open. However, at the end of the day, it seems imperative that historians explore Jackson's Indian policy within the broadest context of his life, times, and culture. We should also admit the possibility that humans, even demigods in decline, might have changed over time. Blindly faithful apologies and shorthand condemnations only threaten to befog even further an increasingly hazy view of the man.[103]

[handwritten annotation]

[103]James D. Richardson, ed., *A Compilation of the Messages and Papers of the Presidents,* 10 vols. (Washington, D.C., 1897–1914), 2:541, 3:1083; Takaki, *Iron Cages,* pp. 94, 103–4.

Daniel Feller

Andrew Jackson versus the Senate

F RICTION BETWEEN THE executive and legislative branches of government
was built into the U.S. Constitution and has proved endemic throughout the nation's history. Relations between the president and the U.S. Senate, who share responsibility for executive appointments and treaties, have
at times been especially troublesome. Andrew Jackson's presidency (1829–37)
was one of those times. The Senate rejected many of Jackson's nominees
to office, including some of his most intimate favorites—men like Martin
Van Buren and Roger B. Taney—and in 1834 the Senate formally censured
Jackson himself, an event that to this day remains unparalleled in the annals of American government.

Why Jackson had such trouble with the Senate is a question not often
asked. "Partisanship" is the ready answer, and it is true that Jackson's administration inaugurated an era of party conflict more raucous and ran-
corous than ever before. Mention of the Senate in Jackson's day immediately brings up images of the so-called great triumvirate—Henry Clay of
Kentucky, John C. Calhoun of South Carolina, and Daniel Webster of

In citations to Andrew Jackson manuscripts, parenthetic numerals in form (12-3456) show
reel and frame locations in *The Papers of Andrew Jackson: A Microfilm Supplement* (Scholarly Resources, 1987); those in form (DLC-37) give reel numbers for the Library of Congress microfilm of its Andrew Jackson Papers collection; those in form (T123-4) give series and reel
numbers for official National Archives microfilm publications.

Massachusetts—marshaling the Whig party legions in battle array against the president.

Yet this answer alone fails to satisfy. Jackson was already fighting the Senate long before the Whigs organized and the triumvirate gathered in 1834. In fact, he had fought it right from the beginning. Jackson's first Senate (1829–31), in which neither Clay nor Calhoun served, contained twenty-seven professed Jackson men to twenty-one opponents. Yet that Senate gave Jackson much more trouble than his immediate predecessor John Quincy Adams had with his last Senate, which contained an antiadministration majority of exactly the same size. And although other presidents before and since have faced hostile Senate majorities none have been censured. Partisanship also cannot explain why Jackson had such difficulty with the Senate at the same time that he commanded a majority in the electorate, in the House of Representatives, and in the state legislatures. Lastly, partisanship is a circular explanation that in part reverses cause and effect. It presumes that senators opposed Jackson because of their party. But parties were not ready-made during Jackson's presidency. They were still in formation, and Jackson's confrontations with the Senate helped draw party lines by driving some Jackson men into opposition. Senatorial resistance to Jackson, then, did not merely reflect partisanship. Rather, it helped create it.

The true explanation lies deeper. Jackson's administration was one of those in which the endemic competition for power among branches of the American government reached a tipping point. As at other such moments —for instance, in the crises of the Andrew Johnson and Richard Nixon presidencies—partisanship was part of the story, but never the whole story. There was an institutional component as well. In Jackson's case, a president seeking for the first time to wield his popularity as a governing mandate ran into a Senate determined not only to fortify but also to expand its own independent prerogative. The victory was Jackson's, and its result was a substantive, though in part temporary, reordering of the balance of power in which the president, through the new instrument of party, gained a lever of control over the formerly autonomous Senate.

The conflict between Jackson and the Senate began over appointments to office. Under the Constitution, a president "shall nominate, and by and with the Advice and Consent of the Senate, shall appoint" subordinate executive officials, commissioned military officers, and federal judges. He also "shall have Power to fill up all Vacancies that may happen during the Recess of the Senate, by granting Commissions which shall expire at the End of their next Session." This grant of authority masked several crucial ambiguities. The most important concerned whether, since the Senate's consent was necessary to appoint executive officers, it was also necessary to remove them. This and other questions were aired in a floor debate that erupted almost immediately in President Washington's first Congress. The debate ended by leaving the power of removal in the president's hands alone, though by implication rather than positive declaration.[1] After some false starts, Washington and the Senate also settled upon what might be called the "doctrine of separate spheres"—the rule that the two branches should act on appointments separately and independently and that neither should presume to question or interfere with the proceedings of the other. As Washington put it, "[A]s the President has a right to nominate without assigning his reasons, so has the Senate a right to dissent without giving theirs."[2]

As it turned out, Washington and his successors used the removal power sparingly, and the Senate, for its part, rarely rejected presidential nominations to office. Although the threat of nonconfirmation always hung over the president, it was a threat rarely exercised. When the Senate did reject a nominee, it was usually for one of several specific reasons. Sometimes the Senate intervened to enforce its understanding of the complex rules of seniority that governed promotion in the military services. Sometimes diplomatic or consular nominees were rejected as a way of registering opposition to the office itself; for unlike other executive offices, such posts were created not by statute but by specific appointment. Usually in such cases, the nominees were reconsidered and approved after the disagreement over policy was ironed out.

The number of nominees rejected in the republic's early years was quite small. Military officers aside, the Senate rejected five of George Washington's nominations, one of John Adams's, and nine of Thomas Jefferson's. The number rose to twenty-seven in James Madison's administration, thirteen of them tax assessors and collectors under the wartime internal revenue laws.

---

[1] *Annals of Congress*, 1st Cong., 1st sess., pp. 385–99, 473–608. The debate was joined over a provision in the act creating a Department of Foreign Affairs, which in final form said that the department's chief clerk would act in the stead of the secretary "whenever the said principal officer shall be removed from office by the President of the United States" (1 Stat. 29 [1789]).

[2] Joseph P. Harris, *The Advice and Consent of the Senate* (New York, 1968), p. 39.

Twenty-one of James Monroe's civil nominations were refused, but only four of John Quincy Adams's—though in the lame-duck session after his defeat for reelection, the Senate in effect killed many more by postponing them until Jackson's inauguration.[3]

By contrast, the Senate rejected forty-nine of Andrew Jackson's non-military appointments, seventeen of them in a single session in 1834. Not only was the number of rejections unprecedented, but so, too, was the importance of the offices. Among those rejected were two ministers to Britain (the most important post in the diplomatic service), a cabinet officer, a senior Treasury official, and a territorial governor—the first time appointments to any of these offices had been refused.[4]

Trouble over appointments erupted at the very outset of Jackson's presidency. Jackson came into office intent on overhauling the federal bureaucracy, or, as he loved to put it, "cleansing the Augean Stable." A relative outsider in Washington, he believed, as did many of his supporters, that his election had rescued the republic from the clutches of aristocrats and corruptionists. An officeholders' cabal, Jackson believed, had swindled him out of the presidency in 1824 and conspired again to thwart the "cause of the people" by working to defeat him in 1828.[5] "The late political struggle," Jackson informed prospective members of his cabinet shortly before the inauguration, "exhibited the people acting against an improper use of the patronage in the hands of the executive branch." It would therefore be his duty "to dismiss all officers who were appointed against the manifest will of the people, or whose official station by a subserviency to selfish & electioneering purposes was made to operate" against the freedom of elections. In his inaugural, Jackson announced that the people had mandated "the task of *reform*" in government, including the dismissal from office of "unfaithful or incompetent hands."[6]

---

[3]These figures are tabulated from *Journal of the Executive Proceedings of the Senate* (hereafter *Senate Executive Journal*), vols. 1–3. The tally counts only rejections, not nominations that were tabled and not brought to a vote. It also excludes nominees who were reconsidered and confirmed within a few days of rejection.

[4]Tabulated from ibid., vol. 4.

[5]Jackson to John C. McLemore, Apr. 26, 1829, and Jackson to Ralph E. W. Earl, Mar. 16, 1829, in *The Papers of Andrew Jackson*, ed. Daniel Feller et al. (Knoxville, 2007), 7:183, 7:98.

[6]"Outline of principles submitted to the Heads of Department," Feb. 23, 1829, in Feller et al., *Papers of Andrew Jackson*, 7:60; First Inaugural Address in *A Compilation of the Messages and Papers of the Presidents, 1789–1897*, ed James D. Richardson, 10 vols. (Washington, D.C., 1896–99), 2:438.

He began with the Treasury bureau chiefs. These functionaries—the treasurer, register, five auditors, and two comptrollers—were responsible for keeping the government's accounts and overseeing its expenditures. Discharging administrative and adjudicatory tasks supposedly beyond the reach of party politics, they served for terms of indefinite length and had hitherto been considered nearly untouchable. Less than three weeks into his presidency (and just four days after the Senate broke for an eight-month recess), Jackson deposed three of them: second auditor William Lee, fourth auditor Tobias Watkins, and second comptroller Richard Cutts, all appointees of President James Monroe. In their places, he appointed Isaac Hill, Amos Kendall, and William B. Lewis. Kendall and Hill were newspaper editors distinguished for their strident pro-Jackson partisanship in the 1828 campaign; Lewis was Jackson's Tennessee neighbor and political factotum. A few weeks later, Jackson replaced treasurer William Clark, a Quincy Adams appointee, and register Joseph Nourse, who had served since George Washington appointed him in 1789.

Meanwhile Jackson undertook a cleansing of federal commissioned officers in the states—district marshals and attorneys, land office registers and receivers, and customs collectors, surveyors, and assessors. Under the Tenure of Office Act of 1820, all of these officials were commissioned for terms of four years, but were also "removable from office at pleasure."[7] The fixed terms allowed a president to put in his own men by rotating officers out as their commissions expired, without resorting to outright removals. Yet Monroe and Adams had disdained even this power. Adams made a point of routinely renominating incumbents to new terms and of refusing mid-term removal for any reason short of malfeasance or proven incompetence. Monroe in his second term removed only three civil officials before their commissions expired: two land surveyors and an internal revenue collector. Adams in four years removed two district attorneys, a customs collector, and a land office register.

In contrast, by the time Congress convened for its first regular session of Jackson's presidency in December 1829, he had already removed thirteen district attorneys, nine marshals, twenty-three registers and receivers, and twenty-five customs collectors, replacing them all with recess appointees. Historians have bandied figures to minimize the extent of Jackson's removals,

---

[7] 3 Stat. 582 (1820).

mainly by setting them against the many minor functionaries and small-town postmasters who were not displaced. But these offices were often inconsequential and were, in any event, not direct presidential appointments.[8] Measured against all past experience, Jackson's removals were extraordinary. He dismissed more officials in his first few weeks than his predecessors had in years. The anti-Jackson press boiled with protests against what they called "proscription" and with lurid tales of faithful public servants let go without warning or cause—their careers blasted, reputations ruined, and families left destitute. "There has been a great noise made about removals," Jackson noted sourly. "Now every man who has been in office a few years, believes he has a life estate in it, a vested right, & if it has been held 20 years or upwards, not only a vested right, but that it ought to descend to his children, & if no children then the next of kin—This is not the principles of our government." In his opening message to Congress, Jackson defended his removals and condemned long tenure in office for turning government into "an engine for the support of the few at the expense of the many."[9]

Jackson's purge raised again the question of the Senate's role in removals. In 1830, the Senate debated the constitutionality of removals and interim appointments at length. Opposition members, adherents of the late president Adams and of presidential aspirant Henry Clay, offered resolutions demanding to know the cause of certain removals. The implication was that removal without specific cause—that is, without evidence of incompetence or malfeasance—was an abuse of executive authority. But these challenges never rose above the level of partisan attacks, and the administration

---

[8]In "The Federal Civil Service under President Jackson," *Mississippi Valley Historical Review* 13 (1927):517–40, Erik McKinley Eriksson estimated Jackson's removals at one-tenth of all federal officeholders, a highly questionable yet oft-quoted figure. Different methods of classifying offices and of defining "removal" can yield very discrepant results. I use the term narrowly here, as it was usually used in presidents' official messages to the Senate, to mean only commissioned officers displaced during their stipulated terms. Adopting a broader definition, and including diplomats and consuls serving for indefinite periods, Carl Russell Fish came up with 164 civil removals under Jackson, compared to 101 for his six predecessors together (Fish, "Removal of Officials by the Presidents of the United States," *Annual Report of the American Historical Association for the Year 1899* [Washington, D.C., 1900], pp. 67–86). Whatever the basis of computation, the image of a thorough purge was clearly not, as Eriksson suggested, merely the creation of anti-Jackson publicists. Jackson's political manager William B. Lewis pledged just after the election that Jackson was "resolved on making a pretty general sweep," "a radical change," and "a complete overhauling" among the officeholders (Lewis to James A. Hamilton, Dec. 12, 1828, Martin Van Buren Papers, Library of Congress).

[9]Jackson memorandum book, ca. May 1829, in Feller et al., *Papers of Andrew Jackson*, 7:193; First Annual Message, in Richardson, *Messages and Papers*, 2:449.

majority in the Senate rebuffed them all and sustained the president's power of removal.

Where Jackson first ran into trouble with a majority of the Senate, including a crucial group of his own supporters, was not in his removals, but in the men he chose to replace them. Beginning with Amos Kendall and Isaac Hill, Jackson named a slew of partisan newspaper editors—"electioneering skunks," John Quincy Adams called them—to various high offices. These selections troubled even such trustworthy Jacksonians as Thomas Ritchie of the influential *Richmond Enquirer,* who complained privately about them to Jackson. As an obvious reward for political services, appointments of newspapermen seemed designed to corrupt the freedom of the press. Furthermore, some of the editors had indulged in partisan invective that passed the bounds of permissible slander—which in those days took some doing—and several were of dubious private character. The most notorious was Henry Lee (half brother to the later illustrious Robert E.), a Jackson campaign scribbler who a few years before had ignited a scandal by impregnating his wife's younger sister. Dispatched by Jackson over the summer with a recess appointment as consul general to Algiers, Lee was such a pariah that other diplomats bound abroad changed their sailing arrangements to avoid being in the same boat with him.[10]

Although partisan lines were still ill-defined—especially in the Senate, whose members were chosen by state legislatures and did not have to declare their allegiance before the voters—twenty-six or twenty-seven of the forty-eight senators in Jackson's first Congress could usually be relied on to back the administration. But when Henry Lee's nomination came up in March 1830, everyone broke ranks. Jacob Burnet of Ohio, a Clay man with a sense of humor, called for the yeas and nays, which were usually taken only on close or contentious votes. The roll was called and the result recorded: forty-six senators against, not one in favor.[11]

The Senate also rejected Ohio editor James B. Gardiner for a land office appointment by 46 to 0. Another Ohioan, Moses Dawson, was defeated 42 to 5. Two New Hampshire nominees, protégés of second comptroller Isaac Hill, went down by votes of 43 to 1 and 36 to 9, and to crown the sequence the Senate rejected Hill himself by 33 to 15. These were not mere

---

[10]Charles Francis Adams, ed., *Memoirs of John Quincy Adams,* 12 vols. (Philadelphia, 1874–77), 8:215; Ritchie to Martin Van Buren, Mar. 27, 1829, in Feller et al., *Papers of Andrew Jackson,* 7:129–32; Cornelius P. Van Ness to Van Buren, July 11, 1829, Van Buren Papers, Library of Congress.

[11]*Senate Executive Journal,* Mar. 10, 1830, 4:66–67.

rejections but repudiations, in which loyal Jackson men joined the opposition in droves.

The crucial maneuvering in Jackson's first Senate centered on several less objectionable nominees, including two from the editorial corps, Treasury auditor Amos Kendall and New York City customs surveyor Mordecai Manuel Noah. Jackson exerted all his leverage to get them through, making it plain that he regarded votes against confirmation as personal affronts to himself. Most of the professed Jacksonians in the Senate gave way, but three of the more independent—John Tyler and Littleton Tazewell of Virginia and William Smith of South Carolina—refused, evening the Senate balance to within a vote or two. Twice—once with Noah, once with an Indian agent named Wharton Rector—Jackson resorted to the maneuver of renominating men who had just been rejected, claiming that better information or a fuller Senate would produce a different result. Rector was rejected again, but Noah on his second try and Amos Kendall on his first were both confirmed by the tie-breaking vote of Vice President John C. Calhoun.

Although in the end only a handful of nominees were defeated, Jackson's first congressional session ended with tempers high. Opposition senators denounced the Jackson majority for their servility in approving most of the appointments, while the Jacksonians, many of whom thought no more highly of the nominees than did their adversaries, complained of executive manipulation and dictation. "The *dragooning of Party*" saved Kendall and Noah, reported Sen. Daniel Webster of Massachusetts, despite "a burning fire of discontent" within Jacksonian ranks. "Some of the proceedings in relation to appointments have evinced an ingenuity and adroitness in mismanagement which I had never witnessed or imagined," Massachusetts Jacksonian Marcus Morton complained. In the case of Noah, "it was *wrong* to nominate him—*wrong* so long to postpone the nomination—*wrong* to reject it and *wrong* to renominate him." Isaac Hill's "nomination was *wrong*—the postponement was *wrong*—the rejection was *wrong*." As for Amos Kendall, "I could only say that his nomination was *wrong*, that the postponement was *wrong* and I am not quite certain that I am not *wrong* in saying even this." Vice President Calhoun, to whom Morton vented his disgust, came under fire from both sides—from Clay men denouncing his subservience and from Jackson men suspecting his secret disloyalty.[12]

---

[12]Webster to Warren Dutton, May 9, 1830, in *The Papers of Daniel Webster: Correspondence*, ed. Charles M. Wiltse et al., 7 vols. (Hanover, N.H., 1974–86), 3:69; Marcus Morton to John C. Calhoun, June 12, 1830, in *The Papers of John C. Calhoun*, ed. Robert L. Meriwether et al., 28 vols. (Columbia, S.C., 1959–2003), 11:202–3.

Jackson, for his part, felt aggrieved at what he called "the extraordinary course pursued by the Senate." He was especially peeved at Tazewell and Tyler of Virginia. Jackson had offered Tazewell the mission to England a year before and remarked to Amos Kendall, "It is always pleasant when our course is approved by such enlightened minds, as Mr. Tazewells." But that was before Tazewell voted against Kendall for fourth auditor. "Our friend judge Tazewell remained to vote against all the printers," Jackson steamed in May 1830. "I do suppose he does not mean to continue in public life. The people of Virginia have denounced the course of Tazewell & Tyler in the Senate, *some most bitterly.* . . . The people will correct those evils."[13]

To Jackson, voting against his nominees was a violation of senators' obligation to "the people." To some senators, it was a fulfillment of their basic trust. An opposition senator, David Barton of Missouri, urged his colleagues to resist Jackson's removals and "restore this Senate to what it was designed by its makers to be—a body elevated by its long term and comparatively independent tenure of office, entirely above the party politics of the day, and standing aloof, as the great barrier of public safety, against the rage of popular passion on the one side, and the encroachments of Executive will on the other." John Tyler did not share Barton's opposition politics, but he did share his conceptions of duty and senatorial independence. For his vote in the Senate, "I am under no promise, no commitment," he affirmed. "The barking of newspapers and the brawling of demagogues can never drive me from my course."[14]

Jackson in return resolved to allow no senatorial encroachment on his prerogative. Anticipating a challenge, he armed himself after Isaac Hill's rejection with an opinion from Attorney General John Berrien authorizing him to retain the defeated comptroller in office under his recess appointment until the end of the Senate session. Another issue concerned what the Senate was entitled to know about his reasons for making appointments. In March, an opposition senator, Samuel Foot of Connecticut, offered a resolution asserting the Senate's "unquestionable right . . . to call in respectful terms upon the President . . . for such information as may be in his possession, and which the Senate deems necessary" to decide on nominations.

---

[13]Jackson to Kendall, July 2, 1829, in Feller et al., *Papers of Andrew Jackson*, 7:319; Jackson to John Overton, May 13, 1830, Tennessee Historical Society, Nashville (15-0994).

[14]*Register of Debates in Congress*, 21st Cong., 1st sess., p. 150; John Tyler to Henry Curtis, Feb. 22, 1830, in *The Letters and Times of the Tylers*, ed. Lyon G. Tyler (Richmond, Va., 1884–96), 1:407–8.

Foot's resolution was tabled. Still, the Senate on several occasions asked to see the credentials of Jackson's nominees. Jackson complied, but by session's end he determined to submit no longer. "The letters of recommendation to the President & heads of Departments for office belong to the Executive," he noted. "The Senate have no right to call for them. The President has the constitutional power to appoint—he does this on the best information he has obtained, and it is anough [*sic*] for them, informally, to know, that the officer was deemed both honest, fit, & capable." Further requests for such documents should be denied.[15]

As both the senators and Jackson braced for trouble, relations between the two branches by the time Congress adjourned in May 1830 had become severely strained. During the next three years, they grew much worse. Through the remainder of Jackson's first term, he conducted a kind of running warfare with the Senate, a continual skirmishing in which each side sought to seize a little more of the disputed ground that lay between the president's right to appoint and the Senate's right to reject. To convey the nature of this skirmishing, it will suffice to relate one incident, or series of incidents, concerning Jackson's attempt to fill a land office in Mississippi.

It began in 1830, when Jackson decided to provide for one of his late wife's innumerable nephews, one Stockley Donelson Hays, by naming him surveyor of public lands for Mississippi and Louisiana. Hays was an impecunious (and some said bibulous) Tennessee lawyer and a former army officer who had fought with Jackson in the War of 1812. Expecting charges of nepotism, Jackson urged Hays to "get, & send on here, as early as he can, testimonials of his sobriety & capacity as a surveyor—This will be necessary, for so sure as an opportunity offers if one should, to give him a survayers [*sic*] District, that in order to mortify me his appointment will be opposed in the Senate." For Hays's sake, Jackson was willing to bend on protocol. He had Sen. Felix Grundy of Tennessee arrange a private meeting with Mississippi's two senators, George Poindexter and Powhatan Ellis. Both were Jacksonian, though Poindexter was already suspected of coolness toward the administration. Jackson pled Hays's case and gained, as he thought, the two men's acquiescence. The next day, December 20, he sent Hays's name to the Senate.[16]

[15]John M. Berrien to Jackson, Apr. 16, 1830, RG 60, National Archives and Records Administration (NARA), Washington, D.C. (T412-3); *Senate Executive Journal*, Mar. 18, 1830, 4:72; Jackson memorandum, ca. Mar. 1830, Jackson Papers, Library of Congress (15-0266).

[16]Jackson to Robert J. Chester, Nov. 7, 1830, Tennessee Historical Society (16-0669); Jackson memorandum on Stockley Donelson Hays, [Dec. 20, 1830], Jackson Papers, Library of Congress (16-1504).

There, Poindexter (who had his own candidate for the job) objected that Hays's appointment violated the established rule of choosing federal officers from among residents of the state. Jackson felt betrayed but kept his temper, coolly pointing out to Poindexter that the surveyor's post was as much Louisiana's as Mississippi's and that a Tennessean under such circumstances might be considered a neutral choice. Further, said Jackson, while Poindexter's claim of state privilege reflected common practice, it rested on no "matter of right strictly speaking," since offices existed only "for the public good."[17]

But the Senate sided with Poindexter. Hays's nomination was referred to a committee with instructions to look into his qualifications. Jackson duly sent in the sheaf of endorsements Hays had procured from Gov. William Carroll and other Tennessee luminaries. On the other side the committee, prodded by Poindexter, took testimony from Tennessee congressman David Crockett and others that Hays was unqualified, insolvent, and "intemperate to a degree of sottishness." On February 3, 1831, the Senate formally resolved, on Poindexter's motion, "That it is inexpedient to appoint a citizen of any one State to an office which may be created or become vacant in any other State of the Union within which such citizen does not reside, without some evident necessity for such appointment." The vote was 22 to 10, and among that majority were such good Jacksonians as Thomas Hart Benton of Missouri, William R. King of Alabama, and Levi Woodbury of New Hampshire.[18]

Jackson was incensed at what he saw as a brazen encroachment on his right to appoint whom he wanted. But the nomination was doomed, so he salvaged what he could and came to a settlement with Poindexter. Gideon Fitz, the incumbent register of the land office at Mt. Salus (also called Clinton), Mississippi, was elevated to the surveyorship, and Jackson nominated Hays for register at Mt. Salus in his place. For his part, Poindexter, on grounds of Hays's intended move to Mississippi, declared himself "willing to regard him as entitled to fill an office among us." The Senate confirmed Hays on a party-line vote, 25 to 19. Poindexter voted aye, despite, as Jackson

[17]Jackson to Poindexter, Dec. 20, 1830, Mississippi Department of Archives and History, Jackson, Miss. (16-1509).

[18]George Poindexter to David Barton, Jan. 12, 1831, RG 46, NARA; Jackson memorandum on Stockley Donelson Hays [Mar. 8, 1831], Jackson Papers, Library of Congress (DLC-73); *Senate Executive Journal*, Feb. 3, 1831, 4:150–51.

acidly observed, having recently called the nominee "a confirmed and ha-
bitual sot, every way unqualified."[19]

Hays, apparently ungrateful, spoiled this compromise by dying just seven
months later. The Senate being out of session, Jackson deliberately threw
down the gauntlet. He filled the vacancy at Mt. Salus with a recess appointment to another Tennessean, Samuel Gwin, another former comrade-in-
arms and the son of an old friend. When the new Congress convened in
December 1831, Jackson duly nominated Gwin, and the Senate duly rejected him by the large margin of 25 to 13. Again a number of Jacksonians,
including Thomas Hart Benton, sided against the president. In explanation
of its vote, the Senate pointed to Poindexter's resolution against nonresi-
dent appointments adopted the year before.

Jackson exploded. He composed a furious, nearly incoherent protest,
excoriating this "direct attempt" by a minority of the whole Senate—the
twenty-two members who had voted for Poindexter's resolution—"to alter
the constitution of the united States, by controling his constitutional power
of appointing from the great body of the people such persons as he thinks
fit." Admit the principle, said Jackson, and the Senate could limit his appointments "to a state, to a county, a village & even to a certain sect of chris-
tians, to the exclusion of others." It could dictate the appointment of particular persons—could, in effect, seize the power of appointment for itself.
The Senate, said Jackson, had a constitutional right to reject, but if a nominee was "honest fit & capable, they are bound by that solemn instrument,
to confirm him, whithersoever in these united States he may reside." For
the president to allow this "act of usurpation & violation of the constitution" would be "a dereliction of duty, as well as trechery to his constituents."
Therefore, until the Senate recanted, he would consider no Mississippian
for the Mt. Salus vacancy.[20]

In the end, Jackson thought better than to deliver this challenge. On
advice of Treasury Secretary Louis McLane, who hoped to avoid provoking "a direct issue with our *friends*," he held his fire and waited. In January,
an opposition senator moved an inquiry into the "moral worth" of James B.

---

[19]George Poindexter and Thomas Hinds to Jackson, Feb. 15, 1831, RG 46, NARA
(17–0533); Jackson to Thomas H. Williams, Apr. [7], 1831, Jackson Papers, Library of Congress (17-1079); *Senate Executive Journal*, Feb. 19, 21, 1831, 4:158, 161.

[20]Jackson to the Senate drafts, ca. Dec. 1831, Jackson Papers, Library of Congress (DLC-
73; 18-1530).

Gardiner, the Ohio editor whom Jackson appointed to negotiate an Indian treaty after his unanimous rejection for a land office. Jackson prepared another scathing protest—but withheld it. A few days later, Clay men and Southern nullifiers united to reject Jackson's nomination of Martin Van Buren for minister to England; Vice President Calhoun, now definitely in opposition, cast the deciding vote. Raging privately at the Senate's "factious opposition, who have degraded that august body, once the admiration of the world, lower than a Spanish inquisition," Jackson let the post—the most important in the diplomatic service—go unfilled rather than submit another nominee.[21]

Jackson waited nearly six months after Samuel Gwin's rejection for the Mt. Salus land office, until June of 1832. Then he nominated him again. Deeming the second attempt "an act of justice," Jackson fortified it with a batch of letters and petitions from Mississippi (whose procurement he had carefully orchestrated) in support of Gwin, "not doubting," Jackson told the Senate, that they would "embrace with cheerfulness an opportunity, with fuller information, to reconsider their former vote upon his nomination."[22]

The Senate, with cheerfulness, tabled Gwin's nomination by 27 to 17 and left it there, allowing his rejection earlier in the session to stand as the last word on the subject. Gwin had actually been exercising the office this whole time, under the recess appointment Jackson gave him back in October 1831. That appointment automatically expired when the Senate adjourned in July. Jackson paused just long enough to check his legal ground with Attorney General Taney and then filled the vacancy with another recess appointment —to Samuel Gwin.

The Twenty-second Congress reconvened for its second session in December 1832. Now it was Poindexter's turn, in resolutions offered on the Senate floor, to denounce the president's "palpable violation of the Constitution of the United States and a dangerous usurpation of power" which, if unchecked, would strip the Senate of all voice in appointments. Jackson played his waiting game. He held off until February 19, 1833, less than two weeks before a mandatory adjournment, before sending Gwin's name in

---

[21]Louis McLane to Jackson, [Dec. 26, 1831], Jackson Papers, Library of Congress (19-0422); *Senate Executive Journal*, Jan. 13, 1832, 4:199; Jackson to the Senate draft, Jan. 16, 1832, and Jackson to James A. Hamilton, Jan. 27, 1832, in *Correspondence of Andrew Jackson*, ed. John Spencer Bassett, 7 vols. (Washington, D.C., 1926–35), 4:398–400, 402–3.

[22]*Senate Executive Journal*, June 12, 1832, 4:255.

again, accompanied with yet more testimonials from Mississippi proving him acceptable "to the great body of the people" there.[23]

Gwin by now had occupied the Mt. Salus land office for sixteen months despite being rejected once. The Senate promptly rejected him again, 20 to 19. Jackson nominated another Tennesseean, Blackman Coleman, in his place. The Senate rejected him. On March 2, 1833, the session's last day, Jackson nominated William L. Willeford of Tennessee. He was rejected— and for good measure the Senate threw in rejections of two other Tennesseans Jackson proposed for land office appointments in the new Chickasaw Cession in Mississippi.

At this point, with time fast expiring, Jackson pronounced his refusal to nominate any further as long as the Senate adhered to its unconstitutional rule against out-of-state appointments. Late in the day of a marathon closing session, when nearly half its members were gone, the Senate took up Poindexter's February 1831 resolution and rescinded it. The roll call was 17 to 9—five votes fewer for recission than the twenty-two-member rump majority who, as Jackson complained, had adopted the resolution in the first place. Absences explained most of the reversal, though three senators— Benton of Missouri, King of Alabama, and Samuel Smith of Maryland— who had backed Poindexter two years before now voted to rescind. Jackson immediately sent in Gwin's name for a new land office, just created, in Mississippi, and he was confirmed.[24]

Jackson basked in his "triumph over the factious senate headed by Poindexter."[25] Yet all of this was but prelude, for in the next congressional session, the so-called panic session of 1833–34, the skirmishing between Jackson and the Senate finally broke out into open war. The collisions over appointments continued. But the main focus of controversy was an issue that, for the first time, combined the question of appointments with a major policy dispute that arrayed the president and a majority of the Senate against each other. That issue was the Bank of the United States.

More than a year earlier, in 1832, Jackson had vetoed a bill to recharter the Second Bank of the United States. But its existing charter did not expire

---

[23]Ibid., Dec. 31, 1832, 4:293–94, Feb. 22, 1833, 4:315. Sen. George Bibb of Kentucky offered a resolution similar to Poindexter's (Mar. 2, 1833, 4:326). Both were tabled.

[24]Ibid., Mar. 2, 1833, 4:329–33.

[25]Jackson to Robert J. Chester, Mar. 3, 1833, in Bassett, *Correspondence of Andrew Jackson*, 5:27–28.

until 1836, and after the veto, the Bank continued to function under its authority as the lawful custodian of federal funds. It also, notoriously, wielded its money and influence in political efforts to procure its own recharter and to unseat Jackson in the presidential election of 1832. The election, in which Jackson handily defeated Henry Clay, and then the South Carolina nullification crisis commanded Jackson's attention through the winter of 1832–33. But as soon as those matters were resolved and Congress adjourned in March 1833, he turned his sights on the Bank.

Jackson determined to draw the Bank's fangs by withdrawing the government's deposits from its keeping and putting them (for lack of any better place) in selected state banks. Removing the deposits was an action that, under the Bank's charter, could be taken only by the secretary of the Treasury, who was immediately to report his reasons to Congress. In spring of 1833, Jackson canvassed his cabinet on deposit removal. Most members opposed it, but Jackson got the support and arguments he wanted from Attorney General Taney. Treasury Secretary Louis McLane, who disliked the idea, was moved upstairs to the State Department and succeeded by William John Duane, a known foe of the Bank. On September 18, having laid his ground carefully, Jackson read a paper to the cabinet announcing his decision to begin the removal. Virtually instructed to give the necessary order, Duane, to Jackson's astonishment, flatly refused. He also refused to resign, so Jackson dismissed him and put in Taney, who had helped draft the cabinet paper, as acting Treasury secretary. Taney promptly ordered the removal.

The new Congress convened in December. The recalcitrance Jackson had met from previous Senates was nothing compared to the fury he encountered in this one. The Bank responded to the deposit removal by sharply contracting its loans, triggering business distress; and Congress found itself besieged by petitioners imploring relief and generally blaming the president. In the Senate, the Clay-Calhoun opposition axis, forged the year before, was in the majority. Many of its members had favored rechartering the Bank of the United States, but even some critics of the Bank rebelled at Jackson's peremptory mode of acting against it. He had deliberately shut out Congress by executing the deposit removal while it was out of session, and he had run roughshod over his own cabinet, effectively reducing the Treasury secretary from his statutory role as a quasi-independent custodian of the federal purse to a mere subordinate functionary, a lackey of the president's will.

The Senate began by requesting from Jackson a copy of his cabinet paper of September 18. This was no secret document. Released to the press and extensively circulated after the cabinet meeting, it had been crafted purposely for public consumption in order to rally support for Jackson's policy. Still, Jackson invoked what later presidents would call "executive privilege" and refused the Senate's call. Pointing to the constitutional separation of powers, he instructed the Senate that what went on in his cabinet council was officially none of their business.[26]

The next clash came over appointments. The charter of the Bank of the United States, pursuant to its character as a quasi-public institution, provided that five of the twenty-five directors were to be presidential appointees, requiring Senate confirmation and serving one-year terms. Hitherto, the designation of government directors had been routine. Notwithstanding their differences, Jackson had nominated Bank president Nicholas Biddle as a government director for 1830, 1831, and 1832. But to build his case in 1833 for removing the deposits, Jackson had solicited confidential reports on the Bank's dealings from four of the current government directors, Peter Wager, Henry D. Gilpin, John T. Sullivan, and Hugh McElderry. As Jackson saw it, apprising him of the Bank's sordid machinations was precisely the function of government directors. As Bank management saw it, it was spying.

At the beginning of the session, Jackson nominated the four dissident directors to new terms. In February 1834, the Senate took them up and rejected them all, the vote falling along party lines. Jackson sent the names back. He began by disclaiming "all pretension of right on the part of the President officially to inquire into or call in question the reasons of the Senate for rejecting any nomination whatsover" and proceeded to do exactly that. The Senate, said Jackson, had approved the same men the year before, and nothing since had been alleged against their private character. Therefore, the Senate must be unrighteously punishing them for performing their solemn duty of tattling on the Bank. Yet he would never stoop to appoint directors to be mere "subservient instruments or silent spectators of [the Bank's] abuses and corruptions." If candidates were to be disqualified by the Senate for fulfilling their public trust, then there could be no government directors at all, the Bank would go unchecked, and "the judgment of the American people" would assign the blame.[27]

The Senate referred this message to a committee chaired by Jackson's old nemesis, John Tyler of Virginia, who by now sat squarely in the opposition

---

[26]Richardson, *Messages and Papers,* 3:36.
[27]Ibid., 3:41–48.

camp. Tyler reported that just as Jackson's reasons for nominating were none of the Senate's business, so the Senate's reasons for rejecting were none of his. Indeed, it was impossible to determine the motives behind a Senate decision and improper to try, as each member was a free agent responsible only to himself. It was enough for the president to know that the Senate, "in the exercise of an unquestionable constitutional right," had rejected his choices. If he then failed to fill the offices, it would be his fault. Tyler also took exception to Jackson's peculiar practice of renominating men whom the Senate had already rejected.[28]

Evidently, other senators agreed with him, for on the second go-around the four directors were rejected by 30 to 11, a larger margin than before. Three former supporters—John Tipton of Indiana, Gabriel Moore of Alabama, and John Black of Mississippi—went over to the opposition and a number of others absented themselves.

Meanwhile, before the second vote on the directors, the Senate issued Jackson its ultimate rebuke. On March 28, 1834, it adopted two resolutions offered by Henry Clay. The first, by 28 to 18, declared Taney's reasons for removing the deposits (which he had duly communicated to Congress) to be "unsatisfactory and insufficient." The second, by 26 to 20, censured Jackson himself, declaring "that the President, in the late Executive proceedings in relation to the public revenue, has assumed upon himself authority and power not conferred by the constitution and laws, but in derogation of both."[29]

Jackson replied with a long and forceful protest. The Senate, he complained, had issued what was meant to stand as the moral equivalent of an impeachment verdict. Yet it had done so without the requisite participation by the House of Representatives, without any specific charges, without evidence, without trial, and without the two-thirds majority necessary for a real conviction. The Senate had no right to pass judgment on him in this extrajudicial fashion, "palpably repugnant to the Constitution." As always, Jackson framed the contest within the larger question of popular rule. The Senate was a body "not elected by the people and not to them directly responsible," while he as president was "the direct representative of the American people." Censure, therefore, was an aristocratic bid to stifle the popular voice in government and "concentrate in the hands of a body not directly

---

[28] *Senate Executive Journal*, May 1, 1834, 4:394–97.
[29] *Journal of the Senate of the United States of America*, 23d Cong., 1st sess., Mar. 28, 1834, pp. 196–97, (hereafter *Senate Journal*).

amenable to the people a degree of influence and power dangerous to their liberties and fatal to the Constitution of their choice."[30]

The Senate stood its ground. By votes of 27 to 16, it branded the protest a breach of Senate privilege, refused Jackson's request to have it entered on the *Senate Journal*, and denied his right to officially challenge or criticize Senate proceedings.[31] In law, of course, the censure meant nothing. Jackson continued to exercise his office—and through the remainder of the session he and the Senate continued to battle over appointments. The Senate cut a broad swath through Jackson's nominees, rejecting land and customs officers in Indiana and Mississippi, a Louisiana marshal, an Ohio district judge, and another minister to Britain. In retaliation, Jackson took to nominating the sons and brothers of rejected nominees to fill their offices: Martin Gordon, Jr., in place of Martin Gordon for customs collector at New Orleans; George H. Flood in place of Thomas Flood for register of the Zanesville, Ohio, land office. They, too, were rejected. The Senate crowned this series by rejecting Roger Taney, who had ordered the deposit removal, for secretary of the Treasury, the first time a cabinet nominee had ever been refused.

In the next session, in 1834–35, the carnage continued. Jackson tested the Senate by putting up John T. Sullivan and Henry Gilpin, two of the defeated Bank directors, for army paymaster and governor of the Michigan Territory. Both were voted down. In another calculated provocation, Jackson between sessions removed Gideon Fitz from the troublesome Mississippi land surveyorship that had triggered the imbroglio with Poindexter and replaced him with Russell M. Williamson. The Senate, before voting on Williamson, demanded the reasons for Fitz's removal. On similar occasions Jackson had sometimes yielded ground to save his nominees, but this time he refused. "As the representative and trustee of the American people," he told the Senate, he would submit no longer to "these unconstitutional demands" that subordinated the executive to Senate "domination and control."[32] The Senate rejected Williamson. Jackson then put up William Willeford, refused by the Senate two years before for the Mt. Salus land office. He, too, was rejected. Finally, just before adjournment on the session's last day, the Senate took up Jackson's nomination of Roger Taney, rejected as Treasury secretary the year before, for a vacant seat on the Supreme Court. It was indefinitely postponed.

---

[30]Richardson, *Messages and Papers*, 3:69–93.
[31]*Senate Journal*, 23d Cong., 1st sess., May 7, 1834, pp. 252–53.
[32]*Senate Executive Journal*, Feb. 11, 1835, 4:468–69.

But when the next Congress—Jackson's last—convened in December 1835, the Senate's resistance collapsed. The Mississippi wound still festered: Williamson, nominated again for the surveyorship, and a receiver at the Mt. Salus land office were both voted down. But they and a navy captain were the only nominees the Senate rejected in the first session. In the second session, in 1836–37, it rejected not one. No decision was even close enough to prompt a roll call. Never since George Washington's day had the Senate been so supine.

And this was despite the fact that Jackson flaunted his advantage brazenly. Like ghosts from the grave, defeated nominees from previous years were now resurrected, named to new offices, and meekly confirmed. Rejected Bank director and territorial governor Henry Gilpin came back as a federal district attorney. Wharton Rector, twice rejected for an Indian agency back in 1830, returned as lieutenant colonel of a new dragoon regiment. Rejected customs collector Martin Gordon was made superintendent of the New Orleans mint, and his rejected son, Martin Gordon, Jr., received another customs post. Former House Speaker Andrew Stevenson, who had been rejected for minister to Britain in 1834, was now renominated and, over Henry Clay's despairing protest, confirmed. Leading the resurrection list was Roger Taney. Rejected as Treasury secretary in 1834 and indefinitely postponed for associate justice in March of 1835, Taney was named just nine months later by Jackson to succeed John Marshall as chief justice of the Supreme Court and was readily confirmed, 29 to 15.[33]

The ultimate humiliation for Jackson's opponents came on January 16, 1837, just six weeks before his presidency ended. On motion by Thomas Hart Benton, the Senate voted, 24 to 19, to expunge the 1834 censure of Jackson from its own official journal. The clerk was summoned to retrieve the original manuscript, and, while opponents decried the "foul deed" of desecration, he drew black lines around the censure and wrote over it in thick letters "Expunged by order of the Senate," as if to obliterate it even in memory.[34]

What had happened to produce this startling reversal? Simply put, the Jacksonians, by this time calling themselves Democrats, had won a majority in the Senate. But theirs was a new kind of majority, produced by a new method—a systematic purge of the Senate membership, conducted through the state legislatures on orders from Washington.

---

[33]Ibid., Mar. 3, 1836, 4:513–16, Mar.15, 1836, 4:520, Mar. 16, 1836, 4:523.
[34]*Senate Journal*, 24th Cong., 2d sess., Jan. 16, 1837, pp. 123–24.

The chief instrument of the purge was the expunging resolution itself. The only method of controlling a senator once he took office was for his state legislature to instruct his vote. The underlying premise, to which not every one subscribed, was known as the "doctrine of instructions." It said that since senators represented their states and were chosen by state legislatures, they were duty-bound to do their bidding. Legislatures had accordingly issued instructions on particular matters from time to time, though such orders were in no sense legally binding. Senators, generally more disposed to think of themselves as independent agents than legislative puppets, had heeded them or not as they chose, and in recent years the practice of instructing had fallen into disuse.[35]

The Jacksonians revived legislative instructions and, more important, converted them from an occasional expression of local opinion into an instrument of national policy. Many legislatures, prompted from Washington, had adopted resolutions on the Bank issue; and in fact Jackson in protesting the censure pointed out that some of the senators voting for it were under instructions to support his policy. But it was the expunging campaign that perfected instructions as an effective weapon. Benton first announced his intent to move an expunging resolution in 1834, hard on the adoption of the censure itself. Immediately, the legislature of New Hampshire, the most tightly organized Democratic state in the country, instructed its senators to vote for it. Over the next two years, as Benton's expunging measure was twice introduced and twice tabled, legislatures in Maine, Alabama, North Carolina, New Jersey, Virginia, Ohio, Illinois, and New York decreed their senators' support. Some instructions dictated the exact wording of the measure that senators were to vote for. Virginia's resolutions commanded its senators to obey or resign. North Carolina's, aimed at anti-Jacksonian Willie Mangum, accused him of misrepresenting the state and pointedly instructed him by name.[36]

Historians have treated the expunging resolution as a mainly symbolic gesture, but it was far from that. Jackson had been searching throughout his presidency for a way to wield his unquestioned popularity as an effective disciplinary tool, to transform his personal following into a functioning political party. He had never found it. Time and again state legislatures had

---

[35]C. Edward Skeen, "An Uncertain 'Right': State Legislatures and the Doctrine of Instruction," *Mid-America* 73 (1991):29–47.

[36]*Senate Journal*, 23d Cong., 2d sess., Mar. 3, 1835, p. 224; 24th Cong., 1st sess., Mar. 21, 1835, p. 233.

sent senators to Washington, often professed Jacksonians, who then opposed him at every turn. Jackson could not touch them once in office, and his occasional efforts to intervene in their selection proved embarrassing failures, even in Tennessee. Rather than being confined to an anti-Jackson bailiwick like New England, senatorial rebellion thrived deep in Jackson's home territory. In Mississippi, Jackson's popularity reigned supreme. He carried the state overwhelmingly in 1824 and 1828; in 1832, his election was not even contested. Yet Mississippi produced Jackson's most pertinacious Senate opponent, George Poindexter, and another pro-censure senator, John Black. Jackson carried Virginia by more than two to one in 1828 and by nearly three to one in 1832. Still, both its senators voted for censure. Altogether, eleven Senate votes for censure in 1834—nearly half the total—came from states where Jackson had defeated Henry Clay just sixteen months earlier.

What issue then was to define a Jackson man, to place him definitively in or out of the ranks? Since Jackson himself was willing to tolerate dissent within his following—indeed, within his cabinet—on nonessentials, it was not easy to say. Jackson wanted to draw the line on the Bank, but there, as the fiasco with Duane had shown, Jacksonians were not sufficiently united on how to follow up the veto to make it a good test of fealty. The Senate's censure solved the problem by making the issue not the Bank or the deposits, but Jackson himself. The beauty of the expunging resolution lay in its simplicity. It posed the question directly, in stark yes-or-no fashion: do you support the president? At every level, from the local political meeting to the state legislature to the Senate itself, the answer became the measure of party fidelity. Those who answered yes were welcomed in the Jackson fold. Those who did not were cast out. The expunging campaign quite literally defined the membership of the Democratic party.

It also struck a blow at senators' vaunted independence, most immediately by altering the Senate's composition to strip it of three of Jackson's most articulate and resolute critics. The Virginia and North Carolina ultimatums worked as intended. Rather than disobey explicit instructions or violate their conscience by submitting, Willie Mangum of North Carolina and Benjamin Leigh and John Tyler of Virginia resigned, to be replaced by dependable party men. Only honor compelled these resignations: because the expunging instructions carried no legal weight, a man willing to brave the party tide could defy them and keep his seat. Several senators did so. But it was no longer possible to do so and remain, in any one's estimation, a Jackson man. Senators who bucked instructions were casting the dice on a party change in the legislature. If Democrats held control when their terms expired, their fate was certain.

The Senate majority that finally expunged the censure on January 16, 1837, was not, then, a fortuitous or random majority. It was not, as John Tyler had declared the Senate to be, an aggregate of individuals exercising separately their right of private judgment. It was a majority bound and instructed, a majority committed in advance to exercise the will of the party, as announced by Jackson and Benton and enforced through the state legislatures.

The result was a distinct alteration in the role and self-conception of the Senate. The Senate's distinguishing feature had always been independence: independence from executive dictation and independence from popular control. That independence was in effect written into the Constitution, and a half century's tradition had fortified it. If anything, it had grown stronger, not weaker, under the listless leadership of Jackson's immediate predecessors. Men like Tyler and Tazewell of Virginia prized above all what the former called their "example of perfect disinterestedness." They posed themselves in the hallowed role of high-minded, impartial arbiters of the republic's fortunes. Refusing to heed the voice of a president, a party, or even a popular majority was not merely incidental to this role: it was its very essence. His election to the Senate was no party triumph, John Tipton of Indiana insisted in 1832. "*I never considered it so*—and I authorize you to deny it in any way that you deem best." Tipton claimed to support Jackson and "*most*" of his policies. Yet he was "opposed to *removals unless on well founded charges. . . . I am at a loss to know why any man could think I am a partisan.*"[37]

There was no place for such thinking in the new world of party politics. "Speak of me always as a Jackson man," John Tyler could say as late as 1832. But to Tyler this meant only that he favored Jackson for president, not that he felt bound to follow his lead on any point of policy. Compare this to Jackson's comment, a full year earlier: "I want strength in the senate, of good men and true, not such men as Tazewell and Tyler." In Jackson's mind, men like Tyler, who refused ever to place party fealty above personal predilection,

---

[37]John Tyler to Littleton Tazewell, Nov. 16, 1832, in Tyler, *Letters and Times of the Tylers*, 1:443–44; John Tipton to Calvin Fletcher, Jan. 18, 1832, in *The John Tipton Papers*, ed. Nellie A. Robertson and Dorothy Riker, 3 vols. Indiana Historical Collections, vols. 24–26 (Indianapolis, 1942), 2:508–10.

were worse than no Jackson men at all. The aim of the expunging campaign was to get rid of them.[38]

It succeeded, and the Senate would never be quite the same again. It did not, of course, entirely shed its distinctive esprit and character, much of which it retains to this day. But from Jackson's presidency on, senators had to reckon with public opinion in a way they had not previously. Men who had once proudly taken no counsel but their own now looked to instructions from below, in their state legislatures, and from above, in the White House. Their doings were also becoming more exposed to public view. This was no accident. Since the beginning of government, the Senate's executive business, concerning nominations and treaties, had been routinely conducted in secret. Proceedings in executive session were disclosed only when a Senate majority for its own reasons chose to do so. Jackson relentlessly assailed Senate secrecy as a shield for aristocratic cabaling, and under his hammering the facade of confidentiality (for matters of importance usually had a way of becoming known) wore increasingly thin. Formal eradication of secret sessions would await a later day, but in Jackson's administration the presumption underlying them—that the people had no intrinsic right to inspect, day by day, what their senators were doing—came for the first time under direct attack.

The story of Jackson's war against the Senate ends on an ironic coda. In 1842, John Tyler, Jackson's old adversary, was himself president of the United States. Never an orthodox party man, Tyler brought to the presidency the same stubborn sense of independence that had marked his Senate career. Elected vice president by the Whigs and then elevated to the White House by William Henry Harrison's death, Tyler soon renounced the Whig program and found himself president without a party. Approving Tyler's abandonment of the Whigs and observing the Senate's rough handling of his nominations, Andrew Jackson, now in retirement, offered advice: "I could recommend to Mr. Tyler to do as I did, whenever the Senate rejected a good man, on the ground of his politics, I gave them a hot potatoe, and he will soon bring them to terms, and if not, if they leave the office not filled, the vengeance of the people will fall upon them."[39]

---

[38] Tyler to Mary Tyler, Apr. 20, 1832, in Tyler, *Letters and Times of the Tylers*, 1:429–30; Jackson to John Coffee, Apr. 24, 1831, in Bassett, *Correspondence of Andrew Jackson*, 4:268–69.

[39] Jackson to William B. Lewis, Feb. 28, 1842, in Bassett, *Correspondence of Andrew Jackson*, 6:141–42.

Tyler tested the Senate's mettle on March 3, 1843, when he nominated, renominated, and then re-renominated Caleb Cushing for secretary of the Treasury and Henry A. Wise for minister to France. Three times in one day the Senate voted the two men down, by majorities that were decisive on the first try, overwhelming on the second, and on the third just short of unanimous. The scene, although it exceeded anything in Jackson's tenure, would never have been possible without his precedent. Yet no vengeance befell the Senate, for Tyler had no following behind him. With no popular constituency to rally, no party club to wield, he could challenge the Senate, but he could not command it. Andrew Jackson had fashioned new tools of Senate discipline, but they did not function automatically. How his successors would use them, the sequel would tell.

— about careers but not about sectarianism

Contributors

Michael Les Benedict is emeritus professor of history at the Ohio State University, where he taught from 1970 until his retirement in 2005. Professor Benedict is a recognized authority in Anglo-American constitutional and legal history, the history of civil rights and liberties, the federal system, and the Civil War and Reconstruction. He is the author of several books, including *The Impeachment and Trial of Andrew Johnson* (1973) and *A Compromise of Principle: Congressional Republicans and Reconstruction* (1975).

Daniel Feller is professor of history as well as editor and director of the Papers of Andrew Jackson at the University of Tennessee's Department of History. Professor Feller's scholarly interests encompass mid-nineteenth-century America as a whole, with special attention to Jacksonian politics and the coming of the Civil War. He is the author of *The Jacksonian Promise: America, 1815–1840* (1995) and *The Public Lands in Jacksonian Politics* (1984). Professor Feller is currently at work on a biography of Benjamin Tappan, a Jacksonian politician, scientist, social reformer, and freethinker.

Paul Finkelman is President William McKinley Distinguished Professor of Law at Albany Law School. A specialist in American legal history, race and the law, and First Amendment issues, Finkelman is the author or editor of numerous articles and books, including *A March of Liberty: A Constitutional History of the United States* (2002), *Slavery and the Founders: Race and Liberty in the Age of Jefferson* (2001), *Baseball and the American Legal Mind* (1995), and *American Legal History: Cases and Materials* (2005). Professor Finkelman teaches constitutional law and American legal history.

Robert P. Forbes is associate director of the Gilder Lehrman Center for the Study of Slavery, Resistance, and Abolition. He received his doctorate from Yale in 1994. He has also taught at Wesleyan and Rutgers. He is the coauthor of a biography of Francis Kernan, a nineteenth-century U.S. senator from New York, as well as several articles and numerous encyclopedia entries. His book, *Slavery and the Meaning of America: The Missouri Compromise and Its Aftermath*, is forthcoming from the University of North Carolina Press.

William W. Freehling is Singletary Professor Emeritus at the University of Kentucky and senior fellow at the Virginia Foundation for the Humanities, Charlottesville. He is the author of several prize-winning books, including *Prelude to Civil War: The Nullification Controversy in South Carolina* (1966), *The South versus the South: How Southern Anti-Confederates Shaped the Course of the Civil War* (2001), and the two-volume *Road to Disunion: Secessionists at Bay, 1774–1854* (1990 and 2007). He is currently finishing a book of essays on the Civil War era and a study of Abraham Lincoln's early presidency.

Tim Alan Garrison is associate professor in the Department of History at Portland State University. Professor Garrison received his doctorate from the University of Kentucky in 1997. His fields of expertise include U.S. legal and constitutional history and Native American history. Professor Garrison is the author of *The Legal Ideology of Removal: The Southern Judiciary and the Sovereignty of Native American Nations* (2002). He is currently researching the Catawba Land Settlement Act.

Jan Lewis is professor and chair of the Federated Department of History, Rutgers University–Newark. Professor Lewis received her doctorate from the University of Michigan. She is the author of *The Pursuit of Happiness: Family and Values in Jefferson's Virginia* (1983) and a coeditor of *The Revolution of 1800: Democracy, Race, and the New Republic* (2002). She serves as chair of the American Historical Association's Committee on Women Historians and on the advisory boards of the International Center for Jefferson Studies and the *American Historical Review.*

Peter S. Onuf is Thomas Jefferson Memorial Foundation Professor in the Corcoran Department of History of the University of Virginia. Professor Onuf's many publications include *Origins of the Federal Republic: Jurisdictional Controversies in the United States, 1775–1787* (1983), *Statehood and Union: A History of the Northwest Ordinance* (1987), and *Jefferson's Empire: The Language of American Nationhood* (2001), as well as several coauthored and edited publications. His current research interests are the history of federalism and sectionalism: *Liberal Histories, Nation-Making and the Coming of the Civil War* (with Nicholas G. Onuf).

Jenny B. Wahl is professor and chair of the Economics Department of Carleton College. She received her doctoral degree from the University of Chicago. Professor Wahl has previously held positions at St. Olaf College, George Mason University, and the U.S. Treasury Department. She has published in the areas of demography, tax policy, American economic history, and U.S. labor law and is the author of *The Bondsman's Burden: An Economic Analysis of the Common Law of Southern Slavery* (1998). She teaches courses in labor economics, law and economics, and American economic history.

Index

Italic page numbers refer to illustrations.